BRĀHMAṆISM
IN SOUTH-EAST ASIA

BRĀHMANIṢM IN SOUTH-EAST ASIA

(FROM THE EARLIEST TIME TO 1445 A.D.)

By

DAWEE DAWEEWARN, M.A., Ph.D.
Department of History,
Ramkhamhaeng University,
Bangkok, Thailand

Foreword

Dr. UPENDRA THAKUR
Professor and Head,
Department of Ancient Indian & Asian Studies,
Magadh University, Bodh-Gaya, India

HUMANITIES PRESS INC.

Sole Distributors for U.S.A. & Canada
HUMANITIES PRESS INC
771, First Avenue Atlantic Highlands,
N.J. 07716.

ISBN 0-391-02581-3
Brāhmaṇism in South-East Asia
(From the Earliest Time to 1445 A.D.)

PRINTED IN INDIA

Published by S.K. Ghai, Managing Director, Sterling Publishers Pvt. Ltd., L-10, Green Park Extension, New Delhi-110016
Printed at Sterling Printers, L-11, Green Park Extension, New Delhi-110016

FOREWORD

I have a great pleasure to contribute this Foreword to Dr Dawee Daweewarn's book, *Brāhmaṇism in South-East Asia*, which portrays a complete picture of Brāhmaṇical religion in South-East Asia from the earliest times to 1445 A.D., i.e., till the fall of Majapahit, the last great Hindu kingdom which flourished in Java. Though some aspects of this study have been treated by scholars in their monographs and books this is for the first time that a comprehensive work has been done on Brāhmaṇism in South-East Asia which dominated the scene for about 1300 years.

It is well-known that the two Indian religions—Brāhmaṇism and Buddhism—with its many sects and sub-sects flourished in South-East Asia during this period. The numerous inscriptions and art-objects that have been discovered in different parts of this region throw considerable light on the various aspects of these religions. Unfortunately, these inscriptions have not been studied from religious point of view : they have been chiefly utilised as sources of political history. However, on close scrutiny, one finds that most of these inscriptions, particularly those in Cambodia, are religious in character and their chief object is to describe some religious foundations. In this respect, the invocatory stanzas of the Sanskrit inscriptions are particularly interesting from religious point of view as they often express theological and philosophical ideas drawn from various Indian texts. For instance, of all the countries of South-East Asia, the philosophical activities were most pronounced in Java where religious texts of great importance have come down to us which form an invaluable treasure of Indo-Javanese literature. Though in the case of Cambodia, which constituted one of the strongholds of Hindu culture in South-East Asia, it is difficult to say on the basis of the fragmentary documents if philosophical activities were so important as in Java, nevertheless, the average of these stanzas, contained in epigraphic records, would appear more philosophical than average of the invocatory stanzas of the Indian, Cham and Javanese inscriptions. These records as a whole present a clear picture of the general tendencies of these religions in those countries, some of which patronised Śaivism, some Vaiṣṇavism, some both and yet others Buddhism. For instance, Śaivism was the most popular religion in ancient Cambodia and the documents on it are more numerous than those on Vaiṣṇavism and Buddhism, and the ideas we gather from them are for that reason more comprehensive. Thus, almost all the currents of Indian thought are fully reflected in the Sanskrit inscriptions, and the authors have extensively drawn from the Upaniṣads, the Purāṇas and the Āgamas. The influence of Vedānta philosophy which we notice in various countries, specially in Cambodia, towards the second half of the 10th century, seems to have some association with a particular movement in the Śaiva circles in India during this period. Besides, the Yogic theories also seem to have exerted a strong influence, and the proficiency with which the authors of the inscriptions express the religious and philosophical ideas points to the deep cultural influence of India in that part of the world.

As we know, the Philippine islands, Malay and Indonesia were greatly influenced by Hindu religions and philosophy since the early years of the Christian era. While Java has conserved its monuments and inscriptions, Bali with its Hindu-Balinese religion is a store-house of Hindu-Javanese or Old-Javanese culture, deeply imbibing all the best in Indo-Javanese sources. Voluminous treatises on pre-Islamic, Indo-Javanese religious organisations, institutions, etc., in Java known as the *Tantu Panggelaram* and the *Koravāśrama* betray tremendous Hindu influence in all walks of life. This impact was so absorbing and encompassing that even the change of religion, i.e., culture, in Java took centuries to take roots, and it has been rightly suggested that "this process is still far from completed in the eyes of orthodox Muslims". It is therefore not at all surprising to find the Muslims of Java maintaining still its Hindu mythology partly in its literature, and fully in its shadow-play. In spite of the continuous efforts by the powerful Muslim organization *Muhammadiyah* for well over half a century to purify Islam, it has received not much success : On the other hand, it has to face stiff resistance in the form of voices "in favour of maintaining the *Kajavêu* the inherited Javanese way of life. Javanese syncretism make themselves heard louder and louder".

Legends current in Bali tell us how fugitives from Java fled to the East to escape the sword of the advancing Muslim conquerors, and crossed to Bali where they planted their religion and literature. Whatever the credence of these stories the fact remains that as early as 1000 A.D. the Javanese and Balinese royal families intermarried and that Java had conquered Bali more than once, and the Balinese during this period had avidly absorbed Indo-Javanese culture. Thus, Indo-Javanese literature could best be studied in Bali, a graphic description of which has been presented by C. Hooykaas in his informative article entitled "The Treasures of Bali". This influence is again to be seen in the shadow-theatre (*Vayang Kulit*) in Java and Bali, the themes of which can easily be traced to Indo-Javanese sources. Though awkward for a Muslim society, a performance in both the islands is a religious requisite. While in Bali it is requirement during a temple-festival, in Java it is not admitted to the mosque, but in both the islands it enjoys court-favour. This all round influence is further suggested by the Old Javanese *Rāmāyaṇa Kakawin* (Balinese script); Kāvya

Bharata-Yuddha (Balinese script) and the Śaiva-Buddhistic Kāvya *Sutasoma* dealing with *Kalmaśapāda* (same production) as well as the Balinese poems like the *Dukuh Silandri, Basur* and *Jayaprāṇa* which bear the important literary manifestations of an unmistakably Hinduised and still Indonesian people. In fact, we have numerous treatises on religion, philosophy, metaphysics, manuals for priests and so on that are usually mere transliterations into Latin script from the existing palm-leaf manuscripts, but also not unfrequently freshly-composed expositions.

The present work, as rightly suggested by the author, is "not a startling discovery of hitherto unknown sources, but a patient compilation and scientific interpretation of information contained in known sources", suggesting fresh approaches to the topics discussed here. I have no doubt that the work will attract notice of both indigenous and foreign scholars and would go a long way in cementing the age-old cultural tie between India and South-East Asia. Moreover, it will serve for long as a guidebook to the inquisitive researchers in the field.

Upendra Thakur

Magadh University,
Bodh-Gaya

ACKNOWLEDGEMENTS

In preparation of this work my grateful thanks are, first and foremost due to my respected teacher and supervisor, Dr Upendra Thakur, Professor and Head, Department of Ancient Indian and Asian Studies and Dean, Faculty of Arts, Magadh University, Bodh-Gaya, Bihar (India), who not only suggested this topic to me but kindly supervised this work to its completion. Apart from his invaluable professional guidance at all stages of this investigation, his encouragement and personal kindness have sustained me in moments of difficulties. I have no words to express my sincere gratitude and respect to him, but for whose constant advice, assistance and personal guidance the present work would not have been possible.

I am deeply indebted to Dr M.D. Aquique, Lecturer in the Post-graduate department to Ancient Indian and Asian Studies, Magadh University, Bodh-Gaya, who ungrudgingly helped me and gave numerous suggestions from time to time in handling historical materials of various kinds.

I acknowledge with gratitude all kinds of help that I received from Dr Artsa Tulku, lecturer in Tibetology, Magadh University, Bodh-Gaya and Dr M.K. Sharan, lecturer in Ancient Indian and Asian Studies, Gaya College, Gaya, in preparation of the present work.

I must acknowledge gratefully the efforts of all those great savants whose work in any shape or form have been utilised here. The immense help and light that I have derived from them are not a mere matter of formal acknowledgement.

I would like to express my gratitude to the staff of the National Library, Calcutta; The Indian Council of World Affairs Library, New Delhi; Asiatic Society, Calcutta; National Library and Siam Society, Bangkok (Thailand); Mannulal Magadh University Library, Bodh-Gaya; the Seminar Library, Department of Ancient Indian and Asian Studies, Magadh University, Bodh-Gaya; Patna University Library, Patna; Banaras Hindu University Library, Varanasi; and the Library of Silpakorn University, Bangkok (Thailand) who very kindly extended to me their cooperation and help during the course of my research work by providing me with the relevant materials and references.

I would also like to record the friendly assistance of Sri Ram Deep Prasad, Bodh-Gaya and Sri D.N. Thakur, Estate Officer, Magadh University, Bodh-Gaya in connection with the writing of this work.

For photos, I am thankful to Miss Prabhapun Phoodchavee and Miss Supaktra Noibuatip of Thailand, and for maps to Mr Tanya Borisudhi.

Lastly, for financial assistance I am thankful to Mr Y. Togo, the Manager of the Toyota Motor Company of Thailand; Phra Buddhivongsamuni, the Abbot of the Royal Marble Temple, Bangkok-3, Thailand; Phrakru Baideekasingchai, the Royal Marble Temple, Bangkok-3, Thailand; Mr Tawee Khankaew, the Manager of S.K. Gems, Soi Suanplu, Bangkok, Thailand and Miss Mesinee Baison, Bangkok-8, Thailand.

Dawee Daweewarn

INTRODUCTION

The present work entitled *Brāhmaṇism in South-East Asia* is a survey of the conditions of the Brāhmaṇical religion from the earliest time upto 1445 A.D. An attempt has been made to give a comprehensive account of this important facet of the Indian religious set-up in the countries of South-East Asia on the basis of a variety of original and secondary sources. Some aspects of the subjects were undoubtedly treated by competent scholars in many books and monographs but a complete integrated study of all of them was not available in such a comprehensive way as to deal fully with this theme in all its essential formative trends and evolutionary courses. It is surprising that upto this time no work dealing exclusively with Brāhmaṇism in South-East Asia has been written in any language. This led us to embark upon this study. The main feature of this work is not a startling discovery of hitherto unknown sources, but a patient compilation and scientific interpretation of the information contained in known sources. Therefore, without laying claim to any original discovery, we are content with advancing some new interpretations and suggesting some fresh approaches to the topics treated here.

The term 'South-East Asia' was coined during the last world war as a term of military usage but now it has become geographical. The area of South-East Asia, may be broadly defined as nearly the whole of Indo-Chinese peninsula and East Indias, called by the Indians respectively as Suvarṇa-bhūmi and Suvarṇa-dvīpa. To be more precise it comprised the territories now known as Burma, Thailand (Siam), Malaya peninsula, Cambodia (now Khmer Republic), Laos and Vietnam on the mainland, and the islands of Sumatra, Java, Madura, Bali, Borneo, etc.

The countries of South-East Asia have a glorious past of which any civilised region may justly be proud. The relics of their glorious past can yet be seen in its ancient cities and the achievements of the prominent kings—Mengrai, Ram Kamheng, Chulalongkorn (Thailand); Aniruddha and Kyanzittha (Burma); Jayavarman II and Jayavarman VII (Cambodia); Śrī Mara and Harivarman (Champā); Fa Ngum (Laos); Kritinagar, Airlangga and Vijaya of Java; Malavarman of Borneo, etc., were the main builders and organisers of Buddhism and Brāhmaṇism in their respective areas. There are remains of splendid cities, temples and monasteries and places hallowed by the memory of the great thinkers and preachers. Their fertile plains, rippling with bouncing harvests, and teeming with multitudinous population, have witnessed the majestic and interminable drama of the movement and migration of peoples.

Though, the materials for the study of the present work are scanty, nevertheless an attempt has been made to utilise all possible sources such as literature both indigenous and foreign, religious, legal, and secular, the Buddhist and Pali works and the accounts of foreign travellers. Besides these many non-South East-Asian sources have proved very helpful to us. Coming to the archaeological sources we have a large number of art objects and stone sculptures, epigraphic records etc., discovered in the excavations conducted at various places in South-East Asian countries.

Although the sources are numerous and varied, none of these, however, gives us a complete and comprehensive account regarding the Brāhmaṇism in South-East Asia. Nevertheless basing on these sources we have attempted to portray as complete a picture as possible of the topic under discussion.

To have a clear idea of the subject we have divided our work into five convenient chapters. Chapter 1 discusses the origin and evolution of Brāhmaṇism in India. Chapter 2 offers a historical sketch of Brāhmaṇical cults in South-East Asia. Chapter 3 tells us about the Brāhmaṇism and art. Chapter 4 enlightens us on a minor deity of Brāhmaṇical pantheon—Gaṇeśa and Chapter 5 portrays the Brāhmaṇical culture in South-East Asia.

CONTENTS

ABBREVIATIONS

An. Rep. A.S. Burma	:	*Annual Report of the Archaeological Survey of Burma.*
An. Rep. A.S. India	:	*Annual Report of the Archaeological Survey of India.*
A.S. Memoir	:	*Archaeological Survey Memoir.*
ASR	:	*Archaeological Survey Report.*
BCAIC	:	*Bulletin de la Commission archaeology de l' Indo-China.*
BEFEO	:	*Bulletin de l'Ecole Francaise d'Extreme Orient.*
EFEO	:	*Ecole Francaise d'Extreme Orient.*
Ep. Birm.	:	*Epigraphia Birmanica.*
HCFE	:	*Hindu Colonies in the Far East.*
HCGI	:	*Hindu Culture in Greater India.*
IA	:	*Indian Antiquary.*
IAC	:	*Indo-Asian Culture.*
IC	:	*Inscription du Cambodge.*
ICC	:	*Indian Colony in Champa.*
ISCC	:	*Inscription de Champa et du Cambodge.*
JAOS	:	*Journal of the American Oriental Society.*
JASB	:	*Journal of the Asiatic Society of Bengal.*
JMBRAS / JRASMB	:	*Journal of the Royal Asiatic Society, Malay Branch.*
JOI	:	*Journal of Oriental Institute, Baroda.*
JOR	:	*Journal of Oriental Research.*
JRBRS	:	*Journal of the Royal Burma Research Society.*
JSEAH	:	*Journal of the South-East Asian History.*
JSS	:	*Journal of the Siam Society.*
Mon. Ins.	:	*Mon Inscriptions.*
Skt.	:	*Sanskrit.*
VIJ	:	*Visheshvaranand Indological Journal.*

LIST OF PLATES

1

Brahmanism in India—Origin and Evolution

This chapter is intended to present a brief account of Brāhmaṇism in India, from its rude beginnings down to the sixteenth century A.D. But this task is beset with many difficulties. Sufficient data are lacking to enable us to follow, even with a tolerable degree of certainty, the rise and development of the various religious movements in India. Opinions differ widely and the differences are accentuated, and not unoften embittered, by sectarian jealousy and fanaticism. The Indians are particularly sensitive to any matter concerning their religion. Amid the passions and prejudices that have slowly gathered force, it is not easy to get a detached view of things, which is essential to the writing of a historical survey of religious growth.

Indian tradition acknowledges two main strands in Indian religion—the Vedic or the *Nigama* and the Tāntric—Paurāṇic or the *Āgama*. There has been interaction between these two. The Vedic tradition is mainly the Aryan tradition, and the Āgama tradition is basically the pre-Aryan tradition. But there has been a final blend of these two sects of ideologies, which differed in their original forms, in some very deep or fundamental points. We are not, however, concerned with that, as it was pre-historic. What is remarkable is the attitude of the Hindu thinkers all through the centuries in trying to fit in these two systems together. And the result has been something which is unique in the world. It fills us with admiration for the comprehensive spirit which was displayed in making a new fabric out of the warp and weft of the diverse sects and ideas. The fabric is the fabric of Brāhmaṇism in all its wonderful variety.

For the sake of convenience of treatment we may divide this review of Brāhmaṇism in India into the following well-defined chronological periods :

The pre-Aryan period (c. 3000-2000 B.C.)

The beginning of religion of Indian society have been pushed back by two thousand years or even more by the discoveries at Mohenjo-daro. Mohenjo-daro, 'mounds of the dead', is the local name of a high mound situated in a narrow strip of land between the main bed of the Indus river and the western Nara canal in the plains of Larkana District in Sind. Here a city was built about five thousand years ago, and was destroyed and rebuilt no less than seven times. The ruins of these successive cities afford us a glimpse of a civilization which was indeed of a very high order, at least from the materialistic point of view. The people who lived in these cities cannot be definitely affiliated to any known race of men in India. It is certain, however, that they had long emerged from primitive barbarism and developed an urban life with all its amenities. Of their religious culture some traces are left in their icons which include the Mother Goddess, the phallus, and a male god, seated in yogic posture, who has been regarded as Śiva.[1] In the absence of any written documents, our knowledge of this religion must necessarily remain vague, but there are enough indications that the worship of Śiva in the form of phallus, which is a prominent feature in later Brāhmaṇism but is condemned in the *Vedas*, is possibly to be traced to this source. Once this is conceded it is easy to assume that many traits of later Brāhmaṇism specially those which cannot be directly traced to the *Vedas*, might have been a legacy of these unknown people. Their cult of the Mother Goddess may not be exactly the same as Śakti-worship of later days, but both seem to be inspired by the same fundamental belief in a female energy as the source of all creation. The worship of tree, fire, and water seems to have been in vogue. The seal-amulets, containing figures of a variety of animals, have been taken as evidence for the worship of animals, but they might be symbols or carriers of deities who were the real objects of worship. These are no doubt, matters of dispute, but the cumulative effect of the discoveries at Mohenjo-daro and the neighbouring regions may be summed up in the form (i) that some fundamental ideas of Brāhmaṇism as well as some primitive beliefs and observances, still current in India, may be traced as far back as the third millennium B.C., (ii) that the worship of Śiva and Śakti may be regarded as the oldest form of Indian theistic religion.[2]

This old religion and culture was widely spread in Sind, Baluchistan, and parts of the Punjab. How and when it receded to the background is not definitely known to us. It is generally held that the influx of the Aryan race into India was the cause of the downfall of this older culture and civilization of the Indus Valley. This may be regarded as the only

1. Marshall, J., *Mohenjo-daro and the Indus Civilization.*
2. Cf. Hopkins, E.W., *Religions of India.*

satisfactory hypothesis in the present state of our knowledge.

The Vedic period (c. 2000-600 B.C.)

The civilization of the Aryans and particularly their philosophical thought and religious practices during the first thousand years are known to us from sacred books collectively known as the Vedas. This term denotesnot any particular book, but the whole mass of literature produced by the Aryans during the first thousand years or more of their settlement in India. Although definite dates cannot be assigned to the different texts, it is possible to give a general idea of their chronological sequence. The *Saṁhitās*, *Brāhmaṇas*, *Āraṇyakas*, and *Upaniṣads* represent the four successive stages in the development of Vedic literature. The *Rg-Veda Saṁhitā*, the earliest text, may be referred to a date between 2000 and 1500 B.C., while the principal *Upanṣisads* were composed by 600 B.C. Between these two extreme dates we have to put the other *Saṁhitās*, *Brāhmaṇas*, *Āraṇyakas*, and the principal *Upaniṣads*.

In the *Rg-Veda Saṁhitā*, we first come across the ideas of definite gods, as a normal evolution from the striking phenomena of nature. The same *Saṁhitā* shows that the development of the Aryan religion and philosophy proceeded along two well-marked directions. On the one hand, we find the idea of propitiating the different gods by means of worship, which led to the religious sacraments known as yajña or sacrifice. On the other hand, there was developed more philosophic conception about the nature of these gods, which culminated in the idea that all these gods are but the manifestations of a higher Spirit. The later Vedic literature saw a further development in these directions. The Brāhmaṇas developed the ritualistic side by elaborating the mechanical details of the yajña, while the philosophical ideas were developed in the *Upaniṣads*.[1]

The *Upaniṣads* are works of various authors living in different ages. They do not present a coherent or consistent people who obtained glimpses of the highest truths by earnest meditation. Their process is intuitive rather than logical, and their object is to satisfy the natural yearnings of the human mind for an ultimate knowledge of the reality about God, man and the world around us. The answers given to these questions are many, and it is not always easy so say definitely what the teachings of the *Upaniṣads* as a whole are. The hints, suggestions, guesses, and implications contained in them are so many and so diverse that in subsequent ages they have been quoted as authority by the founders of almost all the religious and philosophical systems in India, even though they differed on essential points.

But in spite of the mystic character of the *Upaniṣads*, certain

1. Hopkins, E.W., op. cit.

fundamental conceptions clearly emerge out of the mass of spiritual and metaphysical thoughts. The first and foremost is the idea of one all-powerful, all-pervading, self-existent, eternal, and incomprehensible. Absolute (Brahman), in whom all creatures find their origin and dissolution.[1]

Secondly, the *Upaniṣads* lay stress on the miseries of life, which are perpetuated by transmigration or rebirth due to our *karma* or actions. But they pin their faith on the ultimate hope of deliverance (*mukti*), which means cessation of miseries and enjoyment of eternal bliss. This can only be obtained by a true knowledge of the universal Spirit or Soul (*Brahman*). Such knowledge can only be derived by purity of life and intense meditation (*nididhyāsana*). By implication, if not by express mention, they deny that the ritualistic sacrifices (*yajña*) can achieve the same result. Lastly, the *Upaniṣads* elaborate the idea of the eternal human soul, as distinct from the body, and, by a bold flight of imagination, regard the individual human soul as identical with the universal Soul or God. When true knowledge comes by meditation, the individual souls merge in the universal Soul, as rivers merge in the ocean. A solution was thus offered of the problems of life and death and of God and man, which are at the root of all philosophy and religion.

In spite of the profundity and brilliance of *Upaniṣadic* ideas, they cannot be regarded as sufficient for the moral or religious needs of the masses. In the first place, they could make their appeal only to the intelligentsia, but failed to impress the average man to whom the attainment of such a profound knowledge appeared as a Utopian ideal. Secondly, while the *Ṛg-Veda Saṁhitā* showed an analytic process in discovering one great God behind the visible phenomena of nature, the *Upaniṣads* follow from the beginning an intuitive method. Their conclusions were not based on an intelligible chain of reasoning and arguments, but held out merely as the experience or realization of great minds. They were therefore to be accepted on faith. Thirdly, although by implication they denied the efficacy of ritualistic yajña for the purpose of salvation, they prescribed no substitute for it, which an average man could normally pursue for developing his religious life.[1]

Thus while the *Upaniṣadic* philosophers soared to a dizzy height and indicated the line on which Indian thoughts were to be developed, in later years, they failed to satisfy all the normal religious cravings of the human heart and the legitimate spiritual needs of the human mind.

1. Vide, Nikhilananda, Swami, *The Upanisads*.
2. Hopkins, E.W. op. cit., also see Nikhilananda Swami, op. cit.

The Age of Revolt (c. 600 B.C. to A.D. 300)

The age that followed the early *Upaniṣads* saw new developments in religious thoughts with a view to removing these deficiencies. They started with the *Upaniṣadic* teachings as their background, but proceeded in different directions to build up different systems of religious belief. The chief characteristics which distinguished them are (i) belief in a personal God to be worshipped with devotion (*bhakti*) rather than an impersonal Absolute (Brahman) to be realized through meditation and knowledge (jñāna), (ii) broad practical view of everyday life, laying stress on morality and discounting the metaphysical discussions about God and soul. Emphasis is laid on the control of will and emotions, and the right actions of a man are regarded as the only means to his salvation, (iii) a rational interpretation of all the problems of human life and an attempt to solve them by a co-ordinated system based on analytical reasoning, (iv) aversion to mechanical sacrificial performances as detailed in the *Brāhmaṇias*, and regard for the sanctity of animal life.

The germs of these developments no doubt lay in the *Upaniṣads* themselves. This is best seen in the rise of the theistic Śaiva system, to the history of which we may now devote our attention.

The god Rudra is mentioned as early as the *Ṛg-Veda* as a terrific god whose wrath had to be appeased by offerings. The idea is further developed in the *Śatrudrīya* (*Taittirīya Saṁhitā*) where he is represented both as a malevolent and as a benevolent god. In the latter aspect he was known as Śiva.

In the age of the *Upaniṣads*, when the conception of an impersonal God was the prevailing idea, we find the first beginnings of a theistic system in the *Śvetāśavathara Upaniṣad*. It expounds the characteristic *Upaniṣadic* doctrines but occasionally identifies Brāhmaṇ with the god Rudra-Śiva. There is only one Rudra, so says this *Upaniṣad*, and they do not recognize another. This God—the great Soul whose work is the universe—always dwells in the hearts of men. Śiva is knowable by faith, love or the pure heart. Having known Śiva one attains eternal peace.[1]

Here we find the beginnings of the theistic system which was further developed in the Bhāgavata school. From the conception of an absolute Brahman to that of a personal God, whom an average man can love and comprehend, the transition is no doubt easy and natural, and almost inevitable. But why the particular god Rudra-Śiva should be chosen for this purpose is not so easy to understand. Long ago, R.G. Bhandarkar, after a painstaking analysis of the attributes of Rudra-Śiva, came to the conclusion that this god had a close connection with non-Aryan tribes, and that the element of phallic worship associated with his cult was entirely

1. *Svet. Up.*. III.2; IV. 14, 16, 17; V. 14.

borrowed from them. The discoveries of Mohenjo-daro, to which reference has already been made above, corroborate this view, and we may now assume, with a tolerable degree of certainty, that Rudra-Śiva was, or was assumed to be, identical with the great God of the pre-Aryan settlers of the Indus Valley, and that, with the large absorption of these people into the Aryan society, he came to occupy a pre-eminent position. The *Upaniṣadic* doctrine of an impersonal God was fused with the devotional worship of a personal God, and a beginning was thus made which led to almost revolutionary changes.

These changes were brought about by the Bhāgavatas, Buddhists, and Jains, who all first come into notice about the sixth century B.C. In spite of early opinions to the contrary, it is now admitted by all scholars that all these religious doctrines grew independently in or about this period and their founders were real historical persons. Gautama Buddha is no longer a solar myth, but is recognized as an historical personage, born in the republican Śakya clan. The traditional date of his death, viz. 543 B.C., is not accepted by modern scholars. They regard 487 B.C. as a close approximation to the real date of his death. As by all accounts he lived for 80 years and became the Buddha at the age of 35, the years 532-487 B.C. may be regarded as the period when the fundamental principles of Buddhism were enunciated by him.

Vardhamāna Mahāvīra, usually regarded as the founder of the Jaina religion, was born in a suburb of Vaiśālī, the capital of the famous republican clan of the Licchavis.[1] The traditional date of his birth, viz. 599 B.C. has not been accepted by modern scholars who place it about 539 B.C. He attained supreme knowledge at the age of 42 and died thirty years later. So the effective period of his religious life may be put between 497 and 467 B.C.

But Jainism seems to be much older than this period. The Jainas claim that there were twenty-three prophets (*tīrthaṅkaras*) before Mahāvīra, and have woven absurdly fantastic tales around them. It is said, for example, that the first prophet lived several millions of years and his stature was about a mile high. Somewhat similar claims are made by the Buddhists, but their stories about the six Buddhas who preceded the historical Gautama are not of an absurdly exaggerated character. The germs of all religions may be traced back to inchoate thoughts or speculations of an earlier period, and to this extent we can accept the claims of a higher antiquity advanced by many religious sects. We have no ground to believe that as a system of religion, with definite dogmas and an established organization, Buddhism existed before Gautama Buddha.[2] As regards Jainism, however,

1. Cf. Thakur, U. *Studies in Jainism and Buddhism in Mithila.*
2. For details, see *ibid.*

there are clear indications that Pārśvanātha, the twenty-third tīrthaṅkara, who is reputed to have died 250 years before Mahāvīra, was really an historical person and he founded a religious sect known as Nirgrantha. Mahāvīra belonged to this sect, but gave a decided stamp to it by his own personality. As an historical religion of recognized status, with a definite system and organization, we can hardly trace Jainism long before the time of Vardhamāna Mahāvīra.

Although the historical character of Gautama Buddha and Vardhamāna Mahāvīra is now freely admitted, that of Kṛṣṇa-Vāsudeva, the founder of the Bhāgavata religion, is still doubted by many. Eminent scholars have held that Kṛṣṇa-Vāsudeva was not a human being, but a popular deity—a solar deity according to some, a vegetation deity according to others, and a tribal deity according to still others. But recent researches leave no doubt that Kṛṣṇa-Vāsudeva of Mathurā was a human teacher; belonging to the republican Kṣatriya clan known as Sātvatas or Vṛṣṇis, a branch of the Yādava tribe which was famous in the age of the *Brāhmaṇas.* The earliest account of this great teacher is found in the *Chandogya Upaniṣad.*[1] where he is represented as the son of Devakī and a pupil of the ṛṣi Ghora Angirasa. Incidentally the *Upaniṣad* has preserved some of the doctrines which Kṛṣṇa learnt from his preceptor. It is a noteworthy fact that these fundamental doctrines reappear in the *Bhagavad-Gītā,* which contains the most authoritative exposition of the principles held by the Bhāgavatas, The reference in the *Chandogya Upaniṣad* shows that Vāsudeva-Kṛṣṇa flourished before the sixth century B.C. As to the incidents of his life we know little beyond what has already been stated above.

The popular tales about Kṛṣṇa, particularly his amorous relations with the gopis, are found only in the *Harivaṁśa* and the *Purāṇas.* His association with Rādhā first occurs in still later literature. To derive the life-story of Kṛṣṇa from books which were written five hundred to thousand years later is against the elementary principle of historical study. No importance therefore attaches to these books, as a source of information for the true life of Kṛṣṇa, although they constitute important landmarks for the development of the Kṛṣṇa cult and the evolution of the Vaiṣṇava religion.

Having briefly surveyed the historical origin of the three great religious movements, we may next proceed to explain their nature and significance in the evolution of religion of India.

At the very start we must remember that all thesere the constitute a revolt against, or at least a decided break from the accepted religious creeds of the day. And, it is not perhaps a mere accident that all of them originated in the free atmosphere of independent republican clans, the

1. III. 17.6.

Śākyas, the Licchavis, and the Sātvatas. The history of the world has again and again demonstrated that nurseries of political freedom often tend to develop freedom in the domains of thoughts and beliefs. Besides, all the three clans lived in regions which may be described as the outer fringe of the strong-hold of Vedic culture and therefore comparatively free from its rigid control.

Further, we should remember that these three religious movements were not isolated events, but there were similar other movements, and all these were merely the products of the age. The bold *Upaniṣadic* speculations were the outcome of a creative intellect and critical spirit which revolted against the mechanical, and sometimes cruel, ceremonials of the *Brāhmaṇa* age. But freedom of thought and a spirit of inquiry once aroused are not likely to observe any limit, and it is no wonder that the sixth and fifth centuries B.C. saw a great outburst of intellectual activity which defied established traditions and was out to seek truth by new experiments. The result was almost a wild growth of new views and ideas leading to the foundation of numerous sects and religious systems. Some of these, no doubt, displayed a high degree of intellectual, spiritual, and moral fervour, but others proved a victim to unbridled passions and lack of all moral or intellectual discipline. Thus, while the tide of free speculations led on the one hand to the rise of the important sects like Buddhism, Jainism, Śaivism, and Bhāgavatism, it culminated on the other in different types of heretical systems like that of Cārvāka in which immoral practices masqueraded in the name of religion.[1]

The revolution was started on a moderate scale by the Bhāgavata religion. It substituted a personal God called Hari in place of the abstract idea of a universal soul. Hari, the God of Gods, was not, however, visible to one who followed the traditional mode of worship, viz. yajñas and austerities. He could only be seen by one who worshipped Him with devotion. By an open denial of the efficacy of sacrifices and austerities, denunciation of the slaughter of animals, and stressing the element of bhakti (devotion) in place of abstract knowledge, it constituted a fundamental break from the accepted creeds and beliefs.

Buddhism, which represents the other extreme of reaction, agreed with the Bhāgavatas in the first two of these important principles, but went still further, both in its disregard for sacrifices and austerities and in its upholding the sanctity of animal life. Moreover, it differed from the Bhāgavatas in several important points. It did not acknowledge any personal God, or, for that matter, any supreme God at all. Consequently, neither bhakti nor metaphysical and abstract knowledge of God had any

1. Vide, Bhandarkar, R.G., *Vaisnavism, Saivism, and Minor Religious System*; also see, Hopkins, E.W. op. cit.

place in it, and highly developed ethical life was offered as the sole means of attaining salvation. Further, it denied the Vedic literature as a divine revelation and refused to accept the social order of the day, particularly the system of caste. This completed the revolution which was begun by the Bhāgavatas.

The Jainas accepted most of these points, but regarded austerity as the essential means of salvation. Besides, their philosophic conception was different. They believed in eternal individual souls which were denied by the Buddhists. But, unlike the *Upaniṣadic* doctrine, they regarded each individual soul as eternal, and they had no conception of one eternal soul in which the individual souls are to be ultimately merged.

The rise of these revolutionary religious sects reacted on the orthodox system and led to the formulation of its doctrines in a more coordinated and logical form. The complacent dogmatism of old was rudely shattered by Buddhism and Jainism, which raised the fundamental problems of religion and approached them with a new and critical outlook. The orthodox leaders, in order to meet their bold challenge, tried to set their house in order by two distinct methods. First, they codified and systematized their philosophical and religious doctrines and tried to put them on the unassailable basis of logic and reason. Secondly, they tried to outflank the heterodox systems by accepting those elements which seemed to be the basis of their universal appeal and widespread popularity.

The religious culture of the period 400-200 B.C. is the result of this interaction between these contending forces; and we may note the following developments as the chief landmarks of the period: (i) The formulation of the six systems of philosophy, viz., Nyāya, Vaiśeṣika, Sāṁkhya, Yoga, Pūrva-Mīmāṁsā, and Vedānta; Among these the Pūrva-Mīmāṁsā is an attempt to give a rational and philosophic interpretation of the Vedic teachings, specially the sacrificial system; (ii) Development of Śaivism into a complete theistic system within the orthodox fold; (iii) Winning over of the Bhāgavata sect for the orthodox faith by the identification of Kṛṣṇa with the Vedic god Viṣṇu, (iv) Popularization of the remodelled religion and philosophy by means of epics like the *Rāmāyaṇa* and the *Mahābhārata*; (v) Buddhism and Jainism were alone left outside the pale of orthodox culture to continue the struggle. They gradually gained in power and popularity and for a time almost completely overshadowed their rivals. Buddhism spread far beyond the frontiers of India, and ultimately became a world-religion.

Buddhism first obtained a dominant position in India under the patronage of the great emperor Aśoka (c. 273-236 B.C.), the grand-son of Chandragupta. It is now a matter of common knowledge that by his missionary propaganda Buddhism not only spread all over India, but even far outside its boundaries, and ultimately became a world-religion, a position which it even now occupies, as its votaries number about one-third of the entire human race. With the dominance of Buddhism, Jainism lost its stronghold in eastern India, but found a secure shelter in the south and west, with powerful centres at Mathurā and Ujjayinī in the north. Buddhism rapidly spread to all corners of India and planted its outposts in Tibet, Ceylon, and Burma as well as in western, central and south-east Asia. By the first century A.D., it had reached China; and from China it ultimately penetrated into Korea and Japan. The foreign races like the Greeks and the Scythians who invaded India during 200 B.C. to A.D. 100 largely adopted this faith.

The adoption of Buddhism by diverse races with varying types and grades of civilization could not but exert a great influence upon its subsequent history. New tendencies are noticeable since the time of Aśoka, which ultimately took a definite shape in the time of Kaniṣka (c. first eentury A.D.). The old and new doctrines are known respectively as Hīnayāna and Mahāyāna. The transition was so gradual that one almost imperceptibly led to the other. Yet some fundamental differences can be easily discerned between the early doctrines of Buddhism, as formulated in the Pāli canon (fourth and third century B.C.), and the principles of Mahāyāna in its fully developed form, as expounded in its Sanskrit texts. The Hīnayānist had no concern for God, and regarded Buddha as a perfect man whose precepts and examples were to be followed by each individual for reaching *nirvāṇa* or freedom from bondage, and cessation of existence, practically annihilation. Mahāyānism regarded Buddha as a god, and evolved an elaborate metaphysics involving a pantheon of gods and goddesses. Devotion to Buddha and worship of his images formed a more essential part than the pursuit of an arduous life of morality. The ideal is not the state of an Arhat, who reaches the perfect state through his own powers, but that of a Bodhisattva, who stops short of Arhatship in order to help struggling humanity on the path to salvation. The Hīnayāna ideal is more or less egoistic, whereas the Mahāyānists are inspired by love for fellow-beings, and theirs is not annihilation, but positive bliss. Consciously or unconsciously the Mahāyāna was making a near approach to theistic systems.[1]

There is little doubt that the transformation of Buddhism is partially due to the impact of the rude uncivilized races that adopted Buddhism. The need of presenting the religion in a form which could easily appeal to their heart and mind could not but alter its character, nor could these races embrace Buddhism without introducing into it many of their

1. Vide Elliot, Sir Charles, *Hinduism and Buddhism*; also see, Thakur, U., *Studies in Jainism and Buddhism in Mithila.*

superstitious rites and practices. The Mahāyāna had to tolerate them and developed a flexible adaptability which chaıacterized it throughout its history. This attitude brought it great popularity and enabled it to stride in triumph across the whole continent of Asia.

We have some means of testing the relative strength of the different religious sects in India during the period 300 B.C. to A.D. 300. More than fifteen hundred inscriptions belonging to this period have been discovered so far. Of these, not even fifty belong to the religious sects other than Buddhism and Jainism. The proportion should not be taken as an exact measure of the relative strength and popularity of the orthodox and heterodox doctrines, because accident must have played a great part in the preservation or destruction of records, and some of the disparity may be due to the habit of engraving numerous records on religious structures, which was more marked in one sect than in another. But even making due allowance for all these factors, no doubt can remain of the preponderating influence of the two heterodox religious sects during the period 300 B.C. to A.D. 300. This view is further strengthened by the fact that if we take the epigraphic records for the five centuries following A.D. 300, we find that the position had almost entirely been reversed, and the orthodox sects like Vaiṣṇavism and Śaivism now occupy the position of dominance which had hitherto been enjoyed by their heterodox rivals.

In conclusion, the fact must be emphasised that in addition to the main religious sects mentioned above, there were a large number of minor ones such as the Ājīvikas, and reference is made to worshippers of not only divine or semi-divine beings like Pūrṇabhadra, Maṇibhadra, Candra, Sūrya, Gandharvas, etc., but also of animals like elephant, horse, cow, dog etc.

The Paurāṇic Age (c. A.D. 300-1200)

The fourth century A.D. may be regarded as a turning-point in the religious history of India. Since that date we find the gradual dominance of Brāhmaṇical religion and the steady decline of Buddhism and Jainism. By the twelfth century A.D., Buddhism, as an independent sect, had wellnigh vanished from India, while Jainism was almost reduced to the position of a local sect in western India.

The most important characteristic features of the religious culture of the period are: (1) Downfall of Buddhism in India; (2) Decline of Jainism; (3) Reconciliation of Vedic faith with sectarianism, and the evolution of synthetic Hinduism; (4) History of Śaivism, Śaktism, Vaiṣṇavism, and minor religious sects and popular beliefs; (5) Introduction of new religions.

Before we proceed to discuss these in detail, a few general observations may be made regarding the religious development of the period.

In the first place, it appears from a study of the history of the period that the fortunes of religions depend to no small extent upon the patronage of royal families. At the beginning of the period, the Guptas were the leading power, and for two centuries they dominated over nearly the whole of northern India. They were powerful adherents of the Bhāgavata sect, and this undoubtedly was the main factor in the history of its rapid progress and development at the cost of Buddhism. Of the dynasties that succeeded the Guptas in various parts of northern India, the later Guptas, the Pratīhāras, the Candellas, the Maukharis, the Kalacuris, the Valabhis, and the Varman kings of Kāmarūpa were either Vaiṣṇavas or Śaivas. The Pālas of Bengal were patrons of Buddhism, but their successors, the Senas, were Śaivas and Vaiṣṇavas. It must be mentioned, however, that the line of difference between Śaivism and Vaiṣṇavism was not very marked, and the official records of the same dynasty bear invocation to either Śiva or Viṣṇu. We have also examples of individual kings like Harṣavardhana, who, although officially professing Śaivism, was strongly inclined towards Buddhism as Hiuen-Tsang informs us. Again, in the same family, different kings belonged to different sects, the most typical example being that of Harṣavardhana, the kings of which were devotees of the Sun-god, Buddha, and Śiva.

In the Deccan, the early Cālukya kings were patrons of Jainism, but the Brāhmaṇical religions, both orthodox and sectarian, flourished under the later kings. The Rāṣṭrakūṭa dynasty also professed Brāhmaṇical religion, though some of the kings patronized Jainism. In the extreme south, Jainism was patronized by the early Pallavas and Hoysaḷas, but the later Pallavas were Śaivas and the later Hoysaḷas most ardent devotees of Vaiṣṇavism. This brief, though very incomplete, historical survey would show the gradual loss of royal patronage suffered by both the Jains and the Buddhists.

Secondly, we must note the rise of a debased element in the religions of the day which is generally, though not perhaps very accurately referred to as Tāntricism. Though more closely associated with the Śākta sect, to be noted later, some of its characteristics such as mystic magical beliefs, degraded erotic practices, and extreme veneration for the guru—sometimes leading to gross indecency and lax morality—are common features to be observed in greater or lesser degree in all the principal religions of the time, except Jainism.

Thirdly, we may note that the worship of images of gods, with elaborate rituals and erection of large temples for them, becomes a characteristic feature of the religions of the period.

We may now proceed to discuss in detail the characteristic features of the period noted above:

(1) *Downfall of Buddhism*

The most potent cause of the decline of Buddhism in India was the loss of royal patronage. In northern India, the patronage of Harṣavardhana and the Pāla emperors gave a long lease of life to Buddhism, but with those notable exceptions the other royal families were staunch adherents of the Brāhmaṇical sects. The passing away of the Pālas in the twelfth century A.D. and the destruction of the Buddhist monasteries by the Islamic invaders dealt the severe and final death-blow to Buddhism. The monasteries were the chief strongholds of Buddhism, while the strength of the Jains lay rather in the mass of lay followers. Hence Jainism survived the downfall of its monasteries, while Buddhism perished in its ruins.

The decline of royal patronage was perhaps as much a cause, as the result, of the growing unpopularity of Buddhism. The chief cause of this unpopularity was the development of the Tāntric beliefs and rituals which we have noted above. Whatever might have been the original ideal behind it, some of the debased forms which are met with from the seventh century onwards can only be regarded as a travesty of Buddhism. Even gross sensuality and carnal passions of man found a religious sanction in some tenets of these schools, and the result was a looseness of sexual morality masquerading in the name of religion. It would be, of course, untrue to say that purer forms of Buddhism did not flourish at the period. But the masses naturally followed what was more suited to their tastes, and their unbridled licentiousness brought odium upon the whole religion and hastened its decline and downfall.[1]

In addition to these causes, another powerful factor was working to the same end. The Mahāyāna form of Buddhism, as we have seen before, made a very near approach to the theistic system. Adaptability was always a great characteristic of Buddhism, and its close rapprochement to Brāhmaṇical religion was dangerous to its separate existence. The leaders of the Brāhmaṇical religion were not yet too rigid and conservative to let slip any opportunity of capturing the great stronghold of a powerful rival. As in old days Vaiṣṇavism was won over by the acceptance of Kṛṣṇa as an *avatāra* of Viṣṇu, so about a thousand years later Buddha was regarded as another *avatāra* of the same God. This well-conceived and bold stroke of policy cut the grass from under the feet of Buddhism which was already steadily losing ground, and the ultimate result was the complete effacement of Buddhism from India as a separate sect.

(2) *Decline of Jainism*

Jainism, alone of all religions, was free from the Tāntric development. The rigid conservatism, to which it owed this fortune, however, paved the way for its decline, as it failed to keep abreast with the changing spirit of

1. For different causes of the downfall of Buddhism see, Thakur, U., op. cit.

the times. The new rituals and practices of Vaiṣṇavism, Śaivism, and other sects proved too alluring, and gradually Jainism lost its importance in Mysore and Maharashtra, where it had exercised a dominant influence for nearly a thousand years. Jainism has steadily maintained its old character and has chosen to die rather than surrender its essentials. Fortunately it still maintains its hold among a very influential section of the community in western India. This may partly be due to the fact that it preserved some essential Hindu practices like caste and winked at the worship of some popular deities like Gaṇeśa.[1]

(3) *Evolution of Synthetic Hinduism*

With the decline of Buddhism and Jainism, the Brāhmaṇical religion gradually rose into importance.[2] But there was no homogeneity in it. It included orthodox Brāhmaṇism, i.e. the remnant of the old Vedic cult, and the different sectarian religions, notably Śaivism, Śāktism, and Vaiṣṇavism. Although these were admitted within the orthodox fold, they still retained their essential characteristics and formed distinct entities.

At the very beginning of the period, we notice a systematization of their faiths and beliefs in a number of texts, known as *Purāṇas* and *Smṛtis*. The *Smṛtis* preserve a link with the old *Gṛhya-Sūtras*, describing the Vedic rituals and sacrifices. The *Purāṇas* present the theology of the new sects with the old philosophical and cosmogonical beliefs in the background.

The orthodox Vedic religion was patronized by the Pallavas, Vākāṭakas, the Bhāgadatta dynasty of Kāmarūpa (Assam), and other royal dynasties, and the inscriptions of the period contain frequent references to Vedic cults and sacrifices. These are, however, not unoften combined with pure sectarian worship.

Indeed, one of the most important traits of the Brāhmaṇical religion of this period is this spirit of reconciliation and harmony between orthodox and sectarian forms. Its most notable expression is to be found in the theological conception of *Trimûrti*, i.e. the manifestation of the supreme God in three forms of Brahmā, Viṣṇu and Śiva—Brahmā, the creator, being undoubtedly a pale reflex of the *Upaniṣadic* Brahman. But the attempt cannot be regarded as a great success, for Brahmā never gained an ascendancy comparable to that of Śiva or Viṣṇu, and the different sects often conceived the Trimūrti as really the three manifestations of their own sectarian, god, whom they regarded as Brahman or Absolute. Still the spirit of reconciliation bore significant results. Henceforth

1. For details of Jainism see, Thakur, U., op. cit.
2. For details see Hopkins, E.W., op. cit.; also see Monier-Williams, *Hinduism*, Chap. VII.

the Hindus may be divided broadly into two classes, viz. (1) extreme sectarians who confined their devotion and worship almost exclusively to their sectarian deity like Viṣṇu, Śiva, Śakti, etc; and (2) general followers of the Brāhmaṇical religion who revered and worshipped all these and other gods, even though they might have been specially attached to one sectarian deity, and also followed some of the important Vedic rituals and practices. Thus the Smārtas prescribed the regular worship of the five gods Viṣṇu, Śiva, Durga, Sūrya, and Gaṇeśa, while the rest of the Hindu pantheon was also freely worshipped by many. The samuccaya doctrine lays down that a Hindu even when seeking Brahman, must perform his ordinary duties, and should have a knowledge of the Karma-Mīmāṁsā as well as the Vedānta. The use of the sacred thread and performance of the *gāyatrī* and other rituals by the sectarians may be ascribed to this spirit.

A further step towards the reconciliation of the different sects may be traced in the attempt to establish the identity of Viṣṇu and Śiva, such as we find in the *Skanda Upaniṣad.* The image of Hari-Hara, like that of Ardhanārīśvara (Śiva-Pārvatī) is a visible symbol of this doctrine. There is hardly any doubt that, in spite of the existence of the extreme sectarians who would not tolerate any god other than their own, the general mass of Hindus, even today, while professing one sect or other, have a general reverence for all the Hindu gods. The epigraphical records prove that this has been the case throughout the period under review.

Lastly, there was an attempt to prove that the six systems of Hindu philosophy are not really opposed to each other, but they all proclaim the same eternal truth. This view is first met with in *Prabodha-candrodaya*, an allegorical Sanskrit drama written in the court of the Candella king Kīrtivarman in the latter half of the eleventh century A.D. In a famous scene in this drama, there is a dispute between the Buddhists, Jains, and followers of other heterodox sects on one side, and the Vaiṣṇavas, Śaivas, and Sauras, aided by the six schools of philosophy, on the other. The basic unity of orthodox Hinduism as against the heterodox sects, which is not vividly brought into prominence in this scene, forms a feature of Hinduism up to the present. Vijñāna Bhikṣu, a Sāṁkhya philosopher of the sixteenth century, also proclaims the essential unity of the six systems of philosophy.

It now remains for us to trace the fortunes of the two great sectarian theistic systems, Śaivism and Vaiṣṇavism, together with Śāktism and other minor religious sects and popular beliefs from the fourth century A.D. onward. At the very beginning of the period, we notice a systematization of their faiths and beliefs in the *Purāṇas*. These texts are many in number, and while some like *Vāyu, Viṣṇu, Matsya, Mārkaṇḍeya, Bhāgavata* and *Brahmāṇḍa Purāṇas* are really old, others were added in much later times.

These *Purāṇas* present the two theistic (and also other sectarian) beliefs in a complete form, a form which they have retained till today.

(4) *Śaivism*

The Pāśupata sect continued to flourish during this period. Hiuen-Tsang and Bāṇa Bhaṭṭa, both belonging to the seventh century A.D., refer to it as one of the prominent religious sects of the time. In addition to the *Purāṇas* such as *Vāyu*, *Liṅga*, *Kūrma*, etc., the Śaiva theism was expounded in the Āgamas. There are twenty-eight of these manuals, each of which has got a number of Upāgamas, the total number of texts reaching to about 200. The Āgamas were composed before the seventh century A.D., and their dualistic teaching formed the foundation of a new Śaiva school which is usually referred to as Āgamic Śaivism.[1] The Advaita philosophy of Śaṅkara gave a new turn to Śaivism. A distinct school flourished in Kashmir, about the middle of the ninth century A.D. mainly under the influence of Śaṅkara's philosophy, and substituted the Advaita philosophy for the dualistic teachings of the Āgamas.

There was a great upsurge of Śaivism in south India, which was mainly due to the devotional poems of Nāyanmārs (Śaiva saints), written in Tamil. These are divided into eleven collections which, together with the Tamil *Purāṇa* called *Periya Purāṇam*, constitute the sacred literature of the saints and form the foundation of Tamil Śaivism. The first seven collections, known as *Devāram*, composed by the saints Sambandar, his older contemporary Appar, and Sundarar, all of whom flourished in the seventh century A.D. or shortly thereafter, are regarded as equivalent to the Vedas and are sung along with Vedic hymns in certain religious processions. The eighth collection, *Tiruvācakam* of Māṇikkavācagar, occupies the foremost place in Śaiva literature. This, together with the tenth collection, *Tirumandiram* of Tirūmular, reflects the theology of the Āgamas, and both are masterpieces of poetic composition. The patronage of the later Pallava kings (from sixth century A.D.) and the mighty Cola emperors (tenth century A.D.) gave a great impetus to Śaivism in the Draviḍa country.

A further development of Tamil Śaivism took place in the thirteenth and fourteenth centuries A.D., perhaps even a little earlier. This was the rise of Śaiva Siddhānta. The Āgamas were now replaced by the fourteen Siddhānta-śāstras, which laid the foundation of this new system.

An influential and very powerful Śaiva sect, known as the Vīraśaivas or Liṅgāyatas rose in the Karnatak and Maharashtra countries. The early history of the sect is obscure, but it was most probably founded, or at

1. For details see Bhandarkar, R.G. op. cit.; also see Monier-Williams, op. cit., Chap. VIII.

least brought into prominence, by Basava, the Brāhmaṇa prime minister of Bijjaḷa who had usurped the Cālukya throne about A.D. 1160. This new sect flourished at the cost of Jainism and Buddhism and was the main cause of their decay in the Deccan and Kannada districts, which constitute now its main stronghold.

The Vīraśaivas have several peculiar characteristics. They give great prominence to the monasteries. In every Liṅgāyata village there is a monastery, and every Liṅgāyata must belong to a monastery and have a guru; he need not visit a temple at all. 'The members of the sect worship Śiva in his phallic form, reject the authority of the *Vedas*, disbelieve in the doctrine of rebirth, object to child-marriage, approve of the remarriage of widows, and cherish an intense aversion to the Brāhmaṇas'.

(5) *Śāktism*

The cult of Śakti, consort of Śiva, attained a great predominance during this period. It is based upon the Sāṁkhya philosophy, according to which Spirit or Puruṣa (here identified with Śiva) is inactive, while Prakṛti (identified with Śakti) is productive and the universal material cause. Hence Śakti is in a sense superior to Śiva.

The system lays stress on the inherent power of sounds and the presence, in the human body, of a large number of minute channels or threads of occult force (nāḍī) and six great centres of that force (cakra), described as so many lotuses, one above the other. Hence arise the supernatural powers of mantras or mystic syllables such as *hrīṁ*, *huṁ*, *phaṭ*, etc., and the working of miracles by mystic forms of yoga. Besides, the Śāktas also believe in the magic power of diagrams (*yantra*) and ritualistic gestures made with fingers (*mudrā*).

The worship of the goddess Śakti was accompanied with sacrifices of animals and occasionally also human beings. But the most characteristic feature of the cult was the cakra-pūjā, i.e. circle worship in which an equal number of men and women sit round a circle and, uttering mystic mantras, partake of the *pañcatattva* consisting of five elements. viz., wine, meat, fish, parched grain, and sex. Many sorcerous practices formed a part of the cult, and a picture of this is given in the Sanskrit drama *Mālatī-Mādhava.* Detailed instructions of these practices are given in the text known as Tantras. Hence Tāntricism is used as a general name for similar rituals which are found in many religious sects. The Śaiva Kāpālikas and Kālāmukhas for example, followed similar rituals and practices, and they are found associated with the worship of many other goddesses.

Taken at its best, the Tāntric doctrine, both in Brāhmaṇical religion and Buddhism, is a philosophy, according to which the Absolute is associated with a dynamic principle for the origination of the universe and the different deities can be located in the different parts of the human body (*nyāsa*) by means of a form of yoga. By worshipping Śakti, Prajñā (Mahāyānist goddess), or other goddesses, in the manner indicated above, it seeks to attain, in a supernatural manner, and in an incredibly short time, objects of either material nature (wealth, longevity, invulnerability, etc.) or spiritual character (power of evoking Buddha or union with some divinity even in this life). Some Tantras, however, at their worst, uphold theories which are revolting and horrible.

(6) *Vaiṣṇavism*

We have noted above the three basic elements of Vaiṣṇavism, viz. the original Bhāgavata doctrine, the Pāñcarātra system, and the Gopāla (cowherd)-kṛṣṇa saga, culminating in the Rādhākṛṣṇa cult. During the period under review the Pāñcarātra first comes into prominent notice and is later superseded by the third element.

The most important development of the system is the growth of Pāñcarātra *Saṁhitās* which give a complete exposition of the faiths, beliefs, and practices of the Vaiṣṇavas. The traditional number of these *Saṁhitās* is 108, but nearly double that number of texts are named. Their dates are uncertain, but may be placed between A.D. 600 and 800. They show a considerable influence of the Tāic ntrelement and lay stress on the Śakti of Viṣṇu. Otherwise, they show a normal development of the teaching formulated in the Nārāyaṇīya section of the *Mahābhārata*.

But the Pāñcarātra system shows from the beginning the influence of the third element. The *Viṣṇu Purāṇa*, which is an important text of the system, contains the detailed story of cowherd Kṛṣṇa and his youthful sports. The *Bhāgavata Purāṇa* heralds a new departure. It concentrates its attention almost solely on the cowherd-life of Kṛṣṇa and dwells specially on his amorous sports with the *gopis* which are described here in all their details, while in the life of Kṛṣṇa such as we find in the *Harivaṁsa* and *Viṣṇu Purāṇa* they are hardly noticed at all. But the most distinguishing feature of the *Bhāgavata Purāṇa* is the exalted tone of *Bhakti* or devotion which is displayed throughout the work. The fervent emotionalism which characterizes mediaeval Vaiṣṇavism has its origin in this really great work.

The date of the *Bhāgavata Purāṇa* is uncertain, but it is generally regarded as a late work. The various dates suggested range from the seventh to the ninth century A.D. It must be noted, however, that even the *Bhāgavata Purāṇa* does not mention Rādhā, though it undoubtedly contained elements which might easily give rise to this cult. For, according to it, among the *gopis* there was one who was the special favourite of Kṛṣṇa. But it is difficult to say when this Rādhā cult actually came into being. It was a well-known thing in Bengal by the time of Jayadeva, the Bengali poet, who composed his immortal *Gīta-Govinda* in the court of Lakṣmaṇa Sena during the last quarter of the twelfth century A.D. Rādhā is mentioned in a verse quoted in the *Dhvanyāloka* (c. A.D. 850) and in the *Gopālatāpanī Upaniṣad* and *Brahmavaivarta Purāṇa.* But the dates of the last two works are not known, and they may not be earlier than the eleventh century A.D. A ruined temple, discovered at Paharpur in Bengal, contains sculptured representations of Kṛṣṇa's life, and in one of these, Kṛṣṇa is accompanied by a female. This has been taken to be a representation of Kṛṣṇa and Rādhā, but there is no positive evidence in support of it. The date of the temple is also uncertain but it may belong to the sixth or seventh century A.D. The name of Rādhā occurs in Hāla's *Saptaśatī*, and if the verse is really as old as the time of Hāla, it furnishes the solitary evidence of the prevalence of the cult in the early centuries of the Christian era.

It is generally believed that the *Bhāgavata Purāṇa* was written in South India. Whether this is true or not, there is no doubt that the pure devotional element of Vaiṣṇavism flourished in the Tamil country. The most remarkable specimen of this is contained in the songs of the famous Āḷvārs, the Vaiṣṇava counterpart of the Śaiva Nāyanmārs, mentioned above. Their number is usually reckoned as twelve, and although their dates are uncertain, they may be all placed between the fifth and ninth centuries A.D. Their devotional songs, called *Prabandham*, written mostly in Tamil, are known as the *Vaiṣṇava Veda*, and their images are worshipped along with those of Viṣṇu.

The next great landmark in the history of Tamil Vaiṣṇavism is the rise of a school of philosophers known as *Ācāryas*. Nāthamuni, the first of these, flourished about the end of the tenth or the beginning of the eleventh century A.D. He organized the Śrī-Vaiṣṇavas, and popularized the cult among the masses by collecting the songs of the Āḷvārs, setting them to Dravidian music, and having them regularly sung in the temples. But he was also a great theologian, and his school took up the task of giving a philosophical background to the Vaiṣṇava theories and creeds. Nāthamuni was followed by three *Ācāryas*, of whom the last, his grandson Yāmunācārya, was a great scholar.

The philosophy of Rāmānuja was further developed by Madhva or Ānanda Tīrtha (thirteenth century A.D.), the founder of another sect. He conceived God as altogether distinct from the individual spirit. He travelled all over India, fighting the philosophical doctrines of Śaṅkara and establishing the Vaiṣṇava creed on a definite dualistic basis.

Rāmānuja had followed more or less Vāsudevism of the old Pāñcarātra system, recognizing Vāsudeva with his four *vyūhas*, and his identity with Viṣṇu and Nārāyana. But Madhva ignored Vāsudeva and his *vyūhas* and referred to the supreme Spirit mostly as Viṣṇu. Thus a general Vaiṣṇavism took the place of the old Bhāgavata school.

The southern Vaiṣṇavism laid little stress on the cowherd element of Kṛṣṇa and altogether ignored Rādhā. Far different, however, was the case with Vaiṣṇavism in northern India, which was first put on a philosophic basis by Nimbārka who flourished after Rāmānuja, probably in the twelfth century A.D. His philosophy is a compromise between those of Rāmānuja and Madhva, as he believes God to be both identical with, and distinct from, the individual spirit. But his chief difference from his predecessor Rāmānuja lies in substituting the old and pure *bhakti* (devotion) for *upāsanā* (meditation), and giving prominence to the elements of Kṛṣṇa and Rādhā. Born in the family of a Tailanga Brāhmaṇa in the South (perhaps Bellary District) Nimbārka lived in Vṛndāvana (near Mathurā) and his sect, known as Sanaka-sampradāya, flourishes in northern India.

According to Nimbārka, Rādhā was the eternal consort of Viṣṇu and was incarnated like him in Vṛndāvana. There is also a suggestion, though not a clear statement, that she became the wife of her lord. A further progress of the Rādhā cult is found in Jayadeva's *Gīta-Govinda*, where Rādhā is the mistress and not the wife of Kṛṣṇa.

Among other sects stressing the worship of Rādhā may be mentioned the followers of Viṣṇusvāmin, about whom, however, very little is known. He closely follows the system of Madhva, but introduces the Rādhā element. He may have preceded Nimbārka. It may be noted that Nimbārka worshipped only Kṛṣṇa and his consort to the exclusion of other gods. He thus discarded the samuccaya doctrine followed by the Śrī-Vaiṣṇavas, Madhvas, Viṣṇusvāmins, and generally by all the Bhāgavatas, and became a purely sectarian Vaiṣṇava.[1]

Minor Religious Sects and Popular Beliefs

In addition to the main sects hitherto described, there were during the period under review minor sects worshipping various other deities. Most of these are associated with either Śiva or Viṣṇu. Thus Durgā, Gaṇapati, and Skanda (Kārttikeya)[2] the consort and sons of Śiva, were regularly worshipped under various names, and each had an organized following and a sectarian literature. Similarly there were sects worshipping the Narasiṁha and Rāma incarnations of Viṣṇu.

The worship of Dharma was very much prevalent in Bengal and had an important literature. It is traced to a Buddhist origin, the second member

1. For detailed history of Vaiṣṇavism, see Bhandarkar, R.G. op. cit.; and Monier-Williams, op. cit., Chap. IX.

2. For details see Thakur, U. "Karttikeya in Literature, Art and Coins" in *East and West* (N.S.), Rome, Vol. 24, 1974.

of the Buddhist *triratna* (Buddha, Dharma, and Saṁgha) being converted to a Hindu god. Far greater importance attaches to the sects connected with the worship of Brahmā and Sūrya. Brahmā, though less important than Viṣṇu or Śiva, was the god of a sect which is referred to in the *Mārkaṇḍeya Purāṇa* and the *Pādma Purāṇa.* There is a famous temple of Brahmā in Puṣkara, near Ajmer.

Of the vast Vedic pantheon, Sūrya alone formed the god of a particular sect, and many temples were erected for his worship. This seems to be due to three reasons. In the first place the *gāyatrī-mantra,* daily repeated by the Brāhmaṇas, kept alive the memory of the Sun-god. Secondly, the orb of the sun being daily visible, the idea of his worship could not be dropped altogether. Further, the Magis of Persia brought a cult of the sun into India about the third century of the Christian era. The two streams mingled and saved the Sun-god from the fate of the other Vedic deities. Many inscriptions dating from the Gupta period refer to the worship of the Sun-god, and big temples were erected in his honour.

Outside the circle of sectarian gods mentioned above, there were quite a large number of popular deities who claimed devotion and worship from a clientele which, though not numerically insignificant, are not known to have been organized into sects. Among these may be mentioned Śrī and Lakṣmī (originally regarded as separate personalities), Gaṅgā, Yamunā, Sarasvatī, Saṣṭhī, Śitalā the *dikpālas* (especially Yama, Varuṇa, Kubera, and Agni), and *navagrahas* (Rāhu, Ketu, and seven others whose names correspond to the week days). Reference may also be made to semi-divine beings like yakṣas, nāgas, gandharvas, vidyādharas, and apsarases, who had their iconic forms like the popular deities mentioned above.

Most of the features of Brāhmaṇism noted above continued. Though no noticeable difference marks the Śaiva, Śākta, and other minor religious sects, the Vaiṣṇava cult of Kṛṣṇa and Rādhā showed new and remarkable tendencies, no doubt influenced by the *Padma* and the *Brahmavaivarta Purāṇas* in which Rādhā plays an important part in the life of Kṛṣṇa.

The cult was carried to its extreme form by a Tailanga Brāhmaṇa named Vallabha whose activity falls in the first half of the sixteenth century A.D. His Vaiṣṇavism centres round Kṛṣṇa, the beloved of the *gopīs,* and his eternal consort Rādhā. Elaborate rituals for the worship of Kṛṣṇa and religious feasts and festivals were fully developed—all marked by a spirit of sportive enjoyment. This, coupled with a less exacting demand on spiritual fervour and high tone of morality in the sect, seems to be the secret of its great hold on the masses whose ordinary inclinations find in it a comfortable religious sanction. One of the distinguishing characteristics of this sect is the exalted position of the guru, or the spiritual guide, called the *mahārāja.* God can only be worshipped in the house or temple of the guru, to whom the devotees are enjoined to surrender all their belongings. The highest spiritual object is to join in the eternal sport of Kṛṣṇa and Rādhā. The worldly life offers no bar to this salvation. True to this doctrine, the gurus were married men and led worldly lives. In its degraded form, this sect countenanced antinomian practices, and made Vaiṣṇavism a byword of reproach. The doctrine flourished mostly among the mercantile communities of Gujarat and Rajasthan, though its baneful effects spread far beyond these limits.

Bengal Viaṣṇavism was saved from this degradation by the famous Caitanya or Śrī Gaurāṅga (A.D. 1485-1533), a contemporary of Vallabha. The elements of Rādhā and Kṛṣṇa had taken deep root in its soil, as the songs of Jayadeva (twelfth century A.D.) clearly show. But the merit of Caitanya lies in the fact that he elevated the passions of the couple to a high spiritual plane and stressed the emotional at the cost of the ceremonial side of religion. His piety, devotion, and fervour introduced a pure and spiritual element in Vaiṣṇavism which offers a bright and refreshing contrast to that promulgated by Vallabha. But with the lapse of time, Rādhā gained more and more prominence, and many degrading elements crept into Bengal Vaiṣṇavism also. An extreme form is represented by the Sakhībhāvas, the ideal of the male members of which is to obtain the womanhood of Rādhā even in the physical sense.

The history of religions teaches us an important lesson. It is that any exaggerated importance attached to the female element in religion, or the association of religion with amorous elements, even though inspired or prompted by the highest spiritual motive and backed by metaphysical or mystic interpretations, is sure to lead to the degradation of its followers. This is best illustrated by the fate of the Śakta and Rādhā-Kṛṣṇa cults.

It is refreshing therefore to turn to some sects of Vaiṣṇavism which realized this truth and gave a new tone to the religion by avoiding the fatal process. This was done by twofold means. In Maharashtra, Rādhā was replaced by Rukmiṇī, the lawful wife of Kṛṣṇa, who plays all along a subordinate role to her husband. The great preachers of this sect were Nāmadeva (end of the fourteenth century A.D.) and Tukārāma (seventeenth century), the founders of the popular form of Vaiṣṇavism in Maharashtra. Another mode, propounded by Rāmānanda (fourteenth century), was to replace Kṛṣṇa and Rādhā by Rāma and Sītā. This was further developed by his famous disciples, the chief among whom were Kabir and Ravidāsa, (fifteenth century A.D.). Dadu and Malūkdāsa (c. A.D. 1600), and Tulasīdāsa (A.D. 1532-1623). The religion propounded by them was chaste and pure. The simple, beautiful verses of Nāmadeva, Tukārāma, and the disciples of Rāmānanda are full of piety and devotion, and they have acquired with celebrity far beyond sectarian limits.

2

Brahmanical Cults in South-East Asia—Origin and Expansion

Religion has been one of the most important factors in the building up of Indian civilization. It is no wonder, therefore, that the Indian colonists who founded a new kingdom in south-east Asia transplanted to their land of adoption the religious ideas with which they were imbued at home. Indeed, it is a matter of common knowledge that no other feature of Indian civilization left such a profound impress upon these colonial kingdoms, and even now, when the political supremacy of the Indians in those far-off lands is merely a dream of the past, they contain unmistakable traces of the Indian religion and its handmade art and architecture.

Several circumstances make the study of Indian religion Brāhmaṇism as developed in these countries, one of profound interest. In the first place, although it is a familiar story how Buddhism made extensive conquests in foreign lands, Hinduism had never been known to make its influence outside the boundaries of India. Yet it is precisely the conservative form of Brāhmaṇical religion that became predominant in the new colony, and dominated the entire development of Indian civilization. Secondly, the religious ideas of Indians were confronted there by a system of primitive beliefs and superstitions. Thirdly, the study of Indian religion in the countries of south-east Asia not only affords an interesting insight into the vigour and vitality of the Brāhmaṇical religion, but also shows the completeness with which the foreigners had absorbed Indian civilization. Fourthly, rulers happened to be the patrons of Indian culture. For attaining improved royal status they resorted to patronising *dharma* and for this they sought guidance and encouragement from the priests, poets, philosophers, and saints. In spite of their individual origins from different ancestries or coming to power from various sources they generally believed in a mythological ancestry denoting their becoming ruler by virtue of an element of the divine. Propagation of their adopted *dharma* (*Rāja-dharma*), construction of shrines and bringing the subjects to an upper religious strata used to be their main objectives. They generously granted lands, deserted settlements, revering tax. Most of the kings of south-east Asia assumed the role of the supreme guardian of all the religious foundations of his realm. All these actions of the kings resulted in the uplift of the cultural standard of the people. Of course the missionary zeal of the Indian religious legates too did play its own part but the great impact of Indian beliefs and faiths could not be possible, had the rulers not patronised them and had they not taken active part in expanding them. The king, therefore, was the supreme religious and cultural institution in most of the regions of south-east Asia. Nothing demonstrates more strikingly the absolute hold which the Indian civilisation had over the native mind. It is not only a story of a great triumph, but of a triumph against enormous odds. However, it seems that Brāhmaṇical religion was not probably much behind Buddhism in respect of missionary zeal and proselytising activity.

The Brāhmaṇical religion that flourished in south-east Asia was not the Vedic religion of the old but the neo-Brāhmaṇical religion that was evolved in India almost at the same time as Buddhism and Jainism. The essential character of this new religion was its sectarian character, the chief gods being recognised by them were Brahmā (creator), Śiva (destroyer) and Viṣṇu (protector). They are also called as the great gods of Brāhmaṇical trinity. It is after the name of these gods that the Brāhmaṇical sects like Brāhmaṇism, Śaivism and Vaiṣṇavism respectively emerge as a religious force in the countries of south-east Asia. Confirmation and illustration of what has been said above meet us at almost every step as we proceed with the history of Brāhmaṇical religion in the regions under discussion.

1. *CAMBODIA*

Now let us turn first to Cambodia, Kambuja (Cambodia is the English version of this Sanskrit name) was one of the various south-east Asian countries which felt the impact of Brāhmaṇic culture during the period under review and the Baāhmaṇical gods of trinity, viz., Brahmā, Śiva and Viṣṇu played an important role in the religious life of the Cambodians. The details are as follows:

Brahmā

The cult of Brahmā, known as Brāhmaṇism, is rarely mentioned in the inscriptions of Cambodia. In sculpture also he does not have any important position. His image has been found at Prāsāt Samrong. In Prāsāt Sneg Krabei he is seen occupying the middle place and on his right is four-faced Brahmā and on his left is Viṣṇu. Besides the Brāhmaṇa monuments,

Brahmā can be seen in the monuments of the Buddhist also.

Śiva

Śiva is one of the three gods of the trinity who occupies the most important position among the Brāhmaṇical cults of Cambodia. It is held that the cult of Śiva was introduced in Funan by Kauṇḍinya[1] but this view is not supported by the available facts. Tke earliest evidence in this context can be dated to the 5th century A.D. The Chinese annals tell us of the prevalence of the cult of Maheśvara (Śiva) in the country in this century.[2] We can, however, presume that this cult by then must have become quite popular so as to attract the attention of the Chinese observers. The first inscriptional evidence of the prevalence of Śaiva doctrine, however, is provided by Phṇom Bayang inscription dated A.D. 624.[3] The inscription is as follows:

Yam āntarañ jyotir upāsate budhā
niruttaraṃ brahma parañ jigīṣavaḥ
tapaśśrutejyāvidhayo yadarpaṇā
bhavanty anirdeśyaphalānubandhinaḥ
na kevalaṃ tatphalayogasaṅginām
asaṅgināṃ karmaphalatyajäm api
nisargasiddhair animādibhir guṇair
upetam angīkṛtaśaktivistaraiḥ
dhiyām atitaṃ vachasām agocharam
anāspadaṃ yasya padaṁ vidur budhāḥ

When translated into English this will read as follows:

"Whom (Śiva) the sages, desirous of conquering the supreme (condition), the absolute brahman, worship as the internal light;

"Through whom the practices of austerity, study and sacrifice, provided they are offered to Him, bring about undefinable results, not only for those who are (still) attached to the acquisition of the fruits of those works but also for those who are completely detached and have renounced all fruits of action;

"Whose foot[4] without stand, endowed with tenuity and other qualities

1. Ghosh, M.M., *A History of Cambodia*, p. 50.
2. Cf. Chatterjee, B.R., *Indian Culture Influence in Cambodia*, p. 221.
3. Barth, A. and Bergaigne, A., *Inscriptions Sanscrites de Campa et du Cambodge*, V.
4. This inscription relates the installation or the restoration of a Śivapada. As to what is exactly meant by a Śivapada (the foot of Śiva) we do not precisely know, as several parts of the inscription have suffered damage, but it was probably something corresponding to the Viṣṇupada of Gaya (the Viṣṇupada of Gaya is the footprint of God Viṣṇu). But the symbol of Śiva's foot-print is almost unknown in India.

which are inherent in Him, and which develop through the action of the energies. He assumes, foot that surpasses the power of all thoughts and all words, is known only to the sages".

It can be distinctly noted that Śiva is perceived here as a personal god, but the tone of the inscription is distinctly Vedāntic.[1] He is also identified with the absolute Brahman. Moreover, herein the idea of Yoga is also discernible.[2] Śiva is the 'internal light' meditated upon by sages and this internal light is the Universal Self. The perception of this immanent principle leads to that of the transcendent principle, the *Pārabrahman* or *Paramātmān.*[3]

The immanent and transcendental aspect of Śiva[4] gave rise to the concept of Aṣṭa-mūrti.[5] The eight forms are represented by Earth, Water, Fire, Wind, Ether, Sun, Moon and *ātman* or *yajamāna.* Through these eight forms, and especially through the last one, the essence of Śiva penetrates the cosmos.[6] A Cambodian inscription of the 11th century, however, mentions that it is Śiva's light which shines in Earth, Water, Fire, Wind, Ether, Sun and Moon.[7] The light here is undoubtedly ātman for the 'internal light' referred to in the Phnom Bayang inscription of A.D. 604 and A.D. 624 is nothing but the universal ātman.

The Aṣṭa-mūrti concept, besides playing a speculative role in Cambodia, also influenced the cult. It gave birth to eight liṅgas. Epigraphy tells us also that to the god were offered garlands of eight flowers.[8] These customs were also prevalent in India and are attested to by texts bearing on Śaiva cult.[9] There are, however, certain minor variations in the Śaiva practices of the two countries. While in India seven liṅgas were raised around an eighth liṅga, in Cambodia probably eight lingas were themselves raised

1. Chatterjee, B.R., *op. cit.*, p. 42.
2. Bhattacharya, K., Religious Speculations in Ancient Cambodia, R.C. Majumdar Volume (1970), p. 79.
3. Zieseniss, A., Studien zur Geschichte des Śivaismus, Bijdragen, 98, pp. 86-88.
4. The Indian belief is somewhat similar. The Vedic Puruṣa is also immanent and transcendent (*Ṛg Veda,* X, 90). This idea is developed by the older Upanṣiads like the *Bṛhadāranyaka* and the *Chāndogya,* and the later theism reproduces it in the very term of the hymn (Cf. *Svetāśvatara Upaniṣad,* III, 14-15). In the current terminology too Śiva is *Viśvarūpa* and *Viśvādhika,* cf. *Liṅga Purāṇa* (Veṅkaṭeśvara ed.) II.17.4; II.18.4.
5. Bhattacharya, K., "The Aṣṭa-Mūrti concept of Śiva in India, Indo-China and Indonesia", *IHQ,* XXIX, p. 233ff.
6. *Śiva Purāṇa* (Veṅkateśvara ed.), VII, 2, 3, 28.
7. Coedes, G., *Inscriptions du Cambodge,* VI, p. 229.
8. Bhattacharya, K., *loc. cit.*
9. Subrahmanya Sastri, K.M. (Ed.), *Somaśambhu-paddhati,* p. 174, Śloka-243.

around a new central liṅga.[1] Probably the central liṅga represented the supreme and formless Śiva, whereas the surrounding eight liṅgas were his manifestations. In this connection it may be noted that the inscriptions refer to seven forms of liṅga which are the following: - 1. Ratnaliṅga, 2. Jaṭāliṅga, 3. Mamliṅga, 4. Suvarṇaliṅga, 5. Mukhaliṅga, 6. Hemaliṅga, 7. Svayambhūvaliṅga.

The Sanskrit inscriptions of Cambodia emphasise the omnipresence of Śiva[2] and say that His universal light shines beyond darkness.[3] He is compared to Ether[4] and is variously called as nirguṇa (without qualities), niṣkala (devoid of parts), kavala (unique), atanu (bodyless) and śūnya (void).[5] It is through his śakti (energy)[6] that he manifests himself in diverse forms and hence he is multiple.[7] The beginning and the end of the creation is also attributed to Śiva[8] though he himself is regarded as endless.[9] The trinity (Brahmā, Viṣṇu and Rudra) emanates from him.[10] Thus the entire creation is a reflection of Śiva, being different only in external aspects. This "identity in difference is referrred to in the Prāsāt Khana inscription (of the reign of Rājendravarman, A.D. 944-968.[11] At another place, i.e., in an inscription from Koh Ker (reign of Jayavarman IV A.D. 921-941)[12], Śiva is conceived as the cosmic pillar or the axis of the universe. The same cosmic pillar, which is a manifestation of Brahman-Prajāpati-Puruṣa-Agni, is also conceived as a column of fire[13] which is quite akin to the luminous liṅga referred to by Bāṇa.[14] in early medieval India.

An inscription from Bantey Srei (of A.D. 969), which regard Śiva as pure consciousness, seems to allude to the growth of a monistic doctrine.[15] It seems that these ideas which were conceived in India precisely at the same time[16] found their way into Cambodia quite quickly. That ideas

1. Bhattacharya, K., *R.C. Majumdar Volume*, p. 80.
2. Coedes, G., *op. cit.*, III, p. 106.
3. Barth, A. and Bergaigne, A., *op. cit.*, XVII, A, 1.
4. Coedes, G., *op. cit.*, I, p. 148.
5. *ibid.*, p. 19.
6. *ibid.*, III, p. 182.
7. *ibid.*, I, p. 19.
8. *ibid.*, III, p. 46.
9. *ibid.*, I, p. 13.
10. Barth, A. and Bergaigne, A., *op. cit.*, LV. 1.
11. *Bulletin de l'Ecole Francaise d'Extreme-Orient*, XI, p. 405.
12. Coedes, G., *op. cit.*, I, p. 62.
13. Bosch, F.D.K., *De gouden Kiem*, pp. 236-39. This book was translated into English in 1960 under the title *The Golden Germ*.
14. Gopinatha Rao, T.A., *Elements of Hindu Iconography*, II. 2, p. 364.
15. Bhattacharya, K., *op. cit.*, p. 82.
16. Cf. Chapter of the *Śiva and Liṅga Purāṇa* that proclaim the Śivādvaita.

quickly travelled from India to Cambodia is attested by the fact that the Śaiva cult, which, according to the comparative testimony of Śaṅkarāchārya's commentary on *Brahmasūtra*, II, 2, 37, and Vāchaspatimiśrā's Brāmatī, seems to have been formed in India in the first half of the 9th century A.D., is already found entrenched in Cambodia under the reign of Yaśovarman I (A.D. 889-900).[1] Some kind of monism, was however, already present in Cambodia in the 7th century A.D. This becomes quite obvious from a perusal of an inscription, of the reign of Īśānavarman I (1st half of the 7th century A.D.)[2]. Two inscriptions, one belonging to the 8th A.D.[3] and the other to 9th[4], also illustrate this point. In this connection it is worth mentioning that the prameśvarāgma, mentioned in two Cambodian inscriptions[5], betray a monistic tendency. In both the cases Śiva and śakti are regarded as the creators of the universe and it is pointed out that śakti emanates from the māyā of Śiva.[6] And the Phnom Sangk Kong inscription says that Śiva is one with the śakti, as fire is one with the flame.[7] Now, since the śakti is essentially identical with Śiva, in the last analysis the universe is but manifestation of Śiva.

In Cambodia Āgamic Śaivism was also firmly established. The inscriptions mention the Āgamic dikṣās of Śivāchārya and the pañcākṣaramantra.[8] It seems, however, that the Āgamic influence was more or less confined to the ritual. Only one inscription in Cambodia professes a purely Āgamic doctrine. An inscription from Phnom Sandak, dated A.D. 1110, contains the following verse in its second part ;

yasyāh prasade jagatām vimuktir
vallābhyataḥ patyur aṅadibandhāt
bhāvānyatāyām api bandhavṛddhir
vidyaiva sā vo'vatu viśvarūpa

"May the multiform knowledge protect you ! Though in one of her aspects, she increases the bond, it is through her that the creatures find their deliverance from the beginningless bond, due to the favour of the Lord".[9]

1. Bhattacharya, K., *Les religions brahmaniques dans l'ancien Cambodge*, pp. 43ff.
2. Barth, A. and Bergaigne, A., *op. cit.*, VI, A, 1.
3. *Bulletin de l'Ecole Francaise d'Extreme-Orient*, XXXVI, p. 8.
4. Coedes, G., *op. cit.*, I, p. 19.
5. Bhattacharya, K., *op. cit.*, p. 48.
6. Dasgupta, S.N., *A History of Indian Philosophy*, V, p. 28.
7. Coedes, G., *op. cit.*, VI, p. 229.
8. Bhattacharya, K., *op. cit.*, pp. 72-73.
9. Coedes, G., *op. cit.*, VI, p. 301.

This verse clearly illustrates an Āgamic doctrine. The aspect in which śakti increases the bonds is that of *rodha,* obstruction, or *tirodhāna*, obscuration. These hurdles aim at unleashing the intrinsic faculties of the creatures. The Lord, Mṛgendra explains, uses pain in order to lead the creatures to their deliverance.[1] He throws down successively the bonds by renewing at each stage his twofold operation : obstruction and administration of grace.[2]

The influence of Śaṁkhya can also be discerned. An inscription from Trapang Don On, dated A.D. 1129, says as follows:

namaś śivāya yacchaktir ādyā puruṣasaṃgatā
prakṛtisthā dvitiyā vā yābhyāṃ vyāptaṃ idañ jagat

"An adoration to Śiva ! His first śakti is united with the puruṣa, his second śakti dwells in the prakṛti, and both of them pervade this universe".[3]

The first śakti is united with the puruṣa and the latter is identified with the puruṣa of the sāṁkhya. The second śakti is identified with the mūla-prakṛti (original prakṛti), that is, the undifferentiated matter.[4] The Ban That inscription of the first half of the 12th century A.D. also betrays sāṁkhya influence.[5] Finally, the Baksei Camkrong inscription (A.D. 984) seems to allude to the evolution of the prakṛti, as it is described in the Sāṁkhya.[6]

Similarly the influence of yoga is also reflected from the Cambodian inscriptions. An inscription from Phnom Da, dated A.D. 1054 relates the installation by a yogin, identified with Śiva, of a liṅga drawn from the entrails of his body.[7] This inner liṅga is the absolute Śiva, who is the object of meditation of the yogins following the path of jñāna (knowledge) whereas the outer manifestations of Śiva are worshipped by those who follow the path of karman (action).[8] The absolute Śiva can be realised only through yoga.[9]

From the foregoing discussion it becomes crystal clear that the Śaiva cult in all its philosophical aspects was very much dominant in Cambodia.

1. *Mṛgendrāgama*, VII, 18.
2. *ibid.*, 11ff.
3. Coedes, G., *op. cit.*, III, p. 182.
4. *Śiva Purāṇa*, VII, 16.
5. *Bulletin de l'Ecole Francaise d'Extremè-Orient*, XII, 2, p. 8.
6. Coedes, G., *op. cit.*, IV, p. 89.
7. Barth, A. and Bergaigne, A., *op. cit.*, V.
8. *Liṅga Purāṇa*, I. 75. 18ff.
9. *Bulletin de l'Ecole Francaise d'Extremè-Orient*, XXV, p. 311.

Equally dominant was the worship of Śiva there. During the whole period of the Sanskrit inscriptions, worship of Śiva was the most prominent cult and probably some sort of "state religion".[1] So great was the influence of this god that in the early 7th century A.D. King Īśānavarman I renamed the capital of Kambuja as Īśānapura, which means the city of Śiva. Even the rise of Mahāyāna Buddhism hardly affected the fortunes of Śaivism. In fact, we have evidence to suggest that in the 9th and 10th centuries, when Mahāyānism was in ascendance[2] Śaivism had become very important. The inscriptions of this period clearly indicate the existing popularity of the Śaivite texts as well as Śiva worship.

In the Śiva temples of Cambodia the method of worship was almost similar to the one prevailing in India. Only privileged persons could find access to the liṅga, libations were poured over the phallus and sacred books like the *Rāmāyaṇa*, the *Mahābhārata* and the *Puraṇās* were recited.[3] The rituals also included music and dance which was bound to make a strong appeal to the masses. The Śaivite temples also served free meals to worshippers, probably to those amongst them who were poor. To this class of worshippers, the inscription of Loley afforded much consolation.[4]

In Cambodia Śiva was worshipped under different names some of which are the following: (1) Bhadreśvara, (2) Śaṁbhu, (3) Prahanateśvara[5], (4) Naimiṣeśvara, (5) Piṅgaleśvara, (6) Giriśa (7) Tribhuvaneśvara, (8) Kedāreśvara, (9) Āmrātakeśvara, (10) Vyayeśvara, (11) Vardhamāna, (12) Siddheśvara, (13) Nṛtyeśvara, (14) Gambhīreśvara.

Besides the inscriptional evidences, the prevalence of Śaivism in Cambodia is also attested to by the following facts : (i) A peculiar of Śiva with five heads and ten arms, kept in the Ayuthia Museum (Thailand), was found. He is seen dancing in the central temple of Kut Suen Teng wearing a decorated mukuṭa and ordinary jewels accompanied by divine females and others. (ii) A stele bearing a pair of engraved footprints and bearing an inscription meaning Śiva's two lotus feet which has been found[6] indicate that Śaivite footprints were probably an object of veneration. (iii) A representation of Śiva and Pārvatī riding Nandin wherein Śiva is holding a trident and sitting in a yogic posture is present at Thom Ngua Deng. Two devotees are sitting before him whereas two devīs are standing behind the Nandin. (iv) In a

1. Chatterjee, B.R., *op. cit.*, p. 222.
2. *ibid.*
3. Eliot, C., *Hinduism and Buddhism*, III, p. 100.
4. Majumdar, R.C.; *Sanskrit Inscriptions of Cambodia*, p. 87.
5. Sharan, M.K., likes to read it as Prahasiteśvara (*SSIM*, p. 235, fn. 1) a reading which is totally unwarranted.
6. Chhabra, B.C., *Expansion of Indo-Aryan Culture during Pallava Rule*, p. 76.

bas-relief of Angkor Śiva is represented in Naṭarāja form.[1] (v) The Ardhanārīśvara form of Śiva which is alluded to in an inscription,[2] is also represented in sculpture.[3] (vi) An idol of the female Śaivite deity Mahiṣāṣuramardinī and representations of Pārvatī are also available. The existence of certain other Śaivite goddesses is also beyond doubt.[4] (vii) The people were conversant with the Pañcākṣara Mantra Namaśśivāya.[5] (viii) The symbol *Om* was very popular and even the coat of arms carried this symbol.[6] The sacred manuscripts also had this symbol inscribed on them".[7]

Śaivism was connected with Tāntricism also in the country. Tāntric Brāhmaṇa Hiraṇyadama performed a religious rite according Brahmavināśikha. He taught Śivakaivalya from this book and *Nayottara, Sammoha* and *Śirachheda.* Śaivism united Cambodian religions and the Cambodian nation. King was believed to be a representative of some god. The Vat Vihar inscription mentions Śiva and Pārvatī. The figure of Pārvatī is depicted in sitting pose on the left thigh of Lord Śiva.[8] In śaka 801, Indravarman installed statue of Lord Śiva.[9] Ceremonial golden image of Lord Śiva which was carried in procession was prepared by Amarābhāvā, a favourite of kings Indravarman and Yaśovarman.[10] A lot of consolation is afforded in the inscription of Loley to those persons who could not afford to make costly offerings to Lord Śiva.[11]

From inscriptions we learn that the administration of Śaivite temples was faultless and smooth. Slaves of Śaivite temples were free from royal corvee except in the cases of foreign invasion. Free meals, are referred to be served to worshippers.[12] Lifting of Mount Kailāśa by Rāvaṇa has been portrayed in Bantey Srei. Śiva and Pārvatī have been shown sitting together on the mount while Rāvaṇa is lifting it. Statues of Umā-Maheśvara, Śiva and Durgā were installed by Yajñavarāha.[13] Śiva with Gangā and Moon on his head have been installed variously. Rajendravarman's

1. *Bulletin de l'Ecole Francaise d'Extreme-Orient*, 1961, pp. 85-86.
2. Coedes, G., *op. cit.*, II, p. 149; IV, p. 89.
3. *Bulletin de l'Ecole Francaise d'Extreme-Orient*, 1961, pp. 85-86.
4. *ibid.*, pp. 91-92.
5. *ibid.*, p. 73.
6. *Indian Antique*, 1947, pp. 40-56.
7. *ibid.*, p. 47.
8. Majumdar, R.C., *IK*, p. 8.
9. *ibid.*, p. 61.
10. *ibid.*, p. 158.
11. *ibid.*, p. 87.
12. *ibid.*
13. *ibid.*, p. 271.

Mebon inscription contains installation of phallic and statues of Pārvatī, Viṣṇu, Brahma and Rajendreśvara (representing himself).[1]

In the light of above discussion we can conclude that the cult of Śiva was in great favour among the people of Cambodia. Many royal inscriptions begin with invocations to God Śiva. The kings erected the images and liṅgas of Śiva. Śaivite speculation and worship in Cambodia developed almost exactly as it did in the land of its origin. It seems that in this case the Indian ideas and practices passed into Cambodia almost unchanged and were accepted in their totality.

Viṣṇu

The cult of Viṣṇu known as Vaiṣṇavism flourished side by side with Brāhmaṇism and Śaivism in Cambodia. Like Śiva, the God Viṣṇu also received patronage from some of the kings of Cambodia and also had his followers in the country. But unfortunately, for various reasons, Viṣṇu found less wide acceptance than Śiva among the peoples of Cambodia.

The images purporting to be of Viṣṇu represented, in fact, the king who was thought to be absorbed into the god-head at the end of his earthly existence. This is evident from the fact that many images of the god-head aim to appear as portraits of actual rulers. Names of the statues usually composed by fusing the name of the human counterpart with that of the god indicates that it was a personal royal cult of the king as god. The Cambodian king Suryavarman II had the great Angkor Vat constructed during his lifetime for it was here that he was to be deified in form of a statue of Viṣṇu with the posthumous name of *Paramaviṣṇuloka*.

The two oldest inscriptions of Funan are Vaiṣṇavite in character. One of these begins with an invocation to Viṣṇu and contains mention of the pious donation of king Jayavarman's chief queen Kulaprabhāvati. She is recorded to have installed a golden image of a god in Kruṁbanagara inhabited by Brāhmaṇas. She also built a hermitage with a tank and dwelling house. The other inscription records the consecration of a footprint of Viṣṇu called *Chakratirthasvāmin* by Guṇavarman who was the son of Jayavarman and Kulaprabhāvati.

In India, about the year A.D. 450, Brāhmaṇic gods appear in combined forms as we learn from the rocks of Badami and Mahaballipura. Along with Śiva, Viṣṇu was worshipped by the names of *Hari-Hara*, *Hari-Śaṁkara* and *Śaṁkara-Nārāyaṇa*. He was worshipped in Chenla under the names of Puṣkarākṣa, Puṣpavatasvāmī and Trailokyeśvara. Viṣṇu is generally seen with one head and four hands holding auspicious objects like the disc, lotus, club and counch in India but in his Cambodian portrayal he is seen with as many as ten hands at places.

1. *ibid.*, p. 219.

During the reign of Jayavarman-II and Jayavarman-III Vaiṣṇavism flourished tremendously. On Mahendraparvata, the early capital of king Jayavarman-II, many monuments were dedicated to Lord Viṣṇu. The king's two queens were Vaiṣṇavites, one of whom (queen Bhāsvāminī) was daughter of a Brāhmaṇa and the other (Kambujarāja-Lakṣmī) was the sister of Viṣṇuvala who was known also as Lakṣmīndra.[1]

Viṣṇu is mentioned in the early inscriptions of the Chenla period. A present of the *Mahābhārata*, the *Rāmāyaṇa* and the *Purāṇas* is recorded to have been made to a temple situated on the bank of the river Mekong by the sister of king Bhavavarman-I who was the first king of Chenla.[2] Around the 5th century A.D., Vaiṣṇavism is believed to have entered the south East Asian countries.[3] Vaiṣṇavite cult and also Bhāgavata priests existed in Cambodia during this period. During the reign of king Yaśovarman-I, the Pancharātra, the Bhāgavata and the Satvatas constituted the principal Vaiṣṇavite sects and several Vaiṣṇavite temples, known as Vaiṣṇavāsramas were constructed during this period. Images of Viṣṇu in Si Thep of the Menam basin which was a part of the Khmer empire as early as the end of the 6th century A.D., and also of the reign-period of the Angkor rulers, have been found.[4]

We do not find any mention of the worship of Viṣṇu in the 10th or 11th centuries and it appears from this that it lost its hold during this period. The reign period of king Suryavarman-II (after king Jayavarman) may be regarded as a golden age of Vaiṣṇavism in Cambodia. The *Devarāja cult*, a Śaiva belief, was replaced with Viṣṇurāja cult which was a Vaiṣṇavite belief. The architectural manifestations of Beng, Meles, Chause, Tevoda Thommanon, Bantay Samre and Angkor Vat are the masterpieces of this period.

King Yaśovarman, Indravarman, Suryavarman-II and Jayavarman-III were the important Vaiṣṇavite kings of Cambodia. Someśvara Bhaṭṭa, the celebrated commentator of *Tantravārtika* and performer of 100 thousand and ten million *homas* taught the doctrine of Vedic rituals to the priest of Rajendravarman.[5] The greatest Vaiṣṇavite temple in the world, the Angkor Vat, was constructed by king Suryavarman-II. Though considered to be a Buddhist, Jayavarman-III made provisions for sacrifices to Brāhmaṇic gods.[6] The *Vahnigṛhas* established by him are believed to be sanctuaries for the Vedic worship of fire.[7] In Angkor Thom inscriptions we find

1. *ISC*, No. 15, V. 2.
2. *ibid.*
3. Majumdar, R.C., *IK*, p. 18ff.
4. Coedes, G., *Les Etats . . .*, p. 413.
5. Majumdar, R.C., *IK*, p. 261, V. 239.
6. *ibid.*, p. 459, V. 95.
7. *ibid.*, p. 475, VV. 122-26; Cf. also Ghosh, M.M., *History of Cambodia*, p. 213.

reference to *Viṣṇugṛhas* which we were meant for the reception of the Vaiṣṇavas. In these *Viṣṇugṛhas* the sick and poor received food, accommodation and medicine.

Many references to Lord Kṛṣṇa (an incarnation of Lord Viṣṇu) are contained in the inscriptions of Cambodia. The temple of Prāsāt Khna was dedicated to Kṛṣṇa though it was constructed during the reign of king Suryavarman-I who was a Buddhist king. In the neighbourhood of the temple of Prāsāt Nam Khem, Kṛṣṇa is shown lifting Mount Govardhana and at another place Viṣṇu in the form of Vāmana is depicted measuring the whole world with his three steps.

Amṛtagarbha, son of Jayendravarman, erected Hari Mandira (Viṣṇu temple) in A.D. 883. Baset Stele inscription of king Jayavarman-I records consecration on Viṣṇu's image under the name of Açyuta by one Dharmapāla who was a Bhāgavata. During the reign of king Yaśovarman, the principal Vaiṣṇavite sects were the Pañcarātra, the Bhāgavata and the Satvata. From the inscriptions of Prāsāt Kok Po and Trapan Ron we learn that Bhāgavata sect flourished. Pañcagavya, a Satvata priest is described as the principal master and highly honoured consul of the king. Many Vaiṣṇavite temples, known as Vaiṣṇavāśrama, were constructed during this period.[1] Guru Yajñavarāha and his brother Viṣṇukumāra dedicated a wing of the temple of Banteay Srei to God Viṣṅu and therefore both are supposed to be Vaiṣṇavites. In decorating the new central temple of Baphuon, constructed for the Devarāja, King Udayadityavarman-II made great use of Vaiṣṇavite epics like the *Rāmāyaṇa* and the *Mahābhārata*. To the Vaiṣṇava temple of Kok Po, king Jayavarman had made a rich donation. The ruling class maintained the doctrine of incarnation to support their Devarāja cult. As a matter of fact the incarnation-doctrine is a purely Vaiṣṇavite belief.

By fusing the names of men with God Viṣṇu, new names were coined to name the image of god-head which appeared in the portraits of actual rulers. At Prāsāt-A-Ban in the central sanctuary, the figure of Viṣṇu, riding his vehicle Garuḍa, has been depicted. And many other monuments of the country used to be decorated with the figures of Garuḍa. The Phra Narai statue at Banteay Srei and Phum Pon are the counterpart of Indian Nārāyaṇa-Viṣṇu. Bas reliefs of Angkor Vat are full of the figures of Viṣṇu myths and legends of Rāma.[2]

Viṣṇu has been shown resting on the snake Anantanāga in the Kusi Cheng temple of Khampheng Yai. In the decorative lintel at Phnom Krabes also he is seen in the same state. Here he is with his wife Lakṣmī. He holds a lotus in the left hand and his head is adorned with a *mukuṭa* while Brahmā rises up from his naval.

1. *BEFEO*, (1961), p. 97.
2. Coedes, G., *Les Estats . . .*, p. 236.

In ancient Cambodian sculpture we find Viṣṇu image with all his traditional symbols—Śaṁkha, Cakra, Gadā, Padma and Mahī. He has also been portrayed in the figures of the ten incarnations. (1) Matsya (fish) Matsya-Avatāra; (2) Kūrma (tortoise) Kachhapa-Avatāra; (3) Varāha (boar) Varāha-Avatāra; (4) Narasiṁha (man-lion) Narasiṁha-Avatāra; (5) Vāmana (dwarf) Vāmana-Avatāra; (6) Parśurāma (Brāhmaṇ with battle-axe) Paraśurāma-Avatāra; (7) Rāma (Puruṣottam—full fledged and ideal man) Rāma-Avatāra; (8) Balarāma (man with plough) Balarāma-Avatāra; (9) Buddha (preacher of renunciation, love and non-violence) Buddha-Avatāra; (10) Kalki (he is yet to come and save people from gross injustice, inequality, greed and other sins) Kalki-Avatāra.

In inscriptions Viṣṇu has been called by the following names—(1) Hari; (2) Kṛṣṇa (3) Mādhava (4) Nārāyaṇa, (5) Padmanābhā (6) Trivikrama, and (7) Vāsudeva.

Viṣṇu and Narasiṁha (man-lion), Viṣṇu's Yoganidrā (sleep of contemplation), Viṣṇu's Trivikrama (three strides) or Vāmana-Avatāra and Varāha-Avatāra are also some of the forms of which Viṣṇu has been portrayed. The cylindrical coiffure of the pre-Angkorian images of Viṣṇu is believed to have had for its immediate model, the sculpture of the Pallavas of South India though a distinct Iranian influence has also been suggested for both styles.[1]

Śaivism and Vaiṣṇavism did not subdue each other completely in Cambodia. The last Śaivite temple of the country was Baphuon and the last Hindu temple of the country, Angkor Vat, on the basis of general construction and decoration etc., is dedicated to Viṣṇu though its forms were Śaivite. Though Kauṇḍinya was a Śaivite Brāhmaṇa and worshipped God Śiva, he had high regards for Viṣṇu. It was because of his liberal attitude that king Jayavarman's chief queen and his sons became fervent worshippers of this god. The two servants of Viṣṇu—Garuḍa and Hanumāna were also given high regards in Cambodia during the time of Kauṇḍinya-II.

The Pañcarātra Sect

The Pañcarātra (or Bhāgavata or Satvata) cult "was in its evolutionary stages in the centuries immediately preceding the Christian era. The progress continued in the subsequent times and the Gupta period was marked by a great development of the creed, when its tenets were systematized. It is in this period that it was gradually transformed into Vaiṣṇavism".[2] The identification of Kṛṣṇa-Vāsudeva, originally one—second in order of precedence—of the five heroes (Vīras) of the Vṛṣṇi clan, worshipped by the

1. Coedes, G., *op. cit.*, p. 93.
2. Banerjee, J.N., Presidential Address, *Indian History Congress*, Patna, 1946, Section I.

Pañcarātras, with the cosmic god Nārāyaṇa of the Brāhmaṇas and the Āditya-Viṣṇu of the *Vedas*, was instrumental in that process.[1] It is not, therefore, by sheer coincidence that the Pāñcarātra or Bhāgavata cult is found to have spread to Cambodia, precisely in that epoch and under the same form.

It is an inscription of Fu-nan, that of Prince Guṇavarman[2], dated approximately the second half of the 5th century A.D., that constitutes our first landmark. This inscription commemorate the erection of a Viṣṇu-pada, placing the donations to the sanctuary at the disposal of the Bhāgavata priests (viprair bhāgavataiḥ). The next mention of the Bhāgavatas in Cambodia is found in the Baset Stele Inscr.[3] of Jayavarman-I (c. middle of the 7th century A.D.). It records the consecration of an image of Viṣṇu under the name of Açyuta, by one Dharmapāla, said to be a Bhāgavata. This inscription is particularly interesting for its mention of the Pañcarātra cult (pañcarātrarcā), the five sacraments (pañcabhir yajñaiḥ), the five diurnal rites (pañcakāla) and the five elements (pañçabhautika), terms of technical import in the pañcarātra.[4]

That the Bhāgavatas flourished during the reigns of Jayavarman-II (802-850 A.D.) and Jayavarman-III (850-877 A.D.), is proved by an inscription of Prāsāt Kok Po[5], which mentions a Bhāgavata *kavi* as having obtained the complete favour (ativalla-bhatāpannaḥ) of Jayavarman-II and having been the guru of his Viṣṇuite son, Jayavarman-III. The same inscription also shows that Bhāgavatism flourished during the reign of Indravarman-I (877-889 A.D.), for two religious foundations are ascribed to Amṛtagarbha, a descendant of the Bhāgavata kavi mentioned above, and himself a Bhāgavata. The second of these foundations took place in 883 A.D.

During the reign of Yośovarman-I (889-900 A.D.), the Pañcarātras figure as one of the principal religious sects in Cambodia, alongwith the Śaivas, the Pāśupatas, and the Buddhists. An āśrama called Vaiṣṇavāśrama was dedicated to them at Prāsāt Komnap, not far off from the capital city of Angkor. The Śaivas and the Pāśupatas, on the one hand, and the Buddhists on the other, had their āśramas at Prei Prāsāt and Tep Pranam respectively.[6] Pañcarātra, Bhāgavata and Satvata, are evidently used,

1. Raychaudhuri, H.C., *Materials for the Study of the History of the Vaisnava Sect*, p. 172f.
2. Coedes, G., Deux inscriptions sanskrites du Fou-nan, *BEFEO*, XXXI, p. 2ff.
3. Coedes, G., Inscriptions du Cambodge (*IC*), II, pp. 193-5.
4. Schrader, F.O., *Introduction to the Pāñcarātra*, pp. 76, 112.
5. Coedes, G. et. P. Dupont, Les Inscriptions du Prasat Kok Po, *BEFEO*, XXXVII, p. 387ff.
6. Coedes, G., A la recherche du Yaçodharacrama, *BEFEO*, XXXII, p. 84ff.

in the stele of foundation of the Vaiṣṇavāśrama, as different names of the same sect, also designated by the generic name of Vaiṣṇava. One need not consider the three terms as standing for three different sects as Coedes seems to do.[1] The Prāsāt Komnap inscription is important for a delineation of the Vaiṣṇava practices in the ninth century Cambodia, especially when they are placed side by side with their Śaivite and Buddhist counterparts as depicted, respectively, in the Prei Prāsāt and Tep Pranam inscriptions. Strict chastity was enjoined on the Viṣṇuite hermits. The Buddhists of bad morals and ignorant were declared ineligible for dwelling in the hermitage. Similar remarks were not made regarding the Śaivites,—a fact which leads Coedes to conclude that the latter "seem to have held continence of knowledge less in esteem". The Śaivite and Buddhist hermits used to go out in quest of alms, but not, perhaps, the Viṣṇuites.

During the reign of Rājendravarman (944-961 A.D.), the Pañcarātras occupied an important place in Cambodia. In the Pre-Rup stele inscription (961 A.D.)[2], the court poet referred to the fourfold emanation (caturvyūha) of Viṣṇu, the most distinctive feature of the Pañcarātra. Besides, the Kuk Sla Ket inscription[3], referred to a royal servant, versed in the Pañcarātra, the quintessence of which lies in the five diurnal rites (adhītī pañcarātre. . .pañcahnikapuñjite) and observing the five kālas (pañcakālavit).

In the catholic atmosphere of the regin of Jayavarman-V (968-1001 A.D.), Bhāgavatism flourished along with Śaivism, the official creed, as also Buddhism. The fourfold emanation is referred to in an inscription of of Prāsāt Kok Po.[4] According to the Prāsāt Trapang Run inscription[5] the consecration of the king was performed by a Satvata priest, Pañcagavya, who continued to be his ācārya. Indeed, Jayavarman-V, though an ardent Śaiva, extended his patronage to the Viṣṇuites as well as to the Buddhists, and seems rather to have been an eclectic in his religious outlook. (His posthumous name was Paramavīraloka, apparently of Buddhist inspiration). A rapprochement between Śaivism and Vaiṣṇavism is clearly reflected in the records of the reign. Thus, the Pañcagavya, mentioned above, had a son 'profoundly versed in the Śaiva doctrine (śaivasiddhāntaniṣṇātaḥ) but he performed the function of the consecrator (dhātā) of an image of Viṣṇu, erected by his father. Nārāyaṇa, the fervent Vaiṣṇava, in the Prāsāt Kok Po inscription erects a Nandin and a Mahākāla (Śiva) at the door of a sanctuary of Viṣṇu. Viṣṇuvara (Pṛthivīndrapaṇḍita), the

1. See, on this point, Raychaudhari, *op. cit.*, p. 21.
2. Coedes, G., *IC*, pp. 77, 105, V. 4.
3. *ibid.*, V., p. 119ff.
4. Coedes et Dupont, *op. cit.*, pp. 400, 407, V.I.
5. Finot, L., *BEFEO*, XXVIII, p. 58ff.

noble Bhāgavata (Bhāgavatārya), author of at least three Viṣṇuite foundations during the reign, is described, in a Banteay Srei inscription[1] as a relation and spiritual friend (saṃvanddhī dharmavāndhavaḥ) of the Śaivite guru of the king, Yajñavarāha. It is, thus, somewhat curious to note that an inscription of the same king should refuse the recognition of the Bhāgavatas as a regular religious order.[2]

The Prāsāt Kok Po and Trapang Run inscriptions, referred to above, further show that Bhāgavatism flourished during the reign of Jayavīravarman (1002-1006 A.D.). In the latter of these two records, the Satvata priest Pañcagavya, whom we have already met during the reign of Jayavarman-V, is described as the principal master (ācāryapuṅgavaḥ) and highly honoured counsellor (atimato mantrī) of king Jayavīravarman.

Sūryavarman-I (1002-1050 A.D.), the Buddhist king, also patronized the Pañcarātras, for an inscription, posterior in date, records that a Pañcarātra priest, Kavīśvarapaṇḍita, was, during this reign, the guru of the hermitages at Īśvarapura (Banteay Srei), Śivapura (Phnom Bayang), Sūryaparvata (Phnom Chisor), and Jalāṅgeśvara (Pos Preah Nan), and later on became a guru and adviser (mantrin) of the king.[3] It is interesting, however, to note that the same person is stated to have erected an image of Bhagavatī and consecrated a liṅga of Śiva.

We have traced above, on the basis of the available data, a history of the Pañcarātra sect in ancient Cambodia. That history, evidently, remains incomplete. But we should remember that the archaeological exploration of Cambodia is "far from being accomplished" and that "new inscriptions are coming forth every year from the soil of Angkor".[4]

We have seen how the essential elements of the Pāñcarātra were known in Cambodia. We have also references to the fourfold emanation, the most significant feature of the doctrine. It would be useful to quote the verses in which those references occur, for, as we shall notice presently, they show some considerable divergence from the orthodox Pañcarātra. The verse of the Pre-Rup Stele Inscription reads thus:

pāra satvarajastamaskam api yo nityan niviṣṭaḥ pada
traigunyena caturvvidhena vividhābhivyaktir āvirbhavan
viśvākāradharo nirastasakalākaro pi dedīpyate
vandantāṃ bhagavantam ādipuruṣan taṃ Vāsudevaṃ vibhum

"To Him, who, in spite of having reached for eternity the supreme world in the condition free from *sattva*, *rajas* and *tamas*, appears (in

1. Le temple d'Iqvarapura, Mem. Archeol, *EFEO*, 1, p. 93, VV. 2-3; Cf. Coedes, et. Dupont, *op. cit.*, p. 393ff.
2. Coedes, *IC*, II, p. 67; II. 10-13 & II. 5.
3. *ibid.*, pp. 132-33.
4. Coedes, G., *Les Etats bindouises d'indochine et d'Indonesia*, p. 9.

this world) under diverse manifestations, through the quadruple triad of qualities, and who, in spite of having abandoned all forms, shines in the form of the Omnipresent to that god Vāsudeva, primordial and eternal puruṣa, let our homage be rendered".

The Prāsāt Kok Po Inscription has the following verse:

Namaś caturbhujāyāstu caturdhā viṣkṛtātmane
nistraiguṇyaguṇāyāpi catustraiguṇyadhāriṇe

"Homage to the god with four arms, who is manifested four times—to Him, who, in spite of having for quality the fact that He is without the three guṇas, possesses the quadruple triad of qualities".

In the two verses quoted above, there is no doubt that the four primary vyūhas, or emanations of Viṣṇu, are referred to. But the manner in which this doctrine is expressed (*traiguṇyena caturvidhena, catuṣtraiguṇyadhāriṇe*), is peculiar. Evidently, the Cambodian poets conceived the four vyūhas to be endowed with the three natural qualities of *sattva, rajas* and *tamas*. According to the Pañcarātra, however, the six ideal guṇas of *jñāna, bala aiśvarya, vīrya, śakti* and *tejas*, make up the body of the first emanation, Vāsudeva; while from Vāsudeva emanates Saṁkarṣaṇa; from Saṁkarṣaṇa, Pradyumna, and from Pradyumna, Aniruddha, each endowed with a couple of those attributes, namely, *jñāna* and *bala, aiśvarya* and *vīrya, śakti* and *tejas*, respectively. These six ideal guṇas, as Schrader, points out, "are *aprākṛta*, not belonging to nature"—for nature does not exist as yet—and have consequently nothing to do with the three well-known guṇas (sattva, rajas, tamas); that is to say, the old dogma that God is necessarily "free from (the three) guṇas" (nirguṇa) does not exclude His possessing the six ideal guṇas, which, on the contrary, must be ascribed to Him, because without them there could be no Pure Creation, and, all further evolution depending thereon, no creation at all. . . The six guṇas are the material, or instruments, as it were, of Pure Creation, in their totality, and by pairs...".[1] The attribution of the three natural guṇas to the four emanations of Viṣṇu, is therefore, a divergence that is worth considering. No further light on the question can, however, be thrown in the present state of our knowledge.

One more point may be discussed in this connection. Though the concept of the fourfold emanation of Viṣṇu was not unknown to the Cambodian poets, there is yet no positive evidence to show that the concept of the secondary emanations, giving rise to the twenty-four mūrtis[2], played any

1. Schrader, p. 31ff.
2. Gopinatha Rao, T.A., *Elements of Hindu Iconography*, Vol. I, Pt. I, p. 227ff.

part in that country—a fact which remains in spite of Dupont's[1] ingenious hypothesis of "an undifferentiated sthānaka mūrti of Viṣṇu", contributing to "distinct identifications of detail, according to circumstances".

Besides the member of trinity, there were other Brāhmaṇical gods and goddesses prevailing in ancient Cambodia of which we find numerous references. Amongst the gods most important were Āditya or Ādityasvāmī,[2] (2) Gaṇeśa[3], (3) Indra, (4) Śāligrāmasvāmī,[4] (5) Svayaṁbhūva[5], (6) Skanda-Kārttikeya[6], (7) The nine planets, (8) Yama, (9) Nāga.

1. *Āditya or Ādityasvāmī*

The origin of Āditya is attributable to Āditi. It is said that they were the sons of this Āditi. They are referred to as the solar deities in the *Purāṇas*. They are among the very ancient Indian deities referred to also in the *Vedas*. The number of the Ādityas in the earliest references is seven but in the *Śatapatha Brāhmaṇa* the number is eight. In a village named Sūryanarkoyin (Tanjore District) of South India, there is a temple of Sun God. This god is worshipped there alongwith his attendants,

2. *Gaṇeśa or Gaṇapati* (*Chief of Gaṇas*)

He was chief of demi-gods and attendant of Śiva. This son of Śiva-Pārvatī is one of the best known Indian divinities in the west. He has an elephant's head. One of his tusks is broken. His belly is fat and he rides on a rat. Before the 5th century A.D., he is not attested but is one among the latest of the Brāhmaṇic pantheon. He has survived as a primitive non-Aryan elephant-god but in Brāhmaṇism he has become mild and cultured known also as lord obstacle—Vighneśvara, he is worshipped in the beginning of all undertakings to remove hindrances particularly in literary and educational fields he is patron of grammarians and manuscripts.

1. Dupont, P., Viṣṇu mitres de l'Indochine occidentale, *BEFEO*, XLI, p. 250f. The existence of the triads (consisting of three undifferentiated images of Viṣṇu) at Prāsāt Damrei Krap and Prāsāt Rup Arak on the Phnom Kulen, poses, indeed, as Dupont points out, an important problem of religious interpretation. In the absence of epigraphy, it is hardly possible to solve this problem satisfactorily. But to represent these triads as standing for any of the triads of secondary emanation of Viṣṇu, would perhaps be going too far. For, whether the concept itself was known in Cambodia is still doubtful, while, on the other hand, no similar representation exists even for the well-known fourfold primary emanation.
2. Majumdar, R.C., *IK*, p. 50.
3. *ibid.*, p. 74.
4. *ibid.*, p. 50.
5. *ibid.*, p. 185.
6. For details about Karttikeya see Thakur, U., *Some Aspects of Ancient Indian History and Culture*, p. 241ff.

Printed books often begin with the auspicious formula—*Śrī Gaṇeśāya Namaḥ*, meaning reverence to lord Gaṇeśa.

3. *Indra*

Indra is the king of all gods and minor deities. He is the Vedic war-god and is considered to be the guardian of the eastern quarters of the universe. He is also called Devarāja. He is said to play instrumental role whenever he feels that his throne is at a stake by the pious deeds and penance of any human-being. There are numerous stories about his sending various distraction agents to test and to disturb the penance and pious deeds of sages. He rides his vehicle Airāvata, the elephant with numerous trunks.

In Indo-Khmer monuments he is portrayed riding this vehicle. He is depicted as the central figure in the decorative lintel at Prāsāt Chh Teai Tha and in the temple of Vat Phu. His images also appear in the temple of Prāsāt Sneng Krabei and at Prāsāt Kraham. The two great gods Viṣṇu and Śiva are portrayed on their vehicles Garuḍa and Nandin while Indra is seen on Airāvata in the decorative lintels of Prāṣāṭ Nong Thong.

4. *Skanda Kārttikeya*

The war-god Skanda, also called Kumāra (the prince) Kārttikeya and in the South Subrahmaṇya, was probably originally a non-Aryan deity. He was the son of Śiva and Pārvatī and his sole function, according to orthodox tradition was to slay the demon Tāraka, which scarcely account for his great popularity. From the beginning of the Christian era, the cult of Skanda was widespread in North India though it declined somewhat in medieval times. In South it was even more important for the name and attributes of the god were imposed on the chief deity of the ancient Tamila, Murugans by which name Skanda is sometimes known in Tamil country. Murugan, in his original form, was a mountain-god worshipped in Bachhanalian dances, at which he was impersonated by a medicine-man holding a spear (Velan), whom the dancers identified with the god. He aroused passion and erotic frenzy in girls and women and the dances in Murugan were evidently orgiastic. The Tamil Murugan was armed with spear, and joined his fierce mother Korravai in her cannibal feasts on the battle-field; hence his identification with the Āryan Skanda is evident even today. Skanda is usually depicted as a handsome youngman, often six-faced and mounted on peacock.

5. *The Nine Planets*

The nine planets to whom the Hindus offer prayer and give reverence are—Sūrya, Candra, Bhauma, Buddha, Bṛhaspati, Śani, Rāhu and Ketu. Their images are generally found in South Indian temples of the Śaiva sect. In India the most prominent images of these planetary deities are installed in the Raghunatha temple of Jammu. In Cambodia also their images have been found at various places.

The stele at Vat Clang contains some other gods including Agni. As in India during the Vedic period to this modern time, fire worship—Homa, was prevalent in ancient Cambodia. Yaśovarman-I and Indravarman have referred to the sacrifices to sacred fire. King Yaśovarman-I is recorded to have given orders for offering Homa (*Havana*) to god Viṣṇu in aśramas daily.

6. *Yama*

Yama is the god of justice. In Northern India a day earlier to Dīpāvali (the great festival of lights), an earthen lamp—dīpak, is lighted in honour of this god. This lamp is designated—*Yoma kā diyā*. Also in śrāddha (last funeral rites), this god shares the offerings. After death he is considered to allot seats in the heaven or hell as per the individual performance in this world. He is guardian of the South. In the *Vedas* he is referred to be the death-god. He was not the cheerful lord of the paradise but the stern judge of the dead, ruling only over the purgatories where the wicked suffered until their rebirth. Yama is sometimes aided by his clerk Chitragupta in assessing the deeds of the dead.

7. *Nāga*

Half human with serpent's tails, the Nāgas are very ancient object of worship. They are believed to reside in the underground city of Bhogavati. They guard great treasures sometimes bestowing them on mortals whom they favour. Wholly human forms have been taken by them at occasions. There are many dynasties in ancient India which claimed their descent from the union of a human hero and a Nāgin. These people were probably the dark primitive tribes whom the Āryans met during their expansion. Nāga tribe is still existing in Assam to this day. Snake-cult is very much widespread in India and it appears that the Nāgas (tribe) must have certainly some connection with the Nāga-cult.

Next only to the cow, the snake was perhaps the most revered animal of ancient India. Legendary serpents Śeṣa and Vāsukī give the snake-prestige but the cult is believed to have sprung up from very primitive time as we see that snake is revered all over the world by uncivilised people as an emblem of both death and fertility. On the festival of Nāgapañcami during the rainy season the Hindus in India make offerings of milk and fried paddy to snakes and hills are respected as the homes of snakes.

The following goddesses, all of whom are of Indian origin, were worshipped in ancient Cambodia : (1) Bhagavatī, (2) Chaturbhuja[1]. (3) Devī[2], (4) Durga[3], (5) Gaṅgā[4], (6) Gaurī[5], (7) Indrāṇī, (8) Lakṣmī[6]. (9) Sarasvatī or Bhāratī or Bāgeśvarī[7] and (10) Umā.[8]

1. *Devi*

In *Mārkaṇḍeya Purāṇa* we find mention about the heroic deeds of Devī. In her own words she relates the significance of her various names. She destroys the great demon Mahiṣāsura and since then she got the name Mahiṣāsuramardini. After eating up all the asuras born in the family of Viprachitta, she got the name of Raktachanda. After relieving the world from drought and famine she adopted the name Śatākṣi (with hundred eyes). She gave protection to the vegetables necessary for maintaining life and was called Śākambharī. She killed the Asura named Durgama and adopted the name Durgādevī and after killing the Asura named Aruna she got the name Bhramarī.

This goddess is worshipped in eight different forms. She has varying designations as per age: (1) Sandhyā—when she is 1 year old baby; (2) Sarasvatī—2 years old; (3) Canḍikā—7 years old; (4) Śāmbhari—8 years old; (5) Durgā or Bālā—9 years old; (6) Gaurī—10 years old; (7) Mahālakṣmī—13 years old, and (8) Lalitā—16 years.

1. *Durgā*

Durgā is very frequently represented in some terrific aspects. She represents the destructive force of death which counterbalances growth and production. Devī's special forms are related to the Śaiva and Śākta forms and thus her several forms are associated, though indirectly, with Śaivism. In the *Āgamas* we find the mention of Navadurgās. These nine forms are : (1) Agnidurgā, (2) Harasiddhī, (3) Jayadurgā, (4) Kṣemaṅkarī, (5) Nīlakaṇṭhī, (6) Rudrāṁaśdurgā, (7) Ripumaridurgā, (8) Vanadurgā, and (9) Vindhyavāsinīdurgā.

3. *Gaṅgā*

Rivers were also sacred to the Hindus. Very special sanctity is given to

1. Majumdar, R.C., *IK*, p. 35.
2. *ibid.*, p. 185.
3. *ibid.*, p. 74.
4. *ibid.*, p. 67.
5. *ibid.*, p. 151.
6. *ibid.*, p. 573.
7. *ibid.*, p. 151.
8. *ibid.*, p. 185.

river Gaṅgā. She is believed to have sprung from the foot of Viṣṇu, flowed in the sky as Mandākinī (Milkyway), fell to earth from the matted hair of god Śiva. Gaṅgā is often personified as a goddess. River Sarasvatī is also sacred and is believed to have flowed underground and joined the Gaṅgā, at its confluence with Yamunā at Prayāg (Allahābad). Other rivers considered sacred by the Hindus are Kṛṣṇā, Kāverī, Godāvarī and Narmadā.

4. *Gaurī, Umā and Pārvatī*

Goddess Gaurī is worshipped under different aspects. She is represented as Umā and Pārvatī. As Gaurī she is seen standing on the back of an alligator. For wealth and prosperity people worship her in this form. The abode of Pārvatī is between the Agni-kuṇḍas. She has four arms. In these four arms she holds Akṣamāla, Śiva's image, Gaurī's image and Kamaṇḍalu. Pārvatī is depicted with lord Śiva. She rides Nandin alongwith Śiva. In Cambodian monuments this form of Pārvatī and Śiva images is very popular.

5. *Goddess Lakṣmī or Mahālakṣmī*

Goddess Lakṣmī represents the auspicious motherly force. She is considered to have come out of the milky-ocean at the time of its churning known as the myth of Samudra-manthan. She signifies production and life-increasing objects. She is the consort of the great God Viṣṇu who is himself the maintainer and supporter of the world. She is also called Śrī and represents fortune and prosperity, good luck and temporal blessings. She is portrayed as a woman of matured beauty seated on lotus, holding another lotus in her hand and attended by two elephants who sprinkle water on her with their trunks. As wife of Viṣṇu she has incarnated herself many times (as Sītā spouse of Rāma and as Rukmiṇī the chief queen of Kṛṣṇa, and Rādhā the favourite of Kṛṣṇa's youth).

In India every Hindu, specially the business community worships her ceremoniously in the night of Dipāvalī. This worship is called Lakṣmi-poojā. And in Cambodian temples Lakṣmī is portrayed alongwith Viṣṇu. We find this portrayal in many patterns. She is seen caressing the feet of Viṣṇu who is lying on the serpent Anantanāga in the Kshīrasāgara (ocean of milk). She also appears in sculptures standing between two elephants who are pouring showers of water on her with their trunks. Both these poses are very popular representations of this goddess here in India also. In Gajalakṣmī pose she appears in the sculpture of Sung-Nom and a few other places. We know from epigraphical records that one image of Lakṣmī was sent to the Chinese emperor in 519 A.D., by Rudravarman, son of king Jayavarman as a symbol of good luck.

6. *Sarasvatī*

She is the wife of Brahmā. She has autonomous role as the patron of art, music and letters. In *Ṛg Veda* she is referred as sacred river but in later Vedic literature this goddess is identified as hypostatic goddess of temporary importance. She is depicted as a beautiful young woman with a Vīṇa or Indian-flute and a book in her hand. A *haṁsa* (swan) attends her. She is traditionally known as the inventor of the Sanskrit language and Devanāgari script. Students, writers and musicians have always been worshipping her and her cult is still in existence.

The Devarāja Cult

Almost all ingredients of Cambodian social, political and religious s tructure was patterned on the lines of prevailing Indian situation with the exception of this Devarāja cult and the system of the Sañjakas. Of course the Devarāja cult contains some aspects of the Aśvamedha Yajña so far the objective of attaining greatness is concerned.[1] But while the Devarāja or the Royal God in Cambodia was an eternal prototype of the mortal king as a sort of deification of royalty and kings wanted to personify themselves with the liṅgas which were installed after the ceremony and temples erected to install the liṅgas, the Indian rulers never attempted to do so. So far as partial similarity of the features of this cult with Indian tradition is concerned, we have on record some stray references from which it can be presumed that the rulers of Cambodia might have drawn inspiration. It is also just possible that the Indian priests in their own interest of gaining popularity and prominence in royal courts besides monetary gains, might have persuaded the rulers to adopt this belief.

From the *Rājatarangiṇi* of Kalhaṇa we learn that a man named Surā ins talled an idol in a Viṣṇu temple constructed by him. He named this temple as Sūryavarmasvāmī.[2] In the *Pratimā Nāṭaka* of Bhāsa mention has been made of the Pratimā-Manḍapa.[3] Here King Daśaratha's idol is referred to have been kept alongwith the images of other ancestors. Huviṣka's Devaśālā at Mathurā was a famous store of the images of Kuṣaṇa kings. Kaniṣka's image was also kept at this place. A Gurjara Pratihāra inscription records the construction of a Viṣṇu temple by Ālha and the idol named Vaillabhattasvāmī.[4] We know that in South India also the temples contained idols of gods which were named after the donors.[5]

1. *JOI*, Vol. XXI (June, 1972), p. 325ff.
2. *Rājataraṅgini*, V., p. 23.
3. Keith, A.B.; *Sanskrit Drama*, p. 120.
4. Bhandarkar's list no. 35.
5. *EI*, Vol. IV, p. 1.

The Kuṣaṇa rulers were very often called Devaputra. The king was an embodiment of divinity in their consideration during this period. The words Devaputra and Devarāja are almost synonymous. Devarāja was a phallic representation of lord Śiva.[1] In the *Suvarnaprabhapattana Sutta* it has been suggested that the rulers should be called Devaputra. It was believed that the kings were residents of the heaven before their birth and they took birth on the earth as embodiments of one of the thirty-three divinities. Manu also gives the position of divinity to the kings. Kings were given another name after their death. Such different naming suggests that the souls of the dead kings had attained divinity. Harṣavarman-I adopted the name of Paramarudraloka, Jayavarman-IV Paramaśivapada, Harṣavarman-II Brahmāloka, Suryavarman-I Nirvānapada and Jayavarman-VII adopted Mahāparamasaugata. Among the Bengalis up to this time when speaking of a departed relation we find the prefix *Iśvara* before calling their names. The belief of the Bengalis is that the dead person merged in god.

Religious life in Cambodia was almost disintegrated as they believed in numerous religions and cults. Integration of political life was aimed and for this the Devarāja cult came as a saviour. Not only the minor cults started believing in the Devarāja, even the Buddhist kings established monuments as a proof of their belief in this new great cult. The belief was thus accomplished and the aim was achieved as we know that during the days of attacks from outside people forgot about their minor religious differences and rose in a body supporting the king.

Besides this there can hardly be any doubt about the national character of this cult. Jayavarman-II the great conqueror and liberator of the nation from the subordination of Java desired to declare his nation's autonomy. Since the Cambodian people were religious minded and had now a nation, a capital and a king, the desirability of a national faith and cult was necessary to give them national understanding in their political life which was so much religion oriented.

The Khmer kings, it appears, had knowledge of this cult from before and it might have been borrowed from Java. In the inscription of Changgala and Dinaya situated in central Java contact between the royal dynasties and god Bhadreśvara has been indicated. There in Java also the royal god was symbolic of the dead rulers and for keeping contact with the spirits of the dead rulers, royal priests were necessary. This role, as we observe, was played by Bhṛgu in Champā, Agastya in Java and Hiraṇyadāma in Kambuja. Brāhmaṇa priests were considered as mediators between the king and the god.

According to the Sdok Kak Thom stele inscription of Udayaditya

1. Monier Williams, *Sanskrit English Dictionary*, p. 493.

Varman-II, written in Sanskrit and also in Khmer, considered to be the most important of all the Cambodian inscription so far as its historical content is concerned, when king Jayavarman-II assumed office as king he aspired also to become a Chakravarti *Rājā*. This aspiration of the king was similar to the ambitions of Indian kings. For this he invited Brāhmaṇa Hiraṇyadāma from India for teaching *Tāñ trik Vidyā* to his own royal priest Śivakavalya.

The deity enshrined was named after the deceased king. Such temples had their plinth at elevated places either natural or artificial to give an i dea of Mount Kailāśa which is supposed by the Brāhmaṇas to be the abode of the gods. The ego residing within the enshrined idol was considered to descend on the successors after performing proper rites. The transference of the ego of the dead king to the succeeding king continued in the whole lineage.

The Devarāja or the royal god was eternal prototype of the mortal king as a sort of deification of royalty. King Jayavarman-II was the founder of this concept and cult in Cambodia as we have seen earlier. It was he who invited the Brāhmaṇa Hiraṇyadāma from India for this purpose although it is not proved whether he installed the liṅga giving a name to it in any monument. It appears that it was from the time of king Jayavarman-IV that monuments with a name immediately associated with the name of the founders started being constructed in Cambodia. The terms Devarāja and *Kāmrateñ Jagata Tā Rājā* are found in inscription of the 1052 A.D. only whereas they were applied to the royal liṅgas in A.D. 803, some 250 years earlier. Jayavarman-II or his son Jayavarman-III did not erect any monument or put inscription which can be directly attributed to their personal belief in this cult. It were king Indravarman and king Yaśovarman who constructed such monument in A.D. 877-889 and 899-900 A.D. respectively.

The transformation of the names of the deity was a general practice as is gleaned from the following examples—Yaśovarman-Yaśodharapura; Rājendravarman-II—Rājenderaśekhara, Rājābhadreśvara[1]; Jayavarman-IV—Tribhuvaneśvara[2]; Jayavarman-VIII—Jayavarmeśvara.

The cult was not merely ritual rather it was tāntric in character. The inscription of Sdok Kak Thom by Udayadityavarman which refers to the inauguration of this cult by Jayavarman-II reads: "His Majesty Parameśvara (Jayavarman-II) installed the royal god (Devarāja) in the town of Śrī Mahendraparvata and established this family (i.e., the priestly family of which the history is given). There is a permanence of the god. Here is the history of the branches of this family. His Majesty came from Java to reign in the city of Indrapura.

1. Majumdar, R.C., *IK*, p. 232.
2. *ibid.*, p. 165.

"Śivakaivalya, venerable and learned Guru (spiritual guide) was the royal priest of Parameśvara. . . .His Majesty reigned then in the town of Hariharālaya. His Majesty came thereafter to reign at Mahendraparvata. Then a Brāhmaṇa came whose name was Hiraṇyadāma. He came from a *janapada* (town) and was well versed in magical science.

"His Majesty invited him to perform a ritual in order that Kambujadeśa (Cambodia) might no longer be dependent on Java and a Chakravarti (sovereign over all kings) might rule in Kambuja. This Brāhmaṇa performed a ritual. . .and installed a royal god (Devarāja). The Brāhmaṇa taught several *mantras*. He recited them from beginning to end in order that they might be written down and taught to Śivakaivalya. He also directed Śivakaivalya to perform the rituals of the royal god. His Majesty Parameśvara and the Brāhmaṇa took solemn oath that only the family of Śivakaivalya and no one else should perform the worship of the royal god. The priest Śivakaivalya initiated all his relations into this worship. Then His Majesty returned to Hariharālaya and the royal god also was brought there. His Majesty Parameśvara died at Hariharālaya. The royal god was there and in all the capitals where successive kings took him as their protector."

All the religious ceremonies connected with the institution of the cult remained entrusted to the priests and the rites contained some elements of black magic also. As we know that Śivakaivalya learnt from Hiraṇyadāma, *Brāhmavināśikha, Nayottara, Sammoha* and *Sirchheda* also. Īśānamūrti, Ātmaśiva and Sadāśiva were the important ācāryas and ācāryahomas, who could perform Yajñas also besides presiding the religious functions connected with the inauguration of this cult. The purohitas received land and money as donation. They also got a plot for construction of their own accommodation.

Rulers are known to have transferred their capitals from one place to the other for administrative and strategic conveniences. Whenever they did so, they carried also the Devarāja along with them. Since many important aspects of political life of the country depended upon the Devarāja cult, it appears that this cult played very important role in Cambodian state policy. It remained being carried from one generation of the king to the other. The king was considered divine and the spiritual sanction of his divinity was accepted. The king's office became hereditary in character and firmly established into the statehood. He was apotheosized after his death and his ego was preserved which was not allowed to diminish even after his death. The temples were erected commensurate with the king's greatness.

TĀNTRICISM :

The *tantras* are represented in broadly two classes—the orthodox and the hetrodox. Āgamas and Yamalas and also their supplement are parts of the orthodox tantra while the heterodox tantras are composed of Buddhist and Brāhmaṇical texts like Kulachāra, Vāmachāra, Sahayajana and Vajrāyana.

Like Śaivism and Vaiṣṇavism, tāntricism in its general sense of systematised ritualism had a particular character. Its application to Śakti worship was significant in its early phase while the element of fear played the most important role.

In Mālawa at Gandhara we find the mention of tantra in inscription for the first time. This fragmentary inscription is dated in the Malawa year 480 corresponding to A.D. 423-424. This inscription records that Mayūrākṣa, a minister of Viśvavarman caused to be built for the sake of his religious merit, this very terrible abode...filled full of female ghouls of the divine Mother, who utter loud and tremendous shouts in joy (and) who stir up the very oceans with the mighty wind rising from the magic rites of their religion'[1]

Tāntric literature became more extensive in Cambodia in the 8th century A.D. and the following tantras became authoritative in the country: 1. Chandrahasa, 2. Jhana, 3. Kirana, 4. Lalita, 5. Makuta, 6. Mukhovimukha, 7. Nisavasa, 8. Parameśvara, 9. Prodjita, 10. Raurava, 11. Svyambhūmata, 12. Siddhi, 13. Santana or Sattavane, 14. Sarodgita, 15. Vijaya, 16. Vathula, 17. Virabhadra, 18. Virasa Vireśa.

Śirachheda, Vināśikha, Sammoha and Nayottara, the four tāntric texts were studied as authentic Śaiva Śāstras as early as the 7th century A.D. in Cambodia.[2] All these texts find mention in the Sdok Kak Thom inscription. For establishing the mystic rites of Devarāja cult these constituted the Vaktraçatuṣkam of God Tumburu and were therefore introduced.

Thus, we see that Brāhmaṇism, on the whole, made a deep impression upon the people of Cambodia, who readily took to the worship of Brahmā, Śiva, Viṣṇu, Durgā, Caṇḍi, Śrī and other gods and goddesses. Amongst these the cult of Śiva was predominant throughout the history of Cambodia though Buddhism also prevailed there.

2. *CHAMPĀ*

In Champā the Brāhmaṇic religions prevailed and the trinity of gods were represented in various inscriptions of the country. The details are as follows :—

Brahmā

Brahmā is referred to as creator in several inscriptions (no. 12, v. 24;

1. Banerjee, J.N., *Paurāṇic and Tāntric Religion*, p. 127.
2. Bagchi, P.C., *Studies in the Tantra*, p. 22.

No. 62, v. 3), but does not seem to have held a very prominent position in Champā. He is also called Caturānana, having four faces and in several inscriptions of the 13th century A.D. he is referred to as Svayamutpanna or self-created. In inscription no. 21 he is said to have made the golden peak of mount Meru. King Jaya Parameśvaravarman installed an image of Svayamutpanna at Phanrang in 1233 A.D., and rich endowments were made to the god by the king himself, his heir apparent Nandabhadra, his commander-in-chief Abhimanyudeva and by king Indravarman. The evidence of iconography is in full accord with that of epigraphic records in respect of the inferior position of Brahmā. Only two small images of Brahmā have been discovered in Myson. These were originally placed in temples A and B as secondary gods. Brahmā also figures in bas-relief decorations of temples, but, mostly as a subsidiary god.

The characteristic features of the image of Brahmā are his four faces—of course only three being visible in most cases—and his vāhana, the goose. His common attributes are rosary and lotus—stems. In a bas-relief in the Touranne Museum he is represented as standing, with four heads and eight arms holding a sceptre in one of them.

The scene figuring the birth of Brahmā has been referred to in connection with Viṣṇu. Here Brahmā wears a sacred thread, and holds a discus and a long necked bottle in his hands. Brahmā is usually seated on lotus though in one case the serpents form his bed.

The real importance of Brahmā lies in the fact that he is regarded as a member of the trinity. We meet with the conception of the trinity of Brāhmaṇic gods in one of the earliest records of Champā. The Myson inscription of Bhadravarman dating from 5th century A.D. begins with a reverence to Umā and Maheśvara as well as to Brahmā and Viṣṇu. This decided leaning towards Śiva is further developed in inscription no. 39. Here Śiva is represented as the surpeme god, and the two others pay homage to him. Finally the three gods stand together, Śiva in the middle with Brahmā on the right and Hari on the left.

The same idea is conveyed by iconographic representations on decorative panels. The tympanum at Trach Pho[1] has a Mukhaliṅga in the middle with Brahmā seated on a serpent to the proper right, and Viṣṇu, seated on a boar, to the proper left. Both these gods are turned towards Śiva with joined hands, and two attributes of Viṣṇu viz., a discus and a club are shown in the background. In the tympanum of U'u Diem[2], Śiva and Umā riding on a single bull occupy the centre; Brahmā and Viṣṇu, with joined hands, and seated respectively on a lotus and a Garuḍa, are in the upper right and upper left corners, while two other figures, an armed soldier and Kārttika (?), occupy positions just below these figures. At

1. Parm, *IC*, Vol. II, p. 411.
2. *ibid.*, Vol. I, p. 518.

Thuy Trieu, however, Viṣṇu occupies the central position with Brahmā on the left and Śiva on the right. Śiva rides on a boar, and both the gods have their hands joined in an attitude of prayer.

Viṣṇu and Śiva were both claimed to be the chief of the trinity by their respective followers.[1] An attempt at compromise resulted in the conception of a new god Śaṅkara-Nārāyaṇa. Here the two gods are placed on the same level in theory, and this is expressed by a concrete image, half of which is Śiva, and half Viṣṇu. Such an image is clearly referred to in inscription No. 24,[2] but unfortunately no actual remains of such a figure have yet been discovered.

The idea of association of the chief gods also probably led to the practice of decorating the temple, dedicated to one god, with figures of the other group. Thus the temple of Phong Le dedicated to Śiva has its front decorated with images of Viṣṇu. Similarly figures of Lakṣmī and Brahmā appear on the tympanums of Śaiva temples. The principal tympanum in a temple, however, usually figures the god or gods to whom the temple is dedicated, though a Śaiva temple in Myson has the scene of the birth of Brahmā, and a temple at Phanrang, dedicated to Brahmā, shows the trinity with Viṣṇu as the chief god.

Śiva

Of the three members of the Brāhmaṇic trinity Śiva occupied an unquestioned position of supremacy in the Indian colony of Champā. The causes as well as the process of gradual elevation of one of the gods above his rivals are but imperfectly known to us, but there can be no doubt about the fact. Of the 130 inscriptions discovered in Champā 92 refer to Śiva and the gods associated with him, 3 to Viṣṇu, 5 to Brahmā under the

1. M. Parmentier observes as follows:

"A close study of the evidences furnished by epigraphy and iconography seems to indicate that from the 12th century A.D. a silent religious revolution in favour of Vaiṣṇavism was taking place in Champā. The references to Vaiṣṇava cult or Vaiṣṇava temples before this period are few and far between. But from this period onwards we find an increasing number of them. Again, whereas the figures of Viṣṇu and Lakṣmī hold but a minor place in the decoration of temples of the earlier period they gradually occupy an increasingly preponderant position in the later period. Lastly, Śiva is clearly subordinated to Viṣṇu in the image of the trinity under discussion.

M. Parmentier thinks that the position of Śiva as the Supreme god was lowered in the eyes of the Chams on account of the constant reverses sustained by them in the hands of the Annamites and other enemies. They naturally discarded Śiva who was unable to afford them the necessaly protection, and turned to other gods in the hope that they might succeed where Śiva had failed. This might also account for the rise of Brahmā into importance at the cost of Śiva (Parm., *IC*, Vol. II, pp. 432-433).

2. The god "Srisana Viṣṇu", mentioned in no. 71, may also, refer to such an image.

name Svayamutpanna while two refer to both Śiva and Viṣṇu. This analysis of the known inscriptions is an eloquent testimony to the predominance of god Śiva. The same conclusion is forced upon us when we remember that the two principal groups of temples in ancient Champā, viz., those of Myson, and Po-Nagar are dedicated to Śaivite gods. Further, the preeminence of Śiva is clearly indicated by the fact that the god was regarded as the tutelary deity of both the city and the kingdom of Champā. Thus according to the inscription no. 41, the city was created by the rays issuing from the pair of feet of Śrīśānabhadreśa, while in the inscription no. 94, the same god is referred to as the origin of the kingdom of Champā. These brief allusions are fully explained in the inscription no. 31 which describes how Uroja, sent to the earth by Śiva, established the kingdom of Champā, having at first placed a liṅga of that god as the protector of the city. In the inscription no. 42 we are told that the god Śrī Īśāneśvara lives here triumphantly together with his multitude of servants for the sake of the prosperity of Champā.

The god Śiva was known by various names. These may be roughly classified as (a) Names denoting his position of supremacy over other gods: Maheśvara, Mahādeva, Mahādeveśvara, Amareśa, Adhīśa, Devadeva, Īśvaradevatā, Īśvaradevādideva, Vṛddheśvara, Parameśvara.

(b) Names denoting general greatness, mastery etc.: Īśāna, Īśānadeva, Īśāneśvara, Īśānanātha, Īśāneśvaranātha.

(c) Names denoting the beneficent nature of the gods: Śambhu, Śaṅkara, Śaṅkareśa, Bhāgyakānteśvara, Dharmeśvara.

(d) Names denoting the destructive or fierce character of the god: Śarva, Bhīma, Ugra, Rudra, Rudramadhyeśvara, Rudrakoṭīśvara, Mahārudradeva.

(e) Names arising out of mythological attributes or characteristics: Śulī, Bhava, Paśupati, Vāmeśvara, Vāmabhūteśvara, Yogīśvara, Guheśvara, Jayaguheśvara, Vijayasiṁheśvara, Bhūmivijaya, Indralokeśvara, Suvarṇākṣa, Ṣaṇḍhaka.

(f) Names connected with liṅga: Devaliṅgeśvara. Mahāliṅgadeva, Śivaliṅgeśvara, Śivaliṅgadeva, Mahāśivaliṅgeśvara, Dharmaliṅgeśvara.[1]

The various names attributed to Śiva would convey a fair idea of the conception of the god in the mind of his devotees at Champā. Fortunately we are not dependent upon such a slender means alone for our knowledge in this respect. The inscriptions contain hymns and praises addressed to Śiva, as well as a large number of incidental allusions, and these enable us to enter more fully into this subject.

Śiva is expressly referred to as 'the chief of the trinity' and the 'supreme god of gods' in quite a large number of inscriptions. Thus Śiva is said to

1. Cf. Majumdar, R C., *Ancient Indian Colony in the Far East*, Vol. I, Chap. II.

have obtained the position of the head of the gods by means of his extraordinary power and fame. He is the preceptor of gods. He is the supreme deity extolled and reversed by all the gods beginning with Brahmā or Indra. The gods as a class, derive their strength from Śiva. Brahmā and Viṣṇu bow down to him, saying 'Thou great god, of gods; please grant a boon to us'. Lastly, the brilliant picture of the assembly of gods, sets the final seal of supremacy to the god Śiva. With Indra in front, Brahmā to the right, the Moon and the Sun at the back, and the god Nārāyaṇa to the left, Śiva sits in the middle, glowing with splendid rays, while those and other gods bow down before him and sing a chorus of praise and thanksgiving beginning with '*om*' and ending with '*Svadhā-svāhā*'.[1]

Quite in keeping with this position of unique supremacy among the gods, Śiva is endowed with a number of the highest divine attributes. He controls the creation, maintenance and dissolution of this world, while he himself has neither beginning nor end. He is not only the creator but also the preceptor of the three worlds, *bhūh, bhuvaḥ* and *svaḥ*; he is the knower of all things and the fixed cause of the universe. He is the primeval being, calm, pure, supreme and sublime. He is possessed of anima and other divine faculties; he cannot be cut or pierced; he is without cause and without atoms; his body is imperceptible; he permeates everything, penetrates everywhere, and embodies the entire world in himself. There is none in the world who knows Śiva in his true aspects, for his true nature is beyond the domain of thought and speech. He is the supreme energy and the source of the supreme end of life. His image, identical with the universe, is manifested by his forms, earth, water, fire, air, sky, sun, moon and sacrificer. He is constantly devoted to the welfare of all beings. He is the one lord of the world and grants supremacy to gods and men. From him are born all creatures and to him they ultimately resort.[2]

Śiva has dual aspects. He is the destroyer and burns all forms including gods. On the other hand, he removes the sin of the world and delivers men from the ocean of existence by destroying the seeds of *karma* which lead to successive rebirths. He is the object of meditation of the ascetics and even thoughts of him alone are capable of yielding infinite bliss.

But Śiva is not conceived in the abstract alone. He appears as a concrete divine figure with familiar myths and legends clustering round him. The old popular god of Indian masses reappears in a foreign land with his well-known features. He has matted hair, three eyes, five or six faces, and holds the trident in his hand. He originated from the nether world and is a resident of heaven. But sometimes he lives in the Himālaya

1. For a similar presentation of Mahādeva, cf. *Mahābhārata*, Anuśāsanaparvan, Ch, XIV.
2. Majumdar, R.C., *op. cit.*

or Malaya mountains and sometimes sports in the Mānasa lake with his Śaktis. Besmearing his body with ashes he rides on a bull and dances in cemetery. He married Gaurī, the daughter of Himālaya, but maintains the Gaṅgā on his head. He is not, however, a frivolous god. He is learned and intelligent. He practises austerities without desiring any reward therefrom. Indeed, he has no desire of his own. His body is purified by means of miracles, yoga, japa, huṅkāra etc. He is attended and worshipped by men and gods as well as the semi-divine beings like siddhas, cāraṇas, yakṣas etc.

Some of the great achievements of Indian Śiva were quite familiar in Champā. The famous episode of burning Kāmadeva (Cupid) to ashes is again and again referred to. Being struck with the arrow named Sammohana by Cupid, he reduced the latter to ashes by means of burning fire proceeding from his third eye, but later on again restored him to life. This well-known allegorical myth, depicting Śiva's absolute control over sensual passions, is a favourite theme of Sanskrit poets, and has been immortalised by Kālidāsa in his famous title *Kumāra Saṁbhava.* Apparently this aspect of Śiva's character made a deep impression upon his devotees at Champā.

The second memorable achievement of Śiva, stressed in the inscriptions of Champā, is the destruction of the demon Tripura and his three cities in the sky. As has already been noted, the details of this event agree closely with those given in the *Mahābhārata.*[1]

The third mythological incident about Śiva is the story of *Upamanyu.* This has been narrated at great length in the Anuśāsanaparvan of *Mahābhārata* which agrees with the inscriptions of Champā in extolling Mahādeva in the most extravagant terms and placing him above all other gods including Brahmā and Viṣṇu.

Liṅgapurāṇa, an extremist Śaiva book of the same type, is probably the source of another story in the inscription of Champā. It is said that on one occasion there was a contest for supremacy between Brahmā and Viṣṇu when a luminous liṅga appeared before them. The two combatants agreed to trace the source of the liṅga. Brahmā took the form of a swan and went upwards, while Viṣṇu in the form of a boar went downwards. For a thousand years they tried but could not reach the end of the liṅga one way or the other. Mahādeva then appeared before the discomfited gods and received homage from them, and they promised eternal devotion for him.[2]

The Hoa-Que Inscription from which we learn the above story contains an elaborate praise of the liṅga form which virtually credits the liṅga with

1. Cf. inscription no. 17, V. 4.

2. For the story cf. *Liṅgapurāṇa*, I, 17, 5-52. *Vāyupurāṇa*, Ch. 55.

the same attributes as those given to Śiva himself. The liṅga is primeval, having no beginning or end, and revered by gods and men. The liṅga assumes various forms for the sake of prosperity of this world, and those who even once bow down to these liṅgas realise their desires.

In Champā, Śiva was represented both as a human figure as well as in his liṅga form. The latter occurs more frequently, as in India, than the image of Śiva. The ordinary liṅgas are placed on a pedestal (śnānadroṇī) which is usually square and sometimes richly ornamented with human figures or other decorative designs. In a few instances the pedestal is round and the *yoni* is represented therein. Very often several liṅgas, sometimes as many as seven, are found on the same pedestal.

The liṅgas are of the usual cylindrical shape. Sometimes a head is sculptured on this liṅga. This is undoubtedly the mukhaliṅga so frequently mentioned in the inscriptions of Champā. M. Finot supposes that this head represents that of the king who founded the liṅga and identified himself with Śiva. But M. Aymonier seems to be right in his view that the head represents Śiva himself. For, according to inscription no. 39, after Brahmā and Viṣṇu had bowed down before the liṅga of Śiva, he "showed them his face, issued from the middle part of the liṅga". But it is quite probable that the face was deliberately made to resemble that of the king. In support of this view we can quote the inscription no. 39 in which we are told that three brothers erected the images of Śrī Mahā-Rudradeva and Bhagavatī out of devotion to, and in imitation of the features of their father and mother. In India we meet with similar mukhaliṅgas, sometimes with four faces.

As a human figure Śiva is represented in a variety of forms.

1. Ordinary human figure with two heads: Two mutilated early Śiva figures of this type found at Tra-kieu are given in *Ars Asiatica* (Vol. IV). The god is represented as a strongly built figure standing in a defiant attitude. The head is covered with rich curls of matted hair magnificently arranged in conical shape. A richly decorated diadem surrounds it at the base, while a brilliant mukuṭa (crown) covers the upper part. Stray locks of hair fall on the breast. The nāgas (serpents) serve as the ornaments of the ears and also take the place of the sacred thread. This last is attached to the lower of the two necklaces around the neck. Belts of pearls etc., surround the waist and the upper part of the abdomen. The upper part of a dagger is seen from above the belt. The figures being mutilated, the position of hands and feet cannot be ascertained. One arm shows trace of a bracelet made of serpents. In the face, the eyebrows and moustache are very prominent. There are crosses and circles in the diadem which might represent the sun and the moon but the third eye is not represented on the forehead.

The images of Śiva found at Myson are less decorated and much simple in design.[1] The god is represented as standing. The upper part of the body is nude, while two garments fixed by a belt round the waist cover the lower part. The lower garment reaches almost upto the ankle, but the upper one stops at the knee. There is a rosary round the wrist of the right hand while the left hand holds a vase. The hair is arranged in three stages on the head. The god has a smiling face with fine moustache and the third eye is represented on the forehead. Very often Śiva is represented as seated, in an attitude of meditation.[2] Sometimes there is a beautifully decorated halo behind the head.[3]

In a few instances even the normal human figure of Śiva has got an uncanny appearance. The Śiva found at Yan Mum[4] may be cited as an instance. The god is represented as seated, with a trident in one hand and an elephant's goad in the other. He has three eyes and the sacred thread. But he is attired like a king and the expression of his face is almost ghostly. Sometimes, as at Dran Lai, Śiva is represented as seated on Nandin, very much in the same style as one sits in a chair.[5]

(2) Śiva is sometimes represented as a human figure with extra hands in various attitudes. The following varieties may be noted:

(i) Standing—six arms, the two upper joined behind the head, others holding a triśūla, lotus, sword and a cup. (ii) standing on Nandin, in an attitude of attack; holding a lance in two hands—has twenty-four or twenty-eight arms; attributes:—Aṅkuśa (elephant-goad), nāgī, bell, pitcher, bag and bow. (iii) Dancing the Tāṇḍava—Sometimes surrounded by nāgīs playing on harp and drum. (iv) Seated—holding a rosary in one hand and trident in another.

(3) In decorative designs, specially on the tympanum, Śiva is represented as dvārapāla (gate-keeper of temples). In these cases he has mostly a terrible appearance with projecting eyes and long teeth. He is armed with a club, and wears a crown, eardrops of skulls, upavīta and bracelets of serpents. Sometimes the dvārapāla is represented as standing on a bull and brandishing a sort of wedge-shaped iron instrument, while a small figure on the head of the animal and turned towards the main figure holds a sword in the right and a buckler in the left hand.

The images of Śiva at Champā are too numerous to be treated in minute details. The following summary of Parmentier would give a fair idea of the general position.

"As an idol, Śiva is more frequently represented as a liṅga which, on the other hand, seldom figures in decorative designs. As to the figure of Śiva, it is more often represented as a normal human being, rather than

1. Parm, *IC*, Vol. I, p. 362.
2. *ibid.*, Vol. II, pp. 404-05.
3. *ibid.*, p. 290.
4. *ibid.*, p. 309.
5. *ibid.*, p. 401.

of monstrous appearance. The figure is usually seated, but, in rare cases, standing. In the earlier period he is represented with a corpulent body; in the later period, as an ascetic. It is only in the form of dvārapāla that he takes a terrible appearance. But this form of sculpture gradually disappeared. It is in the decoration of tympanum again in the earliest period, that the god is represented as fighting or victorious. It is specially in these cases that the god has monstrous forms. This is only partly caused by the multiplication of hands which vary from four to thirty. It is only in exceptional cases again that the god is represented with a multiplicity of heads. On the other hand he has very often the third eye on the forehead. His usual vāhana (vehicle) is Nandin, and he has the Brāhmaṇical sacred thread as his distinctive sign. He is sometimes covered by serpents in the shape of ornaments. The usual attributes of the god are the sword, the rosary, the lotus-stem, the triśūla, and the vajra. Among other attributes, less generally found, may be mentioned discus, lance, bow, arrow, pen, purse, wallet, comb, cup, bowl, horn, bell, and elephant-goad. Sometimes the Oṁkāra is marked on the head-dress."[1]

One of the oldest liṅgas of Śiva came to be regarded as the national deity and maintained this position throughout the course of history. The liṅga was established by king Bhadravarman towards the close of the fourth or the beginning of the fifth century A.D. and was named Bhadreśvara, for it was customary to designate the god by a term composed of the first part of the donor's name and the word Īśvara. This liṅga named Bhadreśvara or Bhadreśvarasvāmi was placed in a temple at Myson which soon became a national sanctuary and the centre of a group of magnificent temples. The king endowed the temple with land whose boundaries are described in three inscriptions. This temple was burnt sometime between 478 and 578 A.D. but restored by king Sambhuvarman who confirmed the endowments previously given by Bhadravarman. Following the custom set on foot by the latter he associated his own name with that of the god, and called him Śambhu-Bhadreśvara. Successive kings, such as Prakāśadharma and Indravarman II and many others vied with one another in richly endowing this 'god of gods', and composing hymns of praise in his honour.[2] In course of time a mythical origin was attributed to the Liṅga. It is said, in an inscription, dated 875 A.D., the Śiva himself gave it to Bhṛgu, and Uroja having got it from the latter established it in Champā. We are told that Śambhu-Bhadreśvara, the greatest of gods, and the only one fit to be worshipped, was the guardian deity of Champā, all the kings of which have become famous in the world through his grace and favour.

From the middle of the eleventh century A.D. Śrīśāna-Bhadreśvara came to occupy the position of national god. It appears extremely likely that we

1. *ibid.*, pp. 411-12.
2. Cf. inscription No. 17, p. 35.

find here the old god Śambhu-Bhadreśvara under new names, for the god Śrīśāna-Bhadreśvara is also said to be installed by Uroja. Henceforth king after king declares himself to be an incarnation of Uroja, and restores or endows the temple of Śrīśānabhadreśvara which Uroja had formerly established on the Vugvan mountain. The temple suffered much in the hands of the enemies, particularly the Cambodians, and was therefore repaired and endowed by a succession of kings[1], sometimes with the booty taken from the Cambodians themselves. An idea of the wealth and grandeur of the god and its surroundings may be formed from the numerous lists of articles granted to the god by the kings of Champā in perpetual endowments.[2]

It is thus absolutely clear that Śambhubhadreśvara or Śrīśānabhadreśvara was regarded as the national deity of Champā from beginning to end, and most elaborate arrangements compatible with the wealth and resources of the kingdom were made for his worship. There were apprarently the system of 'Devādasīs' (female dancers), who dedicated their lives to the service of the god which forms so characteristic a feature of Indian temples even today. The enormous wealth of the temples of Champā would also remind one of the temples of India the wealth and grandeur of which have been so vividly described by Sultan Mahmud and the writers of his time.

In addition to the Śiva-liṅga which attained the position of the national deity there were many others though of less importance. The most remarkable among these was a mukhaliṅga of Śambhu in Po-Nagar. We learn from an inscription of the 8th century A.D. that this mukhaliṅga was established by a king named Vicitrasagara. We find reference to this liṅga as late as the 12th century A.D. but it never acquired the status of a national deity like Śambhu-Bhadreśvara or Śrīśāna-Bhadreśvara.

The kings of Champā seem to have regarded it as a pious duty not only to maintain and endow the famous liṅgas of olden times but also to establish new ones. In such cases the almost universal practice was to associate his own names with the new image. Below is given a list of kings and the names of gods established by them:[3]

1. Bhadravarman—Bhadreśvara, 2. Śambhuvarman—Śambhu-Bhadreśvara, 3. Indravarman—Indra-Bhadreśvara; Indra-Bhogeśvara; Indra-Parameśvara, 4. Vikrānta-Varman—Vikrānta-Rudra; Śrī Vikrānta-Rudraśvara; Śrī Vikrāntadevādhibhaveśvara, 5. Jayasiṁhavarmadeva—Jaya Guheśvara, 6. Bhadravarmadeva—Prakāśa-Bhadreśvara; Bhadra-Malayeśvara; Bhadra-Champeśvara; Bhadra-Maṇḍaleśvara; Bhadra-Pureśvara: 7. Indravarman—Indra-Kānteśa; 8. Harivarman-Harivarmeśvara; 9. Jaya

1. Cf. inscription nos. 59, 61, 62, 68-73, 79, 81, 84, 87, 94, 101, 109, 117.
2. For list of articles see Majumdar, R.C., *op. cit.*, pp. 182-83.
3. Cf. ins. nos. 2, 7, 23, 24, 36, 39, 44, 74, 75, 81, 103, 112, 116.

Harivarman—Jaya-Hariliṅgeśvara, 10. Jaya Indravarman—Jaya-Indra-Lokeśvara; Śrī Jaya-Indreśvara; Śrī-Indra-Gaurīśvari, 11. Indravarman—Indravarman Śivaliṅgeśvara; 12. Jayasiṁhavarmadeva—Jayasiṁha-Varmaliṅgeśvara.

In addition to these instances where the kings associated their own names with the gods established by themselves, there are other cases on record where kings and nobles associated the names of their beloved relations with the gods founded by them. Thus king Jayasiṁhavarmadeva installed the goddess Horoma for increasing the religious merit of his mother's younger sister, queen Haradevī. The latter installed Indra-Parameśvara for the sake of religious merit of her husband Indravarman. She also installed Rudra-Parameśvara and Rudroma for increasing the religious merit of her father and mother. These names are also probably to be explained in the same way, though nothing definite can be laid down as we are ignorant of the names of her parents. The inscription no. 38 records the consecration of a liṅga, called Indradeva, in honour of king Indravarman, by a dignitary of the realm. Again, Īśvaradeva, brother of a minister, installed the God Īśvaradevādideva. The inscription no. 12 mentions two gods Īśāneśvara and Prabhaśeśvara, and it is extremely likely that these two gods are associated with the kings named Īśānavarman, and Prabhāsadharma referred to in that inscription. There are similarly other cases, where the names of gods are apparently derived from some kings, though we are unable either to identify the king or to decide whether the king himself founded the image or somebody else installed it in his honour. Two conclusions however stand out prominently from the above analysis. In the first place, the kings of Champā vied with one another in installing images of Śiva as it was regarded pious to do so, and secondly, they identified or associated themselves with the gods by adding their names to that of the god, and also at times by making the image of the god resemble their own.

The practice of associating the name of the king with that of the god founded by him was certainly not unknown to India. The Candella king Pṛthvideva installed an image of Śiva named Pṛthvideveśvara.[1] Two queens of the Cālukya king Vikramāditya II, named Lokamahādevī and Trailokyamahādevī installed two images of Śiva called Lokeśvara and Trailokeśvara respectively.[2]

A number of deities came to be associated with Śiva. The most prominent among them was of course the Śakti of Śiva, known variously as Umā, Gaurī, Bhagavatī, Mahābhagavatī, Devī and Mahādevī. She was also called Matṛliṅgeśvari and Bhūmiśvarī. She was the daughter of

1. *Ep. Ind.*, Vol. I, p. 38.

2. *Bom. Gaz.*, Vol. I, Pt. II, p. 190.

Himālaya and the incomparable and loving spouse of Śiva, worthy of being adored with joy by that god.[1]

The cult of Śakti worship seems to have been most prevalent in the southern region known as Kauthāra. Here was established the goddess Yapu Nagara or Bhagavatī Kauthāreśvarī, in the temple of Po-Nagara which became a national sanctuary of the Chams comparable to that of Śambhu-Bhadreśvara or Śrīśanabhadreśvara.

We learn from an inscription of king Harivarman that an old image of Bhagavatī in Kauthāra, famous all over the world, remained empty for a long time.[2] In other words the image was carried away by savage tribes or destroyed by enemy troops, and the temple remained empty for a long time. Then in 817 A.D. king Harivarman made a new stone image of the goddess, adorned with a variety of ornaments, and offered her gold, silver, jewels, clothes of variegated colour and other articles. He further dedicated to the goddess fields in the Kauthāra country together with male and female slaves, buffaloes etc. Within half a century the stone image was coated over with a plate of gold, and ornaments with costly jewels were added to the head and ears of the image. In the year 918 A.D. king Indravarman established a golden image of the goddess. This was unfortunately carried away by the Cambodians some time between 944 and 947 A.D. The war apparently taxed the resources of the king to the utmost, for in 965 A.D. he replaced the golden image that was lost by a stone one. About a century later, in 1050 A.D. king Parameśvaravarman made rich gifts to the goddess, viz., vase inlaid with gold, a diadem, waistband, silver vase, an umbrella decorated with peacock feathers, a vast silver canopy and several golden pitchers and vases.[3] In 1084, king Paramabodhisattva, together with his sister and eldest son, gave to the goddess, among other things, elephants, a golden crown, a necklace decorated with jewels, and various other ornaments and utensils of gold and silver.[4] In 1160 A.D., king Harivarman, after having triumphed over all his enemies, both foreign and internal, first of all honoured the goddess called Yapu Nagara by giving her great riches.[5] Again, in 1167 A.D., king Jaya Indravarman VI, together with his queens and daughters, made rich donations to Bhagavatī Kauṭhareśvarī. In 1233 A.D., king Jaya Parameśvaravarman granted land and slaves to the goddess Pu-Nagara. The slaves belonged to both the sexes and to various nationalities such as the Khmer, Cham, Chinese and Siamese. Probably the image of the goddess was destroyed soon after. For we learn from two inscriptions (nos. 97-98) that princess Sūryadevī,

1. Cf. ins. nos. 4, 22, 26, 30, 32, 39, 50, 97.
2. *ibid.*, no. 26.
3. Cf. ins. no. 55.
4. *ibid.*, no. 64.
5. *ibid.*, no. 76.

daughter of king Jaya Indravarmadeva gave a sum of money for making a statue of the goddess Bhagavatī Kauthāreśvarī. She also gave various ornaments of gold and silver to the goddess and prescribed regulations for the dancing girls employed in the service of the goddess (1256 A.D.) Later kings of Champā also continued the donations to the goddess.

The general conception of Śakti is beautifully illustrated by the long hymn with which the inscription no. 55 begins. Her power is conceived to be equal to that of god Śiva. She is in her very essence at one with whatever is in the world of God during its creation as well as in its dissolution. She is the primordial energy of the existent and the non-existent. But, as we have seen above, these are exactly the attributes of Śiva himself. Hence the Śakti and Śiva are conceived as essentially one and the same: "Thou hast as body, half of that which has moon as its diadem i.e. Mahādeva; thou art of beautiful appearance and form part of the body of the lord of embodied beings'.

Here we have evidently the conception of 'Ardhanārī'. Bergaigne concludes from it that the image of Bhagavatī Kauthāreśvarī, also named goddess Yāpu Nagara, was that of an Ardhanārī i.e. an idol which represents Śiva and Durgā in the same body, prominence being given to the female part under tāntric ideas. This may or not be true, for the epithets in question might refer to the general conception of Śakti and not to the particular image.

It is true that an image of Ardhanārī has been actually found at Dong Phuc. The female side in this statue is emphasised by the dress and developed breasts while the male part is indicated by fine moustache. The identity of 'ardhanārī' is revealed by the third eye on the forehead.[1]

But the image of the goddess of Po-Nagar at Nha Trang ' is of a quite different character. It is a beautiful statue of black stone. The goddess, seated cross-legged, has developed breasts, and the folds on her belly indicate her maternity. She has ten hands. Two of these are placed on the two knees with palm upwards.[2] The eight other hands behind the two carry dagger, lance, bow, arrow, elephant-goad, shield, discus and conchshell. The goddess, adorned with bracelets and necklaces has a rather sombre expression. This statue of the goddess has been supposed by Aymonier to be the one erected by Indravarman in 965 A.D. More likely it is the statue erected by princess Suryadevi about 1256 A.D.

Sometimes, in bas-relief, the goddess is represented as standing on Nandin. In a bas-relief at Myson the goddess is represented as dancing, holding different attributes in her ten hands. These attributes are generally

1. Parm, *IC*, Vol. II, pp. 413-14.
2. Parmentier thinks that these indicate the two Mudras of *dana* (gift) and *abhaya* (assurance).
Parm, *IC*, Vol. II, p. 412.

speaking the same as those of Śiva. Another bas-relief at Chien Dang represents the goddess in a fighting attitude. She has six arms and holds a bow and an arrow.

The number of images of Bhagavatī, so far discovered, does not correspond to the importance which the inscriptions attribute to that goddess. But in one respect the monuments corroborate the epigraphic records. It appears equally from both that Umā or Bhagavatī was more regarded as a female counterpart of Śiva than as a separate goddess. She has got the same attitudes, attributes and characteristics as those of Śiva. She has a third eye on the forehead, a large number of arms varying from four to ten, and even the same vāhana viz., the Nandin. Only, unlike Śiva, she does not wear the sacred thread which is peculiar to the male sex only.

Another Śaiva deity, Kārttika known also as Kumāra, seems to have enjoyed a great popularity in Champā. He is referred to in four inscriptions (nos. 9, 24, 36 & 39), from one of which we learn that an image of the god was placed with those of Gaṇeśa and Umā in a Śaiva temple. He is conceived as a great hero who repelled all his enemies and this no doubt refers to the part he played as commander-in-chief of the gods in their wars against the Asuras.

Four or perhaps five images of this god have been discovered so far.[1] In two of these the god has his usual vāhana the peacock. In two others, however, the god rides on rhinoceros, a conception unknown in India though familiar in Kambuja. In one instance the god is represented as standing on the peacock with the peacock's train at his back. In other cases the god is represented as squatting on his vāhana. The vajra and sword are his principal attributes. The hair of his head are beautifully arranged in four parts, a fashion peculiar to this god. Sometimes the god figures in the tympanum of a temple in the train of Śiva.

Lastly, a word must be said about Nandin, the vāhana of Śiva and Umā. Separate images of Nandin are found in large number in the vestibules of temples. The figure is that of a recumbent humped bull, looking towards the god in the temple. Sometimes the pedestal of the image was richly decorated and a number of bells were tied round the neck of the bull in the form of a necklace.[2]

Viṣṇu

Although not so prominent as Śiva, Viṣṇu also played an important part in Champā. Viṣṇu was known by various names, such as Puruṣottama, Nārāyaṇa, Hari, Govinda, Mādhava, Vikrama and Tribhuvanākrānta.[3] He was given high attributes. Viṣṇu is the preceptor of the whole

1. Cf. Parm, *IC*, Vol. II, pp. 417-18.
2. *ibid.*, p. 419.
3. Cf. Ins. Nos. 11, 24, 33, 39, 63, 121.

world and without beginning or end. He is revered by the gods, *asura* and *munis.* He is valorous in battle and protects the whole world. Some mythological feats of Viṣṇu are referred to. He churned the ocean by means of the Mandāra mountain and lifted the world by his two hands. He defeated the asuras, Madhu and Kaiṭabha for example, and crushed other enemies.

But as in India, the incarnations of Viṣṇu probably claimed greater homage than the god himself. Two of these, Rāma and Kṛṣṇa, are again and again referred to. Viṣṇu is said to have divided his essence under the form of four Rāmas viz., Rāma and his three younger brothers and we have already seen how the events of the *Rāmāyaṇa* were localised in Champā. Prominence is given to the heroic feats performed by Viṣṇu in his incarnation as Kṛṣṇa. He held aloft mount Govardhana, and destroyed Kaṁsa, Keśī, Cāṇūra, Ariṣṭa and Pralaṃba. Again, Kāmdeva (Cupid) is referred to as the son of Viṣṇu, apparently in the incarnation of Kṛṣṇa, for, according to the Purāṇas, Kāma is the son of Kṛṣṇa.

The kings of Champā took delight in comparing themselves to Viṣṇu, and sometimes even regarded themselves as his incarnation. Thus Jaya Rudravarman was regarded as incarnation of Viṣṇu and his son, king Śrī Jaya Harivarmadeva, Śivanandana regarded himself as a unique Viṣṇu whose glories surpassed those of Rāma and Kṛṣṇa, firmly established in all directions.

The concrete conception of Viṣṇu is that of a god with four arms. His vāhana is Garuḍa, but he sometimes lies down on the fathomless bed of the ocean of milk (kṣīra sāgar), served by Vāsukī, the serpent king, with infinite hood.

The epigraphic records is in this respect fully corroborated by the actual images of Viṣṇu discovered at Champā. The one erected by prince Nauk Glaun Vijaya and found at Bien Hoa[1] is seated cross-legged in Indian fashion and richly decorated. He has four arms. Two of them hold two clubs, while the other two hold a discus and a conch shell. He wears a sacred thread, a unique feature as it is absent from the other images of Viṣṇu in Champā, about seven or eight in number, which have so far been discovered. The chief attributes in the hands of these images, other than those mentioned above, are lotus, sceptre, and arms such as sword, club, axe and bow. In very rare cases Viṣṇu has only two hands, he has generally four, and never more than that. He is usually represented as seated.

In some decorative panels Viṣṇu is represented as riding on Garuḍa or seated cross-legged on its back.[2] There are also images of the Anantaśayana of Viṣṇu. The god is lying at ease on the coils of serpent Vāsukī,

1. For the image see Parm, *IC*, Vol. I, p. 554.
2. Parm, *IC*, Vol. II, p. 422.

whose seven hoods guard his head. From the navel of the god rises a lotus on the petals of which is seated Brahmā in an attitude of meditation. That the scene is laid on the bed of the ocean is indicated by wavy lines with fishes.[1]

We find also an image of Kṛṣṇa in the act of protecting the cows and cowherds by holding aloft the mountain Govardhana over their heads.[2]

Lakṣmī

Lakṣmī, the Śakti of Viṣṇu, also referred to as Padmā and Śrī, was a well-known goddess of Champā. She is frequently referred to in inscriptions and emphasis is laid on her proverbial inconstancy. She is the ideal housewife and faithfully follows Viṣṇu. The favourite Indian convention of regarding Lakṣmī as the symbol of sovereignty was also not unknown. She is said to have been born in the Kailāśa mountain, though the Indian tradition regards her as arising from the ocean of milk on the occasion of the churning of the ocean.[3]

The inscription no. 21 gives the long history of an image of Lakṣmī, originally installed by king Śambhuvarman, and reinstalled by king Vikrantavarman in 731 A.D. The altar of this goddess, we are told, was made of gold and silver.

Three images of Lakṣmī have been so far discovered. Lakṣmī figures largely in the decorative panels. A tympanum at Dong Duong represents the goddess with two hands as seated between two elephants who are pouring water upon her head from a vase held aloft by their upraised trunks. In another tympanum the goddess is represented as seated on a coil of serpents, the thirteen heads of which surround her on all sides. She has four arms; three of them carry conch, discus and a club, while the fourth points to something by the extended fore-finger. The goddess is frequently represented as having only two arms, and holding stems of lotus plant[4]

Garuḍa

Like Nandian, the vāhana of Śiva, Garuḍa, the vāhana of Viṣṇu, was also a familiar object in Champā. It not only figures in connection with Viṣṇu as its vāhana, but a large number of separate images of it occur in decorative panels in various parts of temples.

According to Brāhmaṇic legends, Garuḍa is the king of birds and the

1. *ibid.*, p. 423.
2. *ibid.*, Vol. I, p. 259.
3. Cf. *Viṣṇupurāṇa*, Bk. I. Chap. VIIIff. But the Indian tradition also seems to have been known in Champā.
4. Parm, *IC*, Vol. II, pp. 421-27; *BEF*, Vol. I, pp. 18-20.

great enemy of snakes. He is represented in Champā with the head of a bird, but with the rest of the body very often like that of a lion. He has beak, tails and wings of a bird; as a king he is crowned with mukuṭa and richly decorated with jewels; and being divine in nature he wears the sacred thread. Sometimes Garuḍa is represented as if on the point of taking his flight, and his legs are in different planes. Sometimes the legs are in the same place and hold a number of snakes. The snakes are often represented as forming a dais for Garuḍa, and are treated more as companions of the latter than his victims.

The head of the Garuḍa is not always a faithful reproduction of that of a bird. Sometimes it looks like that of a monkey, and sometimes it is almost human. Sometimes Garuḍa is represented with the head of a monster crushing a large number of snakes with his teeth.[1]

Although the great gods of the trinity, viz., Brahmā, Viṣṇu and Śiva almost monopolised the homage and worship of the people, the lesser gods of the Hindu pantheon were not altogether forgotten. Thus the inscription no. 24 begins with "a reverence to all the gods", and the inscription no. 31 frankly recognises their importance in the following words:

"In some places Indra, Brahmā and Viṣṇu, in some places Vāsukī, in some places Śaṅkara, in some places ascetics, Sun, Moon, Agni, Varuṇa, and in some places image of Abhayada (Buddha) appeared for the deliverance of creatures".

While the list of gods in the above passage is by no means exhaustive, it is worthy of note that deities like Indra, Vāsukī, Sun, Moon, Agni and Varuṇa are placed on the same level as the great gods, and regarded as deliverer of human beings. It shows that side by side with the pompous worship of Śiva and Viṣṇu there were popular cults of various gods and goddesses.

The view is corroborated by the opening lines of Myson inscription (no. 4) of Bhadravarman. The inscription begins with "reverence of Umā, Maheśvara, Brahmā and Viṣṇu", and this is immediatety followed by "reverence to the Earth, Wind, Sky, Water and Fire" i.e., the five elements of nature. Apparently these were regarded as divine in nature. Inscription no. 17 refers to these five together with Sun, Moon and sacrificer as the eight forms of Śiva.

The epigraphic records introduce us to a number of these gods. A short account of them is given below:

(1) *Indra*

Indra is referred to in a large number of inscriptions. He is referred to

1. Parm, *IC*, Vol. II, p. 262, 273ff; 475.

as the chief or king of the gods who killed Vṛtra and other asuras, and worked the miracle of creating the three worlds. He is said to have performed severe austerities and a large number of great sacrifices (yajña) in previous births. Having gained the kingdom of heaven by virtue thereof, he protected it according to rules of dharma. His son is also extolled for the prowess of his unconquered arms. The popularity of the god is indicated both by the large number of references in inscriptions as well as by the fact that not less than twelve kings assumed the name Indravarman. Many kings of Champā are also referred to as Indra personified or Indra fallen from heaven to earth in order to rule over the country.

Two images of Indra have so far been discovered in Champā, one at Tra Kieu and the other at Myson. These are two small human figures and only identified with Indra by the figures of elephant, the vāhana of Indra, before the pedestal. In one of them Indra has probably the Vajra (thunderbolt) in his hand[1].

(2) *Yama*

Yama, the god of death, is conceived as a terrible figure, but he faithfully maintains the law in his kingdom. He is referred to as Dharma and Dharmarāja.

(3) *Candra*

Candra is referred to as god and the victim of Rāhu.

(4) *Sūrya*

The Sun-god is often coupled with the Moon (Candra). They both form part of the grand assembly of gods. Two small images of Sūrya have been discovered at Myson. They are identified by means of the figure of horse, the vāhana of Sūrya, The god holds the sword in his hands[2].

(5) *Kubera*

Kubera is described as a friend of Maheśvara and a mine of wealth. He is also called Dhanada and is praised for his liberality. He is called 'Ekākṣapiṅgala', apparently in allusion to a story described fully in the *Rāmāyaṇa* (Uttarakāṇḍa Ch. XIII). A temple of Kubera was erected in the seventh century A.D. by king Prakāśadharma. This god was worshipped by the people for increasing the wealth and guarding against evils. The god referred to as Arthetvara in no. 92 may be the same as Kubera.

1. Parm, *IC*, Vol. II, p. 430.
2. *ibid.*

Yakṣas, the mythical attendants of Kubera are also frequently mentioned.

(6) *Sarasvatī*

Sarasvatī is conceived as a goddess or merely regarded as a symbolical expression for knowledge and learning cannot be determined.

(7) A god called Vanāntareśvara seem to have been worshipped in the later period, but its identity is at present unknown.

(8) Two gods Mandara and Praṇaveśvara are referred to but their identity is unknown.

In addition to these gods, there were other beings of the nature of demi-gods who are frequently referred to in the inscriptions of Champā. Chief among these are the divine sages (*ṛṣis*) who are placed on the same level as the gods. Among them Bṛhaspati, the preceptor of the gods, and Kaśyapa, the preceptor of the gods and demons are mentioned by name. The former is extolled for his eloquence and knowledge of śāstras. Next to the divine sages mention may be made of the Sīddhas, Vidyādharas, Cāraṇas, Yakṣas, Kinnaras, Gandharvas and Apsaras or celestial nymphs.

A number of evil spirits also figure prominently in the mythical conceptions of the people. Prominent among them are the daityas and asuras who are the eternal enemies of the gods in heaven. There were also the uragas, rākṣasas, pretas, and piśācas. Images of apsaras are found in decorative panels. They wear rich mukuṭas and are represented as flying figures with lotus-stem in their hands.[1] The rākṣas are represented by demoniacal figures, with clenched teeth and a multiplicity of heads and arms.[2] Figures of nāgins are also to be seen in the decorative panels. They resemble the Indian figures, having the body of a serpent with a female bust.[3]

3. BURMA

Burma, though a Buddhist country, could not escape the influences of Brāhmaṇical religion. Although Brāhmaṇism was not the religion of the state nor of the people in general, the records and finds of a number of images however, show that there was a considerable number of followers of the Brāhmaṇical religion, not exclusively Brāhmaṇas, but of other three castes as well, who were free to perform their own religious ceremonies. Brāhmaṇical influence is also indicated by certain ancient place-names[4] of both Upper and Lower Burma. One such name is Bissunomyo, which is equivalent to Viṣṇupura or the city of Viṣṇu. The name was in ancient times applied to old Prome or Hmawza which had obviously been a centre

1. Parm, *IC*, Vol. II, p. 431.
2. *ibid.*
3. *ibid.*
4. Duroiselle, Apocryphal, *Geography of Burma, An. Rep. A.S. Burma*, 1923, p. 15.

of Viṣṇuite influence. The tradition of the foundation of the ancient city of Prome as contained in the *Mahayazawin*, a late Burmese chronicle, is associated with Viṣṇu and his vāhana (vehicle), Garuḍa, as also with Caṇḍī and Parameśvara equivalent to Durgā and Śiva respectively.[1] The *Mahayazawin* does not mention the name of Viṣṇu but refers to a *ṛṣi*. The name of the *ṛṣi* is supplied by the great Shwezigon inscription[2] which records briefly the story of the foundation of Sisit (or old Prome). Old Prome or Hmawza is also referred to as Śrīkṣetra which is the sacred name of modern Puri on the opposite side of the Bay of Bengal, and is associated with a Taungdwin; a town, said to have been founded in 837 A.D., was called Rāmāvatī after the name of the epic hero, Rāma, who is recognised as one of the ten incarnations of Viṣṇu. But the surest proof of the prevalence of Brāhmaṇism in Burma is the archaeological discoveries of Brāhmaṇical gods and temples, of such discoveries we have. Though not at all comparable with other parts of South-East Asia, an interesting record of old Brāhmaṇical temples in ancient Burma, we have only one, the Na-hluang Kyaung that stands at Pagan. The main deity of the shrine is Viṣṇu himself, four images of whom stand on the four sides of a square obelisk at the centre of the vaulted temple.

The existence of a Brāhmaṇical population (mainly Vaiṣṇavite in creed) in Burma at an early period cannot, therefore, be doubted. It can easily be surmised that this Brāhmaṇical community would have their own gods whom they could worship in accordance with their own religious rites. In those localities where the Indian element was permanently represented either by a more vigorous commercial intercourse or by settlement and colonization, it was likely that their gods would have permanent habitat there in temples. The temples having been usually built of brick gradually fell into decay and finally disappeared with the singular exception of the one that is now standing at Pagan. But, most of the images which had been once enshrined in these temples are now emerging out of the debris of ruins of centuries. Thus, at old Hmawza, a locality known in ancient times as Bissunamyo, at least three different types of stone images of Viṣṇu have been discovered, one of which belongs to the 6th or 7th century A.D.[3], along with images of Gaṇeśa, Brahmā and other Brāhmaṇical deities. At Mergui in the Tennasserim province images of Viṣṇu, Gaṇeśa, Hanumāna and Brahmā have been found.[4] Three stone slabs, belonging stylistically to about the latter half of the 9th century A.D. have in recent years been brought over from Thaton to the Rangoon Museum. Two of these slabs

1. *An. Rep. A.S. Burma*, 1910, p. 18.
2. *Ep. Birm.*, Vol. I, part II, p. 90.
3. Thakur, U. *Some Aspects of Ancient Indian History and Culture*, Ch. XXII.
4. Rangoon Museum Exhibits Nos. 1/6, 2/6, 3/6.

depict in bold relief the Anantaśayyā episode of Viṣṇu and the third represents Śiva with Pārvatī seated by his side.[1] At Thaton, the walls of a pyramidal stage of a Buddhist pagoda are decorated with rectangular stone panels purporting most probably to depict a Brāhmaṇical mythological story. Of the slabs that still remain, two certainly represent Śiva with his trident. In Arakan where Brāhmaṇical influence had been more pronounced from earlier times, archaeological exploration has discovered in recent years images of Viṣṇu, Durgā, Sūrya and other deities of the Brāhmaṇical pantheon. Coins and terracotta tablets bearing the Śaivite symbol of the trident and the representation of the bull (Nandi) have been found in large numbers at Mrohaung and other localities in Arakan as well as in other places of both Upper and Lower Burma. Coins with the Vaiṣṇavite symbol of a conch-shell are not also infrequent.

Thus, the above references do not by any means exhaust the list of finds of the Brāhmaṇical cults and articles of worship in Burma. These clearly indicate that, side by side with Buddhism, Brāhmaṇism was also prevalent in Burma. The details of the cults of the Brāhmaṇical trinity are given below:

Brahmā

Brahmā, the first god of the Brāhmaṇical trinity, has been able to command very little influence in Burma. He seems to have had no temple and, as an independent deity, very few adherents too. He has been represented, as we have seen, with Viṣṇu and Śiva on the Anantaśayyā reliefs from Thaton and Hmawza; but independent images of Brahmā are rare, and only five or six extant examples are known. Of the more interesting of them, one is at present housed in the Rangoon Museum, another is in the Pagan Museum and a third is represented in low relief on the face of the interior pillars of the Manuha temple, Pagan. Broken fragments of images of Brahmā have here and there been found, for example, in the ruins of the Zegu pagoda, Hmawza,[2] as well as at the precincts of the Shwesandaw pagoda, Pagan, but even such finds are rare.

The Rangoon Museum Brahmā[3] is carved in bold and round relief out of a rectangular (about 1′4″×1′) slab of soft greyish sand-stone. Brahmā is seated in *padmāsana* with folded hands raised up to chest-height, a position which, most probably, shows him in an attitude of worship of, or of prayer to, a superior deity. He is represented with three heads with matted locks of hair beautifully dressed in the *jaṭā-mukuṭa* fashion crowned over with a floral ornament.

1. *ibid.*, Nos. 8/6, 9/6, 10/6.
2. *An. Rep. A.S. Burma*, 1908, p. 6. There is housed in the Rangoon Museum a rectangular stone-slab representing twelve seated figures of Brāhmaṇical deities of whom Brahmā and Gaṇeśa alone are recognisable. Exhibit No. 6/6.
3. Rangoon Museum Exhibit No. 5/6.

The Pagan Museum Brahmā[1] conforms exactly to the same description. He is similarly seated in paḍmāsana with folded hands in an attitude of worship; and his three heads are crowned with his matted locks beautifully dressed. But the quality of the stone is better in the present example and the two belong to the strictly different schools. Moreover, stylistically judged, they are separated from one another by a gulf of at least two centuries. The former is the product of a local school of art which is but obvious in the comparatively stiff modelling of the body, in the too much boneless flexible lines of the different limbs, in the rigid pose and, last but not least, in the quaint expression of the face. The local artist tutored by his Indian master seems to have worked out an Indian type. But the latter is undoubtedly the product of an Indian artist who gives evidence of his art and skill in the soft modelling of the body in the pleasing graceful lines and curves of the limbs, in the most easy position of the body and lastly in the soft pleasing expression of the face. The sculpture at once reminds one of similar Indian examples of the late Gupta art traditions of Eastern India, and belongs to a date not later than the 10th century, whereas the Rangoon Museum example seems to be a local product of the 12th-13th century of the Christian era.[2]

There are four images of Brahmā carved in very low relief on the faces of the interior square pillars of the Nanpaya temple at Pagan. This temple is traditionally known to have been the residential house of the defeated Talaing King Manuha, who was brought from Thaton and kept a captive at Pagan by Anawrahta. Manuha built a temple where a huge recumbent image of the Buddha in his parinirvāṇa can be seen, and also a second one just adjacent to the first to shelter himself. These two temples are situated at Myinpagan and are in a good state of preservation. Curiously enough, the smaller one, i.e., the temple that was used for the residence of

1. Pagan Museum Exhibit No. V/74.
2. On the walls of the Thein-mazi temple, Pagan, built about the 11th-12th century A.D. there have been discovered wall-paintings depicting, it is asserted, scenes from Buddhist and Brāhmaṇical (?) mythology. One of the characters that form the subject-matter of these paintings, has been sought to be identified as Brahmā. Taw Sein Ko, late Superintendent, Archaeological Survey, Burma, says on page 30 of his Report of the year 1919; "The figure represented is probably a Brahmā of the Brahmaloka going through the clouds while being seated in an attitude of adoration... He is on a pilgrimage to the worship at the above shrine. He wears a crown surmounted by a high peak which is surrounded by six lower ones, and has four eyes, two noses and two mouths, and holds conical flowers... The nose is high, pointed and aquiline, and is distinctly Pyu." We do not see our way to agree with Taw Sein Ko in identifying this figure as Brahmā. Neither his attributes are here seen, nor has he the four faces (three faces are, in fact, represented) by which he is well-known. It might as well be a Mahāyāna deity.

Manuha, a king fervently devoted to Buddhism, contains on its pillars images of Brahmā carved and modelled in very low and flat relief. The main sanctum of the temple is now empty, and it is difficult to determine whether it was a Brāhmaṇical or Buddhist deity that was worshipped there. It is not improbable that an image of Buddha himself was installed there at the sanctum to whom the four Brahmā images were represented in prayer or worship. Even then, the existence of a Brāhmaṇical deity in the residential palace of a devout Buddhist shows that the captive king had a decided Brāhmaṇical leaning.

Herein Brahmā is seated on a full-blown lotus-seat that shoots off its delicately and richly carved stems with leaves and flowers, a beautiful vegetable decoration of considerable artistic merit, on two sides of the seated image. Brahmā seems to have a soft and flabby body resting on his legs the left one of which is in a squatting position and the right lifted at an angle—a position that is suggestively analogous to what is technically known as *līlāsana*. Unlike the images of Brahmā noticed above, here the two hands are not clasped in prayer, but are raised upwards and hold two lotus flowers. The matted locks of hair are arranged in a beautiful jaṭā-mukuṭa consisting of carefully intertwined plaits curling capriciously and coquettishly. He has also a halo round his head and a sacred thread, treated in a flat plastic volume, hanging from his left shoulder. The four images belong to the same type and conform exactly to the same description; but the type itself is interesting, for, the lotus attribute in the hands and the particular seated attitude of the god are unique features rarely seen in extant images of Brahmā.

Śiva

Śiva, the second god of trinity was denied an important position by the members of the Brāhmaṇical fold in Burma. Nevertheless, he is, often mentioned in inscriptions and his images too were worshipped. The Burmese text *Mahayazawin* while describing the story of the city of Hmawza or old Prome, mentions, along with other divinities, the names of Caṇḍī and Parameśvara, identical with Devī or Durgā and Śiva or Maheśvara respectively. According to the story, Viṣṇu presided at the foundation and he was helped by six other divinities, viz., Gavamapati, Indra, Nāga, Garuḍa, Caṇḍī and Parameśvara, no doubt suggesting thereby that all these divinities including Caṇḍī and her lord Parameśvara, occupied a position subordinate to that of the supreme god Viṣṇu.

In legends and traditions of Burma, Śiva has hardly any place, nor is he mentioned in epigraphic records. But numismatic evidence shows that Arakan, the hilly buffer region between the eastern frontiers of India and Burma, had once been a stronghold of Saivism, or was at least under the sway of a dynasty of Śaivite kings. Here have been and are still being discovered coins bearing Śaivite symbols, viz., the trident of Śiva on the reverse and a recumbent humped bull on the obverse. These coins discovered at different times and at different localities have a family likeness inasmuch as they all have common symbols, and on the obverse face over the recumbent bull is invariably the legend or name of the king. All these names end with the surname "Candra", and this surname was adapted by at least two lines of kings ruling at Arakan, known as the Candra dynasty in local legendary history.[1] Names of a number of Candra kings have also been deciphered on a nāgari stone inscription found at the Shittoung pagoda, Mrohaung, and dated palaeographically in the 9th-10th century A.D.[2] The coins referred to above, may, likewise, on palaeographic grounds be said to range over a period extending from about the middle of the 4th to the 10th century A.D.[3], the majority of them in fact, belonging to the closing centuries. Coins have on their obverse the figure of a recumbent humped bull with legend above in nāgari characters, and on the reverse the trident of Śiva with garlands pendent from the outer blades. On the reverse face of some of them symbols of the sun and moon can be traced. The nāgari legend can respectively be read as Vammacandra, Prīticandra, Pṛticandra and Vīracandra.[4] The names are obviously Indian and the symbols Śaivite. It is thus reasonable to make conjecture that the Candra dynasty of kings of Arakan who ruled from c. 400 A.D. to c. 1000 A.D. belonged to the Brāhmaṇical fold and were evidently followers of the cult of Śiva.

Coins bearing Viṣṇuite symbols on one side and Śaivite on the other have also been found in Arakan as well as in Burma proper. They show on their obverse a conch-shell which is a Viṣṇuite symbol, and on their reverse, a trident, associated invariably with Śiva; here is, thus, a blending of the two cults.[5] Col. Phayre is of opinion that "these were cast...at a time when Hindu (i.e. Brāhmaṇical) doctrines had undermined Buddhism, a state of affairs which may be traced from the history of the country from the sixth century of the Christian era, at intervals until the eighth. These coins probably were not intended for currency but might be used as armlets by votaries of the doctrines represented by the symbols[6]." There seems, however, to be no justification for such a surmise.

Existence of the liṅga cult in Burma has often been urged by Taw Sein Ko, late Superintendent of Archaeology in the Peninsula; but 'no object

1. Phayre, *Coins of Arakan, Pegu and Burma,* p. 40 (Figs. Nos. 9-17), and p. 42 (Figs. Nos. 1-9).
2. *An. Rep. A.S. Burma*, 1926, p. 28.
3. *ibid.*, p. 30.
4. *Coins of Arakan, Pegu and Burma*, Plate II, Nos. 1, 2, 4 & 8; pp. 28-29.
5. *ibid.*, Plate V, Nos. 6 and 7, p. 33.
6. *ibid.*, p. 33.

which can certainly be identified as a liṅgaṁ has yet been discovered in Burma, and what has often been identified as a liṅgaṁ may very well be of the shape of a stūpa'.[1]

Temples and Images

From stylistic point of view the earliest Śiva image in Burma proper seems to be the one discovered at Thaton (along with two Viṣṇuite stone sculptures) but now housed in the Government Museum, Rangoon. These three sculptures along with a fourth, which has not yet been traced, must have originally formed part of the Shwezayan pagoda of Thaton. This pagoda is furnished with four large niches at the four cardinal sides; and their size and measurement is such as exactly to accommodate the large stone slabs, described as coming from Thaton, now housed in the Museum just referred to. These niches which had long been empty have now been used to shelter standing slender figures of modern Burmese. Buddha statues that seem incoherent and out of place in the large spacious niches wherein they have found their place. But even the Shwezayan does not seem to have been the original abode of these gods; and it is pretty certain that there must have once existed at Thaton Brāhmaṇical temples dedicated to the worship of these gods, Viṣṇu and Śiva, and that when these temples were ruined or wilfully destroyed, the images were carried over and installed at the Shwezayan to decorate its walls and niches. For, even a casual observation is sufficient to convince one that they do not serve anything but a decorative purpose there and have nothing to do with the cult for which the Shwezayan stands.

The Shwezayan, a Buddhist pagoda of the kind so common all over Lower Burma, was built not earlier than the 14th or 15th century A.D. It is a solid brick masonry structure with a raised square base supporting three pyramidal stages connected with a flight of steps at the east. These steps give access to different ambulatory corridors which are provided with outer railings on one side and vertical walls on the other. On the four walls of the first or lowest pyramidal stage were once embedded square and rectangular stone-reliefs, 50 or 52 in number, of which only 14 or 15 are now extant. Most of these even are partially broken and all of them are in a very bad state of preservation on account of the thick whitewash that is annually applied on them. These rows of stone-slabs are relieved on each side by a large niche in the middle which, in our opinion already recorded, once sheltered the three large bas-reliefs now in the Rangoon

1. *An. Rep. A.S. Burma*, 1924, p. 24; *An. Rep. A.S. India*, 1910-11, pp. 90-92. But quite recently has been discovered at Kalaganon near Hmawza, a fragment of a stone-slab representing a liṅgaṁ (14" in height) an indisputable proof of the existence of Śaivism at Prome side by side with Vaiṣṇavism and Buddhism (*An. Rep. A.S. India*, 1926-27, p. 182).

Museum along with another not yet traced. The importance of these stone-slabs has scarcely been recognised; no attempt has, in fact, been made to prevent their loss and gradual decay, and nobody has ever tried to identify the subject-matter which these slabs relate. And, now owing to the loss of the large majority of these slabs, the thread of the story has been hopelessly lost and the remaining slabs hardly give any clue to their identification. But it seems certain that they tell no Buddhist legend but one frankly of Brāhmaṇical lore or Purāṇic mythology. For, two of the slabs that remain and that are comparatively well-preserved certainly represent Śiva with his trident and jaṭā-mukuṭa. Moreover, the artistic affinity of these sculptured panels with the three larger Brāhmaṇical reliefs of the Rangoon Museum (which, we assume, were once sheltered in the niches of the Shwezayan along with these slabs) is such as to suggest a common cult-relation between the two. To speak plainly, these slabs could not but be Brāhmaṇical. These, as well as the three bas-reliefs, may on stylistic grounds be dated in the 9th-10th century A.D., whereas the Shwezayan can in no way be earlier than the 14th or 15th or even later. It is, therefore, certain that neither the reliefs nor the images have anything to do with the Buddhist temple to which they still belong, and it can, therefore, safely be conjectured that they have hardly anything to do with Buddhism too.

Exactly on the same grounds would we assert that these reliefs as well as the three images referred to above originally belonged to one or more Brāhmaṇical temples, Viṣṇuite or Śaivite, which must have once existed at Thaton, and from where they were removed to the Shwezayan where the reliefs are at present sheltered. We now proceed to describe in brief the fourteen relief panels that are still extant. It is unfortunate that we have not been able to identify any of them and, as years will roll by, the slabs will gradually become more and more weathered and indistinct making the task of identification still more difficult if not entirely impossible.

Slab No. 1 : Half of the entire slab is broken, the other half represents at the bottom three female figures in an attitude of prayer; just in front of them a male figure squats on the ground. At the top there is a representation of a human figure with a big tail; this is perhaps Hanumān, the monkey-god. It may be noted here that images of Hanumāna are not unknown in Burma; for, the Rangoon Museum houses at least one stone-slab of irregular shape and sandy-greyish colour depicting in low relief the figures of the monkey-god with his tail raised upwards. The slab was found in the Mergui district.

Slab No. 2 : The slab which is very badly corroded represents a king or god seated on a throne before which kneels a human figure, partly broken, in an attitude of prayer. Before the personage seated on the throne is brought another royal personage or divinity seated on the throne is brought another royal personage or divinity seated on a chariot carried apparently by two persons.

Slab No. 3 : This undoubtedly represents Śiva seated as if he were kneeling. He holds in his right hand the trident which rests on the palm on his left; and is crowned with his jaṭā-mukuṭa on the head.

Slab No. 4 : This rectangular slab can lengthwise be divided into two portions. At the top, one male figure, probably a royal personage, is seated in an easy position with his left hand on the left knee which is raised, and the right hand placed upon the chest. Over him is the royal umbrella, before him is a female figure standing, probably asking a favour. At the bottom is a kneeling lady; in front is an animal, perhaps a horse, before which is a round disc-form object.

Slab No. 5 : This again undoubtedly represents Śiva with his trident and is in the same position as in No. 3.

Slab No. 6 : This probably represents a sheet of water (a sea or a river) which is suggested by waves upon which a male figure rides a horse. He has an open sword in his left hand; before him stands a female figure who is preceded by a dancing male figure who wears a mukuṭa or crown and holds a *damarū*.

Slab No. 7 : It is an interesting sculpture from artistic as well as from iconographic point of view. It represents an elephant, perfectly well-modelled and in bold relief, upon which are seated more than two male and female figures in troubled and excited attitudes. Behind the elephant are two figures, one male and the other female, fighting between themselves. The whole is done in bold relief, the composition is at once logical and convincing, and reminds one of the mediaeval Orissan reliefs.

Slab No. 8 : Only a portion remains of the slab.

Slab No. 9 : This is also broken, the portion that remains represents two or three figures, very badly corroded. One of them seems to be a Brāhmaṇical divinity who wears a crown or mukuṭa. He stops, it seems, by the indication of his left hand, a chariot of which two wheels only remain. In front of the divinity kneels a woman.

Slab No. 10 : It is a broken piece. A male and a female figure are seated on a throne beneath which is a horse.

Slab No. 11 : It represents at the top a chariot drawn by a horse; on the chariot are seated two female figures. At the bottom are several male and female figures seated in different positions.

Slab No. 12 : It represents at the top a lady, before whom kneel two other ladies, and stands a third of whom only the lower portion remains. Below is the figure of another lady.

Slab No. 13 : It represents a squatting figure with his left hand on the left knee and the right on the chest. He is flanked by two female figures, whose way of dressing the hair and the wearing apparel have close affinities with those of contemporary Orissan sculpture.

Slab No. 14 : This slab represents a king or a divine figure seated on a pedestal under a trifoil arch; before him kneel some male and female figures.

The bas-relief measures 4′×2′4″ and stylistically belongs exactly to the same class as the two Viṣṇu reliefs from Thaton. The sculpture is carved out in bold relief on comparatively hard reddish sand-stone and are frankly the work of an Indian colonial artist. In form and spirit as well as features and ornaments, it is decidedly Indian. The composition of the piece shows high technical as well as artistic efficiency and brings out in prominent relief its affinity with the early mediaeval sculptures from Orissa. But no less interesting is the iconography of the relief which is of a rare type, if not uncommon, even on the Indian continent.

It represents a god seated in līlāsana on a lotus pedestal with a goddess seated between two arms to his left. In size and proportion she takes a minor place in the slab which is almost wholly occupied by the god himself. That she is his consort admits of no doubt; it is evident from the position of the figure and especially from the attitude of the whole body particularly noticeable in the intimate clasp and embrace of the left arm of the god. Her face is roughly weathered, but her richly embroidered cloth as well as her heavy ornaments in her ears and round her neck and hands are quite clear. The dress of the god is also equally rich, and he too, is profusely decorated with ornaments round his neck, arms, wrists, waist and ankles. He wears a crown from which emerges out the jaṭā-mukuṭa, a headdress especially belonging to Śaivite deities; a halo adds dignity to the divine crown. He holds in his two upper hands raised upwards the trident and what we may describe as the vajra respectively, and in his two lower hands, resting on his respective thighs, the rosary (*akṣamālā*) and the *mātuliṅga* fruit. The form of the vajra is indeed interesting in as much as it differs from all known forms of this particular attribute. But whether we call it a vajra or not, it is certain that the slab represents Śiva and his consort Pārvatī or Durgā. The identification finds further support from the fact that the snake which is associated with Śiva hangs downwards from the shoulder of the god, and still further by a representation of the bull (Nandi) shown under the right foot of the god and of the Mahiṣāsura (buffalo-demon) shown on the left corner of the slab under the seat of Pārvatī who is supposed to have killed it. It may, moreover, be noted that the position and attitude of the two figures have a suggestive similarity with those of the famous Śiva-Pārvatī relief at Ellora.[1]

The next important Śiva image in Burma is at present housed at the entrance of the Ānanda Museum, Pagan, where it was removed from the

1. Coomaraswamy, *Indian and Indonesian Art*, Plate LV, Fig. 198.

Nāt-hlaung kyaung. It is about 4 ft. high and is carved out of grey soft sand-stone in bold and round relief. Its form and execution is distinctly South Indian and may on stylistic grounds be dated not earlier than the 12th century A.D. In fact, it is about a century later than the Nāt-hlaung kyaung images, and is of lesser artistic merit. When Col. Yule visited the Nāthlaung temple in the third quarter of the last century A.D., he saw lying on the floor of the ruined structure a seated and a standing image,[1] the former was afterwards carried over to Germany where it has now been sheltered in the Berlin Museum. This is the main image of the Nāt-hlaung temple. The other one was removed to the Pagan Museum. The statue stands on a lotus pedestal in an erect pose; it has four hands, the two upper raised upwards carried the trident and what we may designate as the vajra respectively, while the two lower holds the sword and the mace or gadā. The variation of the distribution of these attributes forms an interesting iconographic feature of this sculpture. The kheṭaka and the gadā that are rarely associated with Śiva form here two interesting attributes, and the shape of the vajra, so unlike its familiar type is also remarkable. An elaborate jaṭā-mukṭa crowns the head, and richly carved ornaments profusely decorate the body. It is undoubtedly a representation of Śiva but its presence in a Viṣṇuite temple is certainly interesting. Mon-Duroiselle has made the most possible assumption, and one cannot but agree with him when he says that "its presence in a Vaiṣṇavite temple, wherein no other Śaivite images have been found would seem to point out to the existence at Pagan of a Śaivite temple from which it was removed after its destruction or its crumbling to ruin."[2]

Recent discoveries at Pagan have brought to light another Śaivite icon, now sheltered in the local Ānanda Museum. It was found on the river-side near Shwe-ōnhmin monastery at Myinpagan and is a large, heavy piece of stone sculpture representing a god seated in rāja-līlā attitude on a double-petalled lotus pedestal, on which is placed the right foot of the god. Under this foot and on the right side of the pedestal lies flat the figure of a male, and on the left there is indicated by scratches a sheet-like object which might well be a piece of cloth or skin. Is it the deer-skin associated with Śiva ? The god seems clearly to have four hands which are all very badly corroded or broken, so much so, that only the akṣa-mālā or rosary can be distinguished in the lower left. The upper right seems to have held the trident. Of his ornaments the heavy kuṇḍala on the ears and the hāra round the neck can easily be distinguished. The headdress is peculiar and seems to have a form flattened at the top. The god is undoubtedly Śiva and the male figure that lies prostrate under his

1. Yule, "*Mission to the Court of Avs*"., pp. 53-54; *As. Rep. A.S. Burma*, 1918, p. 19.
2. *ibid., An. Rep. A.B Burma*, p. 19.

right foot is the apasmāra puruṣa known only in South India as associated with Śiva. The relief is in a very bad state of decay; the face is almost wiped off and the modelling of the body has suffered to extreme. But it is not difficult to make out the style of the sculpture which is decidedly Indian, more correctly speaking, Indian that had an independent local development in the Peninsula. The sculpture is worked out in bold and round relief, and the general treatment though not very refined, shows yet a sure hand in chiselling and a keen sense of the Indian form. The body that is a little bulky and the peculiar seating attitude give to the sculpture an atmosphere of ease, peculiar to a class of Śiva images well known in India. It seems to belong to a period not later than the 11th century A.D. We have noted that the iconography of the sculpture is South Indian, but the more interesting is the fact that the art-inspiration, like that of the Nāt-hlaung images, seems to have come from the North.

The Rangoon Museum shelters an image described as coming from Tenasserim township, Mergui, "This locality was under the influence of Cambodia very probably up to the early part of the 14th century A.D. There is some epigraphical evidence of this and Talaing histories incidentally confirm it. It had been, earlier, colonised by the peoples from South India. It is the Lang-Khia-Siou of the Chinese pilgrims, and no doubt was, earlier still, a part, or dependency, or at least under the influence of the old kingdom of Funan, so often mentioned by old Chinese writers, as early as the 3rd century A.D. At that period Chinese envoys to India and Indian envoys to China passed through this part of Burma."[1]

This icon constitutes a pair with the standing Viṣṇu image. Both are described as coming from the same district; they are similar in form and execution, belong stylistically to exactly the same period, i.e., to the 14th century A.D. and are both carved out of similar pieces of rough porous sand-stone, greyish in colour. Both are frankly late South Indian in character. The figure measures 1'9" in height, the breadth at the base being 11"; the statue itself is 1'3" high and the pedestal on which it rests, 6". It represents undoubtedly a Brāhmaṇical god seated on a raised pedestal with his left leg placed on it and the right leg hanging from it and resting on the ground, a position which is strikingly similar to that of the Viṣṇu image from Ariyambakam. The Mergui statue seems to have had two hands of which one only remains, and is crowned on the head with what seems to be a jaṭā-mukuṭa. This is the only attribute which may suggest it to be an image of Śiva. But the stone is so roughly corroded that we are not even sure if the crown is really a jaṭā-mukuṭa or a kirīta-mukuṭa. The identification of the statue shall, therefore, ever remain open to doubt; but, apparently, it seems to be an image of Viṣṇu, an assumption,

1. *An. Rep. A.S. Burma*, 1917, p. 19.

no doubt, having a support in the fact that exactly similar seated attitude of Viṣṇu is quite common in South India.

But earlier than even the earliest of all the images described here, and one of the earliest in Burma, is the fragment of a stone sculpture, distinctly Śaivite in cult and iconography. It has been discovered from the ancient site of Vesālī in Arakan, a locality where Gupta finds have frequently been made. It forms the lower part of a sculpture and is much damaged. The fragment most probably represents Durgā in the act of slaying the buffalo demon (Mahiṣāsura). "The principal figure, the lower half of which only has been preserved, is standing on a lotus with her right foot and a part of her trident resting on the demon. The demon itself which can scarcely be distinguished owing to its damaged condition is lying prostrate below. It is probably of Gupta date"[1], more correctly speaking, it belongs to the later Gupta period.

These, then, are the few finds of Śaivite images up till now discovered in Burma. Stray and very few as these finds are, and much removed in date from one another, ranging from the 6th or 7th century A.D. to the 14th, the conclusion inevitably follows that they point to the existence of one or more floating mercantile populations who brought their cult and religion with them and had their images locally made for worship. There is no reason or evidence to suppose that they were ever worshipped by the people as a whole, or to hold that Śaivism had ever been the religion of the people or of the State, except in Arakan where a Śaivite dynasty seems to have held sway at least for five centuries, from the 5th to the 10th century A.D. This is amply testified to by the coins discovered there as well as probably by the find of the fragmentary slab described above, which in all probability, is a product of the art and cult patronised by the contemporary Śaivite ruling dynasty.

Viṣṇu

Viṣṇu is the most popular cult of the Brāhmaṇical triad in Burma and referred to in quite a large number of inscriptions. His images too were widely worshipped by the Brāhmaṇical fold and occupied the supreme position.

The earliest Vaiṣṇava tradition in Burma is connected with Hmawza or old Prome, one of the oldest seats of kingship in Burma. The city is said to have been founded by a *ṛṣi* whose name the Burmese chronicles have failed to take into notice *Mahayazwin*, the Burmese text that describes the foundation of the city states that the ṛṣi who presided over the function was helped by six other divines—Gavampati, Indra, Nāga, Garuḍa, Caṇḍī and Parameśvara. Now Gavampati, Indra and Nāga, or a Nāgarāja have often been incorporated in Burmese legendary history in connection

1. *ibid.*, 1916, p. 35.

with the foundation of cities or erection of temples, obviously without having any actual historical significance. But the legend helps us undoubtedly to assume that a strong Indian element with all its traditions of town-planning and temple-building had been at work at the bottom of all such traditions and their actual translation in monuments. Gavampati, who is represented in Mon records as the son of the Lord Buddha, has rightly been styled as the "patron saint of the Mons" as well as the "patron saint of Pagan", and is evidently a creation of the legendary imagination of the Mons. Indra is the king of the *devas* who must invariably be present at all important functions. The Nāga mentioned in the *Mahayazwin* is certainly Katakarmmanāgarāja mentioned in Mon records as having assisted in the foundation of the city of Sisit or Śrīkṣetra (old Prome). Garuḍa is the mythical bird who has the proud privilege of being vāhana of Viṣṇu. Caṇḍī is Kālī or Karāḷī or the wife of Śiva who is mentioned here in the *Mahayazwin* as Parameśvara. The *Mahayazwin* tradition is most probably an adaptation from early Talaing records, but in becoming so it has retained only the epithet—ṛṣi—of the founder of the city, but has failed to mention the name of the ṛṣi. That this was Viṣṇu is evident from the early Mon records in most of which the story of the foundation of Sisit or Śrīkṣetra is given in more or less detail. Let us quote from the great inscription of the Shwezigon Pagoda.[1]

> "The Lord Buddha smiled and Ānanda asked the cause of this smile; and the Lord Spoke Unto Ānanda—Ānanda, hereafter a sage named Biṣṇu, great in supernatural power, great in glory, possessing the five transcendental faculties, together with my son Gavampati, and king Indra and Bissukarmmadevaput (putra) and Katakarmmanāgarāja, shall build a city called Sisit (Śrīkṣetra)".
> Then again—"After the sage Biṣṇu has built the city of Sisit, he shall depart from thence (and) in the city of Arimaddanapura (Pagan) he shall become king Śrī Tribhuvanāditya dhammarāja, etc."

It is thus evident that the ṛṣi is Viṣṇu who is considered to have found the city of old Prome. The Mon records include one Bissukarmmadevaput--son of Viśvakarma, the divine architect—as one who was destined to assist in the foundation of Śrīkṣetra (old Prome), but excludes Garuḍa, Caṇḍī and Parameśvara mentioned in the *Mahayazwin*.

An important corroboration of this tradition is found in the fact that old Prome or Hmawza was known in ancient times as Bissunamyo—an equivalent of Viṣṇupura, that is, the city of Viṣṇu—which undoubtedly points to some sort of Viṣṇuite influence having been at work at this old

1. *Ep. Birm.*, Vol. I, Pt. II, p. 90ff.

royal city of Lower Burma[1] Apart from this, important finds have been made here at Hmawza of images that are distinctly Viṣṇuite in character. But before we turn to these images and to other icons of Viṣṇu found at different localities of Burma, it is interesting to see how and to what extent Viṣṇu has been able to penetrate into the tangle of traditional legendary history of Burma.

Kyanzittha, son of Anawratha, is the second important king of Pagan, who, as seen through the veil of tradition, is a fantastic hero of fairy tales. But, 'in his own inscriptions, with their strong ecclesiastical flavouring he is presented as a grave and religious, but quite human monarch, taking a deep interest in the spiritual and temporal welfare of his people and actively contributing to that by his piety and good works'. In almost all the early Mon records which in most of the cases, relate to his reign and achievements, he is invariably styled as Śri Tribhuvanāditya Dhammarāja, a title distinctly Sanskritic in character. A long birth-legend forms the introduction and framework of most of these records, just referred to. The legend refers to successive re-births of king Kyanzittha—a fact confessedly Buddhist in colour and spirit as is evident from the Great inscription of the Shwezigon Pagoda, Pagan.[2]

But a different version of this birth-legend related to Śrī Tribhuvanāditya Dhammarāja is given in the Myakan inscription of Myinpagan, Pagan, as also in two other inscriptions.[3]

Here, the thread of the story, as recorded in the Great Shwezigon inscription, is taken up, and the Myakan inscription goes on to relate what is more elaborately recorded in the Shwezigon record, i.e., the prophecy of the Buddha to the effect that "the sage Busṇu (Viṣṇu) together with Gavampati, Indra, Bissukarmmadevaput Katakarmmanāgarāja shall build the city of Sisit, and then, from there shall go into existence in Brahmāloka, and then again a thousand six hundred and thirty years after the Buddha's parinirvāṇa shall become king of the Law in the city of Arimaddanapura and bear the name of Śrī Tribhuvanāditya Dhammarāja".

We thus get the birth-legend in two versions. According to the first version which is shorter but more elaborate than the second, king Śrī Tribhuvanāditya Dhammarāja Kyanzittha is presented as having been in one of his earlier incarnations the sage Viṣṇu himself who lived contemporaneously with the Buddha. According to the second version, which

1. *An. Rep. A.S. Burma*, 1923, p. 15ff. Taungdwin, a town said to have been founded in 857 A.D. (?), was called Rāmāvatī, after the name of the epic hero Rāma, who is recognised in South India as one of the ten incarnations of Viṣṇu.
2. *Ep. Birm.*, Vol. I, Part II, p. 90.
3. *ibid.*, Nos. III-V, pp 131 and 141ff; *ibid.*, Vol. I, Pt. II, pp. 138-39.

prefaces the Viṣṇu episode by three of the king's still earlier existences, the king is presented as having been a wealthy and pious man living at Benares in Buddha Kassapa's time. In his next incarnation, he was born in the family of the kings of Patna, and in the third, in the royal house of the Rāma dynasty of Oudh. Next in the time of the Buddha Śākyamuni, he was a sage named Viṣṇu. There is an amount of difference in the two versions; but one thing is common to both, namely, that the king was in one of his previous births a sage named Viṣṇu. It is, therefore, obvious that he wanted to claim his identity with Viṣṇu, and this is certainly significant in view of the fact that Kyanzittha himself was a devout Buddhist initiated into the religion by his master Shin Arahan, and the records of his reign are frankly Buddhist in spirit and colour. Secondly, tradition, even then, was incessant in telling that Sisit or old Prome was built by Viṣṇu himself. Thirdly, Viṣṇu was considered not as a god but as a sage who was living contemporaneously with the Buddha himself, and it is evident from the fact noted above that the sage Viṣṇu held a position in Burma inferior to that of the Buddha, for, Kyanzittha dared not claim his identity with the great spiritual Lord of the creed he professed, but satisfied himself by identifying him as an incarnation of the sage Viṣṇu. In India, by the 11th and 12th centuries to which period our records belong, the Buddha had already come to be incorporated in the Brāhmaṇical pantheon as one of the incarnations of Viṣṇu; and hence occupies a position subordinate to that of Viṣṇu. But there seems to have been an inverted process in Burma, for here Viṣṇu himself (and not the Buddha) did come to occupy a subordinate position. This was only natural, for Burma was professedly Buddhist all the time, while in India Buddhism had come to be supplanted by neo-Brāhmaṇism of the *Purāṇas*.

Viṣṇu as Nārāyaṇa seems also to have been known to the Indian settlers of Burma. Even a casual reader of the early Mon records would be able to observe that Brāhmaṇas are often mentioned in them as taking part as priests in all religious ceremonies of the court. This is not at all surprising, for, from Burma to Champā as well as in Java, Sumatra and Bali, the Brāhmaṇas always played an active and influential part in the courts, no matter whether the religion was Brāhmaṇism or Buddhism. These Brāhmaṇas in the Buddhist courts of Burma were evidently worshippers of Viṣṇu, mentioned in the inscriptions as Nārāyaṇa. The inscription found near the Tharaba gate, Pagan,[1] a record detailing an elaborate ceremony attending the building of a five-fold pavilion (Pañca-prāsāda) in connection, as alleged with king Kyanzittha's royal anointment, has numerous references to Brāhmaṇas who are constantly engaged in

1. *Ep. Birm.*, Vol. III, Pt. I, *Mon. Insc.*, No. I.

bringing water of lustration in vessels of gold, silver, brass and earthen ware and who are invariably mentioned as having worshipped Nārāyaṇa before they were required to perform any priestly duty. Thus:

> "(At) all these seventeen places they (Brāhmaṇa astrologers) made a decoration of plantains and adorned with young plantains (and) sugarcane (and set?) water (in) vessels of gold (and) silver (and) water (in) conchshells wherein (they) put cleaned rice (and) dubhā grass, (and) spread mats, (with) golden flowers, altar oblations and altar candles. Having (arranged them?) they made in honour of Nārāyaṇa, a decoration of plantains (called) "Ox nose" adorned with young plantains (and) sugarcane (and) within it (set) boiled rice in cup-shaped vessels with candles stuck in it, (and) altar oblations, (and) they...(brought?) water (in) vessels of gold (and) silver, spread mats (and) offered...golden flowers (and altar candles?). Then the Brāhmaṇa astrologers worshipped Nārāyaṇa. At the auspicious time...godhūli (being) lagna, the expert Brāhmaṇa astrologers bathed the side pillars, the yas pillars, etc".[1]
> And again.
> "The expert Brāhmaṇa astrologers wore loin cloths, sukhoy cindraw (and) sukhoy ular, with kucom skirts of white. Then they went and worshipped Nārāyaṇa (At) all the ten points they made decorations of plantains (and) altar oblations; water (in) vessels of gold and silver, (and) water in conch-shells wherein (they) put cleaned rice (and) dubbā grass, they arranged nearby."[2]

This ceremonial is again and again detailed in the inscription and almost invariably in the same form. The worship of Nārāyaṇa seems thus to have been in vogue with its peculiarly Brāhmaṇical ritual and it was not only tolerated by the Buddhist court and people, but, as it seems from the context of the inscription, was also considered as an indispensable item of all court ceremonies.

This mention of Nārāyaṇa-worship most probably refers to the worship of Nārāyaṇa-Śilā.[3] The context of the inscription as well as repeated mention of the worship of the god seem to point to the fact that the god was almost in daily worship by the Brāhmaṇas. But nowhere is it given to understand that any image of the god was ever made and worshipped. Had it been so, it would have been possible for us to discover more images of the god than have hitherto been found at Pagan where the inscription has been discovered and of which place the record gives us the story. The only vestiges of Viṣṇu worship in Pagan are the remains of a temple known

1. *ibid.*, pp 41-22.
2. *Ep. Birm.*, Vol. III, pt. I, p. 44.
3. *South Indian Images*, p. 70.

locally as Nāt-hluang kyaung, in which there were once housed images of the ten avatāras of Viṣṇu and of the god himself. Stray finds have also been made of bronze Viṣṇu images, but the mention of Nārāyaṇa in the above record does not seem to point to these bronze or stone images, or to any Viṣṇu temple. It is a matter of common knowledge that the Nārāyaṇa-śilā was and still is the most important object of daily worship in every orthodox Brāhmaṇa house in Northern and Southern India; and it is probable that the god was likewise worshipped by the emigrant Brāhmaṇas also, especially on the eve of their performing any priestly duty.

Images

We have already noticed the association of a strong Viṣṇuite tradition with Hmawza or old Prome. Here have been unearthed several Viṣṇuite images that are most probably the oldest in Burma. We have here to consider three important slabs[1]—all housed at present in the Phongyi kyaung museum near the Hmawza Railway Station—representing three different types of the god.

The first is a rectangular slab of soft sand-stone carved out in comparatively bold relief representing two figures standing side by side but apart from one another. The figure in the right is one of Viṣṇu standing on a Garuḍa with its tail and wings outstretched, a fact very ably represented on the slab with a touch of abstract naturalism. The head and portions of the neck of the human bust of the bird have been lost, but what remains is sufficient to guarantee that the animal represented is nothing but a Garuḍa, the celebrated carrier of Viṣṇu. To the left of Viṣṇu on a full-blown double-petalled lotus, represented no doubt in a somewhat abstract manner, stands Lakṣmī, the consort of Viṣṇu. It is most unfortunate that the upper portion of the slab has been damaged to such an extent that both the figures have lost their heads, and Viṣṇu his upper right hand in addition. Otherwise the figures are very well-preserved and even the details can easily be read. The god has four hands, the attribute in the upper right is lost, the lower right which is raised up to the chest holds a round object, evidently a *vilva* or *mātuliṅga* fruit; the upper left, so far as discernible on the stone, holds the cakra (wheel) and the lower left the gadā (mace)—unlike, indeed, the type generally held by the god. The goddess has two hands, the right one which is raised up to the shoulders holds, as it seems, a bunch of lotus stems, and the left hangs lightly downwards. The sculpture from iconographic point of view is important in more than one respect. First, the holding of a vilva or mātuliṅga fruit—an attribute of Śiva and Lakṣmī—by Viṣṇu is undoubtedly quite unique;

1. Exhibits Nos. 23, 24 and 25.

it is never the custom in India; in the colonies we have yet scarcely any similar instance, nor have we any such reference in any known version of texts on Pratimālakṣaṇaṁ. If it is a vilva, it is likely that the attribute associated with Lakṣmī has here come to be transposed to become an attribute of Lakṣmī's Lord Viṣṇu. Secondly, the position of the gadā or the mace held in the left lower hand is also somewhat peculiar; it is generally held in the hand with all the five fingers with its stout bottom directed upward and tapering top downwards; in other instances, the hand is placed on the top of the gadā which rests on the floor.[1] But here it is held at the neck with its stout bottom hanging downwards but not resting on the ground. But apart from these attributes the sculpture has other interesting iconographic features. Neither in India nor in the colonies we have knowledge of any such image as the present one where Viṣṇu and Lakṣmī stand side by side. Images of Kṛṣṇa and Rukmiṇī or of Lakṣmī with Viṣṇu in his Narasiṁha or Varāha incarnation[2] are frequently seen, but Viṣṇu with his consort Lakṣmī standing side by side on their respective vāhanas is indeed very rare; we scarcely know of any such example. We have no doubt references to Lakṣmī-Nārāyaṇa images in Pratimālakṣaṇaṁ text; e.g. in the *Viśvakarmā-Śāstram* we have:—

"Lakṣmī-Nārāyaṇau kāryyau saṁyukatau divyarūpiṇau
dakṣiṇasthā vibhor-mūrtir-lakṣmī-mūrtis-tu vāmataḥ.
dakṣiṇah kaṇṭhalagno'syā vāmo hastas-sarojabhṛt
vibhor-vāmakaro lakṣmyāḥ kukṣibhāga-sthitaḥ sadā."

In the *Rūpamaṇḍanam*, we read:—

"Ubhau ca dvibhujau kuryyāl-lakṣmiṁ Nārāyaṇa-śritaṃ
daivaṃ śastraiḥ svakīyaiśca Garuḍopari saṃathitam.
dakṣiṇaḥ kaṇṭhalagno'syā vāmo hastas-sarojadhṛk
vibhor-vāmakaro Lakṣmyāḥ kukṣibhāgah-sthitaḥ sadā."

Thus, according to the *Viśvakarmā-Śāstram*, Viṣṇu should be represented to the right of Lakṣmī whose left hand should hold a lotus and the right hand round the neck of her consort; whereas the left hand of the god himself should stretch to the left armpit of Lakṣmī. The attribute or function of the right hand of the god is not mentioned; but it is necessary to present the vāhana as well as the two other attributes śaṅkha and cakra as two āyudhapuruṣas (kartavyaṃ vāhanaṁ devādhobhāgagaṁ sadā; and, śaṅkha-cakradharau tasya dvau kāryyau puruṣau puraḥ). The *Rupamaṇḍanam* explicitly says that the deities should have only two hands each, that

1. *Hindu Iconography*, Vol. I, Pt. I, Plate LVIII.
2. *ibid.*, Plates XL and XLI.

Viṣṇu should stand upon his vāhana Garuḍa, that Lakṣmī should embrace his lord by winding her right hand round his neck and hold in her left a lotus, and that Viṣṇu should stretch his left hand up to the armpit of his consort. The two versions are almost similar, but it is interesting to see how the present icon deviates from all known texts. The god, instead of having two, has four hands and the goddess, who has two hands only, does hold the lotus in her right, not in the left. She does not wind her right hand round the neck of Viṣṇu, nor does Viṣṇu stretch his left to her armpit. This is not all. A further point of departure from Indian icons is the fact that the god and the goddess, both standing, have been given equal importance, their height is almost the same, and though they do not stand on the same plane, it is easily seen that the goddess has not been subordinate to the god which is generally the practice in India. The one factor alone which attached greater importance to the god in his four hands, while Lakṣmī has got only two. These deviations can only be accounted for when it is said that the Indian colonists of the Peninsula had either followed a different textual version yet unknown; or, colonists as they were, they had been less bound down by textual canons than their less fortunate brethren at home. That was why they could easily evolve new forms and types out of their imagination unhampered by any tradition.

The second important piece of icon from Hmawza is also one of Viṣṇu, standing on his Garuḍa and represented on a stone slab having the form of an isosceles triangle.[1] The stone is about sixteen inches high and about a foot wide at the base. The material is a poor kind of very soft porous sand-stone, and the workmanship is rough and clumsy. It is the product of an entirely local school of art which finds expression not only in the typical cut of the face and the simple, almost foolish, smile on the two lips, but most remarkably in the dress the god wears. He stands on his vāhana Garuḍa with two heavy outstretched wings, the left of which alone remains; it is, therefore, difficult to decide whether the bird was represented with a human face and bust as in the mediaeval sculptures of Eastern and Southern India, or with those more realistic features of a bird as in Indian colonial art. But what remains on the stone, seems to favour the former assumption, namely, that the bird represented is really an animal with a human bust and a bird-like lower portion almost exactly as in Indian art. In the present case the wings of the bird have not been so elaborately and so realistically portrayed as in the one discussed above; rather they are done in a more abstract manner and are meant as if to represent the leafy branches of a tree; yet there is sufficient to show that the artist knew his subject well but failed to give an artistic expression to it. The god has four hands; the two upper raised upwards hold the cakra

1. Phoongyi Kyaung Museum-shed near Hmawza Ry. Station, Exhibit No. 25.

and śaṅkha and the two lower hold again a vilva or mātuliṅga fruit and the gadā respectively. He is elaborately decorated with ornaments having wristlets, armlets and a richly carved keyūra round his neck; the head-dress which must have been an elaborate one is, unfortunately enough, broken, but it is most likely that it was of the kind so often seen in Burmese sculptures where it is invariably associated with all important personage and divinities. We are accustomed to see in India and in the colonies Viṣṇu as riding or seated crossed-legged on his vāhana; Viṣṇu standing on Garuḍa is rare; in fact, such representations are hardly seen. It is most interesting that the type has up till now been found in Burma alone, and that is more than one example.

We now turn to the third important Viṣṇuite sculpture from Hmawza.[1] Apparently it is a plastic representation of the well-known mythology of Śeṣa or Anantaśayya of Viṣṇu. It is the most important of the reclining forms of Viṣṇu who is here supposed to sleep on the coils of the serpent Śeṣa that shields the head of the god of gods under its five or seven hoods. By the side of the serpent couch near the feet of Viṣṇu is often represented the kneeling figure of Lakṣmī in a worshipping attitude or the seated figure of Bhūmi devī or Lakṣmī,[2] who holds the right foot of the god in her hands. He is said to have two or four hands and from his navel springs a lotus stalk with a full blossomed lotus flower on which Brahmā is comfortably seated. Brahmā, Śiva and Indra are also sometimes represented as subsidiary deities; and Jaya and Vijaya as two attendants. The attributes of the god are represented in their own form or as personified.

In the present example from Hmawza, the god is represented as lying straight with his two legs crossed at the ankles. The head with the usual head-dress rests on a higher plane and the body stretches not on the coils of a serpent but, so far as it seems, on a lotus couch that rests on a makara the head of which is clearly visible on the left corner at the bottom of the slab. This is peculiarly interesting, for we have not yet been able to discover any sculpture or text where the reclining Viṣṇu is ever represented as having any association with makara. The usual practice, as we have already seen, is to represent him as reclining directly on the serpent Ananta. It is, therefore, striking, and can only be accounted for by

1. This, and the image just described were discovered at a village named Kalagangon near Hmawza. Here have recently been discovered "a few fragments of a Brāhmaṇical sculpture or of perhaps several such sculptures ... but, unfortunately, most of them are too small to admit of any identification" (*An. Rep.A.S. India*, 1926-27, p. 182). Near this village there was a mound called Khin-bha-gon in the course of excavation of which was discovered a band carved in sandstone, and holding a conch which had probably belonged to an image of Viṣṇu. (*ibid.*, p. 171ff).
2. Cf. Rao, G., *Hindu Iconography*, Vol. I, Pt. I.

assuming that the colonial artists either followed a text which is yet unknown to us or that they misinterpreted the whole story as known in India. This will be more evident from the fact that from Viṣṇu's navel rises not one single lotus-stalk but three such stalks with three full-blown lotus on which are seated the three gods of the Brāhmaṇical trinity—Viṣṇu, the main deity, with his four hands holding the different attributes (the right lower which is raised up to the chest holds again a vilva or mātuliṅga fruit), is seated at the centre; he is flanked by Brahmā to the right and Śiva to the left. The latter, as usual in India, is generally seated by the side of Viṣṇu as in an example from Mahabalipuram, or as mounting his bull (Nandi) in the air as in another from Deogarh. Brahmā is here, as elsewhere, seated cross-legged on the lotus rising from the navel of Viṣṇu. He has four hands, the two lower joined in the añjalī pose, and is endowed, as usual, with four heads—three of which are actually represented—crowned over with his peculiar jaṭā-mukuṭa. All three figures, separately haloed by lotus petal designs, are meant to hold equal status, subordinate only to the main deity—Viṣṇu, who is here represented as reclining. The figures are dressed up to the knees and have usual ornaments in the ears, arms, ankles, neck and waist. The position of the right legs of the seated figures of Viṣṇu and Śiva as well as that of the two legs of the reclining figure are interesting. In the former case, it is raised upwards, while in the latter they are crossed. An almost similar position of the two legs of reclining Viṣṇu may be seen in the *Yogaśayanāmūrti* relief from Aihoḷe.[1]

Two Similar sculptures from the iconographic point of view are known from Thaton[2] or ancient Rammaññadeśa, the land par excellence of the Talaings. Unlike the two sculptures from Hmawza just discussed above, these are carved out in bold and round relief on comparatively hard reddish sand-stone and are frankly works, not of local Burman craftsmen, but of Indian colonial artists. Their general features and ornaments as well as the form and spirit that find expression in them are undoubtedly Indian. The artistic and historical interest of these sculptures, are far more than one can possibly imagine. They are by far the most interesting specimens which bring out in more prominent relief the relation of a particular school of the colonial art of Burma with a contemporary Indian school of art on this side of the Bay of Bengal. But here we must content ourselves with a study of them from the iconographic point of view alone.

The two slabs measure $3\frac{1}{2}' \times 1'10''$ and $4\frac{1}{2}' \times 3'$ respectively. The smaller one which is a rectangular slab rounded off at the top represents at the bottom the reposing or Śayanāmūrti of Viṣṇu. His legs are crossed

1. See Rao, G., *Hindu Iconography*, Vol. I.
2. These two and a third from Thaton were brought over to Rangoon where they have found a shelter in the local Government Museum. Exhibits Nos. 8/6, 9/6, and 10/6.

as in the example from Hmawza but in a more easy and flexible manner, and his four hands hold their respective attributes—the two upper which lie flat and reach up to the shoulder seem to hold the cakra (discus) and śānkha (conch-shell) respectively, while the lower right placed upon the lower chest holds a round object, most probably a vilva or mātuliṅga fruit; the lower left, placed alongside the thigh, holds something that is difficult to be recognised. His clothes reach up to the knee and he wears ornaments that are frankly Indian—round the wrists, ankles, waist and neck. The head-dress which consists of triangular lobes pointing upwards had already come to be well familiarised in the mediaeval sculptures of the Eastern school. The three lotus stalks supposed to have sprung from the navel of the god are actually carved out on the stele itself and are represented as having risen from the back of the lying figure. Upon the petals of the three lotus stalks are seated in padmāsana three divinities, Brahmā, Viṣṇu and Śiva; at the top of them are represented three stele, the middle one being more prominent than the other two, signifying obviously the more prominent position of Viṣṇu who is seated just below. Brahmā seated to the right is represented with three heads with his usual head-dress, ornaments and clothes that reach up almost to the anklet. His right hand is raised up to the chest and the left rests upon his left knee. Śiva seated to the left holds in his right hand raised up to the chest probably the mātuliṅga fruit and in his left raised up to the shoulder the triśūl or the trident. Viṣṇu who is seated in the middle holds in his upper right the cakra and in the corresponding left the śaṅkha. The right lower seems to have been represented in the jñāna-mudrā pose and the lower left is unfortunately mutilated. The description thus detailed would at once warrant us to conclude that it is a representation of the well-known Anantaśayyā episode of Viṣṇu. But we are for once put into doubt for missing the coils of the serpent Ananta on which he is supposed to lie; there is not even any suggestion of them. The whole slab is in a fair state of preservation, and the figures are all carved in bold and round relief, the details are all elaborately shown, and had the coils of the serpent been actually represented, we have no reason to miss them. It seems that the artist probably satisfied himself by scratching down on the slab, the outlines alone of the five heads of the serpent which are seen at the top of the head-dress as an ornamental aureole.

Almost exactly of the same iconographic peculiarities is the larger slab from Thaton. It represents the same episode, the Anantaśayyā scene of Viṣṇu who, here too, is seen lying in a reposing attitude with his legs crossed and his upper two hands holding the śaṅkha and the padma respectively. The whole slab is badly damaged and the details are difficult to be made out. Yet the coils of the serpent seem here to have been represented, and the five hoods above the head-dress are more prominently shown.

There is also an attempt at realism in the representation of water which is suggested by crowded lotus leaves, lotus stems and buds in the midst of which the god-rests on the serpent. The same sense of realism is also noticeable in the fact that the main lotus-stalk is here shown to have really sprung from the navel. It winds upwards to a point where it becomes three different stalks with three full-blown lotus on which are again seated Brahmā, Viṣṇu and Śiva with three stele at their back. Viṣṇu in the middle is seated cross-legged, but the two other divinities have their right legs raised upwards with the palm resting on the ground. It should be noticed that the stele at the back of Viṣṇu, though much broken off, is higher and more prominent than those of Brahmā and Śiva, signifying no doubt the superior position of Viṣṇu in the Brāhmaṇical trinity.

There are two other figures of Viṣṇu in the Rangoon Museum. One is a small (about 10 × 4 inches) standing figure of the god with four hands and with a halo round the head which is crowned with a peculiar head-dress. The lower left hand holds the gadā and the right, slightly bent, touches the waist. Two more hands did exist, of them the upper left seems to have held a pointed lotus bud. The material is soft reddish sand-stone, and the sculpture is worked out in bold relief. It probably formed part of a temple as a decorative figure and stylistically seems to belong to the 9th century A.D. The material as well as the style and workmanship of the sculpture seems to relate it with the two Thaton sculptures described above.

The second, a standing figure of Viṣṇu, belonging to at least four centuries later than the one just discussed, i.e., to about the 14th century A.D., was discovered at Mergui but has lately been brought over to the Rangoon Museum. The material is a piece of rough porous sand-stone greyish in colour, and the crude and rough workmanship is late South Indian in character. The piece is little less than two feet in height, and though the figure stands with a stele at the back, it is carved out in comparatively bold relief though the execution is certainly poor. It represents a standing Brāhmaṇical deity with four hands heavily laden with ornaments and crowned over with a peculiar kirīṭamukuṭa. The two legs are covered with anklets almost up to the knee joint, and on the two sides of the conical head-dress seem to have stretched two locks of matted hair. The two upper hands seem to have held the śaṅkha and cakra respectively; the lower right hand seems to be in the abhayamudrā or protection-affording pose, while the lower left is in the varada or boon-conferring pose. It is one of the most common sthānaka-mūrtis of Viṣṇu; but whether it is a yogasthānaka or bhogasthānaka-mūrti it is difficult to decide. In the sthānaka-mūrtis of these two classes the left lower hand is generally made to rest on the left hip, whereas, the same hand in the present example is represented in the varada pose, but in other details the icon closely follows the South Indian canon.

The Nāt-hlaung Temple and its Gods

Earlier than this, but later in date than the images from Hmawza or from Thaton described above, is the group of Viṣṇuite sculptures discovered in and belonging to the Nāt-hlaung yaung at Pagan, the only ancient Viṣṇu temple now extant in Burma. It is an interesting monument, not so much from the viewpoint of architecture, as it is from the viewpoint of history and the cult it represents. "The name", says Mon-Duroiselle, "implies that it was built for housing not figures of the Buddha, but statues of deities inferior to him; in this case Brāhmaṇical figures."[1] In fact, it is a Viṣṇu temple enshrining in the niches of its walls as well as in those of the central obelisk, figures of the different incarnations of Viṣṇu and having as its principal deity one image of Viṣṇu seated on his vāhana Garuḍa placed in the main sanctum, formed by a large deep niche in the middle of the east face of the central obelisk. According to tradition it was founded by King Taung Thugyi who lived from c. 931-964 A.D., a date too early for the style of building itself as well as for the style of the sculptures decorating its walls; nor is there any epigraphic or literary evidence to support so early a date. "The only mention in Burmese of a Brāhmaṇical temple built at Pagan, is found in a late manuscript called *Pugan Mro Phura Samon*, or Record of the Pagan Pagodas, where it is said that it was built by King Anawrahta after his return from the conquest of Thaton (1057 A.D.). This might well be the case, but in the absence of any authoritative corroboration, and in the light of the fact borne out by epigraphs—the Anawrahta was then a very fervent adherent of the Simhalese form of southern Buddhism, it is doubtful whether this bigoted prince would have gone to the length of building a Brāhmaṇical temple". Curiously enough, as Mon Duroiselle has already pointed out, there has been discovered an inscription recording the erection of a Viṣṇu temple at Pagan. The epigraph purports to say that a Vaiṣṇava saint named Irayiran Siriyan, a resident of Magodayarpattanam in Malī Maṇḍalam and a disciple of Śrī Kulaśekhara "made a maṇḍapa, gave a door" in the temple of Nānādeśī Vinnagara Alavar at Pukam, alias Arivattanapuram. Magodayarpattanam in Malī Maṇḍalam is Cranganore in Malabar; Pukam is certainly Pugama of the Kalyāṇī inscription and Pukhan or Pugan of Chinese travellers; and Arivattanapura is obviously Arimaddanapura, another name of the royal city of Pagan. "Nānādeśī Vinnagara means", says Hultzsch, "the Viṣṇu temple of those coming from various countries. This name shows that the temple which was situated in the heart of the Buddhist country of Burma had been founded and was

1. *An. Rep. A.S. India*, 1912-13, p. 186.

resorted to by Vaiṣṇavas from various parts of the Indian Peninsula."[1] As Nāt-hlaung kyaung is the only Vaiṣṇava temple that is still extant at Pagan, and as there is no reference to any other Vaiṣṇava-monument of this place in literature or inscriptions, it is natural to infer, as Mon. Duroiselle has done that the Nāt-hlaung kyaung is the very temple referred to in the Tamil inscription. But from the record itself, it is clear that the temple had already existed there when the maṇḍapa was made and the "door was given to it." Hultzsch refers the inscription to the 13th century A.D. on paleographic grounds, and as the inscription records the gift of the maṇḍapa and the door—not the erection of the temple itself—it is a likely assumption that the temple had been built before the 13th century. It is, therefore, quite likely that the tradition contained in the Burmese manuscript referred to above is true; and that Anawrahta, who flourished in the last half of the 11th century A.D., could have well built the temple—a date which can in no way be deemed early for the architectural or sculptural style of the temple or of the gods respectively. Anawrahta was indeed a fervent adherent of the Simhalese form of Southern Buddhism; but when we read through the contemporary Mon records, and remember that in the Pagan Court the Brāhmaṇas played a very prominent part not only in rituals and ceremonies of the court but also as court-astrologers, and that these Brāhmaṇas who were worshippers of Nārāyaṇa (Viṣṇu) required a place of worship for their own community, we can easily appreciate that Anawrahta himself allowed this prerogative to the most honoured Brāhmaṇa priests of his court who, it may be surmised, had approached him with their request and whom the king wanted not to displease.

From the traces on the outer walls of the eastern or the entrance face of the shrine, as well as from the raised yard in front of the temple itself, it seems that there was originally a porch or a vestibule which was probably identical with the maṇḍapa referred to in the Tamil inscription just discussed. But, unfortunately, this porch or maṇḍapa which did not form part of the original structure has crumbled down to pieces, and the foundation only remains. The doorway has a stone frame of which the lintel has broken down; and, if our surmise can still be pushed, it is this stone-frame door that is referred to in the inscription ('door was given to it'), as having been made a gift of by the Vaiṣṇava saint. The broken lintel has now been replaced by a beam of re-inforced concrete.

In plan, the Nāt-hlaung kyaung is a square raised on a panelled and moulded plinth about five feet high above the ground. Like a good number of other temples in Pagan, the interior of the square is occupied by the usual perambulatory corridor running all round a huge central square masonry structure on three faces of which there were originally figures of

1. *An. Rep. A.S. Burma*, 1902-33. p. 7.

gods standing in niches adorned with pilasters. On the outer walls of the square basement there are, as we have already noticed, a number of arched niches each of which originally contained one stone sculpture. Most of them are now lost; one or two have been carried over to other countries; and a few that still remain in situ are more or less badly damaged. In the niches of the interior square obelisk there were originally standing images of Viṣṇu of which one is comparatively well-preserved. Of the ten outer sculptures that represent the ten avatāras of Viṣṇu, seven only remains; "three of the four niches on the east side are empty, the sculptures having apparently been removed from them and destroyed by iconoclasts; the figures that remain bear visible traces of wilful disfiguration."

Let us begin by describing the main deity of the temple. It has already been noticed that the centre of the interior is occupied by a square obelisk. In the middle of the east face of this obelisk is a large deep niche where the principal figure was once enshrined. The identity of this principal figure was long unknown, and up till the first decade of this century the image itself was even known as lost. Colonel Yule, while visiting Pagan in the last quarter of the century, saw lying on the floor of this temple two images,[1] one standing and another seated, both of stone. The standing one is an image of Śiva now housed in the Ānanda Museum, Pagan[2], while the seated one (4 ft. high) is an image of Viṣṇu on his Garuḍa, and has now found its place in the Berlin Museum.[3] The credit is due to Mon. Duroiselle who for the first time asserted that the principal figure of the temple should be identified with the god now housed in the Berlin Museum[4], and pointed out that Col. Yule was wrong in describing this figure as coming from the niche above the capital on the left sanctum proper. The slab represents the figure of Viṣṇu seated on a lotus throne resting on Garuḍa. The whole piece of sculpture is executed in bold relief; the lotus petals of the seat are shown in sharp beautiful curves, the god is seated in padmāsana in a smiling repose, the carrier-bird Garuḍa poses itself as it were about to fly and both the god and his vāhana are elaborately ornamented from head downwards to the ankles. Beautiful kirīṭamukuṭa flanked by fluttering scarves on two sides crown the head of the god; ornaments round the arms, wrists and ankles are simple, but those at the ears, neck and the waist are profusely and elaborately executed. The presentation of the Garuḍa is peculiar and differs considerably from the two examples from Hmawza discussed above. The bird shows a short stunted human bust resting on two heavy rounded feet with a

1. Narrative of the Mission to the Court of Ava in 1885, p. 53ff.
2. *An. Rep. A.S. Burma*, 1913, p. 18, plate II, fig. 1.
3. Sculptures aus Pagan by Grunwedel, cited in *An. Rep. A.S. India*, 1912-13, p. 136.
4. *An. Rep. A.S. India*, 1912-13, p. 136ff, and footnote, p. 138.

pair of heavy wings scratched in short rounded lines. The god holds in his upper hands the disc and the conch respectively. The palm of the lower right hand which is raised almost to the chest is, unfortunately, mutilated, so much so that the attribute can hardly be made out, but the position of the hand seems to indicate that it was probably a vilva or mātuliṅga fruit as is usually the case in Burma; the lower left holds the club, not at the top but round the middle. It is interesting to find in this example Viṣṇu seated on his Garuḍa as in Indian examples; and the pose and attitude too of the god and his carrier are more or less akin to similar sculptures from India. Interesting is also the lotus-seat that intervenes between Viṣṇu and Garuḍa; it seems that the bird and its flying attitude have practically lost their real artistic and iconographic significance and serve merely as decorations.

Over the two capitals on the two sides of the principal figure are two small niches (2 ft. high) that must have once housed two stone sculptures. Of these two, one still remains in situ. It is a small slab representing likewise the figure of Viṣṇu seated cross-legged (padmāsana) on a lotus-throne resting on a Garuḍa with outstretched wings. The figure is very badly mutilated, but enough remains to show beyond doubt that it is Garuḍa. The god is ornamented with simple but heavy ornaments round the wrists and arms, but they are not so elaborated as in the example just noticed nor is there any mukuṭa of any description whatsoever. The head-dress is most simple and is similar to those so common on the heads of the innumerable Buddha figures of Burma of a later period; the dress is plain and 'resembles (Mon. Duroiselle points out) that of a Buddhist monk'. The iconography of the figure seems all the more interesting when we examine the attitude of the divinity and the physiognomy of the face which is peculiarly Burmese in character. Noticeable are also the two distended earlobes which is a distinctive feature of the Buddha icon. Rightly has it been, therefore, identified as the Buddha avatāra of Viṣṇu. The vāhana Garuḍa, and the attributes, such as the disc held in the second right hand on a level with the shoulder and the club held in the left arm resting on the knee, determine once for all the cult which the god belongs to.

On the northern, western and southern faces of the central obelisk, referred to above, were originally figures of three standing deities cut out in comparatively bold relief in brick within a niche flanked with slender pilasters. The figures are all very badly defaced, and the attributes can hardly be traced without difficulty. The three figures are replicas of one another; they are all of the same pose and attitude with graceful limbs beautifully adorned with ornaments richly carved. The position of the four hands are the same in each and it is most likely that they carried similar attributes too. One of the three is comparatively better preserved and this is described by Mon. Duroiselle as follows: "the right arm is missing. The upper right hand holds what remains of a broken object, probably the disc. The lower left hand holds the conch, the outlines of which are still perfectly seen... This last attribute shows it to be Viṣṇu. Similar traces of the once existing symbols are visible, but much more faintly, on the bricks behind two other statues."[1] The standing position which is most common to mediaeval Viṣṇu images of India, the smooth, refined and elegant modelling of the slender and well-proportioned body, the beautifully executed ornaments, and, above all, the physiognomy of the figures suffice to show that they are frankly Indian in character, belonging to a period not later than the 11th century A.D., and stylistically have very close affinity with the contemporary mediaeval sculptural art of Eastern India.

We now turn to the images in the niches on the outer walls of the temple. The niche at the esatern end of the south wall is occupied by a representation of the varāha avatāra of Viṣṇu. The figure is badly mutilated; the boar-head and the Bhūdevī have suffered most, but the attitude of the legs and the position of the head turned towards the left shoulder on which the defaced female figure of the seated Bhūdevī can easily be noticed, hardly leave any doubt as to its identification. The heavy chignon of the goddess falling on her back and the hands clasped in adoration are represented with a creditable thoroughness of iconographic detail. The hands have mostly broken off; the attributes cannot, therefore, be recognised; but the mace (gadā) held at the middle by the left lower hand as well as the petals of the lotus throne are clearly distinguishable. It may be mentioned here that the attitude of the head has here been to some extent misunderstood. When the head is turned towards the left, it is natural for us to expect from similar Indian examples as well as from artistic requirement that the left leg should be bent and the right kept straight and in order, or vice versa. But here in the present example, though the head is turned towards the left, the leg bent is the right one, not the left.

One of the niches is occupied by a representation of the Nṛsiṁha or Narasiṁha avatāra of Viṣṇu. The attitude of the legs with their knee-joints bent forward as well as the lower hands holding something on the lap is interesting, and is the determining factor for the identification of the divinity. The figure on the lap is completely gone, traces of the stone are only left, but the lines of the lion face of the principal figure with at least six hands that are visible, and the sharp nails of one of the hands that are used to tear off the body of Hiraṇyakaṣipu that can yet be traced, leave no doubt as to its being the Narasiṁha avatāra of Viṣṇu.

1. *An. Rep. A.S. India*, 1912-13, p. 138.

The third niche is occupied by a sculpture representing a two-handed divinity standing erect on a lotus throne with the head slightly bent towards the left. It is crowned with the usually lobed head-dress flanked by fluttering scarves on two sides, but the face is mutilated and hardly can anything be made out. The god is dressed up to the knees and the hands holding respectively the arrow and the bow at once show that it is an image of Rāmāvatāra of Viṣṇu. Iconographic texts would lay down that "Rāmacandra should never have more than two arms; in the right hand the bāṇa or arrow should be held, and in the left hand the dhanuṣ or the bow"[1], and the present example strictly follows the text. But some of the texts demand that an image of Śrī Rāma should be a standing one 'with three bends in the body, in other words, it has to be a standing image of the tribhaṅga variety"[2], an injunction followed in most of the South Indian images of Rāmāvatāra. But here the injunction seems to have been disregarded; nor is the divinity accompanied by Sītā, Lakṣmaṇa or Hanumāna as laid down in certain other, especially South Indian texts.

The fourth niche of the temple is occupied by an image easily distinguishable as Paraśurāma, another avatāra of Viṣṇu. The figure stands on a lotus throne flanked by two full-blown lotuses; it is crowned by the usual head-dress and have also usual ornamental decorations. The attitude of the body is erect but the head is slightly bent towards the right. The hands, two in number, hold respectively a staff-like object perhaps a khaḍga or sword raised upwards, and an axe, resting on the left shoulder. The latter attribute determines the iconography of the sculpture. Here the icon differs a bit from written texts which lay down that Paraśurāma should have the paraśu or axe in the right hand, and the left hand should be in the sūchi pose as if pointing to something'.[3] But the *Agnipurāṇa* would have four hands for Paraśurāmāvatāra holding respectively the paraśu, khaḍga, bāṇa, and dhanuṣ; this helps us to determine that the object held in the right hand of the divinity cannot be anything else than a khaḍga or sword.

On the ten niches, we already know that three on the east side are empty, the icons have not yet been traced and there is very little hope of their recovery. Of the seven icons that remain, four, namely, Varāha, Narasiṁha, Rāmacandra and Paraśurāma have already been identified without any very great difficulty. Of the rest, two are so badly defaced that it is difficult to be certain about their identification. The third is, however, one of the best-preserved images of the Nāt-hlaung kyaung. Mon. Duroiselle sought to identify it, but could not come to a decision.

1. *Elements of Hindu Iconography*, Vol. I, Pt. I, p. 189.
2. *ibid.*
3. *ibid.*, p. 186.

We begin then with this very image whose presence in a Viṣṇu temple is unique and interesting.

We would be surprised at the first instance to know that it is not an image of Viṣṇu, nor of any of his avatāras. It is sheltered in the niche to the proper left of the entrance to the temple. The image can easily be described; but it is better to quote Mon. Duroiselle. "It is standing on a lotus flower from which two other smaller ones spring; the arms are placed close to the body bent upward at the elbows, and each hand holds a lotus bud on a level with the shoulders; it wears a crown; the distended ear-lobes hang down and touch the shoulder under the weight of large ear ornaments. It has bracelets, armlets and anklets; the lower garment is tucked up and reaches as far as the knees; lines showing the folds are visible". Mon. Duroiselle was not able, as we have said, to identify it, but he added, "The number of niches would lead one to suppose that this also represents one of Viṣṇu's avatāras; but it has none of the distinctive attributes of any of these".[1] And, precisely for this reason, it is not one of the avatāras of Viṣṇu, but seems in all likelihood to be an image of Sūrya of the South Indian type. The position of the two hands as well as the lotus buds held in one line with the shoulders are significant; no less significant is the number of the hands, namely two, which is a distinctive feature of standing as well. The high boots covering the two feet and the horses drawing the chariot are, no doubt, missing in the present example; but it need not surprise us in the least, for Sūrya in South India does not generally wear boots nor rides a horse-drawn chariot. The iconographic affinity is, therefore, such that it is only natural for us to identify the present icon as Sūrya.[1] It is certainly surprising, one must admit, to find a Sūrya image in a place where we would naturally look for on avatāra of Viṣṇu. But, the fact can easily be reconciled if we would only bear in mind the very intimate relation of Viṣṇu with the Vedic Sūrya. For, there in the Vedas, he is never a supreme god, but is always 'identified with the Sun and is said to have stridden over the seven regions and to have covered the whole universe by means of the three steps, '—a statement wherein the germ of the later Trivikrama tradition of Viṣṇu is so often traced. The idea underlying this solar explanation is obviously incorporated in the dhyāna śloka—

"Dhyayas-sadā Savitṛmaṇḍala-madhyavarti Nārāyaṇah
sarasijāsanasanniviṣṭah keyūravān makara-kuṇḍalavān
kirīṭī hārī hiraṇmaya-vapur dhṛta-śaṅkha-cakrah".

1. *An. Rep. A.S. India*, 1912-13, p. 138.
2. Cf. *Hindu Iconography*, Vol. , Pt. II, Plates LXXXVI, XCIV (fig. 2), XCVI (fig. 2).

Herein Viṣṇu as Nārāyaṇa is described as residing in the orb of the sun. The idea that Viṣṇu is the sun appears to be still maintained in the worship of the sun as Sūryanārāyaṇa.[1]

Of the two badly defaced images referred to above, one is most probably a representation of the Vāmana or Trivikrama avatāra and the other of the Kalki avatāra of Viṣṇu. The former which is most seriously damaged may be described as standing in a tribhaṅga pose on a pedestal which is undoubtedly what remains of a full-blown lotus flower. The right leg is bent almost at right angles at the knee-joint, and the left one is placed firmly on the ground. The deity seems to have only two hands the right of which holds a kamaṇḍalu and a staff-like object on which the god seems to lean. The attribute in the left cannot be distinguished. The dress seems to have consisted of a loin-cloth (kaupīna) and a waist-band which hangs from a knot along side the left hip. But the attributes that give clue to the identification of the image as Vāmana or Trivikrama is the kamaṇḍalu alone referred to above, and the tuft of hair as well tied up in a knot on the crown of the head. For the canons (e.g., the Vaikhānasāgama) would lay down that a Trivikrama image should be represented as having two arms, "one of which should carry a kamaṇḍalu and the other an umbrella. On the crown of the head there should be a tuft of hair, tied up in a knot; and there should also be a pair of kuṇḍalas in the ears, a deer-skin worn in the upavīta fashion, the sacred thread, a waist-zone and a kaupīna. He should also carry with him a book. All these are intended to show that the image is that of a Vedic student or Brāhmaṇical brahmacārin". Some authorities hold that the image should be represented as a "deformed dwarf; and they therefore, require that the image should be worked in the form of an ill-shaped man with hunch-back, protruding joints of bones and a big belly".[2] The image under consideration, deformed and dwarfish as it is, and wearing as it does a kaupīna, holding a kamaṇḍalu as an attribute, and, finally, having a tuft of hair tied in a knot on the head, seems roughly to agree with both the descriptions. It is likely that he carried a book as another attribute in his left hand.

The other one is Kalki. It can be described as a standing image with two hands holding in the right a khaḍga and in the left some indistinguishable attribute. It has the usual head-dress, heavy ear-ornaments, a heavy necklace and a loin-cloth whose folds can easily be seen. According to the *Agnipurāṇa* Kalki should ride on a horse and carry the dhanuṣ and the bāṇa, but the *Vaikhānasāgama* states that he should have the face of a horse and the body of a man with four hands carrying respectively the śaṅkha, the cakra, the khaḍga and the kheṭaka. Here, the image

1. *ibid.*, p. 76; also see, *IA*, Vol. LIV, 1925, p. 161; J.N. Banerjee.
2. *Hindu Iconography*, Vol. I, Pt. I, pp. 163-64.

neither rides a horse, nor has the face of a horse. The only distinguishable attribute in one of his two hands, and on which the identification rests, is the khaḍga; it is not impossible that the left hand carried a kheṭaka or shield. And once we have made sure of the identifications of six of the ten avatāras of Viṣṇu, namely, the Buddha, the Varāha, the Narasiṁha, the Rāmacandra, the Paraśurāma and the Trivikrama, and when the present one is not obviously an image of any of the three other remaining avatāras of Viṣṇu, namely, the Matsya, the Kūrma, or the Kṛṣṇa, we are led by a process of elimination to identify the present icon as the Kalki avatāra of Viṣṇu. We can also, therefore, assert in the same breath that the three niches that are at present empty must have once sheltered the images of the Matsya, Kūrma and Kṛṣṇa avatāras of the most important god of the Brāhmaṇical triad.

Besides the Viṣṇuite images of the Nāt-hlaung kyaung, a bronze Viṣṇu image, one foot high, had been discovered at Pagan by a phoongyi (Buddhist monk) in a field at Myinkaba (a village near Pagan) which is at present housed in the Pagan Museum.[1] The question would at once arise if the image, small as it is, had really been carried over from the main land by a Brāhmaṇical trader or colonist; and the question is a likely one. But when we consider the stiff rigid modelling of the body, the hard expression of the face, the paucity of ornaments in so late as example (belonging not earlier than the 13th century A.D.), the rough and rigid convention of the different features, and last, but not the least, the conventional curving flame designs at the ends of the two shoulders so common in Burmese images of the later date, we are led to believe that the image had not been an imported one, but had, on the contrary, been locally cast by an indigenous craftsman in the service of a Brāhmaṇical master. And, if our assumption turns out to be correct, we can at once evaluate its iconographic importance. The god stands on a double-petalled lotus pedestal and is crowned on the head by a conical kirīṭa-mukuṭa finished at the top by a round object, obviously a misrepresentation of the kirīṭa-mukuṭa itself. The distended earlobes, a characteristic feature of Buddha images, are noteworthy, and the simple and crude workmanship of the ornaments is interesting. The god has four hands, the two upper hold the cakra and the śaṅkha respectively; the lower right is in the varada pose and the lower left is placed upon a staff-like object, obviously the gadā. The yajñopavīta or the sacred thread across the body is easily recognisable, but interesting is the unarabandha or the belt round the belly. This seems frankly to be a bhogasthānaka mūrti of Viṣṇu, and can well be compared, from the iconographic standpoint, with an exactly similar bronze image from the Madras Museum,

1. *An. Rep. A.S. Burma*, 1913, p. 19.

illustrated in Gopinath Rao's Hindu Iconography.[1]

These, then, seem almost to exhaust the finds up till now made of Viṣṇuite images in Burma proper. We have seen that they have mostly been found at Hmawza, Thaton and deltaic districts in Lower Burma and at Pagan in Upper Burma. It is most unfortunate that none of these images can precisely be dated on any epigraphic evidence. We have, therefore, to fall back upon less precise a data, namely, the stylistic peculiarities of the images themselves, a consideration which we propose to reserve for a later chapter. Here it would suffice to outline in short the period to which these images may possibly be assigned.

The sculptures in the Nāt-hlaung kyaung, Pagan, seem, on stylistic as well as epigraphic evidence referred to above, to date in the later half of the 11th century A.D. The bronze image must certainly belong to a period not earlier than the later half of the 13th century A.D. To the next century, or probably to a little later date, we may ascribe the stone Viṣṇu image from Mergui in the Rangoon Museum. Considered from the viewpoint of these finds just discussed, it can safely be deduced that Brāhmaṇical influx, mainly Viṣṇuite, into the Peninsula began at least as early as the 7th century A.D. and continued with more or less vigour, and in more or less friendly relation with the main Buddhist population, as late as the 14th century A.D. when it seems to have become restricted to the deltaic districts.

Apart from the prevalence of the cult of Brahmā, Śiva and Viṣṇu, we also found the existence of the subsidiary deities of the Brāhmaṇical pantheon in Burma. They are Gaṇeśa and Sūrya. The former (Gaṇeśa) will be discussed later on in the present work. Here, we will only examine Sūrya.

SŪRYA

Archaeological discoveries in Burma have brought to light up to this time at least one image that can definitely be identified as Sūrya. This image has been discovered on a hill known as Shin-nge-det-taung, situated half a mile to the south-east outside the old city walls of the city of Mrohaung in Arakan.[2] But, besides this, we have in one of the niches of the Nāt-hlaung kyaung another image which we have already identified as Sūrya; and our identification rests on assured grounds.[3] These, then, are the two Sūrya icons up till now discovered in Burma; but while the Nāt-hlaung sūrya is definitely of the South Indian type, the Mrohaung example is particularly North Indian, and the two are at least four centuries removed in date from one another, belonging to the 11th and the 7th or 8th century A.D. respectively.

1. *Hindu Iconography*, Vol. I, Pt. I, Plate XVIII.
1. Chap. II, plate X, fig. 14.
2. *Op. cit., An. Rep. A.S. Burma*, 1928, pp. 27-28,

The Mrohaung Sūrya does not stand on his two legs resting on a lotus (cf. the Nāt-hlaung Sūrya) but rides in his chariot drawn by seven horses. The horse in the centre placed in a horse-shoe-shaped niche faces outwards, and the remaining six, three on each side, are represented as galloping. "The figure of the chariot-driver (Aruṇa) is missing. The principal figure is much defaced but enough remains to show that it has two hands both lifted up to the level of the shoulders, each of which carries a circular or round object, the nature of which cannot be ascertained, being mostly broken off. It has a high head-dress, large earlobes and a necklace, and is flanked on either side by what remains of a small standing figure which looks like a female. The one on the right is carrying a bow and that on the left, a staff or an arrow. The two small figures probably represent the two goddesses Uṣā and Pratyūṣā. The interest of the stone lies in its being the first and only one of its kind that has yet been discovered in Arakan or Burma proper".

It is obviously a Sūrya image of the Northern variety, the essential features of which are, 'the seven-horsed chariot of Sūrya with Aruṇa as the driver; the sun-god with his legs covered, wearing bodice and jewels, with his two hands carrying two full-blown lotuses, his head adorned with kirīṭa-mukuṭa; his two male attendants one on each side and two female figures on either side shooting arrows. The figure of the sun and sometimes the figures of both the male attendants, too, have their feet encased in some sort of leggings. Sometimes the legs of these three figures are left uncarved and shown as inserted in the pedestal or what stands for the chariot.[1] The Mrohaung image conforms exactly to this description for here too the legs of the sun-god as well as those of the two goddesses are shown as inserted 'in the pedestal or what stands for the chariot'. Owing to the defaced state of the sculpture, the figure of Aruṇa the driver is missing, but the two full-blown lotuses held in the hands of the main god as well as the kirīṭa-mukuṭa on the head are almost certain. This image is important from another respect too. It supplies us with at least another instance of the Northern type of Sūrya belonging to a period of which only one or two examples have up till now come down to us in India. The reason is obvious, for all Sūrya images and temples to which references are made in Gupta epigraphs seem, with one or two exceptions, to have been lost or destroyed beyond recovery. The earliest Sūrya image up till now known of the Northern type is definitely of the Gupta school and cannot be dated later than the 6th century A.D.; it comes from the Śiva temple of Bhumārā.[2]

1. *IA.*, 1925, p. 164.
2. Banerji, Siva Temple of Bhumārā, *A.S. Memoir*, No. 16, Plate XIV, Fig. G.

From the above perusal it seems that in Burma, Brāhmaṇism found in early times a shelter and claimed a small fraction of the population as its followers. Viṣṇu seems to have been the most popular cult of the Brāhmaṇical trinity. Unlike in Champā and Kambuja, Śiva was denied an important position. Temples dedicated to Śiva and erected for his worship did certainly exist at or near about Thaton as well as in Pagan images have also been discovered here and there, coins bearing Śaivite symbols have been found in several districts, especially in Arakan where a Śaivite dynasty of a long line of kings seems probably to have held sway for a long time, but their number is considerably small and their influences limited. In fact, Brāhmaṇical population in Burma does not seem to have largely subscribed to the cult of Śiva. Same was the case with the cult of Brahmā too.

4. *SIAM*

Siam (modern Thailand), unlike Burma is professedly Buddhist, but it has the unique distinction of maintaining the Brāhmaṇical faith till the present day. Finds of Brāhmaṇical deities and associated objects in considerable number testify to the existence of the Brāhmaṇical population. Brāhmaṇical religion, affiliated to Brahmā, Śiva and Viṣṇu and other minor deities were widely practised throughout the country. Amongst the trinity, Viṣṇu was most popular and occupied the prominent position in the Brāhmaṇical fold. Śiva and Brahmā have lesser importance.

In the present state of our knowledge it is difficult to say when Brāhmaṇism entered into Thailand. However, on the basis of available data we may conjecture that since Siam formed parts of the Kambuja empire about 8th or 9th century A.D., she was naturally very much influenced by the religious condition of that country. It is, therefore, possible that Siam received Brāhmaṇical religious ideas indirectly from India through Kambuja, where Brāhmaṇism was well established by that time.[1] Another inference regarding the introduction of Brāhmaṇism in Thailand may be that it (Brāhmaṇism) dates back to ancient times when historical facts were not recorded.[2] Out of these two theories, the former seems to be more plausible.

The Brāhmaṇical priests and scholars seem to have played a great role in the cultural progress of Thailand like other regions of South-east Asia. The presence of Brāhmaṇas at the court was indirectly responsible for much of the people's belief in Brāhmaṇism and Indian magico-religious practices. Most of the ceremonial activities of the kings and the royal court were conducted in accordance with the Brāhmaṇical concept as

1. Cf. *2500 years of Buddhism*, p. 79.
2. Cf. *Thailand Official Years Book*, 1964-64, p. 312.

interpreted by the court Brāhmaṇas.[1] Brāhmaṇism had a good deal of influence over Thai arts, rites, festivals and ceremonies.[2]

The king's coronation, tonsorial ceremonies for the royal children on reaching their maturity, oaths of allegiance to the king taken by officials, royal weddings, royal cremations, and first ploughing ceremonies were among the ceremonies at which the Brāhmaṇa priest officiated. By means of their astrological computations and horoscopes they cast, set the favourable time for ceremonies, analysed parlance, interpreted dreams of the king, predicted victory or defeat in war, and scarcity or sufficiency of rainfall.[3]

Although the first Thai kingdom of Sukhodaya seems to have preferred Buddhism, they maintained continuity with those Brāhmaṇical traditions and cults that have been characteristics of the Indianized state of Cambodia. This was partly because the populations over which the Sukhodaya rulers first came to extend their sovereignty, did not easily give up the Brāhmaṇical religious and cultural traditions with which they had assimilated during Mon and Khmer influence.

From an inscription on a statue of Śiva, we know that in 1510 A.D., Dharmaśoka, the king of Kamphengphet, introduced the worship of Śiva. He exalted both the cult of Brāhmaṇism and Buddha. From the inscription of Takuapa, we know that as early as the 8th or 9th century A.D., there had been established in Siam, a temple of Viṣṇu.

In Siam, where Brāhmaṇism preceded Buddhism, place names such as *Ban Phra Narai* (village of Viṣṇu) or *Khao Narai* (mountain of Viṣṇu) still point to a strong and early Vaiṣṇava tradition that had once been current in the Peninsula. But more exact are the finds of Viṣṇu images; Viṣṇu often on the back of Garuḍa or with Lakṣmī. Buddha is also often included as one of his ten *avatāras*.

The kings of Thailand had the attributes of a Brāhmaṇic deity. Surrounded and protected by impregnable defences of Brāhmaṇic doctrine, magical regalia, sacred ritual, sycophantic officials, he occupied a sacred and remote position.[4] The king's position in the religious sphere did most to secure his authority, in other spheres. Upon his coronation, he was invested as a re-incarnation Brāhmaṇic god.[5] For many centuries the Thai rulers adopted Khmer Śaivism including the cult of the liṅga, thus providing the court with both the religious rites and supernatural practices. During the reign period of Ram Kamheng, Brāhmaṇism received great

1. Wales, H.G.Q., *Siamese State Ceremonies*, pp 54-55.
2. For details of Brāhmaṇical influence on Thai art, festivals and ceremonies, see Chap. V of the present work; Also see Wales, H.G.Q. *op. cit*
3. Vella, W.F., *Siam Under Rama III*, pp. 29-31.
4. Blanchard, W., *Thailand*, p. 28.
5. *ibid.*, p. 149.

impetus in Thailand. The consort of King Ram Kamheng, lady Nopamas, was the daughter of a Brāhmaṇa priest and astrologer of the Royal court. It is said that Ram Kamheng, though a Buddhist, had a body of Brāhmins attached to his court to advise on matters of state-craft, law and technical matters; to regulate the calender and cast horoscope; to manage the swinging festival, the first ploughing and rites for the control of wind and rain; to look after the regalia and arrange the royal progress; to perform the ceremonies of tonsure, investiture and coronation for royalty; and to discharge a host of other tasks.[1] Another king Lu-Thai (Lidaiya) formally consecreted to the throne under the Brāhmaṇical title 'Śrī Suryavaṁsa Rama Mahadharma Rājādhirāja ! Brāhmaṇism and Buddhism flourished side by side in Siam during his reign period. Both Śramaṇas and Brāhmaṇas were respected. Not satisfied with the erection of the statue of Buddha, the king ordered his artists to make one statue of Parameśvara and another of Viṣṇu and consecreted them on the eleventh day of Purvāṣāḍha in the Devālaya (temple) of Mahākṣetra. The Brāhmins and ascetics rendered perpetual worship to them.[2] Lu Tai yet another king of Thailand, in 1349 A.D. founded an image of Maheśvara (Śiva) and one of Viṣṇu, and placed them in the Devālayamahākṣetra (Brāhmin temple) in the mango grove west of Sukhodaya, where all the Brāhmins and ascetics were to perform the rituals of the cult in perpetuity.[3]

The court Brāhmaṇas were recruited from time to time. With the final destruction of Ayudhya in 1767, those Brāhmins who had escaped the clutches of the Burmese fled to Nagara Śrī Dharmarāja. King Tak, on the re-establishment of the kingdom, recalled them, and endeavoured to collect all that had survived of their ceremonial core. Siamese history of the Ayudhya period contains frequent mention of various supernatural omens which had to be interpreted by the Brāhmins. No king would have thought of embarking on any important undertaking, such as military expedition, without making sure that his soothsayers considered the day to be propitious. King Rama Tibodi I, who promulgated the first Thai laws, is revered as a great law-giver. Most of this early registration was later on altered by additions from the code of Manu.[4]

The above instances clearly indicate that side by side with Buddhism, Brāhmaṇism too flourished in Siam. Although the kings were the followers of Buddhist faith, they paid much attention towards the welfare of the Brāhmaṇas and for the development of Brāhmaṇical gods, like Śiva and Viṣṇu. In short, we may say that these instances show the importance of the Brāhmaṇism in Thailand.

1. Wales, H.G.Q., *Siamese State Ceremonies*, p. 12.
2. Griswald, A.B., *Towards a History of Sukhothai Art*, p. 15.
3. Syamananda, Rong, *A History of Thailand*, p. 48.
4. Blanchard, W., *op. cit.*, p. 27.

Siam, like Cambodia, maintained a number of court Brāhmins at Bangkok until recently when as the result of a revolution a republic came to be established. Joseph Dahlmann who travelled in Siam in the twenties of this century gives the following account of them: "There are about 80 families. Their dwellings are erected round a poorly temple comprising three insignificant structures enclosed by a wall. The Brāhmaṇas differ from the Bonzes by the long flowing hair on their heads. The white ceremonial gown and the conical cap vividly bring to our minds the Brāhmaṇas of the island of Bali. Small as is their number by the side of the thousands of Buddhist Bonzes, they have still many privileges conceded to them, as, in spite of all the changes due to Buddhism, the memory of the old Brāhmaṇical royalty is still so deeply rooted in Siamese tradition. To the Brāhmaṇ community is reserved the consecration of the new king, and royalty is held to be properly transmitted to the new ruler only by the completion of such consecration. Simply and solely for this end is this small group of Brāhmaṇas preserved in the midst of the large community of Buddhist Bonzes. At their head stands a guru bearing the proud title *Mahārājaguru*. With the consecration of the king goes the consecration of the royal elephant, also reserved to the *Mahārājaguru*, for what is the Siamese king without his white elephant ?"[1]

There is a published official account in English of the details of ceremonies and mantras employed on the occasion of the coronation of His Majesty king Prajadhipok in February of B.E. 2468 (A.D. 1926). We have only to note that unlike the Brāhmins of Cambodia the Siamese Brāhmins are not relics of a once powerful religious caste, as Father Dahlmann seems to think, but appear to have been brought in at a later time from Ligor and elsewhere to conduct the court ceremonies, in imitation of other courts, with an Indian ceremonial. The Thai conquerors of Siam sought thus to legitimise their rule in the eyes of the people by observing the same forms as the ancient Khmer monarchy of the land. In 1821 one of the Brāhmins told Crawfurd that he was fifth in descent from his ancestor who first settled in Siam and had originally been an inhabitant of Rāmeśvaraṁ, the sacred island adjacent to South India on the east, to the north of Ceylon. Wales[2] says that some Brāhmaṇas today have a tradition that their ancestors came from Benares, that both these accounts may be true and that there may be now in Bangkok descendants of Brāhmins from both North and South India.

At present the Brāhmaṇas of Siam are known by the name *Phrāms*, which might be a corruption from the Brāhmaṇa. They claimed descent from the persecuted Brāhmins of India, who fled to Pegu and thence to

1. *Indische Fahrten*, i, p. 124 (adapted from the German original).
2. *Siamese State Ceremonins*, p. 61.

Siam during the 5th and 6th century A.D. The Brāhmins of Siam constitute a small community of Bangkok, who live near their temples Vat Bot Phrām, which means 'the pagoda of the sanctuary of the Brāhmaṇas'.[1] The sanctuary comprises only three brick temples in an enclosure. There can be found the colossal images of trimūrti or the Brāhmaṇical gods of trinity, known in Siamese as Phra-Maharazakhruvidhi (=Sanskrit—Mahārāja Guruviddhi).

The Siamese sculptures even now make images of Vamarāja, Māra, Indra etc. The Brāhmaṇic idea of Mount Meru as the centre of this universe is accepted in Siamese religious books and paintings. The greatest symbolic aspects of the glory of Brāhmaṇism still remain in many parts of Thailand, though the country is purely a Buddhist one.

5. *LAOS*

It cannot be said with certainty as to how and when Brāhmaṇism was introduced in Laos. However, we are told that in the sixth century A.D. Funan came to be conquered by its northern vassal state of Chenla which was ultimately divided into two parts, viz., (i) Upper Chenla (i.e., the Lao state to the west of Annam) and (ii) Lower Chenla. Since then Brāhmaṇism became quite popular in Laos and was adopted by a large number of people as their main religion. Since Laos formed parts of the Kambuja empire about 8th or 9th century A.D., she was naturally very much influenced by the religious condition of that country. It is therefore justly said that Laos, particularly Vientiane and Luang Prabang, had received religious ideas of Brāhmaṇism indirectly from India, probably through Cambodia and with the result Brāhmaṇism (Śaivism, Vaiṣṇavism etc.) flourished in the regions, and the people in general were quite familiar with Brāhmaṇical philosophical ideas and religious belief.

The prevalence of Brāhmaṇism in Laos is attested to by inscriptions and archaeological objects of the country. The Phou Lokhon (Laos) inscription in Sanskrit consisting of six lines, comprising three verses in the anuṣṭup metre, is engraved on the north-east face of a sand-stone column which crowns the top of the hill called Phou Lokkon. It records the erection by King Mahendravarman of a Śiva liṅga which still stands on the spot at a distance of 21/2 metres from the inscribed column.[2] The remains of the temple of Wat Phu, on the Liṅgaparvata (liṅga mountain) containing Bhadreśvara (Śiva) are still extant to the south-west of Champasak in South Laos.[3] The specimens of the religious art at Wat Phu

1. Cf. Bose, P.N., *Indian Colony of Siam*, p. 110.
2. Chhabra, B.C., *Expansion of Indo-Aryan Cultures*, p. 69.
3. Marshal, Henri, *Le Temple de Wat Phu*, p. 2.

depict Indra on Airāvata and Viṣṇu on Garuḍa.[1] It was in the seventh century that Jayavarman I had installed a stele inscription at this sanctuary which he named as liṅgaparvata (the mountain containing the liṅga or phallic representation of lord Śiva). An inscription of 835 A.D. speaks of Śreṣṭhapura as a holy place because of its association with the worship of lord Śiva. These instances are the greatest evidence of the presence of Brāhmaṇism in Laos.

Towards the end of the thirteenth or the beginning of the fourteenth century A.D., Brāhmaṇism declined in Laos as in neighbouring Cambodia. Buddhism became the dominant creed, and there are now few traces of Brāhmaṇical religion left in the country, except, of course, a few rituals in public ceremonies, customs and festivals of Laos. The Brahmā-Buddha culture was rooted so deep in their minds that it has left an impressive mark upon their social and cultural life, which guides, to a great extent, their daily life also.

6. *JAVA*

Many forms of Brāhmaṇical religion, affiliated to Brahmā, Śiva and Viṣṇu etc., were widely practised by the majority of the population of Java. About the beginning of the eighth century A.D. we find the Purāṇic form of Brāhmaṇical religion established in Java which is conclusively proved by inscriptions, temples, images as well as literary sources.

We may begin the Brāhmaṇical religion in Java with the Cangal inscription which records that in the year A.D. 732 King Śrī Sañjaya set up a liṅga on a hill, for the sake of the peace of his kingdom. The first verse gives the astronomical details of the auspicious hour when the ceremony took place. The author then eulogises Śiva in the most extravagant terms in the next three verses, while the fifth verse is dedicated to Brahmā and the sixth to Viṣṇu. These hymns refer to the familiar attributes of each of these gods. With regard to Śiva mention is made of his three eyes, the matted hair with the sacred Gaṅgā and the moon on his head, the body besmeared with ashes, and the necklace made of serpents. He is possessed of supreme aiśvarya, and adored not only by the hermits but also by Indra and other gods. He is the lord of the bhūtas and in his infinite mercy maintains the world by means of his eight forms. Brahmā is described as of golden colour, the preceptor (guru) of the world, worshipped by hermits and gods, the source of the three-fold ends of life, viz., dharma, artha, and kāma, and one who has organised society by the rules of the *Vedas*. Viṣṇu is described as lying with his consort on the body of the serpent king, floating on the vast sea, deeply absorbed in his meditation, and adored by the gods for the sake of deliverance.

1. *ibid*, pp. 24-28.

The five verses of the Cangal inscription thus give an admirable summary of the essential conceptions of the Purāṇic trinity. It also clearly indicates that the position of supremacy among them was undoubtedly accorded to Śiva. The records of Airlangga refer to the three principal sects as Śiva (or Maheśvara), Saugata (i.e. Buddhist), and ṛṣi or Mahābrāhmaṇa. Goris has analysed the list of religious sects enumerated in ten different texts. All of them mention one or more Śaiva sects, but only four refer to the Vaiṣṇava sect and three to Brāhmaṇa or Brahmān (devoted to Brahmā).[1]

Again by far the great majority of temples in Java are dedicated to Śiva, and the largest number of the detached images so far discovered are those of Śiva and the members of his family. The same conclusion is borne out by *Amaramālā*, the earliest literary text bearing upon religion that we have so far come across in Java. In giving the synonyms of different gods it begins with those of Śiva and calls him Guru and Īśvara i.e., God par excellence. If we consider the famous Lara-Jongrang group of temples, the great monument of Central Java, we find only a further illustration of the same truth. In this famous group, which will be described in detail in a subsequent chapter, we find the central and the biggest temple dedicated to Śiva with two smaller ones on its two sides for Brahmā and Viṣṇu, and with a temple of Nandi in its front. All these are unmistakable evidences of the supreme position accorded to Śiva in the Javanese form of Brāhmanical trinity.

This great god Śiva was regarded not only as the agent of the destruction of the world, but also of its renovation. He had thus both a benevolent and a terrible nature. These two aspects are represented in Javanese iconography by the two human forms of the god known as Mahādeva and Mahākāla or Bhairava.

The image of Mahādeva has usually one head, though in one instance it has five. He has a third eye on his forehead, his head-dress is adorned with a moon and a skull, and a snake takes the place of the upavīta or the sacred thread. He has usually four arms, rarely two holding fly-whisk (cāmara), rosary (akṣamālā), a book, lotus, water-pot, and trident (triśūla).

The image of Bhairava or Mahākāla has a terrible expression of face protruding eyes and teeth, and wild hair, while the sacred thread is replaced by either snakes or a garland of skulls. He has two or four arms holding mace (gadā), sword (khaḍga) noose, snake and a dagger (or knife), along with the usual attributes of Śiva, such as trident, rosary, and fly-whisk. A variety of the image of this god, which is perhaps called Cakracakra in the attached inscription, deserves particular mention. Here the god sits on the body of a jackal or of a dog, and not only in his seat

1. Cf. Majumdar, R.C., *op. cit.*, p. 101.

surrounded by skulls, but the same form the ornaments of his head, ear, neck and arms. A string of human heads forms his sacred thread, and a number of bells form a belt round his belly. In his four arms are found a trident, a drum (ḍamarū), a dagger, and a bowl made of human skull.

To these forms of Śiva correspond two different forms of his Śakti. The Śakti of Mahādeva is Devī, Mahādevī, Pārvatī, or Umā, the daughter of Himālaya. In her four arms she holds lotus, fly-whisk, rosary, flower, snake, trident or palm-leaf manuscript. A particular form of this goddess is Durgā or Mahiṣāsura-mardinī. She has six, eight, ten or twelve arms, holding various weapons, and is represented as killing the demon who assumed the form of a buffalo.

The Śakti of Mahākāla or Bhairava is Mahākālī or Bhairavī. She is represented as sitting on a dead body, and human skulls form her sacred thread and ornaments of head and neck. In her two arms she holds a trident and a small dish for keeping the blood of the victims. Sometimes she is depicted as a terrible figure with protruding eyes and teeth and a dreadful face, holding fast in her arms the body of the human victim.

The well-known figure of Ardhanārīśvara, combining in one body those of Śiva and Durgā, is also found in Java. The right half of the body is that of Śiva, while the left half is that of Durgā, both being indicated by proper attributes.

The image of Gaṇeśa, the son of Śiva and Pārvatī, is very common in Java, and follows in general the Indian prototype. The war-god Kārttikeya, another son of Śiva, is also well-known in Java. He is generally represented in an ordinary human form riding on a peacock. But sometimes he has six heads and twelve arms, holding various weapons. Lastly, it may be mentioned, that Śiva was also worshipped in the form of liṅga (phallus) in Java.

Viṣṇu, the second member of the trinity, never attained in Java a position or importance equal to that of his rival Śiva, though under some dynasties he enjoyed very high honour and rank. He is usually represented with four arms having the well-known attributes, conch-shell (śaṅkha), wheel (cakra), mace (gadā), and lotus (padma), though occasionally the number of arms is only two. His Śakti, Śrī or Lakṣmi, is usually represented with four arms holding lotus, corn of ear, fly-whisk and rosary. Viṣṇu's rider (vāhana) Garuḍa is also represented in Java, generally with human form, though occasionally the beak, claws and wings of a bird are added. Viṣṇu is often depicted in ananta-śayana posture, such as has been described in the Cangal inscription noted above, and most of his avatāras or incarnations, specially Kṛṣṇa, Rāma, Matsya, Varāha, and Narasiṁha, are represented by images. Sometimes there are two female figures on the two sides of the image of Viṣṇu, which are usually known as Lakṣmi and Satiavana in Bali. The last is probably to be restored as Satyabhāmā. In that case the image may be regarded as that of Kṛṣṇa with Satyabhāmā and Rukmiṇī on two sides.

The devotees of Viṣṇu were undoubtedly less in number than those of Śiva and Buddha, and Vaiṣṇavism ranked in importance next only to Śaivism and Buddhism. This appears quite clearly from the comparatively smaller number of the images of that god found in Java. The religious literature of Java also supports this view, as it contains less traces of that religion than of the other two. Even the Mahābhārata, where Kṛṣṇa, the avatāra of Viṣṇu, plays such a leading part, is strongly Śaivite in character.

The images of Brahmā, the remaining member of the trinity, are comparatively few in number. He is easily recognised by his four heads facing the four directions. He has four arms holding rosary, fly-whisk, lotus and water pot. His rider (vāhana) haṁsa (swan) is sometimes depicted in its normal form, but sometimes also as a human being with the head of a swan above, indicating his true nature. Sarasvatī, the Śakti of Brahmā, is represented with two or four arms, riding on a peacock. The Tengger hill to the east of Singhasāri is referred to as the sacred hill of Brahmā in an inscription dated 1405 A.D.

The image of trimūrti, i.e., of Brahmā, Viṣṇu and Śiva combined together, is also found in Java. It has three heads, all of the same appearance, though in rare cases the central head is indicated to be that of Śiva by the skull and the moon. The image has four arms holding rosary, fly-whisk, lotus, book and the water pot.

Another image, which is very popular in Java, is usually styled Bhaṭāra-Guru. It is a two-armed standing figure of an aged pot-bellied man with moustache and peaked beard, and holding in his hands, trident, water pot, rosary and fly-whisk. This image is usually regarded as a representation of Śiva Mahāyogin (the great ascetic), and his universal popularity is explained by supposing that an originally Indonesian divinity was merged in him. Poerbatjaraka has, however, shown by a comparison with Indian figures that the image represents the sage Agastya. The extreme veneration for and the popularity of the worship of Agastya in Java are reflected in the inscriptions, and Poerbatijaraka's view seems eminently reasonable.[1]

In addition to the principal gods and goddesses described above, we come across the images of various minor gods in Java to which a brief reference may be made. Of the eight dikpālas i.e. minor gods guarding different directions, we meet the familiar images of Yama (the god of death), Varuṇa (water-god), Indra (the king of gods), Agni (the fire-god), Nairṛta, and Kubera (the god of wealth). The first three have distinctive attributes, viz., mace, noose and thunderbolt, while Agni is known by his rider, the ram. The representation of Kubera also follows exactly the

1. Majumdar, R.C., *HCFE.*

lines adopted in Brāhmaṇical and Buddhist pantheons of India, a pot-bellied man, seated on a low cushion with small bags of money scattered around, and holding a lemon in the right hand and an ichneumon in the left. Kubera's wife Hārītī is also known in Java. There are also images of Sūrya (sun-god) holding a lotus and seated in a chariot drawn by seven horses, and Candra (moon-god) holding a flag and carried in a chariot drawn by four or ten horses. Kāma (god of love) is represented as seated on Makara with a bow and arrow in his hand.

It is unnecessary to go further into iconographic details. In short, almost all the gods of Brāhmaṇical pantheon are represented in Java, and the following observation of Crawfurd[1], made more than a century ago, can hardly be regarded as an exaggeration. "Genuine Brāhmaṇical images, in brass and stone, exist throughout Java in such variety, that I imagine there is hardly a personage of the Hindu mythology, of whom it is usual to make representations, that there is not a statue of".

After giving a brief description of the principal features of the Brāhmaṇical religion, we may conclude this account with a reference to the various religious sects that flourished in Java. The classified list of the sects are—(i) Śaiva or Siddhānta, (ii) Pāśupata, (iii) Bhairava, (iv) Vaiṣṇava, (v) Buddha or Saugata, (vi) Brāhmaṇa, and (vii) Ṛṣi.[2] In addition there is reference to Alepaka or Lepaka, a Śaiva sect, and Yogita which cannot be identified.[3] The epigraphic data in general confirm the above list. The Bendosari inscription mentions Bhairava, Sora and Baudha sects. Sora has been identified with Siddhānta, but may also stand for Saura (Sun-worship) which would then give us a new sect.[4]

7. BALI: SUMATRA : BORNEO

Like Java, in Bali too, Brāhmaṇical religion was widely practised by the people. Here (in Bali) Brāhmaṇism is still the prevailing religion. An historical study of the religion in Bali is, however, beset with two difficulties. In the first place, we are unable to trace the successive stage of its development, and secondly, it is difficult to determine how much of it was imported from Java and how much or how little really belongs to the Balinese. The older writers definitely affirm that every vestige of Brāhmaṇical religion and literature that we find today in Bali is derived from Java. Recent researches have proved that this sweeping assertion is untenable, and that Bali possessed a distinct Brāhmaṇical culture before the influx of Javanese elements began in the eleventh century. Still the fact remains

1. *History of the Indian Archipelago*, Vol. II, p. 207.
2. Cf. Majumdar R.C., *Suvarnadvipa*, Vol. II, p. 132.
3. *ibid.*
4. *ibid.*

that since the eleventh century Javanese culture profoundly affected that of Bali, and after the fall of Majapahit empire, large groups of Javanese fled to that island and Javanese religion and literature found there a last resting place. All these so profoundly modified the civilisation of Bali that it is impossible now to distinguish what is Javanese from what is Balinese proper. As a matter of fact the present religious views and practices in Bali may justly be regarded as a fitting supplement and an apt illustration of the picture we have drawn above of the Brāhmaṇical religion in Java.

Nevertheless Brāhmaṇism is stilll a living religion in Bali and we get more details about its actual working than in the case of Java. The following account of Balinese religion should, therefore, be regarded more as a supplement to the sketch we have drawn above than an independent picture.

Buddhism was introduced in Bali as early as the sixth century A.D. But gradually the Purāṇic form of Brāhmaṇical religion, with predominance of Śaivism, exerted its sway. Today the two sects not only exist peacefully side side but there is even a theological and doctrinal rapprochement between the two. The Buddha is regarded as the younger brother of Śiva, and on the occasion of the important ceremonial feasts, there are always four Śaiva and one Buddhist priests. The latter faces the south while three of the former face the other directions, and the fourth sits in the middle. Even at the cremation of princes, the consecrated water brought by a Śaiva priest is mingled with that of a Buddhist. To the mass of people, there is hardly any consciousness of the difference between the two sects, and their view is represented by the popular saying *ya Śiva, ya Buddha* (He who is Śiva is Buddha). In their eyes Śiva and Buddha are one and the same.

The predominance of Śiva in the Brāhmaṇical pantheon is unquestioned, perhaps even in a far greater degree than in Java. Most of the peculiar characteristics and attributes of Viṣṇu are given to Śiva, while Brahmā and Viṣṇu are both regarded, they are rather treated as different forms of Śiva than as seperate gods. Indeed Śiva is more or less regarded as the supreme deity, though his aspect as a member of the trinity is not lost sight of altogether. In other words, the three gods are regarded as mere different aspects of the one indivisible supreme God, though the latter is expressed in terms of one of them viz. Śiva. As in Java, the three gods are known under various names, and their Śaktis are, Umā or Pāravatī (of Śiva in his benificent aspect), Kālī and Durgā (of Kāla i.e. Śiva as destroyer), Śrī or Lakṣmī, the goddess of fertility and protector of agriculture (of Viṣṇu), and Sarasvatī, the goddess of knowledge and fine arts (of Brahmā). Among the host of inferior divinities mention may be made of Indra, Yama, Varuṇa, Kubera, Kāma, Vāsukī (serpent king, a member of Śiva's family), Sūrya, Candra, Rāhu, etc. The incarnations of Viṣṇu and the member of Śiva's family, particularly Gaṇeśa, are also well-known.

The numerous evil spirits or Butas (Skt. Bhūtas) form a characteristic feature of Balinese theology. They are supposed to live in water, trees, or hills, and must be propitiated by appropriate offerings and worship. It has been said that the worship of these spirits occupies the people almost more than that of the beneficent gods.

The Balinese mind is strongly dominated by a religious feeling inasmuch as they have a strong belief in the unbounded influence of gods and Butas, i.e., good and evil spirits over the entire destiny of man. Their whole life may almost be described as an unceasing struggle to befriend the former and to appease the latter. The religious performances thus occupy a prominent place in Balinese life, and their ultimate object may be described as honouring the gods and ancestors and propitiating the evil spirits. The Balinese worship may be divided into two classes, domestic and public. The most important in the first category is Sūrya-Sevana or worship of Śiva as Sūrya (sun). The following account of an actual performance given by an eye-witness may serve as an apt illustration—

"The Padaṇḍa is clothed in white, with the upper part of the body naked, after the Balinese-Indian manner. He sits with his face to the east, and has before him a board upon which stand several small vessels containing water and flowers, some grains of rice, a pan with fire (dhūpa-pātra) and a bell. He then mumbles, almost inaudibly, some words of prayers from *Vedas* (sic), dipping the flowers into the water and waving them and a few grains of rice before him (towards the east) with the fore-finger and thumb of his right hand, whilst at the same time he holds up the pan containing fire. After having proceeded with his prayers for some time during which he makes all kinds of motions with his fingers and turns his rosary, he appears to be inspired by the deity; Śiva has, as it were entered into him; this manifests itself in convulsions of the body, which grow more and more severe, and then gradually cease. The deity having thus entered into him, he no longer sprinkles the water and flowers towards the east alone, but also towards his own body, in order to pay homage to the deity which has passed into it. The bells are not used in the ordinary daily worship, but only at the full and new moons and cremations."[1]

In addition to Sūrya-Sevana, there are other domestic religious ceremonies of the type described in the *Gṛhya-Sūtras* performed on important occasions of a man's life, such as the birth of a child, the cutting of the navel-string when the child is 12 days, 42 days, 3 months or 1 year old; the name-giving ceremony; the piercing of the ears; first menstruation; marriage; conception; death; cremation; funeral; birthdays of family

1. Majumdar, R C., *op. cit.*, pp 140-41.

members; and also on occasions of illness, beginning of harvest etc.

Each house has got a domestic chapel where daily worship is offered to the tutelary deity or deities with flowers and delicacies. These are prepared by the ladies of the family who bring them to the chapels and reverently deposit them before the god with Sembah (bow). The chapel is usually enclosed by a wall, along the side are wooden or stone niches dedicated to particular gods who receive occasional worship.

For public worship, each deśa (district) has three or four general temples viz., (i) pura deśa or the principal temple dedicated to the general and local gods. (ii) pura dalem, the temple for the dead, in or near the cremation ground, dedicated to the goddesss Durgā, (iii) pura segara (Skt. sāgara or sea) on the sea-coast dedicated to the sea-god Baruṇa, (iv) pura Bukit, on the foot or on the top of a hill, dedicated to the gods of the hills.[1] To these may be added the pura Subak, dedicated to Śrī, the goddess of fertility and cultivated fields.

The worship of the piteras or ancestors forms an important part of the Balinese religion. Each dwelling house has got one or more small temples for this purpose, and there are occasional gatherings on sacred spots, believed to be the original dwelling places of these ancestors. At stated periods of the year, the pitaras return to the bosom of their families and are entertained with games and amusements. There are, besides, three religious ceremonies known as *pegursi*, *galungan* and *kuningan* for honouring the souls of the dead and holding close communion with them. In these offerings are placed near the graves, for the souls of those whose bodies are yet unburnt, and also in the pura-dalem, for the souls freed from the body, after burning.[2]

The worship consists mainly of presenting offerings and chanting (or secretly uttering) mantras from scriptures. These vary for different deities and different occasions. The offerings are usually made up of ordinary articles of food (grains, fruits and meat) and drink, clothes, and money. Animal sacrifices are chiefly reserved for Kāla, Durgā, butas, rākṣasas and other evil spirits. Hen, duck, young pig, buffalo, goat, deer and dog are usually sacrificed.

But sometimes we hear even of human sacrifices.

The well-known accessory articles of Indian worship such as ghṛta (clarified butter) kuśa-grass, tila (sesamum) and madhu (honey) are also used in Bali. One of the most important items is the holy water. Although rivers in Bali are named after the sacred rivers in India viz., Gaṅgā, Sindhu, Yamunā, Kāverī, Sarayū and Narmadā the Balinese recognise that those (Indian) rivers are really sacred and the water of these

1. Majumdar, R.C., *op. cit*.
2. *ibid*.

Balinese river is not regarded as holy. The water is, therefore, rendered sacred by the priests by uttering mantras, such as we have seen in the detailed ceremony of Sūrya-Sevana, and is then called amṛta.

Next to Bali, the island of Sumatra has preserved the most interesting remains of Brāhmaṇism. The ruins of brick temples, called *biaro*, are found in large number in the highlands of Padang and Tapanuli and contain Brāhmaṇical images. Stone images of Śiva, Gaṇeśa, Nandi, Brahmā and bronze images of Gaṇeśa and Kubera have come into light from the highlands of Padang, Tapamuli, Palembang and Jambi. These instances clearly indicate that Brāmaṇical religion was widely prevalent in the island of Sumatra.

The existence of Purāṇic form of Brāhmaṇism in Borneo is indicated by the ruins of the temples and detached images. A stone Nandi from Pontianak, the chief town of western Borneo, has come into light. Similarly stone images of Gaṇeśa, Nandi and liṅga were found on the two banks of the river Sekayam in western Borneo. A stone liṅga and Yoni found at Nanga Seravi on the Malavi (western Borneo). From Southern and Eastern Borneo too, a number of Brāhmaṇical images like a stone image of Durgā, Nandi and liṅga have been discovered. An image of Gaṇcśa has been found at Lembang, Sarawak (Northern Borneo). In addition to these images the prevalence of Brāhmaṇical religion among the native Borneo is proved by the fact that the religious beliefs and superstitions of the Dyaks are clearly based upon Brāhmaṇical mythology.[1]

Thus, on the basis of above perusal we may say that Purāṇic form of Brāhmanical religion was widely prevalent in Java, Sumatra, Bali and Borneo. Out of these, the island of Bali has the unique distinction of maintaining the Brāhmaṇical religion till the present day. A vivid picture of the Brāhmaṇical religion, as it was actually practised in South-East Asia, may still be seen in Bali.

1. Cf. Majumdar, R.C., *HCFE*.

3

Brahmanism and Art

We propose to discuss in this chapter the nature and extent of the influence exercised by Brāhmaṇical art in South-East Asia. Of course, the art the Indianised kingdoms produced owes its extraordinary qualities to the genius of the native people, and although the modes may be Brāhmaṇical the expression and the content are local. What the Javanese and Balinese made, springs from their own genius as Angkor did from the genius of the Khmer. The arts of Burma and Thailand reflect the particular genius of the Burmese and the Thai. The Brāhmaṇical modes provided themes and patterns for transformation, opening up before local people avenues of cultural and artistic development.

A vast series of Brāhmaṇical art, ranging from massive architectural complexes to tiny bronzes produced in Cambodia are masterpieces, monumental, subtle, highly sophisticated, mature in style and unrivalled for sheer beauty.

1. CAMBODIA

The best groups of buildings surviving from early Chen La are at Sambor Prei Kuk. Two groups lay at the centre of the city, containing buildings from various periods. The main structures are typical square or octagonal brick tower-shrines, set on high brick terraces, with certain ornamented parts made of sandstone. The temple in the southern group once contained a gold liṅgam and has sculptured scenes set in cartouches or ornament. Aligned with it is the tower which contained the Nandi shrine, the sandstone canopy of which is carved with magnificent relief ornament. Some of the other buildings have chaitya windows framing heads or figures to ornament their towers. The pillars and pilasters are round or chamfered, carved with rings and circlets of relief ornament, and having cushion-capitals of deeply bowed outline like many Indian prototypes. But the chief glory of these buildings is their splendid lintel stones, carved with elaborate relief ornament. At each end, above the dies on which they rest, are fantastic beasts, whose tails are elaborate foliate curlicues, bearing riders; from the open mouth of each beast springs a fictive arch. The lintel's four lobes of ornament are textured with elaborate foliage, and punctuated by three flowery cartouches containing figures riding animals; and from the fictive arch hang fabulous looped strings of jewels punctuated by tassels. This indicates the fundamental motifs—Indian in origin—of all the later Chen La and Khmer ornamental carving which plays such an important part in the architecture. The beasts, called makaras, vomit forth the ornament. And the ornament itself is based upon elaborations of the hanging jewel string and the extravagantly efflorescing garland of foliage, all contained within even, orderly rhythms. The foliage in the early lintel frames shows, especially in the local style of Prei Kmeng, the first intimations of the upward pointing flamboyant shapes which became so characteristic of full Khmer art, sprouting everywhere from eaves and hoodmouldings.

The significance of all this ornament can be traced to Brāhmaṇical prototypes. The jewel strings refer back to the old Brāhmaṇical custom of donors literally hanging their wealth, their jewels upon sacred trees or the railings of shrines. The foliage is derived both from the vases and garlands of flowers offered in a similar fashion, and from the imagery of the shrine as a celestial wish granting tree through whose fabric courses the sap of divine life. The makara is the emblem of time, which vomits all forth, and swallows it again. And since the temple is the earthly, man-made counterpart of the heavens in which the gods dwell, the figures populating the reliefs represent lesser celestials; the courtesans, musicians and courtiers of the gods.

The Chen La style appears at several sites, and follows several phases during the seventh and eighth centuries, declining by degrees into a lesser exuberance. The phases are named after the major architectural sites where they occur Sambor, Prei Kmeng, Prasat Andet, Kompong Preah. At Han Chei there is a small brick tower faced with sandstone, probably the last of the pre-Angkor phase. It is small, its ornament has shrunk to pure foliage and its pillars have diminished capitals, though under the architraves are some figurative pieces of iconography. This whole somewhat unenterprising style of architecture depends on its fine relief sculpture. And indeed sculpture was the major art during the whole Fu Nan-Chen La epoch. Among the few great stone icons which have survived are some of the world's outstanding masterpieces, while the smaller bronzes reflect the same sophisticated and profound style.

The first surviving statues come from the hill, Phnom Da, the 'acropolis' of the then capital of Fu Nan, Angkor Borei. They belong to the early sixth century, a period when the state of Fu Nan was coming under pressure from Chen La. The king to whose reign they belong was Rudravarman, whose patron deity was Viṣṇu. The statues are Vaiṣṇava. Some represent Viṣṇu himself in a characteristic form wearing a tall mitre, with his four or eight arms supported on a frame left in the stone of the block.[1] Like the great majority of Fu Nan-Chen La images they are carefully worked from the back as well as the front. The faces are markedly Indochinese. On at least one of them there is a striking depiction of individual muscles bulging on the shoulders, breast and arms, quite unlike the usual smooth rotundity of the limbs of most sculptures of the Indianized tradition. To account for this, it is possible that Romano-Hellenic influence, already established during the second to fourth centuries A.D. in the north-west of the Indian subcontinent has penetrated to this remote region. A striking Vaiṣṇava image from the same period is that of Kṛṣṇa performing one of his chief miracles, holding aloft in one hand the mountain. Here the image was most likely a 'grotto icon' meant to be placed in the narrow stone cell of a temple. The figure, its braced arm, and the mountain, though all standing out distinctly, are completely engaged with the background. So the sculpture is virtually a relief, but a relief of such great depth that the ground plays no role in the image.

This effect is characteristic and illuminating. Most Indian sculpture is in the form of massively protuberant relief, and in this the Kṛṣṇa follows Brāhmaṇical tradition. The fact that so many of the earlier and the latter Fu Nan-Chen La sculptures are carefully cut from both sides and back might mislead a spectator into imagining that they were carved as true fullround sculpture. This is not so. Even free-standing they are still reliefs, the figures conceived on a rhomboid section, organized so as to present a clear frontal plane, with emphatically receding but distinctly visible side surfaces. The bodies show marked ridge lines dividing the side surfaces from the frontal surface; and all the surfaces are cut as subtly undulating continuities. The deep side surfaces give them a vivid plastic presence; the surface continuity gives them their sensuous vitality. These qualities, however much they may be overlaid by decorative schematicism in later times, are, what give all of Cambodian art its special virtue.

Later the Fu Nan-Chen La sculptures become more numerous. Outstanding among them is a male deity with a horse's head probably of the sixth century, found at Kuk Trap. The figure has a slightly dehanche posture, and at the side of one hip there is a big bow of drapery, which is obviously derived from a similar motif common on the sculptures of Mathura, in western India, during the second and third centuries A.D.

1. Cf. Majumdar, R.C., *HCRE*.

Another very Indian like figure is the torso of a female deity, in a markedly dehanche posture, found at Sambor Prei. The breasts are round, with marked cup like top surfaces, far more characteristic of India than the sloping breasts of other early Cambodian female sculptures. The best of these is perhaps the splendid Lakṣmī from Koh Krieng, probably made in the early part of the seventh century. The majestic goddess standing in a symmetrical, frontal posture makes no attempt to seduce the mind with smiling face or a 'hippy' pose. Nevertheless, the surface of the stone is carved with an intense sensual affection, for the gods and goddesses of Hinduism are meant to be physically adored. The still later, with its more decorative sinuous linear surfaces, lacks the lively monumentality of the Koh Krieng goddess.

The only masculine image which can rival this Lakṣmī in its monumentality is the great Harihara a compound icon of Śiva and Viṣṇu combined half and half of Prasat Andet, dating to about 700. A.D. It forms the chief item of a stylistic group centred on Prasat Andet. Characteristics of the male images are incised moustaches recalling the art of north-western India and a forehead peak on the mitre. This particular image has the same squared off section with deep side recessions, and the same sensuous surface, though the general expression is far more severe. The ankles are broken; but the feet are still present and apart from the forearms and hands, the sculpture is complete. Details such as the brief-loin cloth held by a chain is executed in the shallowest of relief. So is the coiled hair on Śiva's side of the mitre. Jewels are carved in the same way on other stylistically similar sculptures. But most of the body is turned into clear and emphatic volumes, not bulkyslender, in fact, but fully plastic.

There are many more of these grandiose images, male and female, some almost complete, some fragmentary or damaged. They vary in quality, and style evolves gradually towards the recognizable Khmer style of the ninth century. Gradually the volumes of the body, so clearly defined in the style closer to Fu Nan, weaken, and submit to a somewhat decorative, sinuous silhouette that encloses the figure. Earlier the eyes, the everted Melanesian lips and the strong pectorals were defined in terms of clear planes. Later the body becomes predominantly a softly undulant surf ace on which features are carried out almost as linear signs. Humps and hollows are both shallow. The folds or drapery become decorative patterns. But in spite of these changes, the original plastic inspiration remains, ready to blossom when opportunity offers.

The establishment of the Khmer empire in Cambodia was to some extent a function of Indonesian culture. There was, however, no invasion. The success of the Khmers was a native success, and amounted to a complete reorganization of the old Fu Nan-Chen La kingdom. The main architect of this success was Jayavarman II, who had lived a substantial part of his life in Java, at the Śailendra court. Jayavarman established the basic royal cult of the Khmers. He summoned a Brāhmin learned in the appropriate texts, and erected a liṅgam. This liṅgam, in which the king's own soul was held to reside, became the source and centre of power for the Khmer dynasty.

One of the Jayavarman-II's capitals was at Sambor. The temples he built with their sculptures there seem to have amounted to a revival of the old Chen La style. At Banteay Prei Nokar and Roluos (where he died) he also had old style temples constructed. But on Phnom Kulen, where the sacred liṅgam was set up, he seems to have ordered the first attempt to imitate the cosmic mountain in the form of the brick pyramid of his temple. In abouṭ A.D. 800 at another of his capitals, Amarendrapura he seems to have made a three-tiered brick pyramid crowned by a group of five shrines, dominating the plain. Even here the shrine architecture represents a continuation of the old Chen La pattern of tiers of diminishing repeats of the basic cell. But in the elaborate sculptured ornament of his temple Jayavarman made a radical departure. The Viṣṇu figures gradually dispense with the solid aureole supporting the arms. They show the Prasat Andet forehead peak, but their eyebrows gradually lose their clear bows and condense into a single continuous line. Although under Jayavarman the Khmer 'renaissance' cannot be said to have begun, the main lines of its inspiration had been laid down.

The real emergence of Khmer art began under Indravarman (877-89). This king is represented in the inscriptions he commissioned as a scholar as well as a successful ruler. He claims to have studied the monistic Vedānta philosophy of the great Indian Śankarācārya, with a Brāhmin learned in that tradition. He pacified the Khmer kingdom and his authority seems to have been recognized in the most distant parts of South-East Asia. But the achievement for which he is remembered today in his laying of the foundations of Angkor.

The Bakong was a more deliberately impressive work. It was intended to be Indravarman's own holy liṅgam shrine on top of its sacred mountain. The shrine was, like those of Preah Ko, of brick and stucco, and was replaced in the twelfth century. It stands on a series of sandstone terraces with four axial stair ways and a gate tower forty-seven feet high at the foot of each. It forms the centre of what must have been a most impressive group of eight brick shrines, set in an enclosure with gates, pavilions, and causeways over the moats lined with colossal Nāgas, and free-standing Garuḍas. There can be little doubt that the huge terraced pyramid was inspired by, if not so highly elaborated as the great ninth century Buddhist monument in Java, Borobudur.

The most important inventions of Indravarman's artists are the free-standing sandstone sculptures, especially the grouped figures. The Nāgas and Garuḍas of the Bakong causeway have been mentioned. They are, it is true, clumsy compared with later similar inventions. The Nāgas stretch like thick, serpentine rails flanking the approach roads, and the massive Garuḍas punctuate them at intervals. But this very idea—that sculptures of mythical beings should actually come down from the building and articulate into the everyday world the magical space of which the temple shrine is formed represents a major artistic achievement.

The large sculptures which now stand free, such as the Bakong Śiva or the goddesses, must once have been enclosed in vanished brick shrines. They dispense with the stone aureole supporting the arms and hands and exhibit the same sensuous continuity of surface as the great Chen La works, but they have also become more massive. Shoulders are broad, arms and legs especially the males' are thick. Faces have taken on an air of complacency, and the skill of their execution has become a familiar routine. The horizontal elements of brows, eyes, nose and mouth are stressed, and the whole figure is designed on the basis of squares. Movement is almost eliminated in favour of a self-satisfied calm. The tall cylindrical mitre of the males is narrower than the head, and seated into a prominent diadem. A striking feature of the whole style is the way in which, on to the broad, sensuously massive surfaces of the images, the folds of the waist cloth at the front of the belly and thighs effloresce into elegantly sinuous linear relief. On the Bakong Śiva a shallow fan of pleats projects on to the belly above the hip girdle, while below it extends sinuous pointed fans with rippled ends, half way to the knees. Female images show a long, central fan of pleats running to the ankles, and a special petal like swag of pleats folded down over from behind the girdle into a very feminine and suggestive loop, with a curvilinear pointed tail cast on one hip. All these ornamental motifs on the figure sculpture, like all the splendid Khmer foliate ornaments, follow undulant double curves slightly square in form.

The most interesting of Indravarman's sculptures is the colossal group of three figures on the Bakong which probably represents the king with two of his wives, one on each side, in the guise of Śiva with Umā and Gaṅgā. The heads of all the figures are missing and so are nearly all of their arms. But it is possible to see that the whole group was originally carved from a single block. Each of the goddess queens rests a hand on back of one of the god king's thighs, linking the group together. The better preserved of the female figures clearly shows the two long creases' essential to canocical beauty running along the breasts. The bellies of all are broad, encircled by the girdle. The side recessions of the figures are long, running far back in depth. When whole this group must have had a splendid, monumental presence.

With the death of Yasovarman, the great ruler whose plans could have been carried out only by means of fairly drastic, even tyrannous compulsion, heralded a phase of internal conflict in the kingdom. His brother Harsavarman-I reigned from 900 to 921, and built as his own temple mountain the Baksei Chamkrong, a superbly proportioned small pyramid entirely of stone, crowned by a single tower. In 921, however, one of his maternal uncles, Jayavarman-IV, split the kingdom, and set up a rival capital forty miles from Angkor, in the old Chen La country.[1]

The site he chose, now called Koh Ker, was irrigated by a similar though more modest baray. His son followed him as ruler in the new capital and a style of art evolved on many temples there, which, though now mostly destroyed, were chiefly of brick. The sculpture was somewhat less hieratic than Yasovarman's work. Male figures appear as well as female, wearing an enlarged and emphasized version of the deep petal like loop of front drapery worn by earlier female figures. But most interesting are the free standing sculptures found which depart from earlier canons. One of these is a four faced Brahmā, another a male divinity kneeling on one knee with the other cocked up forward. There is a gigantic pair of mythical wrestlers, and two Garuḍa birds chasing a Nāga. It was inevitable that the Khmer genius, which conceived its architecture as situated in an ambient space, should begin to conceive its sculpture in the same way.

In the 920s for the first time temples in many parts of Cambodia were dedicated by individuals other than the king. They belonged, no doubt, to the hereditary aristocracy; their shrines are rich and beautiful reflecting the general prosperity of the country, though the temple mountain remained the royal prerogative. One of the earliest of these independent foundations was the Prasat Kravan, a Viṣṇu temple dedicated in 921 by certain members of the nobility. This shrine, the upper storeys of which are ruined, is remarkable especially for its reliefs carved in the baked bricks of the tower. On the inner walls of the main tower are carved a series of icons of the different forms of Viṣṇu, complete with attendant figures and floridly ornamental haloes. On the walls of the north tower are reliefs of forms of his wife, Lakṣmī. The main figures stand formally, with toes turned outwards on their base lines. Their forms are simple, with only a few jewels and stylized pleats to decorate them. It is probable that these figures, indeed the whole of the shrines, were finished with a layer of fine lime and colour. Painted relief like this, based on a firm outline, comes close to the kind of painting which was practised in many countries of the Indian circle.

The greatest work of Khmer architecture and sculpture in the tenth century is a private foundation twelve miles north of Angkor—Banteay

1. Cf. Majumdar, R.C., *op. cit.*

Srei. On this building a style was perfected which marks a high point in the art of South-East Asia. It has survived the repeated reconstructions of Angkor only on two tiny shrines inside Angkor Thom. Everything about Banteay Srei is distinctive. It is full of inventions, and is splendidly elaborate in the best sense. The man who founded it was a Brāhmin, Yajñavarāha, who was himself of royal descent, and had been tutor to Rajendravarman and his son. His temple consists of three tower-shrines in line on a single terrace inside concentric enclosures which are pierced by gate pavilions. Around the shrines are other buildings, some with stone vaulted roots identified as libraries, and the remains of a pillared hall. On the terraces, groups of free-standing figures of mythical guardian animals are arranged. Pink sandstone was used throughout, and on the whole it is in an excellent state of preservation.[1]

The chief iconic image from the site is a splendid sculpture of Śiva seated, holding his wife Umā on his left knee. The massive cubical forms give a grandiose impression of power. But the bulk of the architectural invention was devoted to the huge gabled doorways. These are crowned with the usual ornate Khmer lintel. Above it usually towers a triple-tier of flamboyant double ogival arches, whose outer ends roll up to form Nāgas and Garuḍas, and whose deep curves erupt along their upper edge into a continuous row of upward pointing hands of foliage. Inside the lowest arch is a pediment bearing a figure relief of mythical scenes. The figures here are very lively, creating a strong sense of space. They converse or quarrel with each other recognizably. The narrative sense is strong. Sometimes the upper pediments contain figurative reliefs; here and there images of deities act as dies at the springing of the arch. The linear effect of the arches spreads beyond their termini into the ornament of roofs and facades. On the exterior gate pavilions an entirely original pattern of double arch is used. It is triangular, crowned with a lozenge panel set in a high, pointed cartouche; its ends curl up into sinuous volutes, and it is punctuated with rosettes. Finally, on the central sanctuaries the crowning tiers, like certain South Indian towers, are people with deities, each in his halo of fine ornament.

The sculptural style of Udayādityavarman's reign is both interesting and progressive. The stone relief carving, both of foliate ornament and of narrative with figures, has beautiful classical self-sufficiency. The ornament is never excessive, though the forms are full of life. The narratives devoted mainly to Kṛṣṇa show that the artists were capable not only of infusing the old conventions with new life, but of inventing entirely fresh compositions full of men and animals in vivid motion. The heads of the Brāhmaṇical icons which come from the various sites show that the artists

1. Rawson, Philip, *The Art of South-East Asia*, p. 39ff.

had a vision of the divine persons which included a strong sense of their physical presence. These are no routine formulae merely chopped out with skill. The correct iconic types are certainly followed, but the execution is imbued with tender solicitude for the actuality of flesh and bone. Even the linear conventions which govern the shaping of eyes and lips, derived ultimately from those of the Banteay Srei style, are carried out with modest care. The surface changes delicately from convex to concave, softly but at the same time with absolute formal accuracy. Such art can only be the result of inspiration and dedicated work in which time is no object.

One of the most interesting pieces of all is a fragmentary bronze bust, from the western Mebon, of the god Viṣṇu lying asleep on the ocean of non being. Head, shoulders and the two right arms survive. It shows the extraordinary, delicate integrity and subtle total convexity of surface which these sculptors could achieve by modelling. Eyebrows, moustache and eyes seem to have been inlaid, perhaps with gold, silver or precious stone, though the inlay is gone and only the sockets remain. This was one of the world's great sculptures. Another magnificent bronze of Śiva, from Por Lobeuk suggests the wealth of metal art that once must have existed in Cambodia at the height of its power. But metal is wealth, and invaders and pillagers have melted down all but a few scattered items. Rarely indeed can such a level of artistic achievement have been attained, only to be so thoroughly obliterated.

The whole enclosure of seventeen hundred by fifteen hundred years of Angkor Vat is surrounded by an external cloister. It is approached from the west by a magnificent road built on a causeway lined by colossal Nāga balustrades. Rows of lions guard the approach, and the causeway rises to a broad cruciform plateau on pillars guarded by Nāgas with raised hoods. At this level it penetrates the first of the two main rectangular enclosures which sanctify the shrine, through a towering gate pavilion whose winged roofs ride down in steps to the level of the enclosure roof. The enclosure is formed by high walls on a plinth, cloistered and roofed with stone.

The inner enclosure is yet another cloistered well, punctuated with corner towers, lesser gate towers, and towers where the three naves meet the doors in the enclosure wall. Inside the inner enclosure, the main entry rises by a magnificent flight of steps, flanked by two further pavilions, from the ground level to the summit of the three terraced mountain, on which stands the quincunx of towers. All are on a cruciform plan with gabled porches extending in the four cardinal directions. But the central tower the Śiva shrine is the most magnificent of them all. The tower spires have eight storeys and a crown, and are square, with a series of multiple recessed profiles and centre projections that makes them look octagonal. They show the full-fledged curved outline of a sprouting bud, which gives the impression that each storey is rising out of the one beneath. This impression, combined with the facade motifs of all the gable ends which have upturned corners and rise well beyond the ridges of their roofs is responsible for the extraordinary dynamic, rising effect of the structures.

The genius of the artists of that age was for relief. Indeed one might say that the Vat is a repertory of some of the most magnificent relief art the world has ever seen. The open colonnaded gallery on the first storey contains over a mile of such work, six feet high. Elsewhere appear those occasional groups and figures of divinely beautiful female courtiers, celestial courtesans, known to Brāhmaṇical tradition as apsarases, who are an essential ingredient in the Brāhmaṇical image of heaven, where all is pleasure without pain. The ultimate foundations of the style remain what they always were, securely Indian, reminiscent of the Pallava and Chola art in south-eastern India.

There is one further element in this relief style which is important, in a way in which it is not in the styles of Banteay Srei or the Baphuon. This is the element of expression derived from and related to the dance. One must suppose that in common with all other Indianized courts of South-East Asia, the Khmer court had imported and developed in its own way the traditions of the Indian dance. Even today similar traditions survive in Java, Bali, Burma, Thailand and Vietnam. The repertoire of costume, posture and significant gesture is bined at Angkor Vat with the use of the great legends of Brāhmaṇism as an immense fund of dramatic expression. But the strength of this figurative art is that it can combine into its dramatic image all sorts of additional elements such as chariots, horses, and crowds of fighting figures in a way impossible to the theatre.

The main sources for the relief subject matter are the *Mahābhārata* and the *Rāmāyaṇa*, as well as legends of Viṣṇu and his incarnation Kṛṣṇa. The wars of classical legend, in which incarnations of the various persons of the Brāhmaṇical deity triumph at length over demoniac adversaries, are obvious subjects for a king who regards himself as earthly incarnation of the deity to commission. The artists' extraordinary skill is everywhere apparent. Unfortunately, we know none of their names, for the only name to be mentioned in this kind of sanctuary must be the king's. But they were capable of creating in relief only about an inch deep an extraordinary complex of scenes: figures involved together in vigorous action, the air thick with banners, umbrellas and floating scarves. It is, of course, an art of outline, where the solid bodies are created mainly out of assemblies of convex curves, with here and there recurving pure concavities. But so skilful is the composition with its echoing and connecting curves that one has the impression that the whole relief forms part of a single massive chain of movement. The ground is filled with figures which, by their complex sequences of overlaps, produce convincing conceptions of spatial depth. Demoniac faces are so characterized; but most of the other faces as well as hands, feet and limbs, remain conventionalized, as they are in most Indianizing art.[1]

The meaning of Angkor Vat is probably best indicated by its facing west. It is a meaning which seems, in the historical context, ironically apt: for to the west lies the region of the dead. And among the reliefs is one panel devoted to the judgment of the dead by Yama, the Brāhmaṇical 'Lord of Death. The dead are, according to their merits, punished in a hell equipped with all kinds of hideous tortures, or carried off to the mountain peaks of heaven where the apsarases, filled with inextinguishable amorous desire, await them. It is clear that Suryavarman intended the Vat to be his own mortuary shrine; it is also clear that he intended it as a kind of premature wish fulfilment. He had constructed his heaven, complete with apsarases, before his death, as a visible demonstration that his nature was divine. Incarnate as Viṣṇu (his chosen personal deity) heaven would automatically be his after death.

The image of the Cosmic Nāga seems always to have been very important to the Khmers. The snake is always associated in Indian mythology both with the origin of things, and with the sources of the life giving water upon which the whole of life, in the high tropics, depends. Angkor itself, designed as a superb irrigation system, must obviously have been under the special protection of the greatest Nāga of them all Śeṣa, the emblem of infinite possibility, upon whom the god Viṣṇu, also long popular in Cambodia, reposes in one of his most important icons.[2]

2. CHAMPA

The Cham art seems to have followed its own course of evolution. Hence, before examining the Brāhmaṇical art of Champa, a few words must be said about the origin of her art. According to Parmentier the Cham art is not derived from any other known art: on the other hand, it is of indigenous growth and is derived from a wooden origin evolved on the soil itself.[3] But it is with great diffidence that we venture to differ from the opinion of one who had probably gone more deeply into the subject than any other living scholar. The derivation of Cham art from Brāhmaṇical art of India seems to us to be such an obvious fact that it appears impossible to accept the conclusions of M. Parmentier without demur.

1. Cf. Rawson, Philip, *op. cit.*, pp. 92-93.
2. Majumdar, R.C., *op. cit.*
3. Vide, Majumdar, R.C., *Champā*, Vol. I, pt. II, p. 271.

It may be stated at the very outset that we are in full agreement with the general principles laid down by Parmentier for guiding fruitful inquiry into the relation between two different systems of art. These may briefly be summarised in his own words as follows:

"In order to infer the relationship between two arts, it is sufficient merely to point out that both present the same tendencies and possess the same general features. But in order to prove that one system of art is derived from another, it is necessary to show that at the time which is either contemporary or anterior to the earliest specimens of the art which is supposed to be derived, the art supposed to be the origin possessed features common to the former."[1]

Having established this general principle, M. Parmentier proceeds to discuss whether the primitive style of Cham art has any common features with the art of Kambuja, Java or India as it existed in the seventh century A.D. He points out that Java may altogether be eliminated from the inquiry as its most ancient monument is posterior to this date. As regards Kambuja, the art of Angkor had not come into existence in the period in question, and the primitive Khmer art was not only very different from, but in a decidedly inferior state of development than, the primitive Cham art. Lastly, an examination of the Indian Brāhmaṇical monuments earlier than the seventh century A.D. has led Parmentier to conclude that with the exception of the curved roof, no typical element of Indian architecture appears in Cham style, nor is any typical motif of the Cham art traceable in the old Brāhmaṇical Indian style.

It is on this point that we must join issue with M. Parmentier. To us the characteristic feature of a Cham temple seems to be its storeyed roof of several stages, in gradually diminishing proportions, each of which is again a miniature of the whole. Now this is the characteristic feature of what is known as the Dravidian style and makes its appearance as early as the seventh century A.D. in the Mamallapuram Raths and the temples at Conjeeveram and Badami.[2] Any one who compares the Dharmarāja Rath and Arjuna Rath with the normal type of temples in Champa cannot but be struck with the essential resemblance between the 'śikharas' of the two. It may not also be uninteresting to note that the Dharmarāja Rath is expressly designated as a temple of Śiva named after the king as 'Atyantakāma Pallaveśvar', as was the case with the Myson temple which was known as that of Śambhu-Bhadreśvara after its founders.

Again, some of the temples of Champa have an elongated curved roof with ogival ends and this had its counterpart in the Gaṇeśa Rath and

1. Cf. Majumdar, R.C., *HCFE*, Chap., on Champa; also *Champa*, part II, p. 272.
2. Cf. Ferguson, *History of Indian and Eastern Architecture*, Vol. I, BK. III, Chaps. III-VII.

Sahadeva Rath. The type of śikharas, viz., the curved ones, resembles Draupadī Rath and is probably derived from those of North-Indian style, as Parmentier himself admits. The basement of the temples at Champa also resembles those at Conjeeveram and Badami. On the whole it seems impossible not to connect the style of Champa with the early Dravidian style both of which rise into prominence more or less about the same time. It is generally held that the rock cut raths at Mamallapuram and the other early temples of that type must have been preceded by similar structures of less imperishable materials and the existence of this style in India and probably even before the 6th century A.D. may therefore be regarded as a certain fact. While we remember that Indians from the eastern part played a prominent role in the colonisation of the Far East, and also the great extent to which Brāhmaṇical civilisation had influenced that of Champa, we need not hesitate to trace the origin of Cham style to Brāhmaṇical temples at Badami, Conjeeveram and Mamallapuram particularly as this part of India was the nearest by way of sea to the kingdom of Champa. It is quite true that the Chams did not blindly imitate the Indian prototypes and added new elements of their own, but the fact that their style was throughout based upon the essential and characteristic features of Brāhmaṇical style, seems to be beyond question.[1]

As in India, the art in Champa was mostly the handmaid of religion, and the people lavished their skill and resources mainly on religious edifices and images of gods and goddesses. The art of sculptor in ancient Champa may be studied under the following heads, viz., (A) human figures, (B) animal figures, (C) ornamental decorations.

Human figures in the art of Champa are either detached images or part of decorative elements in the temples. The images, again, are mostly either of gods and goddesses or of kings and queens.

The images of gods and goddesses have been described before. It is needless to say that they form the best specimen of the artistic activity of Champa. It is, of course, idle to expect that all the idols would show a degree of artistic skill, but some of them at any rate indicate the height of skill to which the sculptors of Champa had attained in this line of activity. The following may be selected as fair specimens.

Two standing images of Śiva in Myson

The images resemble each other to a great extent. The features, at least of the upper part of the body, are well proportioned and the expression of face is pleasing. The main defect of Brāhmaṇic sculptures, viz., the lack of accuracy in physical details, is also manifest in the art of Champa.

1. Cf, Majumdar, R.C., *op. cit.*

Even more beautiful than the preceding is an image of Skanda standing on his peacock. By the clever handling of the artist, the body of the peacock has been made the pedestal and its variegated train, a nicely decorated background, for the image of the youthful god. The pose and the expression of god are really charming. The seated image of a deity in Myson shows good proportions, but unfortunately the head is missing.

Like Brāmaṇical art, again, the images of gods in later periods became more and more deformed till they assumed sometimes a monstrous appearance. This is best seen in the figures of dvārapālas which adorned many temples.

The human figure forms the most distinguishing trait of decoration in the primitive art of Champa. It occurs almost in every part of the temple. in various forms and shapes, such as praying figures, persons mounted on gajasiṁha, apsarases, demons etc. Some of the figures show good proportions and arc really charming. Compare, for example, the exquisite figures of two musicians in Myson one playing upon lyre and the other upon a flute. The Cubic art employs human figures more sparsely. But some of them, the figure of dvārapāla, for example, in the false doorway of Hoa Lai, are fairly good.

The most interesting sculptures in temples occur on the Tympanums of outer doors which are mostly in stone. In the earlier period they were engraved with composite scenes in bas relief. As a general rule the principal figure occupied the centre, while the subsidiary figures were ranged on all sides. Two examples may be noted below.

1. *Tympanum of Myson*

In the centre, a pedestal, with Nandin sculptured in front, bears the image of dancing Śiva. The upper part of the image is unfortunately broken, but enough remains to show that the god had a necklace and several hands. There are three figures on each side of the central image. Of these to his proper right, the one nearest to him is dancing, while two others are playing on musical instruments viz., flute and kind of drum (tabalā). Of the three figures on the other side, a figure with joined hands probably stands for the king or the donor, while the other two, a female figure and an infant, probably represent Durgā and Skanda. Two trees on two sides, with a parrot on one of them, show that the scene is laid in an open ground. The upper part of the sculpture represents gods or apsarases flying through clouds. The whole composition is graceful and charming and reflects great credit on the artists of Champa.

2. *Tympanum of Khuong My Temple*

It represents Kṛṣṇa as holding aloft mount Govardhana in order to afford protection to the cows and cowherds. The mount Govardhana is indicated by a number of boulders with trees, deers and anchorites moving in them. The cows are shown below in several rows in their true perspective. Sometimes the tympanum contains one prominent figure only and this is usnally the case in later periods. These images are as a rule of inferior type. Two good examples are furnished by the image of Umā the Ghanh Lo and an image of Śiva in Po Klong Garai

Animals are figured as vāhana of gods, and they also occur in bas relief scenes. Animal figures also formed an important part in decoration in primitive art. We meet with a large variety of animals such as rhinoceros, lion, elephant, Gajasiṁha, Makara, Nāga, Garuḍa, bull, horse, hare, deer, goose, peacock and monkey. These are all made with a fair degree of success. Although conventional to a certain extent, the figures are not very far removed from nature. Special reference may be made to a monkey in the Myson temple D and the head of a lion in Myson K.

Later on, in Cubic art, for example, decorations by animal figures were reduced in quantity, being replaced in large measure by floral decorations. But, even the few representations of animals in buildings indicate clearly that the Cham artist had not lost their high skill. Some new species appear in this period viz., wild boar, dog and butterfly. In mixed art, the representations of animals are almost wholly absent.

During the second period the animal sculptures cease to play any important part in the decorations of buildings. We find only the friezes decorated by long rows of animals. Moreover, the representations of animals become gradually unnatural, conventional and ultimately hardly recognisable. It may be pointed out here that although the figures of lions are executed with great skill and form an important element in the decorations of temples, this animal was unknown in Indo-China. There can be hardly any doubt that its occurrence in decorations is due to the influence of Brāhmaṇical traditions. The same indeed may also be said of the mythical animals such as Makara, Nāga, Garuḍa, etc. The Gajasiṁha is, however, a peculiar creation of the Chams. It is composed of the body of a lion with the head of an elephant.

The bull appears more as a vāhana of Śiva than a pure decoration and as in India, detached images of this animal are often met with in temples. Certain birds and animals appear only once or twice in bas-relief scenes and do not otherwise play any important part in the art of Champa. Among these may be mentioned squirrel, tiger, parrot, fish and tortoise.

Ornamental Decorations

The Cham artists excelled in floral decorations. Although they treated foliage in a conventional manner, they added an element of grace and beauty which made it highly charming. This is particularly the case in the

Primary Art. The number of specimens collected by Parmentier shows the high degree of excellence that the Chams had attained in this direction. The style is purely Brāhmaṇic and we find here the same "undulating stem of a creeper with large curling and intertwining level.[1] Most of the foliage patterns occur on pillars and pilasters, and are in the shape of scrolls; sometimes, as in India, "the whole scroll is deeply sunk and very clearly and carefully carved". Sometimes the foliage is of an intricate and complex design, but the Cham artists show high skill in handling it. But here, as in other instances, the history of the art of Champa, like that of India, is written in decay. We miss the vigour and refinement of the early patterns in those of succeeding ages which gradually become lifeless and mechanical in the extreme. In the second period when the art of floral decoration was at low ebb and the pilasters were mostly plain, we meet, instead, with geometrical patterns which although lacking the grace and charm of old, are not altogether devoid of aesthetic elements.

Thus the glory of Cham art is undoubtedly the sculpture of this first period, up to the end of the tenth century. Much of it consists of lesser figures that form part of the architectural decor. There are heads of makaras, dragons and other beasts which appeared at corners on the architraves of shrines, and figures of lions which supported bases and plinths. These share the heavy ornateness of the Cham decorative style.

Certain busts of celestials with joined hands served a similar purpose. They are distinguished by their crude finish, and by the deeply cut, somewhat lumpish Cham cartouches composing the crowns they wear. Figures in plaques from the bases of pillars are found, such as a couple of wrestlers carved in relief. But the most striking architectural adornments have a quality all their own. The best is the capital from Tra Kieu which carried a musician and a couple of dancing girls meant to be celestial apsarases. The postures and surface of the two divine beauties have been captured with an extraordinarily sensual charm. They seem to be clothed in nothing but strings and strings of pearls, though probably they are supposed to be wearing clothes of the fine Indian gauze, which appear only in the knotted fans at their hips. The double joined gesture of an arm and the soft roundness of the bodies evoke a vivid response.

Of the major iconic sculptures, the great liṅgam icons standing on carved pedestals are the most austere. The pedestal may show rows of fantastic beasts, deities or dancing celestials, carved in relief. The liṅgam itself may emerge from discs of ornament, one of which represents an opening lotus, symbol of the feminine principle of the universe. A pedestal which probably served as an altar for icons from My Son shrine, shows a

1. Cunningham's description of Gharwa Temple. *ASR*, Vol. III—Quoted in V.A Smith's *Fine Art in India and Ceylon*, p. 166.

series of little figures of ascetics seated, among ornament, under Cham versions of Indian toraṇa arcades, while at its two ends, celestials make expansive gesture towards the images. Several figures of Śiva survive. The bodies are relatively simplified and subordinated to a roughly cut sinuosity. The ornamental haloes feature worm like ornament. The faces bear an expression of ferocity, with the everted Cham lops under moustaches heavily stressed, conveying an impression of uncoordinated vigour. There seems in these to be a strong influence from Indonesian art. One Viṣṇu, from Da Ngi, and certain Buddhist images Lokeśvara show strong elements of Fu Nan-Chen La style. Again it is the charm of the feminine icons which is most likely to find a response today. One, of exceptional beauty, comes from Huong Qua; others, less fine perhaps, from several sites. From Dong Duong comes a half life size Buddha figure, and various other images, including an impressive one of Śiva.

3. *BURMA*

There is a large number of temples in Burma with the images of gods and goddesses. Brāhmaṇical as all these images are, it is only too natural to infer that the artistic tradition responsible for them is esssntially Indian. Such, indeed, it is; but deeper have we to dive to discover the affinity and influence of particular schools and period of Indiaṇ art which might have been responsible for their inspiration. We have to begin with the Arakan images which we consider to be the earliest in Burma.

The two Arakan images studied in these pages are so badly defaced and mutilated that it is difficult to make a correct consideration of their artistic peculiarities. But our task becomes somewhat easier if we admit into our consideration two other stone sculptures, one representing a Nāga king, and a nother a Deva belonging to the same period and coming from almost the same locality, namely, from the ruins of the Mahāmuni pagoda, Arakan. They bear oṇ them a distinct stamp of what we call late Gupta tradition of art. The physiognomy of the face of the Nāga king and the Deva, the misunderstood position of their feet, and the head-dresses that crown their heads are distinctly local; but the soft and lively modelling of their body, the pleasing curves of their face and arms and their sympathetic response in the curves of their ornaments, the easy flow of their lines that glide softly over the hard stone, and lastly, their composition that is at once pleasing and convincing leave no scope for doubt as to their source of inspiration. And what is easily noticed on these two sculptures is equally present and can be made out, though with difficulty, on the Sūrya and the Devī images too. Portions of the body that are intact, distinctly show the same convincing character of its composition, the same soft and lively modelling, and easy flow of lines which are rich and abiding legacies of the Gupta tradition of art. But the exquisitely feminine grace as well as the most subtle and sensitive modelling of the early period of that school are missing in them. This is exactly what it should be, and it helps us to place the Arakan sculptures in a line with the later Gupta sculptures of the 7th and 8th centuries A.D., examples of which are abundant in Eastern India and Assam.

Another remarkable sculpture from the artistic point of view is the Viṣṇu-Lakṣmī slab from Hmawza belonging to a period not later than the 8th century A.D. This finely and delicately modelled sculpture has apparently the grace and softness of a Gupta example; but a closer analysis would show that its source of inspiration is not the one that is responsible for the Arakan images. In fact it owes its existence to a different school of art on this side of the Bay, namely, the Pallava school, and has consequently, those Gupta features in its form and execution that are inherent in the Pallava school. The most arresting feature of this sculpture is the elongated appearance of the two figures and their supple but bold and rounded legs and arms with their bones and muscles so suppressed as to provide them with a soft grace coupled with a dignified composure. These characteristics, as well as a consideration of their physiognomical features and of the relation of their body and garments, cannot but suggest a very close affinity with the Pallava tradition of art.

It is not unlikely, and careful artistic consideration leads us more to infer that these sculptures were works of Indian traders or priests or colonists in pursuit of their respective vocations of life. But side by side there was also a local artistic activity fostered, no doubt, by the Indian masters. These local artists, who are reponsible for many Buddhist images of stone and terra cotta that have come down to us must have also been entrusted with the task of executing Brāhmaṇical images examples of which have survived to this day. At least two such examples are known from Hmawza. The very crude and rough execution of an Indian subject-matter, the physiognomy of their faces, the quaint expression of a foolish smile on their lips and not the least, the dress of the divinity standing on his vāhana Garuḍa have all combined to give an un-Indian character to their appearance. The treatment of the subject-matter is equally foreign to any known school or period of Indian art; the rigid lines and the sharp angularities, the incoherent composition, the schematic surface-treatment of the reliefs and not the least the soulless and meaningless decorations on them are all responsible for the lifeless, almost wooden, atmosphere in which they live. They are mere translations of a canonical test. But here and there cling faint traces, e.g., in the modelling of the body and treatment of the face of the standing Viṣṇu, of the lessons they received at the feet of their Indian teachers.

The three Thaton bas-reliefs as well as the smaller slabs of stone described in a preceding chapter belong to what we may call the mediaeval period. The three larger slabs have attained different standards of artistic excellence and it is most likely that they belong to the same school of art and the same period of artistic activity comprising roughly the 9th and 10th centuries A.D. In the two Viṣṇu reliefs the subject matter is the same and their iconographic representation is practically of the same kind, but there is considerable difference in their artistic treatment. The larger relief is very badly corroded, but it is not very difficult to ascertain that the modelling of the individual figures of both the reliefs is of the same quality : the treatment of the volume by a schematic arrangement of the figures as well as the general linear composition of the reliefs also differ very little. But it is in the treatment of the surface that the main difference lies. The smaller slab is divided into three, strictly speaking four distinct parallel surfaces schematically arranged and each carved individually almost on the same plane and in comparatively less bold relief with the result that there is hardly any scope for the display of light, and shade. It is the treatment of the volume that sets apart each individual surface, not a skilful distribution of light and shade. There is very little scope for contrast in the carving of the different planes of the relief, and the eyes glide from one surface to another slowly and smoothly. But the larger relief at once convinces one of the more technical artistic efficiency of the artist. His sure chisel has been able to carve in different planes and each plane in comparatively bolder relief, and no opportunity has he missed to distribute his larger surfaces on the different planes into as many smaller ones as he could. He has used his subject-matter in a most intelligent and therefore artistic form by introducing elements which he could well leave out. This is evident in the representation of water suggested by lilies and lotuses carved on a lower plane of the relief which on the smaller slab has been left bare. A comparison of the surface treatment of the two reliefs is still better seen in the representation of the lotus seat (padmāsana); on the smaller slab the petals are arranged in one surface and are indicated almost in outlines. While on the larger one the petals are arranged in a double surface and indicated in separate boldly carved petals. The attitude of the two artists is best seen in the comparative treatment of the uppermost portion of the smaller relief and the lowermost portion (i.e. the pedestal) of the larger relief. On the former, the volume of sine has been distributed in three low-carved steles left bare. Such a treatment the artist of the larger relief could never tolerate; this is evident from the fact that he has not even suffered to leave bare the lowermost portion of his large slab of stone, a portion unclaimed by his subject-matter. But artistic consideration has necessitated him to carve it not only in deep square panels displaying a nice systematic contrast of light and shade, but also in long parallel lines. This difference in treatment of the surface alone is responsible for the world of difference in the artistic effect of the two reliefs. Thus, one is neat but schematic, lifeless, mechanical and is, therefore, a mere translation of its subject matter, the other is more lively, more animated more resourceful, more pleasing, more expressive and is therefore, entirely a new creation.

But the most artistic of the three reliefs and one of the best examples of mediaeval relief sculptures in India and Burma is the one that represents Śiva seated with his consort Pārvatī. The whole stele is occupied by the god alone and Umā plays only a minor part throwing herself in the background. But how well-planned complex is the composition that she merges in the linear arrangement of the two left hands and the leg of her lord. Her head and left hand with a portion of her body is carved on the same plane as that of the body and hands of Śiva but the remainder of her whole person shifts itself on a deeper plane in a position that is in rhythmic response with the left side of the body of the god. The linear composition of the relief is effected mainly by the portion of the four hands and the two legs; and this linear movement regulates the mass that is distributed in three bold surfaces, one at the top comprising the two upper hands and the head, one at the right comprising the two right hands, the right leg and the right side of the body, and a third at the left comprising the left hand, the left leg, the left portion of the body of the god and finally the whole person of Pārvatī. There is another surface that comprises the pedestal containing the lotus design, the bull and the buffalo. These four surfaces, we have already said, have been carved in different planes, all in bold and round reliefs. But most remarkable is the complex linear composition referred to above. The two upper hands raised upwards and in angular curves, we find their happy response in the two hands lowered down in delightful lines and soft curves ending in the supple movement of their figures. The surface comprising the head with its halo and mukuṭa comes down to rest on the body up to the waist-zone and then dividing itself into two, takes a linear movement in two directions, the right one is a sympathetic response with the raised right hand and the left one with the raised lower hand and the pedestal below. Thus, in the soft but bold and masculine modelling of the body, in the distribution of the mass, in the very difficult surface-treatment in different complex planes resulting in a rich display of light and shade, and finally in the complex linear composition of the whole relief, this sculpture shows the artistic efficiency of the colonial artists at their very best.

These three reliefs have a close affinity with those lately discovered by Rai Ramaprasad Chandra Bahadur from different sites of Orissa and now deposited in the Indian Museum, Calcutta. In fact, so remarkable is the affinity that one who is not told of the find spot and the story of its discovery, is apt, at a first study of the Śiva-Pārvatī stele, to style it as

Orissan of the 9th and 10th centuries A.D.[1] Moreover, this particular relief has also a considerable iconographic affinity with a Śiva-Pāravatī relief (Indian Museum, ex. No. 33/N.S. 2222) discovered along with the images and reliefs just referred to. In form and appearance, in modelling and composition and in their general treatment and execution, these reliefs, at least the Śiva-Pārvatī and the larger Viṣṇu reliefs, have a striking similarity with the Orissan sculptures referred to, and it is difficult to discard our assumption that these are certainly works of artists who had migrated from Orissa, then rich in her art-tradition and general culture.

The Nāt-halaung images undoubtedly belong to the mediaeval period, about a century and half later than the Thaton reliefs. The South Indian Tamil inscription, palaeographically dated in the 13th century A.D. records the gift by a Vaiṣṇav saint, a native of Cranganore in Malabar, of a maṇḍapa in the temple of Nānādesī Vinnagar Alvar at Pagan. "Nānādesī Vinnagar", says Hultzsch, "means the Viṣṇu temple of those coming from various countries. This name shows that the temple, which was situated in the heart of the Buddhist country of Burma, had been founded and resorted to by Vaiṣṇavas from various parts of the Indian Peninsula."[2] Mon. Duroiselle is perhaps right in asserting that the Vaiṣṇava temple mentioned in this epigraph refers to the Nāthalaung temple which he is inclined to assign to the 13th century A.D. The temple cannot, in our opinion, if we are to judge by the sculptures in its niches as well as by the architectural style, date later than the middle of the eleventh century A.D.[3]

In view of the fact that a Tamil inscription has been discovered in the debris of the temple purporting to relate that the temple had been founded and resorted to by Vaiṣṇavas from various parts of the Indian Peninsula and that the iconography of some of the images (e.g. the Sūrya) are distinctly South Indian, it is only natural to conclude at once that the Nāt-halaung images owe their artistic inspiration to contemporary South Indian school of art. Had it been so, our problem would have been as easy as one can naturally expect under such circumstances. Unfortunately, such an assumption is not borne out by a careful consideration of the sculptures themselves.

These images are very badly defaced, and it is difficult to make a systematic artistic survey of each individual image. But the general features and characteristics are easily recognisable from what remains of some of them, e.g., the Kalki, the Sūrya, the Rāmacandra and the Paraśurāma images. The hard but lively modelling of the body, the regular lines that control the slim arms and legs and the gradual attenuating curve from the

1. Cf. Ray, N.R., *Brahmanical Gods in Burma*, pp 78-79.
2. *An. Rep. A.S. India*, 1932-13, pp 136-37,
3. Cf. Ray, N.R., *op. cit.*, p. 79.

'chest to the waist broadening itself downwards on the hips, at once turn our eyes and attention to the large number of sculptures of the Eastern school of art of the Pālas and Senas of Bengal and Bihar whose rule comprised the centuries from the 9th to the 12th. Our surprise increases all the more when we consider the physiognomy of the face and the body and discover its close affinity with that of the sculptures of the particular school referred to. They have all slim but well proportioned arms and legs, a broad chest that gradually merges itself in an attenuated waist and a pair of well balanced hips. Their head-dresses and ornaments too are strikingly similar, and it is particularly noticeable in the heavy ear-rings, armlets, wristlets and finally in the fluttering scarves over the two shoulders, a feature that is hardly missed in the Buddhist and Brāhmaṇical images of the Eastern school. But we become almost certain of our assumption when we notice the closest affinity of their facial treatment. It is roundish with a pointed chin and the two lips, the lower one of which is slightly modelled in a rounded curve, are drawn downwards to give a smile of bliss and contentment. A not very sharp nose finishes itself up into two faintly modelled curves of eyelashes that give a restful shade to the half closed eyes below and a pointed downward motion to the broad forehead above. Thus from the point between the two eyelashes to the pointed chin there is a downward motion relieved only by the rounded cut of the face. All these are characteristic features of the Eastern school of art revealed in innumerable Buddhist and Brāhmaṇical images found all over the area that comprise the modern provinces of Bihar and Bengal.

It is indeed surprising how in a temple that is supposed to have been built and patronised by Brāhmaṇas from South India and where the iconography of the images is South Indian, the images themselves happen to be works belonging to, or deriving their inspiration from, a school of art in Eastern India. But, howsoever surprising it might be, our finding can scarcely be doubted, and if we are to accept it, the conclusion becomes inevitable that services of artists imported from Eastern India or at least trained in the art tradition of that particular school must have been requisitioned by the South Indian masters who had most probably been responsible for the building and up-keep of the temple itself.[1]

To this tradition of art, though undoubtedly to an earlier date must also belong the seated images of Brahmā now in the Pagan Museum. The figure is badly damaged, but enough remains to show the soft texture of its modelling, the masculine vigour of the physiognomical form, the bold but graceful lines that regulate the mass, the surface treatment of the face that has delighted in a display of light and shade by means of deep chiselling in bold and logical curves which is responsible for the decidedly Indian

1. Cf. Ray, N.R., *op. cit.*, p. 81.

expression of the face, and lastly the well balanced, though not original, composition of the whole stele. The facial and the bodily type and the character of the modelling and general treatment take us so near the comparatively early examples of the Eastern School of art that a very close affinity between the two art traditions cannot but very naturally suggest itself.

But these remarks cannot be applicable to the standing Śiva image of Pagan, belonging undoubtedly to a period not earlier than the 13th century A.D. Unlike that of the Nāt-halaung images the material of this sculpture is a kind of very soft sandstone, and the modelling is somewhat hard and stiff. The two arms modelled in the round are heavy and the legs both heavy and static. The pose and composition are conventional and the treatment of the surface does not show very strong contrast of light and shade. The elaboration of ornamental details which are here conspicuous by their presence is a characteristic feature of late mediaeval sculptures, and the static heaviness invariably reminds one of late South Indian, especially Cola, examples with which the present icon has a close affinity.

Regarding the artistic consideration of other minor images, stone or bronze, we have hardly anything to say more than what we have already said in the preceding pages. They have scarcely any artistic justification, and their interest is mainly historical and iconographical. The Tennasserim images, the bronze Viṣṇu from Myinkaba, Pagan, and the miniature Gaṇeśa and other sculptures are almost all late South Indian, but were in most cases locally cast or carved. They are works not of any particular school or schools of art that flourished in the Peninsula, but of local craftsmen called to serve by South Indian masters who had been there for purposes of trade and commerce.

Considered from the viewpoint of both art and iconography of the images studied and described in these pages, Brāmaṇical element in Burma seems to have made its mark at least as early as the 6th century A.D., and continued to have its share of influence on the people up to at least the 14th. But it should distinctly be understood that this element was more or less confined to the Indian section of the population, and we have as yet no evidence at hand to show that Brāhmaṇism could never replace Buddhism which was the religion of the state as well as of the people in general. Brāhmaṇism was obviously the religion of the Indian minority who had been given the right of freedom of worship according to their own choice and belief. And as Buddhism in Burma was not exclusive at the beginning, it was possible for some of the Brāhmaṇical gods to be incorporated into their legends (e.g., the Mahapienne=Gaṇeśa), as well as in some of the Buddhist temples as subsidiary deities (e.g., in the Shwesandaw, the Nanpaya, etc.)

Brāhmaṇical element in Burma during the early days of her history seems to have been confined to Arakan on one side and to Lower Burma, i.e., the kingdom of Hmawza on the other. In Arakan the artists responsible for these images came along with people who had migrated from Eastern India, and at Hmawza, most probably, from the Pallava country, the former, obviously, by the land route and the latter by sea. Arakan, in those days, formed more a part of the Indian frontier than a province of Burma, and relations and intercourse with Bengal and Assam were far more frequent that we can possibly imagine. Numismatic evidence have proved that a Brāhmaṇical dynasty of kings whose names end with Candra ruled over Arakan from at least the 5th to about the 11th century A.D.[1] Sanskrit inscriptions palaeographically dated from the 7th to the 10th century A.D. have been discovered at and near about Mrohaung, the capital city of Arakan, and the script is decidedly of the later Gupta and early Pāla periods.[2] Old Prome, and for that matter, Lower Burma was during the 6th, 7th and 8th centuries of the Christian era dominated by an Indian dynasty of kings known as the Vikrama dynasty.[3] It was most probably under the aegis of this dynasty that Brāhmaṇism made its mark in Lower Burma, and the images discovered at the site of the capital city are no doubt contemporaneous. But it is difficult to ascertain from which part of India this Hinduised dynasty had migrated into the Peninsula. The Viṣṇu-Lakṣmī slab shows Pallava affinities but evidence of Pallava relations with Burma are but scanty, though the Indian colonies of Champa and Kambuja, Java, Sumatra and Malay owe much to Pallava enterprise. In fact, the earliest epigraphic record found in Indo-China is in the early Pallava script, and the monuments of Champā and Java are definite proof of much that is borrowed from the Pallavas. The Pallavas maintained an active maritime commerce but no evidence has yet been furnished to show any attempt at any systematic colonial or commercial enterprise in this 'land of gold'. There might have been some floating companies planted on the coastal regions of Peninsula, but they have left very little trace and have hardly left any marked influence on the history of any period of Burmese culture and civilization. But mention must here be made of the

1. *Coins of Arakan, Pegu and Burma*, Phayre, *op. cit.*
2. *An. Rep. A.S. Burma*, 1923pp. 27-28 and 1926, p. 28.
3. *An. Rep A. Burma*, 1924, p. 23. Quite recently has been discovered at Hmawza line of inscription in Pyu around the lower rim of a votive stupa. The inscription contains two names, Srī Prabhuvarma and Srī Prabhudevī, which seem to be the titles of the king then reigning and his queen. The name-ending Varman is interesting; for royal titles ending in Varman are frequently met with in South Indian History. Specially in the dynasty of the Pallavas, as well as in those of some of the colonial Indian royal dynasties of Indo-China and Indonesia (An. *Rep. A.S. India*, 1926-27, p. 171ff).

discoveries made at Hmawza (old Prome) of two gold plates, three fragments of a stone inscription, a small votive stūpa, and a gold-leaf manuscript, all bearing Pāli inscriptions in a script very closely allied to the Canara-Telegu script of the 5th and 6th centuries A.D.[1] Stone and terra cotta sculptures bearing unmistakable traces of Gupta influence have also been discovered in the same locality.[2]

4. SIAM

The task of presenting a study of Brāhmaṇical influence on Siamese art is arduous unlike that of Javanese or Cambodian, because in Java and Cambodia, the population after the Indian advent did not undergo noteworthy changes, and art followed a comparatively regular evolution. But, Siam has risen on the ruins of several Indianised kingdoms. Before their conquest and absorption by the Siamese in the thirteenth century, those states had ample time to evolve and develop their own artistic traditions (which later shared in the formation of Siamese artistic ideals) and to produce works whose remains co-exist within the limits of Siamese borders with purely Siamese monuments. Reginald Le May while surveying the sculpture in Siam points to no less than nine schools, viz., (i) Pure Indian, (ii) Mon-Indian, (iii) Hindu-Javanese, (iv) Khmer and Mon-Khmer, (v) Khmer-Thai traditions (U Tong), (vi) Thai (Lopburi), (vii) Thai (Sukhodaya), (viii) Thai (northern), and (ix) Thai (Ayuthia).[3]

Moreover; the Siamese art developed from the very beginning of the epoch when the Hindu and the Buddhist missionaries from India went to Indo-China and preached their own doctrines there. Their activities began particularly with the growth of the Mauryan empire in India which culturally far extended beyond the present limits of the country. It is very likely that emperor Aśoka spread the gospels of Buddhism even in Burma, Siam, and Malay. Likewise, in the later Nāga and Gupta ages the Brāhmaṇical Hinduism got a firm footing in the Indo-Chinese peninsula on account of the renewed colonial zeal of the nations of coastal India and the vigorous foreign policy laid down by the family of Samudragupta. As the result of cultural enterprises from the side of the intellectual Indians a fine and sensitive art had its birth on the fascinating soils of the Menam-Valley, which may even vie in beatitude with the well-known arts of Java, Cambodia, Pagan (Burma) and Bali.

The real spirit of the Siamese art of both the schools of the earlier Mon-Khmers and Lawas, (who were responsible for the growth of the

1. *An.Rep. A.S. Burma*, 1924, pp. 21-23; *An. Rep. India*, 1926-27, p. 171ff.
2. Also see Thakur, U., "Elements of Hindu Culture in Burma". in *India's Contribution to World Thought and Culture*, ed. Lokesh Chandra, pp. 437-444.
3. For details of these nine schools, see Le May, Reginald, *The Culture of South-East Asia*.

ancient culture of Siam up to the 13th century A.D.) and of the later Thais lies Indian *Silpa Śāstras,* but in its strange subtlety, originality and refinement, which have undoubtedly made possible the creation of the fine monuments in ancient and in modern Siam. Many of the unadored and dilapidated relics of Siam are still bespeaking of the grandeur and magnificence of the ancient culture of the country, which certainly occupied a glorious chapter in the history of the Far-East.

The Mons/or the Talaings, the Khmers and the Lawas were responsible for the growth of the ancient culture of Siam up to the 13th century A.D., when the Thais, hailing from Nan-Chao in South China, invaded and gradually conquered Siam. Although the Thais were victorious, they never hesitated to imbibe the cultural wealth indirectly bequeathed to them by the Mons, the Khmers and the Lawas. Thus, the 13th century A.D. stands as the period of cultural transition in the history of Siam and some of her neighbouring countries (viz. Shan-States, Kelantan, Trengganu, Laos, Cambodia, Tenasserim etc.). In this respect the Thais may be compared with the White Huns or the Epthalites of the ancient days who although had entered India as conquerers very quickly turned to be zealous admirers of Brāhmaṇism and eventually became the very guardians of the Brāhmaṇical civilisation and culture by shielding them from the onslaughts of Muslim iconoclasticism. In the very same way, by dint of their superior culture, the vanquished Mon-Khmers absorbed the Tibeto-Burman Thais into their own culture and civilization. For that reason the Thai art may be rightfully declared as an aspect of the re-oriented continuation of the earlier Mon-Khmer and Lawa culture.

The vast ruins of the Mon-Khmer civilisation in Siam may be seen in the ancient cities like Lopburi, Muang Singh, Petchaburi (Sanskrit, Vajrapuri), Phimai (Bhimapura ?) and Viṣṇulok (i.e. the city of Viṣṇu). The Khmer temples are marked with the Indian architectural techniquc having floral decorations and cruciform śikhar's or spires. In short, the Khmer temples can be hardly differentiated from their Indian prototypes.

There are definite archaeological evidences which go to prove that the Khmer Art indirectly got some of its inspirations from Bengal. The Buddhist mahānāvikas (great sea-captains) and missionaries of this country kept on regular cultural and commercial intercourses with Burma, Siam, Mergui, Malay, Indonesia and Cambodia. If the Mauryan missionaries really went to Suvarṇabhūmi, it is very likely that they sailed from coastal Bengal. Now, the art of Bengal influenced the art of Siam, particularly, from the 8th century A.D. onwards when the Mahāyāna and the 'tāntrik' Buddhism first began to develop in Eastern India. This religion of the 'Greater vehicle' (Mahāyāna) travelled to the interiors of the trans-Gangetic India from Bengal being greatly fostered by the dynasties of the Khaḍgas, the Candras and the Pālas. One of the principal items of this eclectic conception was the identification of Śiva with Buddha in a particular iconographic form known as Avalokiteśvara or Lokeśvara. This divinity has been imagined as a sublime manifestation of Dhyānī Buddha Amitābha (literally meaning, the meditating Buddha of the eternal light), who bestows his divine mercy upon mankind, both good and bad. Like Mahādeva he prefers poison (halāhala) to ambrosia for the benefit of the suffering mankind. In the Pāla-Sena epoch, this sublime conception of Avalokiteśvara of Lokanātha became popular in Bengal and the cult possibly reached Siam-Cambodia in the contemporary period when under the patronage of Jayavarman VII, the great temple of Angkor Thom was raised on the evergreen soil of Cambodia. The culminating sculpture beauty of this lay in the four faces of the god carved on the four sides of the temple arch, looking in all directions, perhaps, in sympathetic look over the mundane sorrow. Possibly, due to the introduction of this Mahāyānic idea in Indo-China, Mahādeva is still so very popular in Siam along with Buddha. Apart from this the influence of pure Brāhmaṇism in ancient Siam is reflected in many images of Viṣṇu, Lakṣmī, Gaṇeśa and Ardhanārīśvara discovered in the various parts of the territory.

The temple-architecture of early Siam affords curious blend of the art of many neighbouring countries, like Cambodia, Pagan (in Burma), India and Ceylon, with whom she came into a regular contact. Thus, Percy Brown points out while referring to the architecture of the famous Mahā Thāt (Mahādhātu i.e. Great Relic) temple at Svargalok (Swankalok)[1] that the "tower or śikhara shows an affinity to those erected in the tenth and eleventh centuries by the Pālas of Bengal and its detailed treatment to those of Angkor in Cambodia or the Bhuvaneśwar temples of Orissa in Eastern India."[2] But, at this point, we should admit that, although, the Siamese architecture was often influenced in this way by the building techniques of other foreign nationals it remained, nevertheless, as the fruition of an imagination untouched with any monotony of style or technique. The ruins of the brilliant and massive sanctuaries at ancient Phimai, Śrī Deva, Viṣṇulok, Nakhon Pathom, Vajrapuri, Muang Singh, Lopburi, Sukhothai, Ayuthia, and other places still remain as silent witnesses of the creative magnificence of the early and present inhabitants of Siam.

Possibly, the earliest traces of Brāhmaṇical influence may be discovered in the ruins of Pong Tuk (100 miles N.W. from Bangkok), Nakhon Pathon and in the Peninsular Siam. As Percy Brown points out "a small model found at Kedah recalls the system of roofs reproduced in the monolithic

1. Probably built in the 12th century A.D.
2. *Indian Architecture*, ch. XXXVII.

temples at Mamallapuram (Madras, 7th century) for example those of the rathas of Bhīma and Gaṇeśa."[1]

The architecture of Siam during the period between circa 1000 and 1300 A.D. may be to some extent designated as "Mon-Khmer", as it was also partly influenced by the early art of the Mons, which in its turn was stimulated by the art of Pagan in Central Burma. In short, it may be observed that the Mon-Khmer art of Siam was chiefly inspired by the motifs of Angkor and Pagan. The introduction of "Amalāśila" or "Āmalaka" on the top of the Khmer temple of Mahā Thāt at Lopburi was perhaps a sign of freedom of the Siamese artists from the monotonous architectural formula of the Cambodian Khmers.[2] During this Mon-Khmer epoch the art and architecture of Pāla Bengal probably influenced the art and architecture of Siam. As an example, the bas-reliefs of a temple at Phimai show remarkable Bengali influence of the Pāla period. As Percy Brown remarks "the temple at Phimai, the earliest is richly decorated with carving in bas-relief, some of the patterns both in design and modelling being almost exact replicas of similar ornamentation on the remains of the Pāla structures at Gaur in Bengal of the ninth century."[3] The *Rāmāyaṇic* scenes, which are depicted in the bas-reliefs on the walls of some temples at Phimai peculiarly resemble the *Rāmāyaṇic* scenes as depicted on many temples of mediaeval Bengal.[4] Particularly, the bas-reliefs on a dilapidated stone linted in the ruined city showing the fight between Rāma and Rāvaṇa bear a very close resemblance with many similar temple reliefs of Bengal and Cambodia.

These śikharas of the stone sanctuaries of the period of the Cambodian overlordship in Siam, are generally of cruciform type more or less with the shape of a betel leaf. But the introduction of a sort of "amalāśila" on the apex makes a slight curve on the top. This may be discerned, particularly, in the design and type of the well-known sanctuaries of Wat Mahā Thāt and Wat Phra Prāng Sām Yot at Lopburi.

With the coming of the Thais in the 13th century this temple architecture gradually underwent change with the effect that the śikharas (Phra Prāng) started to be of less and less dimensions in breadth. Thus, after the lapse of few centuries, the Siamese temple arches looked like elongated domes. Here, we can roughly ascertain the chronology of the Khmer Thai and Thai monuments by a study of the breadth of the "Phra Prāng".

1. *op. cit.*, p. 216, For the excavations at Pong Tuk, see Le Reginald.
2. Brown, Percy, *op. cit.*, p. 227. Khmers used laterite stones in this epoch to build their monuments in Siam.
3. *op. cit.*
4. For the description of Phimai, see Major Erik Seidenfaden "An Excursion to Phimai, a temple in the Khorat province", *JSS*, Vol. XVII.

After a study of the numerous śikharas in Siam, one may come to a general conclusion, although not too decisive, to the fact that the broader is the Prāng, the earlier is the age of the temple. At present, the Prāngs or śikharas in Bangkok look like narrow and lofty Śivaliṅgas. In fact, these so-called Śivaliṅga type of Prāngs are the clear reminiscences of the Khmer temples of semi-curvilinear or cruciform śikharas.

A Brāhmaṇical temple of 17th century A.D. is situated in the centre of Lopburi town. The middle stūpa is for the installation of the liṇgam, which shows that the temple was constructed for the worship of Śiva. Brāhmaṇical carvings are found inside the stūpas and on the walls. Śālā Phra Kāla, the original Vat to Viṣṇu, was built in the 10th century. It stands behind a new Vat built in the 11th century of the Buddhist era.

The triple shrine of Phra Prāng Sām Yot (the temple with three śikharas) was doubtless at first a Brāhmaṇical structure turned later to Buddhist uses. The central shrine is slightly larger than those on the sides; all face east and are connected with one another by covered passages along the north-south axis; they are built of limonite stone being used for doorways, pediments, and so on. 'The design is certainly not Buddhist', says Le May, and the three towers ranged alongside one another invariably bring to the mind the Brāhmaṇical trinity of Brahmā, Śiva and Viṣṇu. Non-Buddhist figures, too, have been found on the towers-bearded figures with their hands resting on clubs which also points to an originally Brāhmaṇa construction.[1] Origin of this temple, the shape of its openings, the windows and passages, is unknown to purely Cambodian monuments. Again the decorative sculptures are barely sketched and the details are picked in stucco, a procedure extremely rare in Khmer art, though not altogether unknown. Some vestiges of ancient Snānadroṇis attest the original character of the shrine.

The Phra Prāng Khek, also a triple shrine without the connecting passages and with the lateral shrines definitely smaller than the central, and the Sān Sūng, the Vaiṣṇava shrine, in the neighbourhood of which the pillar with the Mon inscription was found, are other early monuments also worthy of note.

Some temples in Srixatnalai (Sukhothai) in central Siam, particularly the Vat Pra Pai Luang and the Vat Sisawai in old Sukhothai, seem to have been originally built for Brāhmaṇical worship and later adapted to Buddhist uses in the Thai period.[2] This is clear from the plan of the structures as also from the survival of the older decorative sculptures on their walls.

The lower valley of the Mekong and the valley of the small stream

1. Le May, Reginald, *The Culture of South-East Asia.*
2. *ibid.*, pp. 79-81; *BCAIC* (1909), pp. 205-06.

Petchaburi offered the most favourable conditions for the establishment of colonies. Accordingly we find relics of a number of old states with Ratburi on the Mekong at their centre, Muang Singh farthest inland, Kanburi, Phra Pathom between the Kemong and the western arm of deltaic Menam, and Petchaburi more to the south nearer the sea. It is possible that at one time these centres were united under a single state but we know nothing certain of their actual history.

The Vat Kampheng Luang at Ratchaburi is another temple, Brāhmaṇical in origin, as its plan and the surviving images of dvārapālas and of Viṣṇu on Garuḍa, testify, but turned later to Buddhist purposes.

In central Thailand, there are three temples within an enclosure each consisting of a long brick building, with an ordinary tiled roof. Access to them was from one end, while the altar and images were at the opposite one. One of the three buildings contained fifteen large handsome images, all in a standing posture, of brass, with their crowns, amulets, and drapery gilded. The most distinguished was a figure of Mahādeva, nine ft. high. There were several smaller ones of the same deities, with figures of Pārvatī, Padmi, and Viṣṇu, and one statue of Brahmā. A sacred building appeared to be dedicated to Gaṇeśa, whose statue was the most conspicuous. Here were also the four statues of Mahādeva. The third building appeared to be dedicated to the worship of the liṅga, of which there was a large gilded figure in the centre of the altar, surrounded by forty or fifty small brass images—such as those of Śiva, Geṇeśa, Nārāyaṇa, Hanumāna, the Nandi, etc. These images were perhaps brought, at different times from western India.[1]

The modern temples of Bangkok are stylistically in link with the much earlier Khmer and the Thai monuments of the epochs of Lopburi, Dvāravatī, Sukhodaya and Ayuthia. The features which distinguish them from the earlier temples are the distinct Chinese influence, and elaborate embellishment with mosaic and gold, the coloured roofs and elongated freeze corners. The architectural characteristic of the Bangkok Wats (temples) which chiefly display a considerable Khmer influence or the oblong Prāngs (spires) surmounted by tṛśūla or trident.[2] It seems that they are the evolved form of the older Mon Khmer monuments of Petchaburi (Vajrapuri) Lopburi and Viṣṇulok. The Cambodian spires of Khao Wang (palace mountain) and Wat Mahā Thāt in Petchaburi and the Jinarāt temple of Viṣṇulok really look like the earlier forms of the oblong spires of the modern Wats of Bangkok. The cause of the present artistic

1. Cf. Esa, John Crawfurd, *Journal of an Embassy from the Governor-General of India to the Courts of Siam and Cochin-China*, pp. 182-83.
2. Among the Indian scholars K.D. Nag first noticed this Śaivite symbol on one Bangkok temple during his stay in Siam with "Kaviguru" Sir Rabindranath Tagore. See "*India and the Pacific World*".

modification of such śikharas seems to be the influx of the Mongolian art motifs in Thailand since the 13th century A.D. when the Tais or the D'ais began to pour in Siam from South China. There are numerous other Wats with less artistic beauty and glamour in Bangkok.

The unparalleled architectural beauty and lavish decoration of Wat Phra Keo have been described in the inspired language of Young[1] in a classic line which runs as follows: "It certainly looks like a solid mass of gold, and at sunrise and sunset when it catches the rosate hues of the rising or the setting sun, its golden surface can be seen from afar, shining and glittering like a second Sun itself, above the coloured roofs of the temples and the white or many tinted spires that are associated with it". One group is of pointed top and embellished with pure Thai art. Some of the Prāngs or śikharas of this temple illustrate an evolved form of Khmer architecture. They are of oblong shape and look like the artistic reminiscences of the old Khmer temples of Lopburi and Viṣṇulok which were inspired by Brāhmaṇical temples of ancient India.[2] Except the few spires of Cambodian origin which can be also seen in Wat Arun, the shrine of the emerald Buddha is entirely of Thai art, the chief decorative design of which consists of carpet-coloured roofs and delicately elongated freezecorners.

The wall paintings of the outer gallery of Wat Phra Keo are also of unique interest. They depict the scenes of the *Rāmakien*, which are of the Siamese version of the Indian *Rāmāyaṇa*. They were first executed at the instance of Rāma I and were later on renewed by king Rāma III and King Mongkut. The paintings of Wat Phra Keo are the charming creation of the Thai genius for their delicate style and bright colour. These paintings we may describe as the result of the first Thai attempt to produce a complete picture of the *Rāmakien*, stories which occasionally differ from those of Indian *Rāmāyaṇa*. Some comic scenes which have been inserted in the gallery also illustrated the humorous aspects of the Thai mind.

The monstrous Yaks (yakṣas) with their frowning expression, and bearded Chinese Lokapālas with their hanging loins looks conspicuous to the tourists who enter the magnificent chapel. The former is decorated with cheap mosaic, while the latter is made of cement.

Wat Arun or the Temple of Dawn (Sans. Aruṇa) with its lofty towers stands as a unique monument in Bangkok, for which the city itself should be given some artistic prominence in the region of South-East Asia. The

1. Young, E., *The Kingdom of the Yellow Robe.*
2. Le May, Reginald, "*Buddhist Art in Siam*". Coomaraswamy, *History of Indian and Indonesian Art*. There are some other spires in the chapel which look like the Burmese Pagodas. In this connection also it is interesting to note that there is a miniature representation of the Hindu-Javanese temple of Borobudur in the Wat.

gigantic edifice bespeaks the brilliance of the Thai art which is not only marked with a delicacy of decoration but also with a sensitive architectural beauty.

Formerly in the present site of Wat Arun, there was an old temple called Wat Chaeng. The older name is still popular among the Thais and the Chinese who inhabit Bangkok and Thonburi, the latter being situated opposite the river Chao Phya. In the second part of the 18th century the chapel was going to fall in ruins and at that time it was restored by King Phya Taksin[1] (1770 A.D.) who saved Siam by driving out the Burmese invaders. The Wat was later on repaired and rebuilt at different dates by the pious kings Rāma II (1809-1824), Rāma III (1824-51), Mahā Mongkut (1851-1868 A.D.) and Chulalongkorn (1868-1910). Practically it took more than a century to complete the construction of this colossal "Temple of Dawn". At present its importance is so much felt that its picture has become a sacred symbol in Siam. The Wat has really ushered in a dawn in the political history of Thailand as its spires pierced the sky when the Burman vandals fled to the west being chased by the cavalry of Phya Tak. Although Ayuthia, the earlier capital, was devastated into ruins by the invaders, a new era of political and cultural glory dawned in the sky of Thonburi, where the massive structure of Wat Arun stands with silvery Menam (river) flowing by its side.

The religious sculptures of Siam is a thing of elegance, beauty and artistic sublety from very ancient days. Since the time of the propagation of Buddhism in the country numerous images (of stone, stucco, bronze, wood, terra cotta etc.) have been made by the Siamese revealing a display of sensitive and creative art, which may still inspire the artists all over the world.

In the thirteenth century, with the coming of the Thais from South China, the Siamese sculpture underwent a great change. Although, the Thais completely defeated the Khmers of Siam, they did not hesitate to imbibe their art and civilization which illumined the valleys of the Mekong, the Menam Chao Phya, and the Salwin in course of their settlement in the heart of the Indo-Chinese peninsula.

According to Coedes and Le May, the earliest school of the Thai sculpture which developed in the region of Chieng Mai in North Siam between Circa 1100 A.D. and 1400 A.D. was influenced by the Pāla art of ancient Bengal and Bihar. Possibly the Siamese sculpture reached its perfection in the famous period of Sukhothai and her adjacent city Sawankhalok (circa 1300-1400 A.D.). The Thai school during this period,

1. After his victory over the Burmese troops, he was caught for religious insanity and was killed by his General Ghao Phya Chakri, who founded the present dynasty in 1782. He was then known as Phra Buddha Yot Fa Chulalok or King Rāma I.

revealed a little modification of the Chiengsen school, possibly with a slight Ceylonese influence. After the end of the epoch-making Sukhothai period, the Siamese statuary passed through a slow process of evolution, until it gradually gave rise to the Ayuthian school of sculpture.

A large number of Brāhmaṇical images mostly of Viṣṇu have been found throughout Siam. One of the Brāhmaṇical images of Chaiya is a standing figure of Viṣṇu carved in a greyish limestone. It is now in the National Museum in Bangkok, and according to the museum label, its prominence is Wat Sālā (Sālā Tung monastery) at Chaiya. It is a four-armed Viṣṇu in Sthānakamūrti, 27 inches in height. The posterior left arm is missing, the anterior left hand holds a conch-shell, on the hip the posterior right hand holds a heavy sceptre and the anterior right hand appears to be in *abhayamudrā*.[1] As the statue represents Viṣṇu, the attribute in the missing hand must have been either the lotus, the round symbol of the earth or the discus.

The figure wears a small mitre, decorated in bas-relief with an elaborate pattern of leaf and vine, with rosettes on the corners. The face is round and relatively small, the almond shaped eyes are sharply incised, flat and without any interior definition of pupil or structure. They are extremely long and spread to the outer limit of the face. The ears are constructed in a remarkable fashion, presented in frontal view, and joined to the mitre to secure them against fracture. The torso is nude except for a flat torque, with an ornament of opposed S-shaped elements at the centre. This takes on a configuration reminiscent of the Śrivatsa mark, a symbol of beauty and fortune often associated with Viṣṇu. The image wears simple armlets and bracelets.

The costume is a *dhotī*—a large rectangle of untailored cloth which can be draped in so many different ways that it is difficult to analyse this particular disposition with certainty. The same is true of the waist sash which holds the dhotī in place, and the broad sash which is looped through it. As well as we can make out the pattern of circles at the waist as the decorated upper of the dhoti, the lower edge encircles the legs between knees and ankles, and heavy vertical fold of cloth, that falls down in front between the legs, is a pleated lateral edge of the dhotī.

There is an interesting museum within the precinct of Mahādhātu monastery. Among the objects on display in it are two stone sculptures of Viṣṇu which bear a very close resemblance in style and iconography to the Chaiya Viṣṇu.[2] Both images have small round faces with button like eyes; both are four-armed figures with the posterior arm missing. In the

1. Diskul, S.K., M.C. Subhadradis, *Art in Thailand : A Brief History*, p. 7.
2. Le May, Reginald, *The Culture of South-East Asia*, pp. 80-81.

remaining left hand of each is a conch-shell held against the hip.[1] The remaining right hand which has the palm up and the figures extended at hip level, must have held either the lotus or a symbol of the earth. These images wear high mitres, which are similar in shape and decorated with patterns of leaf and vine, both wearing heavy earrings which were originally attached to the shoulders as well as the earlobes. Apart from the earrings, the only jewellery is an armlet and the chest is nude.

All the above three images are totally frontal. Each is designed to be seen in a controlled experience, probably as the occupant of a niche in an architectural programme. Their overriding characteristic is the flat, two dimensional presentation. The surface of the stone pier is unmodified except for the superficial attachment of linear pattern of dress and adornment. All three images have a harsh, broken outline which is in tense opposition to the rigidity and static immobility of the vertical axis.

The Viṣṇu image from Takuapa is a very impressive statue, well over six feet in height. It was lying on a small hillock near the mouth of the Takuapa river on the west coast of the Isthmian tract.[2] It was broken into several pieces, which had been collected and grouped around the base. Despite the loss of the forearms and most of the facial features, and despite the fractures of the body, it is the most powerful and emphatically monumental sculpture yet discovered in Thailand.

Dupon believes that the Takuapa image could be directly attached to the Pallava style of Southern India. Its presence on the Isthmain tract was due to the accident of trade rather than to the development of any artistic tradition which could be identified as distinctive to Peninsular Siam.[3] These were from scattered sites on the Isthmain tract as well as from Petchaburi province at the very head of the Peninsula, and the site of Dong Si Mahāpot in Prāchinburi province in eastern Thailand.

In the heart of Siam, remote from all the chief waterways, in the valley of the mountain torrent Pa sak, lies the ancient site of Sī Tep (Śrī Deva) which has yielded some of the most remarkable monuments of the early period of colonisation; together with fragmentary inscriptions in Sanskrit written in the *grantha*-character of the fifth century A.D. The ancient city of Śrī Deva extended over a square mile, and was surrounded by a mont and ramparts with six gates. The ruins of four temples and another terraced structure are still traceable in the centre of the city. A fragmentary stone statue form Śrī Deva, now in the museum of Ayuthia, gives the clue to the origin of these monuments.[4] In the fine form and studied modelling

1. Diskul, M.C. Subhadradis, *op. cit.*, p. 7.
2. Lunet de Lajonquiere, Le Domaine archaeologique de Siam, *BCAI*, Vol. I, 1909, pp. 170-71.
3. Dupon, "Le Buddha de Grahi et i' "Ecole de Chaiya" *Bulletin de l'Ecole Francaise d'Extreme orient*, Vol. XLII, 1942, pp. 105-06.
4. *BCAIC* (1909), pp. 198-200.

of the body, as also in the shape of the headgear, cylindrical at the base and octagonal at the upper end, the statue clearly stands apart from the usual run of Cambodian sculptures. Again, unlike in such statue, this figure has no ornaments whatsoever in the ears, on the neck or on the waist; arms and feet are missing, but presumably they were also unadorned, we may suppose that in spite of their eccentric situation, these monuments were Brāhmaṇical in origin, and later remodelled by the Cambodians who preserved the older divinities in the new sanctuaries.

The sculptures of Śrī Deva, comprise among others, the magnificent torso of a *yakṣinī*, two very fine statues in *tribhaṅga* with cylindrical caps, and a fragment of a *nandi* ; there is also a *dvārapāla* of clearly Khmer origin, which, while differing altogether from the other pieces, evidences the later Khmer occupation of this area. The other statues, not easy to identify because the arms are broken and therefore the symbols lost, are thoroughly Brāhmaṇical in inspiration; the head-dress, the features, the massive neck, the treatment of the legs and clothing, and the *tribhaṅga* must be noted. The torso of the *yākṣinī* is a masterpiece of technical perfection. Coedes has mentioned Gupta art and its canon as nearest allied to this; but the epigraphy of Śrī Deva points to South Indian influence. It seems that the art of Śrī Deva should be placed as a transtition from Amarāvatī to the later forms of Pallava art of the time of Mahendravarman and his successors. We know that in epigraphy the colonies supply transitional forms of the South Indian alphabe t not so well represented the home country, something similar in monumental art need therefore cause no surprise.

The results obtained by Wales in expedition to Śrī Deva (in 1935) confirm the above conclusions. He had identified a Vaiṣṇava shrine with a ruined brick tower 40 ft. high on a laterite base, 20 ft. from ground level; the inner vault of the tower is constructed by means of successive encorbelments. The statues, a headless four-armed figure, and a large and very noble head are also of the fifth or early sixth century A.D.[1]

The Brāhmaṇical cult predominates the art of the later Indo-Cambodian remains, and images of Brahmā, Indra, Viṣṇu, and Śiva adorn the entrance of almost every temple; Buddha images are not unknown, but usually only as an *āvatāra* of Viṣṇu. There is, however, exception in the sanctuary of Phimai, the image of Gautama takes the place of honour on the lintel of the principal entrance, the Brāhmaṇical gods being relegated to the subsidiary entrances. In any event, this temple in honour of Lord Buddha reconstructed in the midst of an old Viṣṇu temple is clear proof of the rising importance of Buddhism at the cost of Brāhmaṇism.[2]

The Viṣṇu from Si Chon bears a close resemblance to the well-known

1. *London News*, Jan. 30, 1937.
2. *BCAIC* (1909), pp. 190-91.

Viṣṇu image from Takuapa, which is now in the Bangkok museum. Neither image has the customary reserves of stone at the hips, which disguised by the knot of a sash and the handle of the club, and which functioned as a part of a system of supports to protect fragile areas of the image against fracture. Instead, the lower arms are held away from the body and were supported by reserves of stone which were attached to the *socle.* Vestiges of these reserves may be seen on the base near the left and the right feet. Images with this system of reserves appear to be a late development in the series of long-robed Viṣṇu images in both Thailand and Cambodia and probably date from a period extending from the second half of the seventh century till the eighth century A.D.

One male figure with four arms wearing a roughly conical head-dress and a long skirt or dhotī, is a representation of Viṣṇu in *Sthānakamūrti,* which has been found at Wat Jom Tong. While its arms are broken and its attributes are thus missing, it is very likely that they were the conch (śaṅkha), club (gadā), wheel (cakra) and either the lotus (padma) or the symbol of the earth (bhū). Thus, we see that a large number of Viṣṇu images have been found from the different regions of Thailand. Their artistic characteristics are very much similar to that of the Brāhmaṇical images of the post-Gupta art in India.

Besides Viṣṇu images, a number of liṅgas have also been found in Thailand. Na Khom, the foundation of a large sanctuary has yielded a large size liṅga. This liṅga is divided into a cubic base section (Brahmābhāga), an octagonal section in the middle (Viṣṇubhāga), and a cylindrical section on the top (Rudrabhāga). These sections are of relatively equal length and the object is thus a conventionalized rendering of the phallic emblem of Śiva.[1]

Another liṅga has come into light from the area around Wat Sra Si Mum. This crystal liṅga is considered by its owner to be rare and potent treasure. It may have served as a votive object or possibly it was carried as an amulet. Natural objects with a phallic shape, usually stones from the beds of sacred rivers, have been valued by devotees of Śiva in India. They are known to have carried liṅgas on their persons as their chief act of worship. Since it is portable hence it could have been brought to Sichon.

An image of Brahmā, the four headed god, creator of the universe stands in its own shrine in the compound of the 'Eravan', the government-owned luxury hotel. It is an imposing example of what exists in every Bangkok compound and in every up-country village—the Phra Phūm Chao Thi or sacred owner of the land; a propitiation to the lord or spirit

1. Cf. *JSS,* p 6.

of the earth for its use by man (Phūm, may be originated from Brahmā). In most households it is a small temple-shaped structure, often in bright colours, mounted on a pillar. Inside is the carved outline of a Brāhmaṇa god, Thai style, and in precincts plaster figures of horses, cattle or slaves promised in return for favours rendered.[1] Flowers, incense-sticks, fruits and rice may also be offered. This is not taken very seriously in Bangkok but this Brāhmaṇical tradition is still followed, no doubt to avoid running any risk of offending the deities.

At Anlong Pong Tai no less than five Viṣṇus resting on a serpent Ananta, besides numerous liṅgas placed in rows, have come into light. There are as many as ten such rows distributed over a stretch of 130 metres in length. One may say that the whole river bed is bedecked with liṅgas over which the gurgling crystal clear waters are forever performing the holy rite of ablution.[2]

Thus the early Brāhmaṇical images of Siam show the characteristic Indian tribhaṅga and of them rightly Le May observes, 'I would not, however, associate these figures with gupta art. They may be contemporary with it, but I have a feeling that the origin of all the early figures of Viṣṇu and other Brāhmaṇical Gods found in Siam must be sought in Central and Southern India, among the Pallavas, Cālukyas and Pāṇḍyas. They are, to my eyes, the undoubted forerunners of these swaying, lissome, sinuous figures of the Coḷa period in the South.[3] The later Thai art of Siam, however, found its chief inspiration from the Pāḷas of Bengal and Bihar.[4]

5. *LAOS*

On the art and architecture of Laos we find marked Brāhmaṇical influence. The earliest material evidence of ancient Brāhmaṇical influence can be dated to about the 6th century. The Wat Phu Hill, about nine miles from Bassac, was then called, a liṅga-parvata. Here originally a temple of Bhadreśvara Śiva existed. In that temple a liṅga was installed. Later on, the temple was turned into a Buddhist shrine with a monastery attached to it.[5] The specimens of the religious art at Wat Phu depict Indra on Airāvata and Viṣṇu on Garuḍa. These instances provide the greatest evidence of the wide prevalence of Brāhmaṇism in Laos.

The images of the gods and temples, similar to those in India were

1. Cf. Insor, D. *Thailand*, p. 57.
2. Cf. *JSS*, Vol. XXII, 1928, p. 39.
3. Le May, Reginald, *The Culture of South-East Asia*, p. 114.
4. *ibid.*, pp. 163-65.
5. Cottnell, L. *The Concise Encyclopaedia of Archaeology*, p. 268; also Majumdar, R.C., *HCFE*, p. 184.

made in various parts of Laos. The Lao art, in fact, is spectacular and almost similar to Indian art, the Khmer art or the Chinese art which absorbed all the influences coming from these lands from time to time.[1] The anthropomorphic representation of the Buddha in Laos art seems to be nearer the Burmese and Siamese art. This art is entirely religious in character, and both the Buddhist and Brāhmaṇical arts flourished in Laos and formed the main theme of the decorative art.

Similarly the sculpture art in Laos shows several Brāhmaṇical prototypes. "The figures standing over the carytides and the Pātravatī in the background seen on an ancient door at Wat Aram" undoubtedly bear post-Gupta characters. This feature in India may be seen as early as the beginning of the Christian era. The early Indian motif demonstrating the composite figures of animals combining acquatic creatures, is represented at Thāt Luong. Similarly, the Garuḍa and Nāga carved in relief on the Wat Pa Rouck and the representation of dvārapālas at the entrance of many shrines in Laos are Brāhmaṇical themes. Thus, the sculptures of Laos are purely religious in character which include the images of the Buddha, Devadatta, Apsarāses, Kinnaris, Nāgas, Garuḍas etc.[2]

For the study of Laotian architecture we have to depend on religious monuments known as Wat (monastery or temple). It is also known as Pagoda which is of Indo-Portuguese origin. Besides Mahāvihān (mahāvihāra), Thammasālā (Dharmaśālā) etc., the two types of the edifices are important.

i. Sim (Pāli. Skt.=Sīmā), the place for performing *uposatha* (Pātimokkha, performance).
ii. Thāt (Pāli. Skt.=Dhātu), the edifice for putting the relics.

From the construction of the Thāts, Wats and buildings in Laos it is clear that the style was imported from India via Burma and became the model of architecture of all the countries of South-East Asia. According to G. Coedes the characteristic type of building of Laotian architecture is the Thāt (dhātu) which is the counterpart, in Laotian terms, of the Indian sihalesa and Burmese stūpa, combined with the Khmer and Siamese cetiya.[3] The Thāt Luong (the great shrine), situated 5 miles to the east of Vientiane, built in 1560, the chief d'oeuvre of Laotian architecuture representing the wonderful stūpa of the world like Angkor Wat in the Republic of Khmer and Borobudur in Java, is modelled on Indian pattern and in style and general outline it bears close affinity with some of the

1. Souk Boun, *Limage du Buddha dans l'art; Laos*, pp. 1-13.
2. Gangneux, P. *L'ART Lao*, p. 12.
3. Coedes, G. *The Making of South-East Asia*, pp. 174-75.

mediaeval temples of India. Similarly Wat Pa Ruok shows affinity with the Gupta temple at Sānchi and the Wat Ban Tan displays Gupta-Cālukyan features.

Besides, the plan of the big buildings in Laos is often cruciform like the Brāhmaṇical buildings, the window frames showing explicit Brāhmaṇical influence.[1] The Indian sculptural and architectural styles found their way into Laos through its neighbouring countries, and not directly from India. The ancient Brāhmaṇical tradition of medium weight architecture, characterised by the curvilinear roof, has left traces in Laos in the design of apertures, and in several monuments very archaic in appearance, either in their overall composition or their ornamentation. The light architecture constructed with perishable materials has not survived for a direct comparison with the Indian prototypes. The remarkable co-existence of the two great religions of India Brāhmaṇism and Buddhism can be seen even today. The Wat Pra, constructed in the 17th century, is adorned by an image of Lakṣmī standing on a lotus over its dome while the Buddha figure is in the temples. Similar images of different Brāhmaṇical gods and goddesses along with the central figure of the Buddha can be seen in most of the Wats of Laos.

6. *JAVA*

The influence of Brāhmaṇism is most vividly noticeable in the ancient sculpture and architecture of Java. Java is all strewn over with the relics of ancient Brāhmaṇical temples. Most of these temples are in a well-preserved condition and many are in a ruined state. For the sake of convenience of treatment of Brāhmaṇical-Javanese art, we shall study it in two broad periods, viz. (i) Central Javanese period, and (ii) the East-Javanese period.

(i) *Central Javanese Period*

The Indo-Javanese art, like its parent art in India, may be described as the handmaid of religion. All the monuments of this art, so far discovered, are religious structures, and religion has provided its sole aim and inspiration from beginning to end.

The religious structures in Java are known by the general appellation Candi. The word originally denoted any monument over the ashes of the dead, ranging from a single stone column to a complete structure. Krom suggests that the word is derived from Caṇḍikā, a name of the goddess Durgā, who is specially associated with the dead and whose temple is invariably present in a Balinese cremation ground even today.

1. Beytie, De L. *L'Architecture Hindu au Extreme-Orient*, p. 231.

Howsoever that may be, it is evident that the word Caṇḍi gradually came to denote a temple in cremation ground, and ultimately any temple. Before describing the individual temples in Central Java, it will be convenient to begin with a general description of the essential features of its temple-architecture.

The Javanese temple of the standard type may be divided into three parts as follows: (1) basement, (2) main body (referred to sometimes as Body), (3) roof.

The basement, as well as the main body of the temple consists, like the classic entablature, of three distinct parts which we may designate as the base, wall (the central vertical part), and cornice (corresponding to Greek architrave, frieze and cornice). The base and the cornice have also the same essential features in the basement and in the main body of the temple.

The base consists of a flat plinth supporting a bell shaped ogee and a roll moulding, though occasionally one or more string courses (fillets or mouldings) are added to give the whole thing a complex character.

The cornice, consisting of one or more projecting string courses or mouldings, is enriched with ante-flex ornaments which serve to distinguish the different parts and emphasise the corners. Just below the cornice is a frieze-band usually enriched with ornaments. The walls of the basement are usually divided into panels (sometimes sunken) by pilasters, and often richly ornamented with figure sculpture, scroll work etc.

The main body of the temple is usually square (sometimes rectangular) on plan with a porch or vestibule in front and projections on all other sides. The vestibule leads to the only entrance of the temple which has no other opening. The walls on three other sides are divided into panels as in the case of the basement, though sometimes there is a projecting niche in the centre of each. As already stated, the walls stand on a base and support a cornice both of which have the same features as those of basement. The walls of the main body of the temple are, of course, naturally of greater height in proportion to the base and cornice than is the case with the basement.

The roof consists of a series of gradually diminishing storeys, each repeating on a minor scale the general plan of the temple itself, viz., a cubic structure with four niches on four sides. To the four corners are four diminutive turrets which again are miniature reproductions of the temple. In the cases of some great structures, the upper stages of the roof are made octagonal, instead of rectangular, in order to relieve the monotony. The roof was crowned by an ornament, the exact nature of which is uncertain, as no single specimen has been discovered in situ. Judging from the fragments and also from the corner turrets, it appears to have been of the shape of a cushion with a high and pointed final.

Sometimes the cushion supported a bell shaped stūpa ending in a pinnacle.

The interior of the temple is a plain square chamber. Its walls, rising vertically up to a certain height, support a series of horizontal courses of stone which, projecting one in front of the other, form an inverted pyramid of steps, and is terminated by a high and pointed hollow cone, the whole corresponding to the storeyed pyramidal roof outside. Stucco or plaster work is found in some temples. In some cases it was part of the original plan, but in others it is a later addition. Sometimes even colour or paint was used. The decorative ornaments which consisted of well-known Brāhmaṇical motives such as rosette, garland, floral scroll, arabesque, various naturalistic designs and floral or geometrical patterns will be noted here that all these patterns are derived from India and there is no trace of local flora or fauna. One very frequently occurring motive, however, deserves particular notice. The Dutch archaeologists describe it as Kāla-Makara. It really consists of two separate motives Kāla and Makara though sometimes they are found united to form a single combined motive. The Kāla head (also called Banaspati) is shaped like the head of a monster, and is taken to be an effigy of the terrible god Kāla. But it is really derived from the Brāhmaṇical motive of lion's head and Coomaraswamy rightly describes it as a grotesque Kīrtimukha.[1] It is a conventional lion's head with protruding eyes, broad nose, thick upper lip with big projecting teeth on two sides. The Makara is a favourite motive of ancient Brāhmaṇical art. There are differences of opinion regarding its original significance. According to Vogel, it was originally a representation of crocodile. On account of a strange combination of elephantine and fish-like properties Grunwedel describes it as a sea-elephant.[2] In Java the Makara has the body of a fish and the head of an elephant, and is often developed into a floriated ornament.

The Kāla head is usually placed right over a gateway, or above a niche, in the centre of the enclosing arch, ending in a Makara head at its two ends. Makara heads are also placed at the foot of door jambs. These motives are also found at the top of the staircase and various other parts of the building. In short, the Kāla-Makara motive, combined, or separated into two elements, occurs almost everywhere, and is one of the most favourite decorative devices of Indo-Javanese art. Though its elements are originally derived from India, it is according to Vogel, "the outcome of an indigenous combination and development"[3], and should

1. Coomaraswamy, *op. cit.*, pp. 202-03; also cf. Majumdar, R.C., *op. cit.*, p. 170.
2. *Indian Art*, pp. 60-61; Grunwedel, *Buddhist Art*, p. 57.
3. *Indian Art*, p. 62.

be regarded as Indo-Javanese rather than Indian. This may be doubted as the complete design also occurs in India.

The decorative relief and sculptures in Central Javanese temples were always restrained and in perfect correlation with the general architectural plan. They were designed to accentuate and emphasise the outline, rather than overshadow it by exuberance, or distort it by wrongly conceived ornamental patterns.

Two peculiarities of Javanese temples may be noted here. In the first place, columns and pillars are wholly lacking. Secondly, the arches are all constructed on horizontal principle, as in ancient India, and the true or radiating arches are conspicuous by their absence.

These two peculiarities made it impossible for the Indo-Javanese architects to cover large spaces by means of big arches and domes. Hence they could not plan any temple on a very big scale. They sought to make up for this deficiency, either by developing the projecting bays on the three sides into separate side-chapels, with separate roofs, or by surrounding one main temple by a large number of subsidiary temples, so as to give a monumental or colossal character to the whole structure.

Individual temples or groups of temples were surrounded by an enclosing wall. It is also likely that the gate of this enclosure was covered by a structure like South Indian Gopuram. No trace of such a structure has, however, been found in Central Java. Its existence in Eastern Java, in the later period, is proved by actual remains and literary descriptions, and it may be presumed that this element of architecture was also taken from Central Java.

The stone used for the temples is usually trachyte, but a softer kind of sandstone or marlstone has been used in Lara Jongrang, Plaosan, and Sajivan temples. Mortar was used in the upper part of the temple, though not in the base where the shaped and dressed stones were simply set side by side and kept in their position by various devices of connecting stones.

Dieng Temples

It is generally assumed by the Dutch archaeologists that the groups of temples on the Dieng plateau are the oldest temples now extant in Central Java. The arguments which may be brought forward in support of this view are based, in the first place on a number of inscribed stones which formed part of the temples, and an inscribed gold plate which belonged to the treasury of a temple; and secondly, on the architectural motives of decoration. The alphabets of the inscriptions are similar to what we find on one bearing a date 731(=809 A.D.). The decorative motives also belong to the earliest phase of Indo-Javanese art. On these grounds the temple groups of Dieng are regarded as contemporaneous with, if not earlier than the Candi Kalasan which was built in 778 A.D. It must be admitted, however, that these arguments cannnot be regarded as conclusive.[1]

The plateau of Dieng, called in old times Dihyang, has a height of about 6500 ft. and is surrounded by hills on almost all sides. About the centre of this plateau, standing in a line north to south, are four temples called Candi Arjuna, Candi Srikandi, Candi Puntadeva, and Candi Sembadra, all facing west, while there is a fifth, Candi Semar, which lies opposite to Candi Arjuna, and faces east. That these five temples belonged to the same group is indicated by the fact that they were all surrounded by one enclosing wall.

There are three other isolated temples on the same plateau, called Candi Dvaravati, Candi Gatotkaca and Candi Bima. In addition to the remains of other temples, Candi Parikesit, Candi Nga-Kula Sadevo, there is a long underground tunnel, which served as drain-pipe of the Arjuna group of temples.

The names of five of these temples are borrowed from the heroes and heroines of the *Mahābhārata*, Puntadeva, being a Javanese name for Yudhiṣṭhira. These names have, of course, been given in later times and although they indicate the popularity of the great Epic, they do not throw any light on the original nature of these temples, any more than do the similar modern names of the temples of Mamallapuram.

The Dieng temples, generally speaking, belong to the standard type described above. The ornament was very restricted and simple, being composed mostly of plain courses, pilasters, and ogee mouldings. The projections on three sides contained niches. The lotus cushions in these niches with holes in the centre prove that they once supported images of gods which have now disappeared. These niches, the door of the vestibule leading to the temple, and niches on two sides of it (where they occur) on the front wall of the temple, were all crowned by Kāla-Makara ornament.

The images found in the plateau of Dieng belong exclusively to the Brāhmaṇical pantheon. We have images of Śiva, Durgā, Gaṇeśa, Brahmā and Viṣṇu. The temples were thus Brāhmaṇical, and to judge from the extant remains, mainly of Śaivite character. The representation of the three chief gods with their riders is very important from iconographical point of view. For the riders have all human forms and only the head of a bull or a swan, or the beak of a bird on the human body indicates the riders of Śiva, Brahmā and Viṣṇu.

A general view of the architectural remains of Dieng indicates that it was a holy place of pilgrimage rather than a town with a considerable

1. Cf. Majumdar, R.C. *Suvarnadvipa*, pt. II, p. 172.

number of settled population. Beyond the normal requirements for priests and servants of the temples and the occasional rush of pilgrims, there are no vestiges of a large number of dwelling houses, and there is hardly any space for the accommodation of a large population. The Dieng or Dihyang, to call it by its old name, thus resembled the Jaina City of Temples in India, such as Śatruñjaya or Palitānā. We learn from the Chinese account that the king of Java visited it once a year, and presumably the nobles and other classes of people made occasional pilgrimages to this holy place.

To the south and east of the Dieng Plateau we come across the ruins of a large number of ancient temples. To judge from a number of inscriptions scattered about in the neighbourhood, they belong probably to the middle of the ninth century A.D. The isolated remains also indicate that they were mainly Śaivite in character. These temples, built on the standard type, offer sometimes examples of exquisite decoration.

Among these Candi Pringapus has been rendered famous by the enthusiastic description of Brandes. It is a small beautiful temple measuring about 16½ft. × 15ft. It is of the standard type save that the basement consists merely of a plinth and plain walls without any moulding, and that there are no projections on the three sides of the temple. The walls are, sculptures on these panels as well as those on the front constitute the excellence of the temple. Brandes has compared the decoration of this temple with that of Mendut and emphasised the fact that artistic principles of construction did not differ according to the sectarian character of the structures. In conclusion attention may be drawn to the repetition of prominent part in later East Javanese art.[1]

Another interesting group of temples is that on Mount Ungaran known as Gedong-Sanga which lies to the east of Dieng and south of Semarang. The name Gedon-Sanga means nine houses and no doubt refers to the nine groups of temples which are now found on two ranges of hills, separated by a deep ravine which today forms the boundary between Semarang and Kedu. It is a difficult question to decide whether all the temples belong to one series. The difficulty of communication between them, caused by the depth of the ravine, would, no doubt, incline us to regard them as two different groups. But the similarity of architecture is in favour of regarding them all as belonging to one and the same series. It is conceivable that in old times the communication was rendered easier by means of a sort of staircase which is now lost.

The temples of Gedong-Sanga are not arranged in a difinite plan like those of Dieng, but lie scattered about on different plateaus without any symmetry of plan. They belong to the standard type and need not be

1. Cf. Majumdar, R.C. *op. cit.*, pp. 176-177.

described in detail. They were mostly Śaivite in character, but some were devoted to worship of Viṣṇu. Among the various images found in these temples particular mention may be made of a new form of Durgā. Instead of standing she sits on the bull, and holds the *asura*, not by the hair, but by the neck.

The earlier Brāhmaṇical temples in the Prambanam valley are not of great important and may be briefly described. On the Gunung Ijo, on the eastern side, there is a group of eleven temples, consisting of the principal shrine, 3 rows of 3 temples each, and an isolated temple. The main shrine, about 50 ft. square, is of the normal type. The other temples measure about 29½ ft. All these temples have their entrance on the west and are mostly in a dilapidated condition, walls and contained a Śivaliṅga and the temples were thus Śaivite in character. A short inscription, founded in one of the smaller temples, indicates the probable age of the group to be about the ninth century A.D.

Ruins of temples are also met with an Saragedug valley, but these are shapeless mass of ruins. Mention may be made of Candi Abang in the south—western corner, being the only temple made of brick so far found in the Prambanan valley. Of course the large number of bricks lying scattered about in the valley indicate the use of this material for buildings, but very few brick temples have actually been met with in Central Java.

The Lara Jongrang group, usually referred to as Prambanam temples par excellence, and properly so called, derives its name from a stone image of Durgā of that name in one of the minor temples. She is looked upon by the natives as the petrified princess at whose desire the temples were built in one night by an unsuccessful suitor for her hands. The story goes that the unwilling princess consented to marry him only on condition that he would raise six temples over six pits in one night, and as he was prevented from completing his talk only by the artifice of the princess, he cursed her to be converted into stone. The image is still the object of veneration and worshipped by the native people and the Chinese.

The Lara Jongrang group consists of eight main temples, enclosed by a well, with three rows of minor temples round the wall on each side. A second enclosing wall surrounded them, and there is trace of even at hird. The number of minor temples in each row is sixteen, counting twice the last three temples on each side of each row, and temples are found which probably belonged to a fourth row. The wall surrounding them is almost a square, measuring nearly 285 yds. on each side, while the third wall was about 437 yds. square. Little, however, remains of these two walls, or of the minor temples which were all of the same pattern. These all faced sway from the main temple and had an inner chamber of about 8 ft. square reached by a small staircase. There is a well hole in the middle of the chamber which usually goes down right up to the foundation. These pits have been ransacked by treasure seekers, and occasionally ash-urns have been found, but there are no images in any of these temples. It may be noted that each row of these temples stood on a successive higher level so that the innermost stood about 2 yds. higher than the ground level. About 2 yds. behind the innermost row of these minor temples rises the first enclosing wall, about 15 ft. high and 6½ ft. wide. It surrounds a raised terrace on which the main temples stand. The terrace is about 110 yds. square and was accessible by staircases from the four gates, one in the centre of the enclosing wall on each side. These gates have now vanished, and the corresponding openings in the second enclosing wall indicate the existence of similar gates which all faced the four cardinal directions.

There are eight temples on the terrace. Of these six are arranged in two rows of three each, running north to south, and between them are the remaining two, placed close to the surrounding wall and a little to the east of its northern and southern gateways. The western row contains the three biggest temples, all facing east, and the three smaller temples of the eastern row are just opposite to them facing west.

Of the three temples in the western row, the central one is the biggest and the most renowned, and contains an image of Śiva. The one to the north has an image of Viṣṇu, and that to the south, an image of Brahmā. Of the three temples on the opposite row, the middle one contains the image of Nandi, and the other two probably contained images of the riders of the other two gods, though we have no definite evidence on this point. It has been suggested that these two were also Śaivite containing a liṅga and Mahāyogī. There are, however, no actual remains in the other two temples to indicate their sectarian character.

We may now proceed to describe in some detail the Śiva temple in the centre. Its basement has a length of more than 30 yds. The length of the projection in front of it is about 22 yds. of which 6 yds. is covered by the stairways and the small temples in the angles formed by them. Thus the portion of the basement free from the projection is a little more than 4 yds. on each side, which is also the depth of the projection. The height of the basement is about 10 ft.

The basement supports a platform on which the temple stands leaving a margin about 7 ft. wide on each side, which served as a path of circumambulation. The platform is enclosed by a balustrade decorated with reliefs on both sides. On the outer side it consists of a regular series of a projection niche followed by a sunken panel. Each of these niches contains three figures, three females, three males, or a male between two females holding one another in a very intimate way, and is flanked by a chiselled pilaster on each side. The two pilasters support a superstructure consisting of a splendid *Kāla-Makara* between two lions. The *Kāla* head is richly carved, its two curls ending in two *makaras* facing each other. Between the two are lotus plants, coming out of the mouth of the Kāla, and supporting three hanging bells. The figures in the niche undoubtedly represent divine beings while those in the panels, represented as dancing or singing, are perhaps heavenly nymphs or Gandharvas. The figures and decoration on the balustrade are executed with a masterly skill and may be regarded as the very best that the Javanese artist has ever been able to achieve.

The inner side of the balustrade consists of a continuous series of relief sculptures depicting the story of *Rāmāyaṇa* from the beginning up to the expedition to Laṅkā. The story was presumably continued on the balustrade of the temple dedicated to Brahmā. These reliefs which will be noticed at some length in connection with sculpture, constitute the chief importance and grandeur of the Lara Jongrang temples. They may justly be regarded as the Brāhmaṇical counterpart of the Buddhist reliefs on Borobudur and are hardly, if at all, inferior to them.[1]

The main body of the temple stands in the centre of the platform. The base of the temple looks like a second or upper basement, and may be regarded as such, particularly as there is above it the temple base proper, on which the walls of the temples rest. The two bases, or a second basement and the proper base of the temples, are separated by a cornice decorated with antefix ornaments, and thus they were intended to be looked upon as two distinct parts of the building.

The upper basement, or the lower base of the temple—it is difficult to say which would be the more proper designation—rests on a plinth about 1 yd. high. This consists of a plain flat band supporting a series of decorated panels. The decoration consists of a lotus vase, the spiral leaves of which, flowing on either side cover the entire field. Sometimes winged shell is substituted for the vase. This vase-motive, not common in Java, is executed here with a great deal of freedom and masterly skill.

A cornice with projecting antefix ornaments separates the plinth from the upper part of the second basement, about 3 yds. high. It consists of the usual ogee and roll moulding, small courses, all vigorously executed. The band below the cornice is decorated with garland and Kinnara motif, and antefix ornaments, with the same motif, are placed above the cornice. At each corner of the cornice is a magnificent gargoyle. The central vertical part consists of a series of twenty-four sculptured panels. The indentation of the upper basement and the general arrangement of these panels follow those of the lower basement. Similar flat posts, flanked by carved pilasters, separate one panel from another and each of these panels consists of a projecting central part with two sunken panels on two sides.

There is thus no doubt that the Lara-Jongrang temples were Brāhmaṇical in origin and dedicated to the well known Brāhmaṇical trinity. But

1. Majumdar, R.C., *op. cit.*, p. 215.

Śiva is undoubtedly held as the great god, Brahmā and Viṣṇu obviously playing a minor, if not a subordinate role.

In the opinion of some scholars the Lara-Jongrang temples were originally meant as burial chambers, the great Śiva temple being destined for the king, and others for his relations and nobles according to their rank. This view rests mainly upon the popular tradition of the origin of the temples from pits, and is strengthened by the actual finds of well-holes in all of them and ash-urns in some. It is, however, also equally possible that the buildings were originally planned as temples and used as burial places only in subsequent times, or as an after thought, by way of subsidiary use. This view finds support in the actual practices in Bali, from which it would further appear that the main Śiva temple was the royal temple and the subsidiary temples represented the different suburbs and quarters of the capital city, each of which was expected to take care of and provide for the regular worship in the particular temple assigned to it.

The temple of Lara-Jongrang possesses a uniformity of design and decoration which relegates them all to the same period and excludes the possibility of successive addition at different times. All the three great temples are square in plan with prominent projections on all sides. In the biggest one, the central temple of Śiva, the projections have been converted into side chapels. Consequently it has stairways on all the four sides, leading to the main shrine and the three side chapels. But the temples of Brahmā and Viṣṇu have only stairways in front leading to the main shrine. Further in the Śiva temple there are small temples in the angles formed by the basement.

The peculiarity and the special excellence of these temples lie in the dimensions and decorations of the different parts of the temples and each of these requires a separate and detailed description.

The basement consists of the usual roll and ogee mouldings below, and the cornice at the top, but the central vertical portion forms the special characteristics of these temples and its decoration has been called the 'Prambanam motif.' It consists of a projection niche, containing a standing lion, with a sunken panel on each side containing a conventional tree between two Kinnaras or animals. All this is enclosed by a border of beautiful rosette pattern and is flanked by a plain flat vertical post on each side. This entire thing, which forms, so to say, a unit, is separated from its next repetition by a broad flat post with two chiselled pilasters on two sides. The lion in the projecting niche is a freestanding conventional figure looking to the front, and the sides and top of the niche are decorated with *Kāla Makara* ornaments. The Kāla-head is, however, represented by merely gracefully curved outline, without protruding eyes or teeth, and is combined with rich, variegated floral and spiral patterns with a small bell hanging from its centre. The tree in the side panel stands on a vase and is crowned by an umbrella, sometimes with birds sitting on its branches. It is splendidly decorated, specially by lotus in various stages of development, and might have been easily mistaken for a bouquet of flowers, but for the birds. The figures on two sides of the tree are generally Kinnaras usually a male and a female but sometimes replaced by animals or birds.

As stated above, the panels repeating this general motive are separated by a flat post, and the separation is further emphasised by the antefix and other ornaments placed above and beneath this post.

It is necessary to add that while the basement of the six main temples follows this general plan, there are endless minor variations in the execution of details, not only in the different temples but even in the different panels of the same temple. It will be hardly an exaggeration to say that probably no two panels exactly agree in the representation and decoration, either of the niche with the lion or of the panels with trees. This endless diversity takes away the monotony and displays an artistic skill of a very high order, which can be truly appreciated only by a minute examination of the different panels.[1]

The sculptures on the panels are, however, altogether different from those of the lower basement. Here, the central projecting panel contains a human figure in high relief, seated, between two lotus stalks, on a cushion in Indian style, and decorated with rich ornaments. The twenty-four figures in the twenty-four panels are all seated in various mudrās, and distinguished from one another by some easily recognisable attributes. The halo round the head indicates that they represent divine beings. The sunken panels on either side contain two or three persons each, evidently followers of the chief figure.

The identification of the chief figures was for long a perplexing problem. At one time they were supposed to represent the Bodhisattvas, although the temple was manifestly a Śaivite. Miss Martine Tonnet, however, succeeded in demonstrating that these figures represent the dikpālas (protectors of the different directions), such as Indra, Yama, Varuṇa and Kubera.[2] Although the detailed identifications of all the figures, as suggested by Miss Tonnet, may not be accepted, her general view seems to be beyond question.

Of the main body of the temple the base alone remains, the roof and the upper portion of the walls having almost entirely disappeared. The base shows peculiarity in two respects. In the first place, the ogee and roll mouldings are repeated twice, and secondly, instead of being plain as they usually are, the upper ogee and roll mouldings are decorated respectively with lotus-leaf, and ovolo (bead and real ?) ornaments. It may be

1. For details see, Majumdar, R.C. *op. cit.*, p. 218ff.
2. *ibid.*, p. 221.

noted that both these peculiarities, so unusual in Central Java, were further developed in East-Javanese art. Above these upper ogee and roll mouldings rise the walls of the temple, which are too ruined to admit of even a general view of their nature and appearance. They were decorated with projecting niches, of which one fortunately still exists.

The niche resembles that of Candi Kalasan and probably contained an image standing on a decorated pedestal. It was bordered by the usual Kāla-Makara ornament and crowned by a projecting superstructure showing a high pointed roof probably a representation in miniature of the roof of the temple—with two figures on two sides in an attitude of devotion.

The niche was flanked by a tripartite post; a broader one in the centre, decorated with recalcitrant spiral, between two plain smaller ones with only conventional lotus flower at the foot and the top. Beneath the central post was a small niche which contained a detached image of a lion standing on an elephant's head. The space between the niche and the smaller post was decorated with lotus and rosette motif.

The mouldings above the wall are wholly lost and can only be guessed from the scattered fragments. It appears that just above the post with recalcitrant spiral was a moulding of palmettes. The many dwarfish Gaṅgā figures which lie on the ground show that there was a band decorated with these figures as is the case at Candi Kalasan.

One of the stairways leads directly from the ground to the main shrine, while the three others lead to the side chapels. The main stairway begins at a distance of about 8 ft. from the projection of the basement. The lowest step is about 7½ft. broad and so are the remaining seventeen or eighteen that constitute the first flight. Singularly enough, the first flight of steps does not lead the platform round the temple, but to a landing above, from which one has to go down to it by means of two smaller staircases, one on the right and another on the left. This being the case with the other three stairways also, the result is that if any one wishes to move round the temple along the platform he has to climb up and down by the four smaller stairways on the four sides of the temple.

If we follow the main stairway after the first flight, we find the steps reduced in breadth. Just where the smaller steps begin there were on two sides the gateways of the covered side stairs leading down to the floor of the platform. Continuing the ascent along the main stairway and treading over ten of these smaller steps we reach the door of the shrine. It was of massive proportions, and must have produced a striking effect, but only fragments of it now remain. The door as well as the front, back, and sides of the walls of the opening were decorated with Kāla-Makara ornaments combined with figures of lion, lotus divine beings etc.

The door leads to a chamber about 10 ft. square, the front side being a little longer than the rest. The walls of this room have beautifully decorated panels carved with recalcitrant spirals and rosette patterns. Behind this is the main shrine about 23 ft. square, with decorated panels on the walls. It contains an image of Śiva, represented as a human figure with four hands. On two sides of the door leading to this shrine are the two guards Nandīśvara and Mahākāla.

So far about the front of the temple, in the case of the other three sides, the stairways lead directly to the chapel. The walls of these chapels are plain except for five projecting courses in the middle. Three of these are decorated successively with palmette, rosette and again a palmette ornament. These are followed by a roll moulding and a plain flat course. Against the back wall of these chapels are the images of gods, Gaṇeśa, Bhaṭāra-Guru, and Durgā in Mahiśāsuramardinī posture, occupying respectively the western, southern and northern chapels.

The two smaller temples of Brahmā and Viṣṇu need not be described in detail, as the general arrangement is the same save that there are no side chapels, and consequently no temples are of the same size. Each side of the basement measures 17½ yds. of which the projection covers more than 14. The height of the basement is about 10 ft. and the depth of the projection about 5 ft.

The sculptures on the central vertical part of the lower base of the temple (or the upper basement) and the inner side of the balustrade require special mention. As regards the first, the panels in the Brahmā-temple contain a Brāhmaṇa or ṛṣi between two standing figures, and those in the Viṣṇu temple, a divine figure between two females. A definite explanation of these figures is not yet forthcoming. Van Stein Callenfells has suggested that those in the Viṣṇu temple represent the different incarnations of the God.[1]

As to the sculptures on the inner side of the balustrade, those in the Viṣṇu temple represent the episodes from the life of Kṛṣṇa some of which can be definitely identified. As regards the Brahmā-temple, nothing exists in situ, but detached reliefs containing the last part of the story of *Rāmāyaṇa* viz., the banishment of Sītā, the birth of Lava and Kuśa etc. are found scattered about, and they most probably belonged to this temple. In that case we must presume that the story of *Rāmāyaṇa* was continued from the balustrade of the Śiva temple to that of the Brahmā temple.

In addition to the principal image of the god in each of these temples, there are against the back wall three smaller representations of the same god. Evidently the four images in each of these temples corresponded to the four images in the Śiva temple, viz., one in the main shrine and three in the side chapels. The principal image of Brahmā and one of the smaller have four arms each, while of the other two are also different.

1. Cf. Majumdar, R.C., *op. cit.*, p. 223.

The principal Viṣṇu image is four armed. Of the three smaller ones, two represent the Vāmana (dwarf) and Narasimha incarnations, while the third, a two armed figure, holds in one hand a four armed figure of Lakṣmī.

The five other temples within the main enclosure are not only much smaller than, but also different in plan from, the three temples in the western row described above. They are square in plan, but the projections on the side occur only on the main body of the temple, and neither on the basement nor on the base of the temple. The decorations also differ a great deal though we come across panels with tree and vase motive and lion niches.

The central temple of the eastern row contains an image of bull, the rider of Śiva. Against the back wall are the images of Sūrya and Candra, standing on the lotus cushions which rest upon chariot drawn by horses, seven in the case of Sūrya and ten in the case of Candra. Sūrya holds with two hands a lotus flower in front of his body, while Candra holds aloft a soma plant with the right hand and a flag with the left. The latter has a third eye, evidently a Śaivitc characteristic.

In addition to the monuments described above, there are remains of many other temples in different parts of Central Java, in varying degrees of preservation, some of them if not most, were earlier than Lara-Jongrang, but it is not possible to attempt a detailed notice of them all in this work. A brief and rapid review of some of them must suffice for our present purpose.

The temple of Selagriya (Sanskrit Śilāgṛha=stone house ?) near Magelang is situated on a spur of the Sumbing hill overlooking a deep ravine. It is a nice little temple of the standard type though some of the usual mouldings are absent. Its decoration was never completed, but three beautiful images of Śiva Guru, Durgā on Mahiṣāsura and Gaṇeśa adorned the three niches on the projections of the three sides.

The Candi Sten, near Magelang, of which little remains above the foundation, consisted of a group of seven temples in a line, having the main shrine in the centre and three on each side the whole standing on a rectangular brick floor. It has yielded no less than fourteen stone images of Gaṇeśa and was evidently dedicated to that God. The neighbouring temple of Candi Reja, with a brick foundation, is very remarkable in that it contains, in addition to the images of important gods, also those of the minor gods, specially the dikpālas such as Yama, Varuṇa, Vāyu etc.

The Candi Asu (also called Añjing) at the western foot of mount Merapi has several striking peculiarities. It is in an unfinished state, and this enhances its value for the study of the Javanese architecture. For here we find an excellent example of what a temple would look like after the architectural part was over and before the sculptors had begun their task of decorating it. Here we find not only the blank panels, pilasters, and walls, but also blocks of stone put in their proper place, awaiting to be converted into antefix, makara, lion and other ornamental designs. It shows the vigour and grandeur of purely constructive design, and, in a negative way, demonstrates the value of decoration when properly applied. It also shows that the Javanese architects correctly understood the well-known artistic principle that decorations must always be subordinated to the architectural design and never allowed to dominate or distort its main features.

The Candi Asu also shows in several respects the beginnings of those modifications which were afterwards so characteristic of the Eastern style of architecture. The temple stands on a high basement, but there is not sufficient space round it to serve as a passage of circumambulation. The high basement, the raised base of the temple, and the body of the temple itself, all follow one another in unbroken succession. The staircase from the ground does not lead direct to the basement but to a projection on its front side and the corners of this projection are visible on two sides of the top of the staircase. This was ultimately developed into two temples at the two angles formed by the staircase with the basement. In details of ornament also we meet with triśūla-cakra (trident and wheel combined) and the lion's head conventionalised into a floral pattern two characteristic features of the Eastern style. It may be noted that some of these characteristics are also met with in the Lara-Jongrang temples.

Nothing remains of the body of the temple except a portion of one side wall. But the existing ruins give clear indication of bold conception, vigorous execution, and artistic conception of a high order. If the temple were completed, and stood in a fair state of preservation, it would have easily ranked with the most important monuments of Central Java.

Another remarkable monument is Candi Merak which lies to the immediate west of Kali Bogor, above nine miles to the north of Klaten in the Surakerta Residency. It was a mass of ruins until the restoration by Perquin in 1925. It resembles the temple of Ngawen, in having in front of the main shrine an elaborate Gopuram, with the doorway in the centre and two side walls adorned with niches. There are certain characteristic deviations from the usual classic type. In the first place the base and the temple are both square in plan with a projection only in the east where the Gopuram stands. Although there is no projection, the walls of the temples are adorned with niches in the usual way. Secondly, the roof consisting of five stages, has more distinctly the shape of a pyramidal tower. Each stage of the roof has a prominent caitya window niche in the centre, with Kāla-Makara decorations. The two corner towers on each side are also of somewhat peculiar shape.

The doorway of the Gopuram is also of remarkable design. The horizontal lintel, supported by two carved vertical posts, and adorned with a Kāla-head in the centre, supports an elaborate framework above it. The top piece of this framework is a Kāla-head with two elaborate scrolls on two sides, resting on a horizontal bar. The enclosed space is beautifully carved with flying figures, floral design, etc. Between the lintel and the horizontal stone bar is another sculpture and decorative ornaments indicate a high degree of skill and elegance. Among the images is one of Gaṇeśa which shows that it was a Śaiva temple.

A few words must be said about the rock-cut temples in Java. In this respect the Indo-Javanese architects never attained a high degree of success and this is particularly striking in view of the wonderful cave temples wrought in India and the high degree of artistic excellence displayed therein.

The Batu-rong cave in the Beser hill in the neighbourhood of Magelang is a long chamber with vaulted roof, containing a liṅga and yoni on a square footstool. There is a niche on the right wall and some carvings on the back wall. The doorway is about 6½ ft. high and 3 ft. broad.

There is a group of caves in Kuta-Arja. Two of these are in the southern side of Gunung Lanang. A portion of the rock has been polished to make the facades. The larger of the two is 6½ ft. high, about 16 ft. broad, and 18 ft. deep. Both contain liṅga and yoni, formed out of the primitive rock.

About half a mile to the north lies the cave of Gunung Tebasan. It consists of a long antechamber, measuring 40 ft. broad, about 10 ft. deep, and 8 ft. high, leading to two small inner chambers containing liṅga and yoni. To the south of this is the Batu Layang cave (also called Kali Tepus or Tepus) which also consists of an antechamber leading to the main cell beyond it. To the west lies the cave of Selagriya or Batu-ruma on Gunung Meranti. The front of this cave is wholly open and it contains a liṅga and a yoni.

The object which these cave temples were meant to serve is not quite clear. They could not have been possibly designed, like ordinary temples, as public places of regular worship, as they were too far from inhabited localities. Friederich has equated the name Tebasan with *tapas* and referred to the caves as dwelling places of Śaiva ascetic. As is well known, the caves in India were also intended for the residence and worship of the ascetics and Friederich's suggestion appears to be quite reasonable, even apart from the liṅguistic argument on which it rests.[1]

A review of the architectural remains in Central Java shows that they are confined to a limited area, viz., the subdivision of Wanasaba, the Dieng plateau, the residences of Kedu and Jogjakarta, and the adjoining

1. Cf. Majumdar, R.C., *op. cit.*, p. 229.

portions of the districts of Semarang and Surakerta. The further we go to the west of this area the less prominent become the products of Indo-Javanese art. Only removed from Dieng and other holy places are found, and there can thus be hardly any doubt that although Brāhmaṇical culture made its influence felt in these regions they were outside the main sphere of that culture.

Some parts of this outer area, notably the districts of Dara in Pekalongan and Tegal further to the west (specially Slavai, Balapulang, Bumı Java, Banjumudal, Bumil-aju and Bantarkavung) form an exception. Here we meet with stone images of Brāhmaṇical gods and even remains of temples. But side by side there are rude images of Polynesian character in connection with the pre-Brāhmaṇical antiquities of Sumatra and Java. According to Krom we must presume here a mixture of Brāhmaṇical and indigenous influences whereas in the rest of the outer area, there was a pure, though weakened form of Brāhmaṇical culture and civilisation. Krom further believes that the Brāhmaṇical element in this mixed culture is to be derived from Central Java and not from the later kingdom of Prajajaran as is generally believed. According to the same scholar this Indo-Javanese Polynesian culture originated in or shortly after the period of Central Java, and ultimately influenced in its turn the regions further west as far as Suṇḍa.[1]

While the views of Krom appear to doubt quite reasonably the pr esent state of our knowledge, they cannot be regarded as more than a hypothesis. Attention may be drawn to the recent theories on the origin of New-Javanese literature,[2] and a similar explanation may be offered for the mixed culture of a part of Central Java is too imperfectly known to allow generalisations about the nature and extent of Brāhmaṇical influence in its different parts, simply on the ground of the existing archaeological remains.

The Javanese sculpture, like Javanese architecture, presents itself to us in a mature stage, when the artist had mastered the technique and long passed the stage of clumsy primitive efforts. This is, no doubt, due, to a great extent, to the fact that Indian colonists brought with them skilled artists and mature traditions of art.

Following the plan adopted in the case of architecture, we may begin with the sculptures of Dieng. The decorative sculptures offer comparatively few motifs such as garland, lotus petals, foliage and flame. As already noted in connection with the temples, they show a simplicity of design and boldness of execution, and on the sense of dignity and restraint pervades them and indicates an intellectual refinement. The relief figure include the Kāla-Makara and the human busts within the niches in the

1. Cf. Majumdar, R.C. *op. cit.*, p. 230.
2. *ibid.*

roof of Candi Bima. These latter show a high degree of excellence and form the high water marks of Indo-Javanese sculpture of the Dieng perio .

Fergusson[1] regarded these busts as those of Buddha, and Havell[2] looked upon them as representations of Bhīma, the Pāṇḍava hero. That both these views are mistaken has been ably demonstrated by Vogel.[3] We should rather regard them as parts of a decorative device, without any iconographical significance.

Havell has waxed eloquent over the artistic merit of these sculptures. "There is" says he "the greatness of line, splendid generalization and profound abstraction of the best Egyptian sculpture, and all the refinement of Greek art."[4]

Proceeding on the assumption that the busts represent those of Bhīma, Havell shows how ably the artist has represented the "born fighter and leader of men, with a depth of penetration which belongs only to the grandest portraiture."[5]

Few people would perhaps join in the rapturous outburst of Havell. But nobody can deny that the execution of these images shows a high degree of technical skill and artistic conception. The artist excels in power of expression, and his creations are forceful and dignified. He has produced quite a large variety of types of what may be regarded as transition between portraiture and ideal divine figures. There is no lack of frank naturalism, but there is at the same time a conscious attempt to idealise and generalise. The type is not purely Indian, but the influence of Brāhmaṇisation either in conception or in execution, is not so complete as in the sculptures of Prambanam and Borobudur. But the artist has fully imbibed the best traditions of Indian art and mastered its technique.[6]

The bust, now found at Bagelen, but originally belonging to Dieng Plateau is a divine figure, perhaps of Śiva, and exhibits a greater process of Brāhmaṇisation. It has a calm serene expression and belongs to the best type of Central Javanese art. It may be regarded as the finest work of the Indo-Javanese art, found at Dieng Plateau.

To the same class belongs the image of Durgā, found in the same locality. Although inferior to the preceding one in artistic merit, it exhibits an advanced technique and highly developed conception of art. The prostrate buffalo and the sad dejected face of the demon offer a striking contrast to the triumphant smile of the goddess. The representation of the demon just issuing out of the buffalo is also well conceived. It may

1. *History of Indian and Eastern Architecture*, Vol. II, p. 431.
2. *Indian Sculpture and Pa inting*, pp. 142-43.
3. *JRAS*, 1917, pp. 371ff.
4. *op. cit.*, pp. 142-43.
5. *JRAS*, 1917, pp. 142-43.
6. Cf. najumdar, R.C. *op. cit.*, p. 232.

be noted in passing that the goddess holds in her hands the attributes of Viṣṇu viz., conchshell, discus, lotus etc.

The general disposition of the sculptures in Lara-Jongrang and their subject matter have been referred to in course of the description of the temple. It is necessary here only to refer to their artistic excellence.

A highly developed aesthetic sense is noticeable in all the sculptures, both decorative ornaments and relief figures. The Kāla-Makara ornament, on the top of the niches in the balustrade, is a pleasant contrast to the usually hideous and distorted monster's face that we meet with elsewhere. But even this was excelled by the beautiful conventional design of the same which we notice above the niches of the basement. Here the face is almost unrecognisable in the graceful curves and the beautiful complex of intertwining spiral, the whole producing a linear design of infinite beauty.

The same aesthetic sense has transformed the tree-and-vase motive into a floral bouquet whose charm holds in awe of admiration the two Kinnaras seated on its sides. The Kinnara figures, half bird, half human, are very appropriate. To appreciate the beauty of the tree you must have the eyes and heart of a human being but to enjoy it perpetually you must have the wings of a bird. Taken as a whole, the decorative reliefs are very charming and graceful and show a variety of designs.

A high degree of aesthetic sense also pervades the delineation of human figures. The best seems to be the triple figures in the niches on the outer side of the balustrade. Characterised alike by the elegance of forms and the harmonious grouping, they may be regarded as the best jewels in the ornamentation of the temple.

The figure in the neighbouring panels are less elegant, but full of life and movements, bringing into relief the still beauty of the principal figures. In these attendant figures the artist has shown in a remarkable degree his power of delineating movements of all kinds and infusing life and vivacity in them. The man, for instance, who is playing on the mṛdanga (a kind of drum) is depicted as if his whole body is dancing with the tune. The skill with which different postures of the human body are faithfully drawn is also worthy of notice.

All these peculiarities appear again in a still more remarkable degree in the famous series of reliefs representing scenes from the *Rāmāyaṇa*. There are altogether forty-two panels depicting the story of the *Rāmāyaṇa* up to the arrival of Rāma and his monkey troops to Laṅkā. It will be beyond our scope to describe all of them, but a few typical scenes may be discussed.

The very first panel represents *anantaśayana* of Viṣṇu. The god is seated on serpent Śeṣa and the sea below it is indicated by waving lines and aquatic animals such as fishes and crabs. Viṣṇu has four hands. The upper right arm holds the discus and the upper left, the conchshell. The object in the lower right hand is indistinct, while the empty lower left hand is stretched, with palm outside, in the act of greeting the five figures on his left. These represent the gods who have come to request him to be incarnated on earth for killing Rāvaṇa. The foremost of these figures, distinguished from the rest by his peaked beard and peculiar headdress, probably represents Brahmā. He presents an offering (arghya) to Viṣṇu.

Viṣṇu is seated in a peculiar manner. His left leg is doubled up and two ends of a girdle that pass round his body are tied a little below the knee. This method of keeping the body at ease is also noticeable in the sculptures at Sāñchi, and Borobudur. To the right of Viṣṇu, Garuḍa is seated in a reverential attitude, holding with two hands a lotus with long stalk towards his master.

The theme is delineated with admirable force and simplicity. There is a beautiful harmony in the whole composition, and the artist has shown his sense of symmetry and balance. As in the body of the temple, the decorative ornaments are kept in due subordination. The most remarkable thing is, however, the divine figures. Each of these is graceful in its own way, endowed with different features and imbued with different expressions. Taken separately each would have constituted a charming figure by itself, and this is a rare thing in a composition of this kind. The continuation of the scene, in panel II depicts king Daśaratha with his queen and sons, and probably the sage Viśvāmitra.

The panels delineate the tragic scene of the banishment of Rāma. To the left is a long scene depicting the coronation of Bharata with its attendant joyous ceremonies such as music and dancing. To the right, Rāma and Sītā are being driven in a chariot towards the forest.

In the centre the old king Daśaratha and queen Kauśalyā are seated overwhelmed with grief, the king's head drooping over his left shoulder, and the queen closing her eyes with left hand. The sorrow of the royal couple is reflected in the dejected and somewhat startled faces of the two attendants sitting on the right. The placing of this scene between the other two at once brings into prominence the great tragedy of the whole.

Apart from the masterly setting of the whole scene, the details are worthy of a great artist. The sorrow of the king and queen is shown in a simple but very effective manner. Both of them have their faces turned towards the right but not looking at the departing chariot, a sight, too painful for them. The face of Rāma is sad, that of Lakṣmaṇa sadder still, but not so the face of Sītā, in whom the joy of her husband's company seems to outweigh all other considerations. Remarkable is also the attitude of Bharata and his queen. They look morose and sit apart, in strong contrast to the posture in which loving couples are usually represented. Amid the joyous surroundings of their coronation Bharata and his queen alone are sad and unhappy.

The panels represent the episodes of Sūrpanakhā and Mārīci. Beginning from the left, the first scene represents Rāma seated in his hut, while Sūrpanakhā, with her maid, kneels down before him, offering some presents. The forest is indicated by two trees, under one of which Sītā stands, at a distance, looking at the scene with a jealous eye.

The next scene shows the same two figures, Sūrpanakhā and her attendant before Lakṣmaṇa. His outstretched left hand with a pointed finger is a warning to them to retire, while an arrow (or a club or some other weapon) in his right hand completes the threat. Poor Sūrpanakhā, frightened and disappointed, bursts into tears. The difference in the attitude of the two brothers is worthy of note.

The next scene represents Sītā seated in her hut, while Lakṣmaṇa left to guard her, sits below her. Next we find Rāma in the thick forest just letting off the arrow which has pierced the golden deer. Above the deer is portrayed the hideous figure of Rākṣasa Mārīci, uttering the fatal cry. The forest is indicated by trees, plants and shrubs, while the figure of Rāma in the act of throwing the arrow is faithfully drawn, his left hand holding the centre of the bow, with right hand stretched back behind his body. The running deer with his head turned back towards his pursuer is also admirably carved.

Lastly, we may refer to panel in which Hanumān, on his return from Laṅkā, narrates the story of Sītā to Rāma. The artist has very cleverly depicted the different effects of the story on the different persons present. Rāma is overpowered with emotion, but is evidently fully absorbed with the mental vision of Sītā which the narrator's story has conjured up before him. Lakṣmaṇa, too, is deeply moved, but less absorbed than Rāma. Sugrīva and the seated human figure behind him are visibly affected by the pathos of the story which they are listening to with rapt attention. The two monkeys on the extreme right pay no attention to the story and are making merriment, in strong contrast to the rest.

If we compare the attitude of Rāma with that of Sītā when she hears the news of Rāma from the same Hanumān, we can easily mark the difference in the two characters. Sīta is visibly affected, her whole body leaning forward towards the speaker. But while her emotion is only too visible, Rāma presents, outwardly, a calm placid figure, with a slight twist of the left hand (in common with Sītā) as the only external indication of the deep emotion which is agitating his body and mind. Whereas Sītā is looking eagerly towards Hanumān, Rāma is turning away from him. In Sītā the emotional element reigns supreme, while it is subordinated in Rāma to a strong will-power and intellectual force.

In conclusion we may refer to the detached images of the gods specially those of Brahmā, Viṣṇu and Śiva in the temples. They are beautifully modelled, but the expression lacks the ideal abstraction which is the dominant keynote of Borobudur Buddha. The features, though somewhat stiff, are, however, characterised by an elegance and refinement of high order. The image of Mahādeva will serve as an example.

The above review makes it clear that the art of Lara-Jongrang is more naturalistic and is characterised by a greater feeling for movements and human passions. It is more informed by human life and activity, though not devoid of the graceful charm of idealism. It has brought the divinity of idealism to the earth below.

(ii) *East Javanese Period*

The art of Eastern Java may be regarded as a continuation of that of Central Java, and if we treat it separately, it is merely from geographical and chronological considerations. The monuments of this art belong exclusively to the eastern part of Java, and are, with a few exceptions, posterior to those of Central Java described above, but they illustrate the normal development of the principles which underlay the earlier art. Although characterised by certain definite tendencies which gradually assert themselves prominently and transform the entire nature of Indo-Javanese art, it would be wrong to regard the Eastern art as something radically different from the earlier phase of Indo-Javanese art noticed in Central Java.

It is therefore natural to assume that when for some reason or other the political and cultural centre of the Indo-Javanese was shifted from Central Java to the eastern region, the artistic traditions were carried to the new home and underwent there a normal development, though undoubtedly affected by new surroundings and new conditions of life and society.

The oldest temples in Eastern Java are those of Badut and Besuki. The ruins of the former lie about six miles from Malang in the *desa* Badut, sub-division Dau. The ruins consisted merely of a massive heap of stones, but the Dutch Archaeological Department has partially reconstructed the temple from the fragments lying scattered about. There is absolutely no doubt that it was purely Central-Javanese in character. The basement is square in plan but severely plain. The western face of it is intersected by the staircase, the stone crubs of which are richly decorated and end in volutes. The main body of the temple stands on the basement leaving a circumambulating path about 5⅓ ft. wide. It is square in plan with a portico on the west side. The base of the temple has the usual profile consisting of a plinth, an ogee and a roll-moulding which projects boldly to the front.

The staircase leads to a portico the door of which is crowned by a Kāla head, the place of Makara on the two lower ends of the jambs being taken by a peculiar decorative piece of stone. The cella is nearly square and fairly big, measuring about 11½ ft. by 12ft. as opposed to the small size of the shrines usually met with in Eastern Java. A yoni and a liṅga, now set up their, perhaps also originally belonged to it. The yoni is divided into fragments but the liṅga is in a fair state of preservation. In the middle of the chamber is a pit of fairly large dimension. It is about 6½ ft. square, the walls being made of stone. Nothing was however found inside. It has been suggested that it originally contained the stone urn which has been discovered amid the ruins. Perhaps someone originally dug up the pit and brought out the urn.

The walls on the north, south, and east have each a niche in the centre. These originally contained images of gods, two of which, Durgā and Guru, were found and have been replaced. There was also a niche on each side of the portico on the western wall. The niches are crowned by Kāla-heads supporting miniature temple-roofs with divine figures flying through clouds on two sides. The walls on the two sides of the niches are divided into panels and decorated with wall paper designs or cakra-triśūla.

Above the walls is a well-defined cornice with richly ornamented antefix. Practically nothing remains of the roof above. Among the decorative motifs may be mentioned tree, vase with lotus, and Kinnaris. The plan, the method of decoration, the images, and the decorative ornaments—all belong to the style of Central Java. The temple was enclosed by a wall, remains of which can still be traced for a considerably length. To the west of the main temple were three small subsidiary temples, of which very little remains. A Nandi and a liṅga were found among the ruins and probably occupied two of these temples.

A little to the north of Budut we come across the remains of another temple at Desuki within the same sub-division Dau. Only the basement of the temple remains. It is square in plan, each side measuring more than 21 ft. There is a projection on the west side with a staircase, while the walls on the other sides contain three richly decorated panels divided by plain pilasters. There are also two sculptured panels on two sides of the staircase on the western side. The sculptures in the panels are mostly animal figures and vases with lotus. The figures of Durgā, Gaṇeśa, Bhaṭāraguru and a liṅga have been found among the ruins. To the south-west corner of the projection, next the staircase, a liṅga has been built up into the body of the temple itself. The characteristic feature of the temple is that its plan, the sculpture, motifs, and the mode of decoration are purely Central Javanese in character. The basement of the temple was faced with stone-slabs, but the main structure was made of brick.

Some decorative features, e. g. Kāla-head over the main entrance and those over the niches were made of stone.

Before the discovery of the temples of Badut and Besuki the Candi Gunung Gangsir (also called Derma or Keboncandi), made of brick, was regarded as the oldest monument in Eastern Java. It stands on a very high basement, which has a projection only on the front. The bass of the temple looks almost like a second basement, as in Lava-Jongrang. Here, again, there is a central vertical part between decorated upper and lower bands. Pilasters with ornaments at their upper and lower ends, divide this central part in long panels which are decorated with lotus-vases between two sitting naked famale figures.

The first stage of the roof alone exists and it repeats the main features of the temple. The cella is about 12ft. square and ends above in a hollow pyramidal cone under the roof somewhat in the style of Kalasan. A torso riding on a bird is found among the scattered ruins and may be the figure of Viṣṇu or Brahmā, thus indicating the Brāhmaṇical character of the temple.

On the grounds of technique of architecture, the Candi Gunung-Gangsir may be regarded as contemporary or even earlier than Lara-Jongrang. To the same period, or perhaps a little later, may be referred the Candi Sumberananas, to the north of Bihar. It is also made of brick and its lower part, which has alone survived, has the classical profile of Central Java. Images of Bhaṭāra Guru, Brahmā, and Nandi have been found in the ruins of this temple, and their style, particularly that of the last, approximates very closely to that of Lara-Jongrang.

The earliest dated monument in Eastern Java is the tomb and bathing enclosure known as Jalatuṇḍa. It lies on the western side of Gunung Bekel, one of the four peaks of the mount Penanggungan. An area 55ft. long by 44ft. broad, was surrounded by walls on all sides. The back wall was built against the hill side, and the two side walls followed the level of the sloping ground by terraced stage. The front wall has entirely disappeared. These walls were crowned by three spouts, one in the centre and two others on two sides of the back wall. These spouts were made into decorated figures, set in a niche, and we still find a nāga-head on the left and Garuḍa-head on the right side. Over the right hand spout a second niche with decorated top still exists. The water from each spout fell into a cistern, over the walls of which there were gargoyles to carry the surplus water. The walls of the middle cistern, the largest of the three, consist of several decorated mouldings.

A few yards below the middle cistern was discovered the royal cofin which is now in the Batavian Museum. It is a square box on a high round lotus cushion, all made up of one piece of stone. The box has a pyramidal cover and is divided into nine compartments all of which contained bones and ashes. There were, besides, plates and coins, both of gold and silver. The gold plates were decorated with figures of nāga and tortoise with mystic syllables and also inscriptions in honour of Śiva, the lord of Bhūtas, and Agni, the Lord of Dvijas.

There is a second tomb and bathing enclosure of Belahan on the opposite side of mount Penanggungan. It resembles that of the Jalatuṇḍa in many respects and has yielded a number of very beautiful images. The fines of these is a figure of Viṣṇu on Garuḍa. It has been suggested with great probability that this figure of Viṣṇu is a portrait of king Airlangga.

The first notable monument in Eastern Java of which enough remains to give us a fair idea of its architectural peculiarities is Candi, the cremation sanctuary of king Anuṣanātha. The basement of the temple is square in plan with projection in front. It stands on a base consisting of a plinth, the broad central part divided into deeply sunken panels between pilasters, an upper band and the cornice. There is no decoration on any part of the base. From the doorway two small steps lead down to the cella. The walls are quite plain and end in the usual vaulted roof by means of a series of projecting layers. The chamber is empty, the Śiva image it once contained having disappeared. Just in front of the main staircase is a rectangular terrace, more than a yard high. There is a figure, probably of Viṣṇu, and formerly there were, more on this entrance.

To the north-west of Singhasari lies the tower temple known as Candi Singhasari. The main body of the temple stands on the square basement, its lower part being surrounded by a stone ring which crowns the basement. It is about 21½ft. high and square in shape with a slight projecting niche on each side. These niches have separated profiles of their own, and a Kāla-head, placed above them, reaches up to the cornice. The roof above it consists of several stages of which two are horizontal courses. On them is decorated with lions' heads, looking front, placed side by side, and another with a pair of lions sitting back to back between a makara on each side.

Of the figures of gods which once adorned the cella, the side-chapels, and the niches, only a damaged figure of Bhaṭāra-Guru is now in situ, in the southern chapel. Four others, Durgā, Gaṇeśa Nandīśvara, and Mahākāla are now in the Leiden Museum. These are all remarkable for the rich decoration and the nice execution of details which characterise the Singhasari school of art. The presence in the roof of a band with animal motive particularly that of lion's head and makara, formulate a direct Brāhmaṇical influence.

In spite of the political convulsions that transferred the seat of authority from Singhasari to Majapahit there is no corresponding break in the continuity of the art traditions in Eastern Java. This is less to be wondered at when we remember that the royal dynasty of Majapahit derived its claims to rule over Java from that of Singhasari and tried by every means to keep alive the bond between the two. Naturally the art of Singhasari continued to develop in a normal way even under the new regime.

The first notable monument of this period is Candi Javi at the foot of the Velirang. It is the same as temple Jajava which containing the remains of king Kṛtānagara and where the king was represented by the excellent images of Śiva and Buddha. It was begun by king Kṛtānagara himself, but Jayavardhana, the first king of Majapahit completed it. The *Nāgara-Kṛtāgama,* to which we owe this information, also gives an interesting description of the temple when it existed in its full glory. It appears to have been of the shape of a tower temple and contained an image of Śiva; but an image of Akṣobhya was placed hidden in an upper chamber which, however, subsequently disappeared.

The small temple, rather the model of a temple, at Kotes, to the east of Blitar, known also as Candi Papoh is important as it gives us a complete representation of an East-Javanese temple, particularly its roof. The temple itself is square in plan, with projections on all sides, containing the door and niches, and the usual structures at the two angles formed by the front projection and the wall of the temple. The images found among the ruins indicate that the temple was Śaivite in character.

Not far from Paree, to the east of Kadiri, lie the remains of Candi Suravana (old Sura-bana), also called Candi Bloran. The foot of the basement, about 1½ ft. high, consists of a plain plinth, a decorated cornice, and the central vertical part between a decorated upper and a lower band. The central part consists of projecting sculptured panels, divided by plain flat pilasters. At each corner are dwarfish monster figures, and in the centre of each side (except the front), a decorated rectangular block of stone, all of which stretch from the plinth to the cornice. Above this, the basement proper really consists of two parts separated by double ogee mouldings decorated with lotus leaf motif. The lower part is plain, with only a small decorated piece of stone projecting from the centre. The upper part is almost entirely covered on each side by a big oblong sculptured panel, the small margins on its two sides forming two raised decorated pilasters. The sculptures on the big panels illustrate the poem Arjuna-vivāha. The sculptures on the corner pilasters have been explained by Brandes as the scenes from *Rāmāyaṇa,* but this is doubted by Krom.[1] Fragments of images found among the ruins indicated the Śaivite character of the temple.

The greatest and most famous monument in Eastern Java is the temple complex of Panataran (old name Palah). The building activities can be traced throughout the thirteenth and fourteenth centuries A.D. The great

1. Cf. Majumdar, R.C., *op. cit.*, pp. 271-72.

temple which naturally occupies fourteenth century A.D. during the Regency, while the Peṇḍapa-terrace and a smaller temple, which come next in point of importance, belong to the reign of Hayam Wuruk.

The whole temple area, 196 yds. by 65 yds. was enclosed by a wall with its chief entrance to the west. The enclosed area was again divided into three parts by two cross walls. The main temple occupied the rearmost i.e., the eastern part. Three terraces, each smaller than and having a different ground-plan from the lower, supported the main temple.

The elevation of the first two terraces is similar and resembles that of the basement of a temple. Its characteristic features were the decorated pilasters at the corners which project in front along the entire height above the plinth, and support a miniature temple above the floor of the terrace. The reliefs on the central part, in the first terrace, consist of a number of medallions, on three superimposed slabs, decorated with reliefs representing an animal amidst foliage. These animals are of great varieties including even some species medallions, resembling flat pilasters, are covered with reliefs representing scenes from *Rāmāyaṇa*. In the second terrace, the central part is covered by continuous reliefs illustrating Kṛṣṇāyana. It appears that the version of the poem followed by the artist is somewhat different from the existing text, but there is an agreement about the essential points.

The third terrace is square in plan with triple projections in front against the centre of which the staircase is placed. It stands on the second terrace, leaving a passage all round. It has a very simple elevation, viz., the central part with decorated string courses above and below. The central part is divided into a number of sunken panels flanked by pilasters. The panels are decorated by winged nāgas with projecting heads, and the pilasters by winged lions with raised hind legs. The vertical character of the relief of the third terrace offers a striking contrast to the horizontal character of those of the first two, and clearly indicates that it was designed to support a structure above it. In other words, the third terrace may be regarded as the base of the temple.

Although nothing now remains above the third terrace the scattered fragments give some idea of the walls of the temple which once stood on it. A number of *gaṇa* figures as pilasters, served as the base. The upper part stood on a number of richly decorated courses, and had a great niche in the centre of each side, with images, respectively, of Brahmā, Viṣṇu and Śiva, and their vāhanas. There were also decorated panels and images of other gods e.g., Indra, Kārttikeya, Vāyu, Agni, etc., on their proper vāhanas.

While Brāhmaṇical culture and civilisation maintained a precarious existence in Java proper in isolated hill sides, and were gradually degenerated into primitive cults, things were more favourable in the eastern corner, where petty Brāhmaṇical states existed up to the eighteenth century. Unfortunately the monuments in these regions were mostly in brick and have thus left little traces behind. But quite a large number of ruined structures, with images of Brāhmaṇical gods and a large collection of gold, silver and bronze images of Buddhist gods, leave no doubt that the practice of temple building contained in the north, south and south-eastern parts of Eastern Java, where some decorations can still be traced.

A heavy brick wall surrounded the temple, rather a temple-complex or a town. The wall was 12 ft. high, 6 ft. thick, and had a circumference of 2¾ miles. The temple was made of layers of brick inside, and chalk-stone on the outside. The steps leading to the basement were of the shape of half-moon, while the basement itself was like a monstrous tortoise surrounded by two serpents with heads in front and tails at its back. Some writers, however, differ in their description, mentioning an allegator and two dragons in place of the tortoise and two serpents.[1]

The walls were divided by ornamented projecting courses into eight squares, decorated with floral arabesques. In front of the temple was a terrace or a platform. Among the images are mentioned those of Gaṇeśa, Brahmā, Garuḍa, Nandi and a group of life-size figures of Gopīs bending respectfully before Kṛṣṇa.

The images found at Singhasari present the same characteristic features at those of Jago, but are on the whole executed with greater artistic skill. The Gaṇeśa is seated on a cushion surrounded by human skulls, and the terrible and hideous naked figure of Bhairava is represented as seated on a jackal with his foot on a similar cushion. The four hands of Bhairava hold respectively a trident, short dagger, drum, and pot of wine; he wears a garland made of human skulls and is decorated with other ornaments. The Mahākāla has a short stout figure armed with club in one hand and mace in another. Durgā strides on the prostrate Mahiṣa and holds various weapons in her six hands. With her left hand she seizes the head of the asura, a dwarfish figure standing on the horn of the buffalo. The Nandīśvara has a more pleasing appearance. The image of Brahmā is a fine example of a benign god, camly mediating, with his eyes fixed upon a lotus on the palm of his hands, joined in front of his body. The two figures of Nandi are also well executed.

The images of the Majapahit period show the same general characteristics, but gradually a new element is added, the so-called "garland of rays". To the halo behind the head conventional representation of the rays of sun, and gradually these surround the whole image. The figure of Pārvatī, with Kārttika and Gaṇeśa on two sides, is fair example.

In addition to the ordinary images of gods we have to note a series of

1. Cf. Majumdar, R.C., *op. cit.*, p. 285.

remarkable images of gods which are designed as portraits. In India, and some of her eastern colonies like Champā, the practice prevailed of associating the name of the king (or his relations) with that of the god founded by him (or in his memory) and sometimes also of making the image of the god resemble his own. Evidently the same idea of deifying the king is responsible for these portrait-images of gods.

The Viṣṇu image of Belahan is one of the finest in this series. The god is seated on a lotus seat on the head of Garuḍa. The two upper hands hold a cakra (discus) and śaṁkha (conch-shell) while the two lower hands are joined on his lap. The left leg is crossed over the right thigh and the right leg is placed on the shoulder of Garuḍa. The latter is represented as a gigantic figure, trampling down two serpents under his feet.

Viṣṇu has a serene majestic face, but the image is not an idealisation of divinity but realistic representation of an individual. There are good grounds to believe that the figure is that of the famous king Airlangga (11th century A.D.). The modelling of the image is good and the composition as a whole shows skill of high order. A fine Śiva image, now in the Colonical Museum at Amsterdam, is supposed to represent Anuṣanātha. It is perhaps the finest specimen of figure sculptures of the thirteenth century A.D., combining as it does, serenity with ideal beauty.

Another fine example is furnished by the Hari-Hara image of Simping representing the features of king Kṛtarājasa. Two of his hands hold śaṁkha (conch-shell) and gadā (club), and two others akṣamāla (rosary) and triśūla, attributes respectively of Viṣṇu and Śiva. The features are lovely, and the expression is graceful. The rich ornaments, decorations of the clothes, and the natural lotus leaves, among others, relegate it to the school of Singhasari and Jago, and it may be regarded as one of the best productions of this school. An image of Pārvatī, in Candi Rimbi, is of the same size, and so completely resembles the Hari-Hara figure in point of style and decoration, that Krom has regarded it as portrait of the chief queen of Kṛtarājasa, the daughter of Kṛtānagara. These images show that the school of art, to which they belong along with images of Singhasari and Jago, flourished in the early Majapahit period.[1]

Beautiful naturalistic figures, single or in groups, are occasionally met with in the ruins of temples. Their exact meaning and purpose are uncertain, but they show that pure aesthetic ideas were not foreign to Eastern art. The image of mother and child found at Sikuning, is a good example. It may be a representation of the goddess Hārīti or Ṣaṣṭhī (as the halo indicates a divine figure), but the artist has produced a natural, not idealistic figure.

One of the latest specimens of these protrait images is furnished by a

1. Cf. Majumdar, R.C., *op. cit.*, p. 292.

figure of Mahādeva found in Djakarta. The face is strongly marked by Chinese and Javanese elements. The fully developed 'garland or rays' marks it as belonging to late Majapahit period.

7. *BALI* : *BORNEO*

Besides Java, the island of Bali is the most important region in Indonesia from the point of the history of Brāhmaṇical arts. Although very poor in architectural remains, its sculptures offer a fruitful subject of study, of the monuments which deserves detailed consideration from Brāhmaṇical point of view in a rock cut monastery, called Goa Gaja.

The Goa Gaja (=Skr. Guhā Gaja or Elephant's cave) is a cave situated a little to the south of the road from Pliatan to Bedulu. The cave was hewn out of a large isolated block of stone. The entrance consists of an almost rectangular opening. Above this is the Kāla-head with nose and left cheek badly damaged. Its prominent features are protruding eyes, earrings (used by females), and fingers of two hands with nails curled inside.

The cave contains many niches. A Gaṇeśa image is found in one, while another contains a part of the back of a rākṣasa which is now placed in front of the cave. The third niche, to the right end of the main chamber, contains three liṅgas, each surrounded by eight smaller ones and incircled by a band at the centre. Two words are inscribed on two sides of the entrance. The script of one of these may be referred to the eleventh century A.D. to which period the cave also probably belongs.

There are many beautiful temples of moderated size in Bali, but all these are subsequent to the period when Javanese settled in large number in Bali after the fall of Majapahit. It would be convenient for a proper understanding of the subject if we give an idea of the general plan of temple enclosure before describing specific examples.

The temple area is divided into three court-yards, separated from one another by low walls with gate. An interesting peculiarity is that these gates are not placed in the same line of axis nor is any of them placed precisely in the centre of the wall.

This first court-yard is usually empty though occasionally there is either a *bale* or an offering-pillar. From the first court-yard one passes through the principal gateway to the second court-yard. Here we usually find a number of *bales* and the offering pillar. The *bale* is a small square chamber where the offerings are kept. It has usually a stone foundation which supports wooden posts and rafters carrying a simple pointed roof. The posts and rafters are decorated and the scenes from the *Rāmāyaṇa* and *Mahābhārata* are illustrated on the walls. In the Pura Deśa (public temple in a locality) there is a special *bale* called *bale agung*, a long rectangular chamber, which serves as a prayer hall for the village elders on the new and full moon days. A seat for the god is placed at one end of the chamber.

Of the temples, those dedicated to Śiva, Viṣṇu and Brahmā, called Meru, are the principal ones. The sanctuaries of Viṣṇu and Brahmā lie respectively to the north and south of that of Śiva. The height of the temple roof and the number of storeys it contains clearly show that Śiva occupied the highest place in the trinity, and Brahmā, the lowest.

Having thus described the general plan of temple we shall now describe the different parts of it in some detail. In essence, the plan of a Meru resembles that of Javanese temples, and rock hewn Candis of Bali. A square basement with mouldings, a square chamber constituting cella, and a conical pyramidal roof consisting of series of gradually diminishing storeys ending in final representing liṅga or *ratna*—these have been the essential features of Balinese temples in all ages. There have been no doubt modifications, mainly due to materials used. At first perhaps the shrine was closed by wooden walls and the roof was made of wooden frame with thatched cover. Gradually stone replaced wood in all these parts. The next stage, when the walls of the sanctuary were made of stone, the roof remaining the same is illustrated by the temple of Kesiman. The final evolution of a temple completely made in stone is illustrated by the temple at Tonjo. It is remarkable how the roof has an altogether different appearance although the essential features remain the same.

The influences of art traditions of Central Java at about 8th to 10th century A.D. are proved by the image of Śiva from Bedulu. Although somewhat damaged, this fine figure is undoubtedly reminiscent of the flourishing period of Central Javanese art. The political influence of Matarm dynasty over Bali may account for this. To judge from these and other similar sculptures which may all be dated between the 8th and 10th centuries A.D., must regard this as the earliest period in the evolution of art in Bali during which the Brāhmaṇical influence was dominant and indigenous element was conspicuous by its absence.

During the succeeding period, however, the native element comes to the forefront, and we find a distinctive Balinese style. But gradually this Balinese style is influenced by Javanese, evidently on account of the close political relations subsisting between the two islands.

The earliest specimens of this art are furnished by two groups of images found at Pura Sukavana on the Genung Panulisan. Each group consists of two figures, a man and a woman, in one case standing, and in the other case, seated. The standing images wear clothes of variegated patterns, while the seated ones have plain clothes and wear the sacred threads across the upper part of the body. Both appear to be those of a king and a queen, and both groups may represent the identical royal pair.

The date 1101 A.D. engraved on the back makes it not unlikely that they were the parents of Airlangga, viz., Udayana and Mahendradattā. This is, however, by no means certain.

About this class of images Stutterheim has observed as follows: "Some figures of deified kings and queens, very often depicted together standing on the base, show such pronounced Indonesian features that no doubt can remain about the drastic departure from Brāhmaṇical styles. The bodies have no more the slender grace and movement of the Brāhmaṇical gods. Rigidly closed, they stand like mummies."[1]

Stutterheim has very rightly drawn attention to the fact that some of the peculiar features of this style may perhaps be due to the circumstance that the statues were intended to represent deceased kings and queens, and belonged to a special category of art, which may be called the art of deed.[2] That the Balinese art in this period was capable of the producing more graceful figures is proved by the statues found near the cave Goa Gaja.

The images found in cave, and those that are now set up in front of it, were evidently brought from some other places in the neighbourhood. Among these arc several male and female figures, including an image of Gaṇeśa, which served as water spoùts. The female figure is a fine piece of sculpture. The modellin is graceful and shows a developed technique and naturalistic style allied to Indian art. The expression is full of serenity and beauty. Another group, Hāriti surrounded by seven children, though less successful as work of art, shows a fair degree of skill.

The third group of images, called Kutri-group, shows the same style as we meet with in Goa Gaja. The best specimen of the group, Durgā-Mahiṣāsuramardinī, found at Kutri shows that it was one of the finest images in Bali. The goddess stands over the buffalo and holds various weapons in her eight hands. A similar figure Pura Puseh in the neighbourhood offers a strong contrast by its heaviness and lack of grace. Midway between the two stands the figure of the eight-armed Amoghapāśa.

Several sculptures represent a combination of four figures facing the four directions. The head-dress and the ornaments rasemble those of the preceding one. Each figure has got four hands and a third eye, and holds a śaṁkha (conch-shell) and a book in the upper hands. It seems, therefore, each figure represents the Brāhmaṇical trinity, the third eye, the śaṁkha, and the book being respectively the attributes of Śiva, Viśṇu and Brahmā.

A composite scene is depicted on a sacred water-pot found in Pura Puser at Pejeng. It is about 2½ ft. high, drum shaped, and open at the

1. Majumdar, R.C., *op. cit.*, p. 315.
2. Majumdar, R.C., *op. cit.*, p. 315.

top. The whole outer surface is minutely carved. The principal figures are those of eight snakes in four pairs on four sides. The hoods of each pair are intertwined and crowned by a Śivaliṅga. The tail of each snake is interlaced with that of the neighbouring snake in the next group, and the two ends of each pair of tails support a lotus cushion on which a god is seated. The body of the snake is carried by gods, richly dressed and bending under theheavy burden. They are evidently running over the sea, the representation of which covers the lower part. The upper part is filled with landscape plants, trees and birds, and a few figures. The upper and lower rims are covered respectively with lotus petals and conventional floral designs. The whole scene is overcrowded with details and indicates a degraded form of art such as we meet with in Eastern Java. It has undoubtedly a mythological import, the exact nature of which is, however, difficult to understand.

Before we conclude the study of sculptures we may refer to two characteristic specimens. The first is a Śivaliṅga surrounded by eight busts and eight seated figures in two rows. The upper row of busts is enclosed within lotus petals, and the figures in the lower row are seated on lotus cushions. The next is a representation of Narasiṁha incarnation. The style is very peculiar, almost baroque in character.

The sculpture of the latest period is best seen in the decoration of the hundreds of temples scattered over the island. The Balinese not rich or resourceful enough to raise imposing structures, lavished their skill and energy in the exuberant and excessive decoration of temples, specially their gates and walls, by means of sculpture and painting. Among purely decorative elements we find a rich variety of foliage, flowers and geometrical patterns, besides birds, legendary animals, Kāla-heads, and figures, which are often of grotesque, fantastic and demoniac character. Reliefs, depicting stories from old Brāhmaṇical scriptures, adorn the walls. Among the figures in the round, we have not only images of benevolent gods and mythical beings' such as Garuḍa and Kinnara, but also gods of terriffic appearance, dreadful dvārapālas (temple guards), and various types of demons and monsters. In spite of high technical skill and some amount of graceful beauty, the art is marked by a highly conventionalised style and the general tendency seems to be a leaning towards the representation of the weird, the grotesque, and the terrible in a somewhat baroque style. It must be remembered, it was dictated by religious considerations, and used for the definite purpose of warding off evil spirits who are continually threatening the sacred places with destruction.[1] The modern Balinese art is a living one, and an adequate idea of its nature and varied character can only

1. Cf. Majumdar, R.C. *op. cit.*, pp. 331-332.

be given by a large number of illustrations which are impossible within the present scope of this work.

A general review of the architecture and sculpture in Bali enables us to mark several well defined stages in the evolution of its art. At first it was dominated by purely Indian traditions. From the tenth centry A.D. the art was gradually modified by the working of indigenous element, and it was further subjected to influence from Java. The result was that during the same period we find different styles and levels of excellence in proportion to the presence or absence of Indian and Indo-Javanese tradition and influence. This may be called the truly Balinese period as distinguished from the purely Indian period preceding it. Following Stutterheim's classification we have divided this period into early Indo-Balinese and Middle Indo-Balinese periods.

No remains of old Brāhmaṇical architecture have survived in Borneo, even then we have a few specimens of sculpture which enable us to form a fair idea of its artistic achievements. By far the most important specimens of sculpture in Borneo are the images found in Genung Kombeng. The image may be divided into two groups, viz. (i) Śaiva and (ii) Buddhist. But here we are concerned only with No. 1 that is, Śaiva image.

Amongst the largest figure is that of Mahādeva. The god stands on a lotus cushion and has four hands. The upper right hand holds a rosary, the lower a triśūla, the upper left hand a flywhisk, and the other is empty. A high mukuṭa, necklace, a heavy upavīta, a band round the upper abdomen, girdles, armlets, and anklets decorate the body. The thin transparent cloth ends just above the anklet, and its waving edges are seen on both sides. The other figures are those of Guru, Nandīśvara, Mahākāla, Kārttikeya and Gaṇeśa. It appears from analogous examples, that the temple containing these was dedicated to Śiva, whose figure occupied the shrine, and there were five niches for Guru, Gaṇeśa, Durgā (not found), Mahākāla, and Nandīśvara. The figure of Kārttikeya was probably placed in the wall. The presence of head of Brahmā shows that there was also a temple dedicated to that god, and it is a natural inference that a Viṣṇu temple completed the group.

From an artistic point of view the few images indicate a highly developed school of sculpture in Borneo. The image of Mahādeva is perhaps the best. The pose and modelling of this graceful, figure, with the calm placid smiling face which combines the dispassionate abstraction and the benevolence of the great god, reminds us of the figure of the same deity at Lara Jongrang.

Several other objects, excavated at Muara Kaman, now form part of the regalia belonging to the Sultanate of Kutei. Among these may be specifically mentioned a small golden figure of Viṣṇu, worn by the crown prince on ceremonial occasions, and a golden figure of tortoise. Viṣṇu is four armed, holding a discus, conch shell, and mace in three hands, while the fourth the lower right hand, is in varad-mudrā. The workmanship is of primitive character.

4

Ganesa—A Minor Deity of Brahmanical Pantheon

Of all the gods and goddesses of the Hindu pantheon, Gaṇeśa is the most interesting not only on account of his importance, but also because of his iconographical peculiarities. He is depicted with an elephant's head, a bulging belly and in a variety of poses. In point of time the god appears to be a late addition to the hierarchy of Brāhmaṇic deities but, at the same time, it is noteworthy that he achieves a very exalted position in the hierarchy of gods and goddesses within a very short space of time. The general opinion seems to favour the view that his worship began sometime in 6th century A.D. and during the following two or three centuries we witness his rapid rise to prominence, so much so, that by tenth century an independent sect—of course within the fold of Brāhmaṇism—commonly known as the Gāṇapatya comes into being. Gaṇeśa was also borrowed by other religious systems such as Buddhism and Jainism, and his worship spread almost all over Asia (except the western regions) where Buddhism and other sects of Brāhmaṇism became living faiths. Gaṇeśa is still accorded a very high position by the Hindus and it is one of the most important deities worshipped in India today.

The worship of Gaṇeśa, the elephant-headed deity, in the later Gupta and the post-Gupta periods can be said to be an established fact. This has been conclusively proved by the evidence furnished by an inscription on an ancient column at Ghatiala near Jodhpur (Rajasthan). The inscription is dated 862 A.D. and has been taken to be the earliest of its kind in the praise of this deity. The column is crowned by four images of Gaṇeśa, seated back to back and facing the four cardinal points. This shows that by 862 A.D. Gaṇeśa, in the form of the elephant-headed god had risen to that exalted position where he was worshipped independently and invocated for success. However, earlier images of the god are met with in the rock-cut temples at Elephanta, Ellora and Badami in western India. The images of Gaṇeśa ascribable to 6th century A.D. are far and few between. Noteworthy among them are those in the Gupta temple at Bhurma (District Panna, Madhya Pradesh) and Udaygiri hills near

Vidiśā (Madhya Pradesh). They have been adequately noticed by scholars who agree that the worship of Gaṇeśa was in vogue in the Gupta period. In this connection it is interesting to note that Varāhamihara in his *Bṛhatsaṁhitā* prescribed the details regarding the fashioning of the Gaṇeśa images.[1] The work is dated to the beginning of the 6th century and it can therefore be surmised that the images of Gaṇeśa must have existed in the still earlier period.

It appears that the worship of Gaṇeśa began in the Gupta period around 4th-5th century A.D. and spread to other lands quite early. The Buddhist lost no time in borrowing the deity in their own pantheon and Gaṇeśa travelled to distant lands along with Buddhism. Thus in South-east Asia he was worshipped as Brāhmaṇic deity whereas in the Far East, he was adored as a Buddhist deity.

The following account amply shows that the elephant-headed god was worshipped almost all over South-east Asia, and as such he is perhaps the only Brāhmaṇic divinity whose worship was so widely distributed in terms of space and time.

1. BURMA

The Burmese are professedly Buddhist and follow the Pali canon of the Southern school. Buddhism was introduced in Burma in the later half of the 11th century. However, Brāhmaṇism appears to have already penetrated into Burma long before Buddhism. This is evident from innumerable images of Śaiva and Vaiṣṇava gods and goddesses which have so far been found in that country. There is abundant evidence—epigraphical and otherwise—to show the existence of a considerable number of Hindus, particularly Brāhmins, in Burma as priests, astrologers, architects, etc., who probably occupied positions of influence and responsibility. This perhaps took place in the 5th-6th centuries A.D. during the time of the Imperial Gupta rulers. It were these people who introduced and carried with them images of various deities of the Brāhmaṇic pantheon.

A good number of Gaṇeśa images have so far been found in lower Burma, for in upper Burma Mahāyāna Buddhism held sway. Gaṇeśa being the God who removed obstacles and granted success in any undertaking, his images were carried by merchants and traders who went out of India in order to achieve success in trade and commerce beyond the seas. Their journey was extremely hazardous and full of dangers. It is, therefore, very natural that they carried with them small portable statues of Gaṇeśa. Ray rightly observes that, "Gaṇeśa found popular favour mainly with the commercial section of the population".[2] In Burma, especially in

1. Ch. 58, V. 58.
2. Ray, N.R., *Brahmanical Gods in Burma*, p. 66.

the deltaic regions of lower Burma, Indian immigrants settled in large numbers. In this region, which was their commercial stronghold, a number of small images of Gaṇeśa have been found. They are modest in size, crude in execution and are devoid of any artistic merit. They were probably carried from place to place by merchants and traders as they travelled far and wide in the country.

There are two interesting images of Gaṇeśa in the Rangoon Museum. Both are small in size and are carved in low relief. One of them shows the god seated in padmāsana and six armed. The attributes in his hands are not clearly visible. The upper left appears to be holding a discus (cakra) and a noose (pāśa) while the two lower hands hold the bilva fruit and the trunk respectively. Both the images betray poor workmanship.

Ray has noticed fragments of images of Gaṇeśa within the precincts of the Shwesandaw Pagoda, Pagan, where, along with other Brāhmaṇic divinities were placed at the corner of the different pyramidal structures as guardian deities of the Buddhist shrine.[1] However, a most remarkable Gaṇeśa image was recovered sometime ago from the debris of the ruins of one of the temples of Pagan.[2] It is unique and is of great iconographic interest. It depicts Gaṇeśa seated in padmāsana. He has four hands of which the upper right holds a paraśu and the lower right a rosary (akṣamāla) whereas the upper left has a conch shell and the lower left, placed in his lap probably has mātuliṅga. Yet the most interesting feature of the sculpture is the figure of crocodile on the front of the pedestal carved in low relief. Similarly, on the right and left of the pedestal are carved in bas-relief a tortoise and fish respectively. All these are acquatic creatures which have not so far been found associated with Gaṇeśa elsewhere so far. Nor is there any literary evidence to connect the god with them. The image, therefore, is unique on account of these unusual features. It is not unlikely that the Indian traders carved such an image to protect them from acquatic creatures in the jungles of Burma during their travels far into the interior of the country.

There are two more images of Gaṇeśa at Pagan which are only miniature votive tablets. Gaṇeśa thus appears to have gradually achieved an important place in the indigenous religion and mythology of Burma and came to be known as *Mahā-pienne* and as such is still worshipped in the Peninsula.[3]

2. *THAILAND*

Thailand (popularly known as Siam) came into contact with India at a

1. Ray, N.R., *op. cit.*, p. 67.
2. *ibid.*, pp. 67-68.
3. *ibid.*, p. 69.

very early period. The stylistic evidence shows the influence of the Amarāvati school on Siamese art in the early centuries of the Christian era. Later still, the Gupta, Pallava and Pāla elements are noticeable in Siamese art. It appears that the southern part of Thailand came first into contact with India. It was easier for Indian traders to push further eastward from lower Burma into Thailand. This should explain the strong Burmese Brāhmaṇic influence on the Mon art during 6th-8th century A.D.

The Mons were devout Hindus. Notwithstanding the fact that the Thais adhered to Buddhism later, Gaṇeśa was popular among them all. Several statues of the god have been found. Among these those of the Ayuthian period are noteworthy. The early art of Ayuthia (Ayodhya) betrays strong Indian influence. This is borne out by a fine bronze statue which represents the god seated on a cushion in the mahārājalīlā pose with his trunk curved towards left. Under his uplifted right leg is his vāhana, the rat. He wears a knee-reaching lower garment and a sacred thread of snake (nāga-yajñopavīta). His bangles and armlets are simple rings (valayas) whereas the jewelled karaṇḍa-mukuṭa is noteworthy. He has four hands, the arrangement of which, according to Getty, is rather unusual and unique.[1] From the shoulder to the elbow there is one arm, but at the elbow the arm branches into two. Of the two upper hands, the left holds a noose (pāśa) while the attribute in the right is not clearly seen. The lower right holds a broken tusk and the lower left rests on the thigh. However, the god is shown with both the tusks intact. This lapse of iconographical details may be due to the ignorance of the Ayuthian artist.

In the famous Brāhmaṇic temple at Bangkok, there is an interesting bronze statue of Gaṇeśa. He is shown with his legs superposed. He wears a nāga-yajñopavīta. In his right hand is to be seen the broken tusk while in the left is a manuscript. This can be taken, with a reasonable amount of certainty, to be the representation of Gaṇeśa as a scribe (lekhaka) for the sage Vyāsa who is traditionally supposed to have dictated the whole *Mahābhārata* to Gaṇeśa. This is not unlikely in view of the fact that the great epic had already reached as far as Cambodia by 6th century. It may also suggest Gaṇeśa's association with knowledge (jñāna).

3. CAMBODIA

Legendary accounts show that India came into contact with Cambodia at quite an early period. Tradition tells us that about the early centuries of the Christian era a Brāhmin by name Kauṇḍinya journeyed to the coast of Cambodia and established a kingdom there. He Indianized the country

1. Ray, N.R., *op. cit.*, p. 47.

completely, and the Chinese reports state : "They worship the Spirits of Heaven and make images of bronze. Those with two faces have four arms and those with four faces have eight arms".[1] These are obvious reference to Brāhmaṇic gods and demonstrate how deep the Brāhmaṇic influence had penetrated into Cambodia.

Cambodia is extremely rich in sculptural remains and there are innumerable images of Hindu, including Buddhist divinities. Just as in Burma and Thailand, in Cambodia too a number of Gaṇeśa images have come to light. As already observed, the *Mahābhārata* was known in Cambodia as early as the 6th century. It, therefore, seems likely that they knew Gaṇeśa from an early period. This is confirmed by the evidence from the inscriptions of Angkor Borei, dated 611 A.D., which records the grant of slaves to the temple which was dedicated to several deities of which one was Gaṇeśa.[2]

The cult of Śiva appears to have penetrated into Cambodia from Funan where Hindu religion was practised at an early date. Gaṇeśa, therefore, very likely came along with Śiva. There are several temples of Śiva and Gaṇeśa in Cambodia. In this connection it may be mentioned that Yaśovarman I (889-910 A.D.) had erected an āśrama at Neak Buos, an important religious centre which was founded by Jayavarman I. The āśrama was dedicated to the Gaṇeśa of Candanagiri. This has been referred to in an inscription of 9th century but found in the region of Kompong Thom.[3] The 'Sandal Mountains' (Candanagiri) has been identified as the Chocung Prey near which, on a hill in the vicinity of Prah Pada, are the ruins of a temple that is believed to have been dedicated to Gaṇeśa. This inscription is of great interest because it refers to Gaṇeśa as an independent deity of local importance and emphasizes the tradition which followed him from India to Japan of being worshipped in connection with mountains.

One temple at Prāsāt Bak (10th century) was apparently dedicated to the worship of Gaṇeśa. Gaṇeśa is also depicted in the scenes in Bung Meglea and his statues have also been discovered in the vicinity of Kuk Trapeang Kul temple. Several other loose sculptures have also been found from time to time. Gaṇeśa is known as Prah Kenes in Cambodia and his representations can be distinguished on account of certain characteristic features. First and foremost, he is never shown as pot-bellied and bulky. He is usually shown sitting cross-legged and with two hands. The trunk is almost straight and curled down at the end; sometime it is upturned also. Another noteworthy feature is that the pre-Khmer images of Gaṇeśa, as a rule, are not shown with head-dress of any sort. However, towards 8th century we find Gaṇeśa wearing an ornate karaṇḍa-mukuṭa.

1. Le May, R., *The Culture of South-East Asia*, p. 112.
2. Briggs, L.P., *The Ancient Khmer Empire*, p. 46.
3. *ibid.*, p. 139.

They are usually bare to the waist and are shown wearing a nāga-yajño-pavīta.

One of the most remarkable images of Gaṇeśa is in a private collection at Speak Thmar Kendal. It depicts the god sitting in a cross legged posture. He has two hands and wears a tall conical headgear. Curiously enough, he has four hands. It may be especially mentioned that four-headed forms of Gaṇeśa are extremely rare and the only parallel that can be cited is from Ghatiala (Rajasthan) in India where four Gaṇeśa images are carved on the top of a column in cardinal directions.

An interesting stone image of the god was discovered at Thurol Phak Kim Kanda. This is by far the simplest form of Gaṇeśa in which he is shown sitting cross-legged and does not wear any jewellery, not even the sacred thread. T he right hand holds probably the broken tusk while the left one has a bowl of sweets. On the forehead is the third eye, a characteristic of Śiva. This is a pre-Khmer image datable to the pre-eighth century.

A fine stone of the Khmer period (10th-12th centuries) is now preserved in the Musee Guimet, Paris. It shows the god sitting cross-legged and wearing a very elaborately jewelled mukuṭa. He also wears a nāga-yajñopavīta and has snakes for armlets (sarpa-keyūra). Of the four hands, the two at the back are broken, the other two at the front are shown resting in the lap and the attributes in the hands are, therefore, not clear. Though slightly bulky and of ponderous proportions, the statue is well modelled and is a fine specimen of the period to which it belongs.

4. *CHAMPA*

To the east of Funan and Cambodia was situated the kingdom of Champa, which is now occupied by the central and southern Annam. The very name Champa is thoroughly Indian and it is clear from the monuments, statuary and inscriptions found in that ancient country that the early civilization flourishing there was due to strong influence from India. Contact with India started from about the early centuries of the Christian era and the influence of the Amarāvati school is visible on its early artistic creations. As in Cambodia, in Champā too, the principal Brāhmaṇic cult was that of Śiva. In fact, Śaivism was held in such a high esteem by the Cham dynasty, that it claimed direct descent from Śiva. The most important centre of Śaivism was in the Quangdom where, between 4th to 7th century innumerable sanctuaries were erected at Mi-so'n alone. Alongwith Śiva, Gaṇeśa naturally found his way into Champa.

There is epigraphical evidence to show that temples were erected and dedicated to Gaṇeśa. One such sanctuary was at Po Nagar. From the cultural evidence it appears that Gaṇeśa was quite popular during 7th-8th centuries A.D. A most impressive statue of Gaṇeśa was discovered at Mi-so'n where a Śaiva shrine was found.[1] It depicts a standing Gaṇeśa wearing a dhoti-like lower garment (*Sampot*), very similar to the Indian *ardhoruka*, reaching knees. It is held in position on waist by what looks like a cord (kaṭi-sūtra). Originally four armed, two of its back arms are now missing. In the lower left hand is a bowl of sweets which he is eating with his trunk. He wears sparse jewellery and there is no crown on his head, but the nāga-yajñopavīta is seen. The statue is dated to about 8th century. As compared to the Khmer representations of Gaṇeśa, this image appears rather bulky. It is characterised by rather coarse plastic treatment. Another seated image was also found at Mi-so'n.[2] Yet most interesting is the Gaṇeśa image in the Saigon Museum. It is unfortunately in a mutilated condition. It shows the god seated, and with two hands. Curiously enough it has three deep set eyes. He also has a small prabhāvalaya at the back. According to Boisselier, it is the only representation of its kind in the whole of South-East Asia.[3]

In some of the Cham statues of Gaṇeśa we notice uṣṇīśa, the protruberence on the head, which is supposed to be a symbol of great men (mahā-puruṣa-lakṣaṇa). This, in fact, is a characteristic of the Buddha images and it is not, therefore, unlikely that the Buddhist iconography influenced the Brāhmaṇic image. This becomes all the more possible in view of the fact that both the religions flourished in Champa side by side.

5. *JAVA AND BALI (INDONESIA)*

It appears that Java was known to Indians from a very long period, for the *Rāmāyaṇa* refers to the islands as Yava-dvīpa. In all probability the first contacts were made about the beginning of the Christian era, if not earlier. Brāhmaṇism began to spread in these islands during the time of the great Gupta monarchs in 4th-5th centuries, and Śaivism became a most predominant faith. Innumerable sculptures of Brāhmaṇical gods and goddesses have been found in Indonesia. In Java, however, there does not appear to be a cult of Gaṇeśa and no temples were dedicated to him but his images have been found in the temples of Śiva.

Among the statues of Gaṇeśa in Java the most primitive is the one discovered in west Java.[4] The carving is very crude and the statue appears to be unfinished. Some scholars would like to assign it a very early date

1. Jean Boisselier, *La Statuaire du Champa : Recherches sur les Cultes et L'iconographie*, p. 57.
2. Jean Boisselier, *La Statuaire du Champa : Recherches sur les Cultes et L'iconographie*, pp. 57-58.
3. *ibid.*, p. 58.
4. Getty, Alice, *Gaṇeśa*, p. 45.

only because it is so primitive. However, the image appears unfinished and it is therefore extremely difficult to date it with precision. Another early Gaṇeśa statue is a small bronze which is now in the British Museum. It shows the god seated with two hands without any attributes and there is no head-dress. The trunk is somewhat straight. The statue perhaps represents an early attempt at fashioning the anthropomorphic form of Gaṇeśa and may be ascribed to the 6th century. A slight advance is noticeable in the bronze statuette in the possession of G. Coedes. It also has two arms without any attributes. The trunk is straight and the god wears sparse jewellery. He, however, wears a small conical mukuṭa over the head.

The stone statue of Gaṇeśa found on the Dieng plateau is believed to be the most ancient representation of the god in Java.[1] It appears that, stylistically at least, it may be later than the preceding one. It shows the Gaṇeśa sitting, with four hands; the proper right hand holding the broken tusk and the left the bowl of sweets while the upper two held a paraśu and an akṣamāla. He wears armlets, bracelets, a necklace and a nāga-yajñopavīta, but there is no crown on the head.

One of the finest statues of Gaṇeśa from Chandi Banon is now housed in the Djakarta Museum.[2] Practically nothing now remains of Chandi Banon, a Śaivite monument near Borobudur. The statue depicts the god seated and wearing a flowered garment and jewellery. In the right hand he holds a broken tusk and a rosary while in lower left hand is a bowl of sweets. The object in the upper left hand is broken.

The use of skull ornaments in the representations of Gaṇeśa images is a purely Javanese conception. This happened because of Gaṇeśa's association with Śiva who, in the form of Bhairava, wears a garland of skulls (kapāla-mālā). This is best illustrated by Gaṇeśa image of Bara. According to the chronogram in words on its pedestal it is dated 1239 A.D.—in the early Singhasari period.[3] The god carried his usual attributes but a number of skulls are seen on the pedestal. Gaṇeśa is the god who removes all dangers and difficulties. In this case he is himself protected by a large Kāla head against dangerous influences threatening him from the rear. The large canines and the long tongue of the Kāla recall modern Balinese masks. The back hands of Gaṇeśa are at the same time used for the claws of the Kāla. Very similar arrangement of skulls is also seen in the statue from Chandi Singhasari.[4] It shows the god standing with the usual attributes in his four hands. He wears elaborated jewellery in the making of which skulls are used.

1. Getty, Alice, *op. cit.*
2. Bernet Kempers, A.J., *Ancient Indonesian Art*, p. 36.
3. Bernet Kempers, A.J., *op. cit.*, p. 73.
4. *ibid.*, p. 79. pl. 235 now in Leiden Museum.

During 8th-9th century the Śaiva cult was especially flourishing in Bali and consequently Gaṇeśa became quite a popular deity. It is interesting to note that a majority of Balinese images of Gaṇeśa show him a standing posture. Besides, he was usually shown with a third eye, a characteristic of Śiva. A remarkable statue from Djembaram depicts him seated and holding in his two hands a fly-whisk in the right and a bowl of sweets in the left. A bronze image of Gaṇeśa have also been found in Bali. Gaṇeśa is also to be seen sculptured in the group of royal personages whose statues were made posthumously. Probably, they invoked the god to remove obstacles in life after death.

6. BORNEO

It is indeed surprising that Brāhmaṇism should have penetrated as far as Borneo in the 5th century or even earlier. This is evident from an epigraphical record discovered at Kotei which records certain Brāhmaṇic rites performed by Brāhmins. Furthermore, a cave at Kombeng contained several Brāhmaṇical and Buddhist images among which majority were of the Śaiva pantheon. Of these, a fine statue of Gaṇeśa shows him sitting with the usual attributes in his four hands.[1] It is a loose image and appears to have been brought with others from some other temple which was facing destruction at the hands of hostile barbarians. It seems that the idol is taken to be contemporaneous with the Kotei epigraphs of 5th century and is thus supposed to be one of the oldest statues of Gaṇeśa known so far. This dating, however, is not supported by stylistic evidence. Furthermore, it should be borne in mind that the statue originally belonged to some temple on the banks of river Mahakan whence it was brought and deposited in the cave. On stylistic grounds it can be assigned to 8th century.

Another statue of Gaṇeśa from Borneo shows the deity seated with fan-shaped ears and almost straight trunk which appear to be the characteristic of Borneo statues of Gaṇeśa.[2] Another important feature that is common to both is that the crown looks more like the jaṭā-mukuṭa. In the present case it looks as if the hair is combed into a round bun (dhammilla) on the top of the head and is adorned by a tiara. The attributes in his hands are not clear. A very interesting feature of this statue is the urṇā mark, or the protuberance between the eye-brows, an important mark of greatness. The urṇā is usually to be seen in the statue of Buddha in India and its presence in Brāhmaṇic images is, probably, due to the ignorance of the artist who was perhaps used to fashion Buddha images. It may be recalled that another mark—uṣṇīśa—has been noticed in the images of Gaṇeśa in Champa.

1. Getty, *op. cit.*, p. 64, pl. 32b.
2. Getty, *op. cit.*, p. 64, Pl. 32d.

5

Brahmanical Culture in South-East Asia

One of the most distinctive and edifying phenomena of the classical period, alike in Europe as in Asia, was that very large spheres of cultural influence were assiduously created, established and fostered, undeterred by the virility of any of those colonial zones, oriented as these influences seem to have been, towards, sophisticating and tempering the cultural slant of these autochthonous people. This 'acculturation', as sociologists might choose to call it, was not an imposition, but a dynamic reception to ideas which were neither sold nor canvassed for. We also know that in South-East Asia almost all the countries that had been colonized by Indians or had close commercial contact with India were permeated with the Brāhmaṇical culture and its elaborate paraphernalia of rites and rituals, gods and goddesses, and myths and legends, which is still traceable in these lands after so many vicissitudes of a long history.

In such a context, there is hardly any surprise that the Brāhmaṇical heritage was imperceptibly blended with the local clan in South-East Asia, to enable it to become almost the common pool of ancestral heir loom for all these peoples. Sensitive and sympathetic art-historians have labelled the ambit of this temporal efflorescence the 'Indian Asia'. At the root of such a transaction lay the already achieved fusion of Brāhmaṇism and South-East Asian thought and culture, producing the Kaleidoscopic variations patternised out of the absorption of our Epics, *Purāṇas*, cults and beliefs into their religio-cultural pool. Sanskrit was, doubtless, a powerful medium of expression for this cultural well-being; it was in fact a universalised ingredient in the literary, cultural and artistic cross-fertilisation afoot in that age. The entire South-East Asia, came from effectively under the spell of South Indian kingdoms from a comparatively early times, and the Gupta and post-Gupta forces working from Bihar and Bengal in the wake of the peripatetic programmes of Buddhism first and the renascent Brāhmaṇism subsequently, ably participated in this process. South India, by and large, stood out as the most favoured foster-mother for these South-East Asian principalities. The assimilation was so complete ultimately, and the medievel manifestations of this process were so thoroughly transformed in the indigenous content, as to make them a positive though subtle transfusion of the local with the peripheral. The spirit of oneness so engendered was, however, moored to last, and stayed on even after the advent of Islam into these shores, or the still later inroads of western culture.

India gave the whole of South-East Asia its own culture. In Ceylon colonists from western India settled as early as the 5th century B.C. Ceylon was converted to Buddhism in the reign of Aśoka. Indian merchants found their way to Malaya, Sumatra and other parts of South-East Asia during this time. Wonderful memorials and Buddhist stūpa of Borobudur in Java and Śaivite temple of Angkor in Cambodia were established. Cultural influences from China and Islamic world were felt in South-East Asia but the primary impetus to civilization came from India. Generally we use the word colony for the Indianized states but this hardly appears to be an appropriate word since we do not find any real historical edidence of an Indian conquest outside the bounds of India. The so-called Indian colonies were peaceful ones. The Indianised kings were indigenous chieftains who had learnt what India had to teach them.

Cambodia, Champa, Thailand, Burma, Laos, Malaysia and Indonesia, all these were the glorious collaterals of Brāhmaṇic cultural polyphylum, the saga of each of which shows the undercurrents of a traditional homogeneity. We might record at this stage, some important historical details that would link Brāmaṇism with South-East Asia more than anything else.

1. CAMBODIA

Cambodia was the most thoroughly Indianised state in the whole region of South-East Asia, i.e., it bore the deepest impress of Brāhmaṇical religion, culture, language and literature and art. In the domain of language and literature, she (Cambodia) has been able to keep up the Brāhmaṇical tradition. Present day literary compositions, which are nevertheless, a great departure from the epoch of the inscriptions written in old Khmer amply bear this truth. Khmer literature, like Khmer writings is largely cast in an Indian mould, though it is modified with a distinctive native tradition. Technical works on divination, astronomy, medicine and the like also occupy a conspicuous place in Khmer literature. Khmer originality is reflected in stories and legends. In the western sense of the term, practically no Khmer theatre exists. Form of ballet or rhythmical pantomime based on classical subjects from Indian sources—especially the *Rāmāyaṇa* and the *Mahābhārata* are performed. Even in technical works poetic forms are used extensively with a fixed number of syllables to the verse.

The history of the contact between India and Cambodia in the domain of language and literature forms, is in fact, part of a wider field of study, viz., the systematic study of the expansion of Sanskrit outside the borders of India through the ages. This study also yields fruitful results so far the development of Sanskrit language is concerned. Analytical study of Cambodian Sanskrit undoubtedly helps us though indirectly, in the study of the evolution of Cambodian language. At present old Khmer which is revealed entirely in old inscriptions is very little studied. From India ancient Cambodia adopted Sanskrit, Prākrit and Pāli but out of these the highest position was given to Sanskrit. Brāhmi script was maintained by the Brāhmaṇa immigrants who wanted to maintain eloquence of their language. At places we find Pallava script of South India in the inscriptions.

Khmer alphabet is derived from Pallava or the East Cālukya alphabet of South India. Words derived from Sanskrit are so numerous that Aymonier has remarked that an entire dictionary can be made out of the words of Sanskrit origin which are in current use in the Khmer language. Sanskrit words have, however, been generally identified according to fairly well defined rules.

Sanskrit		*Khmer*
Ga	—	K
Ta	—	d
da	—	t
pa	—	ba
ba	—	pa
j	—	s
s and s	—	s
v	—	p

Transformation of words have been done according to the above principle :

Devatā	—	Tevoda (in learned Khmer) Tepda (in popular Khmer)
Puruṣa	—	Baros or Pros
Śāsana	—	Sasna
Svarga	—	Suorkea or Suor
Vak	—	Veaca or Peak
Vimāna	—	Phimean

Besides the above we find that there is a tendency in Khmer language to be brief and monosyllabic:— Liṅga—Lin; Viṣa (poison)—Pis; Dosa—Tus; Velā (time)—Pel; Hasta—Hat; Pati—pti; Śunya—Sun; Vera—Vera—Vrah. Sometimes, by eliminating the vowel between two consonants abbreviations are made:— Garuḍa—Krut; Pati—Pdei; Saras (tank)—Sra. And sometimes the first letter of the word is eliminated and if this is 'n', the consonant of the second syllable is nasalised as we find in Nagara—Angkor.

During the Chenla period the local old Cambodian language received special attention. A number of inscriptions of that period have an appendix in vernacular. Some of them have been written exclusively in vernacular only. It is just possible that the Cambodians were influenced by the South Indian Pallava traditions since we know that king Mahendravarman (600-630 A.D.) used Tamil (vernacular) in inscriptional use. The local language developed by absorbing words from Sanskrit and Prākrit to such an extent that it could easily become a rival of Sanskrit for documentary purpose.

The principal feature of old Khmer language is that most of the words admit of one or two syllables maximum. Bisyllables are generally derived words while words having 3 syllables are very rare. Three and four syllable words have most probably foreign origins. Khmer words are formed of: 1. Prefixation, 2. Inflexion, and 3. Reduplication.

In Khmer we find pure and simple juxtaposition of the root and the affix peculiar to Sanskrit. Affix is joined directly to the root without any modification of the affix or the root itself. This phenomena which is very frequent in Khmer allows us to find out the links between a certain number of derivatives and their roots besides helping in restoration of the ancient forms which have been lost in course of time.

So far the general aspects of the word are concerned, the Khmer language admits of only the morphology of lexicon or the morpho-semanterus (*śabda* in Sanskrit). Morphems (*pada* in Sanskrit), do not exist in Khmer. Morphology is used in formation of words and not for the construction of sentence. In Khmer there is neither number nor gender. For plural number auxiliary words having lexical meaning such as many, numerous etc. are used. Verb also is invariable like other words of a sentence. Verbal tense is also unknown. Verbal aspects are indicated by auxiliary morphems. Grammar plays the role of giving laws of syntactical order (place of words in the sentence) and the particles which accompany them.

The most remarkable fact in the evolution of the Khmer language is the aspiration of the initial consonant. In an initial group of two occlusive consonants the first becomes an aspirated consonant. In combination like 'ko', 'k' becomes 'Kh' in Angkorean epoch. Coedes opines that this aspiration is due to the impossibility of pronouncing a consonantic group given in a loan word such as Kṣatriya or in a word produced by the regular play of prefixation or of inflexion.

George Coedes[1] points out the peculiar form of transformation of Indian words such as phdei from *pati* (husband), '*Phdah* from *Pada*' (abode), 'Khsat' from Kshatriya'. So far this word is concerned it should be noted that certain texts in North Western Prākrit show the treatment of 'Ks' as 'Kh'. There is yet another frequent feature in the evolution of Khmer language. Contraction of a large number of words through the loss of vowels and the re-grouping of consonants are done. This results in reduction of old bisyllable into monosyllable.

Khmer alphabets have, in the beginning, profound South Indian influence, pre-Angkorean characters without legs and are of unequal dimensions. The graphic system of Sanskrit has been adopted and modified. Vocabic signs have been added so far vocabic point of view is concerned, t he language, Khmer is much richer than Sanskrit.

In peaceful contacts between two peoples, financial transactions and co mmercial exchanges require a vocabulary. New ideas, new objects and ter ms thus introduced necessitate infiltration of foreign terms. Indigenous terms and also foreign terms tend to loose their originality or their own c haracter from morphological and semantic points of view. For transmission of social moral, religious and administrative novelties brought by India to ancient Cambodia, the old Khmer language did not have equivalent terms. And thus Brāhmaṇical terminology in these spheres were implanted.

Among the many administrative and political reforms taken up by Kauṇḍinya I, was the introduction of Sanskrit and alphabet of North Indian origin which opened up the treasures of Brāhmaṇical literature both sacred and profane to the people of Funan. Communication with other peoples of East and South East Asia (where some developed form of Sanskrit was being used as *lingua franca*) also became easier.[2]

Most of the place names mentioned in Khmer inscriptions are found in North India. Standard Sanskrit prevailed in the whole region lying between Himalayas and the Vindhyas and even today the languages of this region are originally Aryan. Even in the opinion of Hiuen Tsang, the people of Central India used explicit and correct speech and their expressions were elegant like Devas.[3] Sanskrit came to Cambodia from a region where it had preserved its purest forms through centuries.

Sanskrit loan-words in old Khmer can be divided into following categories: 1. Geographical names, 2. Names of persons and divinities, 3. Administrative terms, 4. Terms relating to calendar and numbers, 5. Abstract terms, 6. Miscellaneous terms.

1. Quoted in Sarkar, K.K., *Early Indo-Cambodian Contacts*, p. 13.
2. Panikkar, K.M., *L'Inde et L'Occident La Haye*, p. 25. Cf. also Ghosh, M.M., *op. cit.*, p. 49.
3. Watters, *On Yuan Chwang*, pp. 1 and 152.

Geographical Names

Geographical names which are purely Indian, are found either in their original form or in a lightly modified form. Indians who came to this land transplanted here the names with which they were familiar from before. We know even in modern times that transplantation of European names in America has been done. The most popular and widely prevalent ending of place names are Pura, Ālaya, Āśrama, Avasa, Āyatana, Deśa, Grāma, Giri, Niketana, Parvata, Taṭāka, and Pattan and Pāda. Place names of divinities, kings, dignitaries and other persons as we see in the following examples:

1. Pura— Śivapura, Īśvarapura, Sarvapura, Ugrapura, Svayambhuvapura, Viṣṇupura, Amoghapura, Cakrāṅkapura, Yaśodharapura, Bhavapura, Indrapura, Bhīmapura, Puruṣpura, Viṣṇupura, Siddhipura, Rājendrapura, Śreṣṭhapura and Vikramapura etc.
2. Ālaya— Hariharālaya, Maheśvarālaya, Śankarālaya, etc.
3. Āśrama— Rājendrāśrama, Rudrāśrama, Sarvāśrama, etc.
4. Āvāsa— Śreṣṭhanivāsa.
5. Āyatana— Siddhāyatana.
6. Deśa— Madhyadeśa, Āryadeśa, Purvadeśa etc.
7. Giri— Yaśodharagiri.
8. Parvata— Mahendraparvata, Siddhiparvata, Sūryaparvata and Yaśodharaparvata etc.
9. Asthāna— Bhavasthāna and Śivasthāna.
10. Pattana— Śivapattana and Nāgapattana etc.
11. Pāda— Śivapāda, Śivaspāda, Īśānapāda, Laksmindrapāda, Īśvarapāda, Viṣṇupāda, etc.
12. Grāma— Viṣṇugrāma.

The term Janapada occurs already in *Aitareya Brāhmaṇa,* Aśokan edicts and the Myakadoni inscription of Śrī-Pulumayi.[1] It was an important territorial unit of ancient India since the time of the Pāli Cannon. It was believed that Janapada mentioned in Sdok Kek Thom inscription was some place in India.[2]

George Coedes has shown that Janapada can also be a place situated in ancient Cambodia.[3] Similarly Nāgapattana may be the same as modern Nāgapattana in South India where a Buddhist vihāra was constructed

1. Raychaudhury, H.C., *The Geography of the Deccan*—in the *Early History of the Deccan*, Edited by G. Yazdani, p. 23.
2. Bagchi, P.C., *Studies in Tantra,* Pt. I, pp. 2 and 18.
3. *BEFEO*, Vol. XLVII, p. 9.

by a Śailendra King during Rajendra Chola's reign. Anga is the same great kingdom in East, Bihar (Bhagalpur area) known to the Indian writers from a very early period. In a Sanskrit verse written in old Khmer it has been pointed out that the village named Videha was given by the king or kings, Śrī Suryavarman to Sukarman who came from Kurukshetra and because of this, this village was called Kurukshetra.

The tendency to replace Sanskrit names by purely Khmer words is also interesting to note. Many names appear only in Khmer form but their meaning shows that they are Sanskrit names translated into Khmer. The following examples deserve mention here:

1. Travan Brāhmaṇa—Pond of the Brāhmaṇa.
2. Balam Vakula—Vakula ground.
3. Vihara Run—Wide Vihāra.
4. Vrai Kapal—Kapala forest.
5. Vanam Purva—Eastern Mountain.
6. Stuk Ṛṣi—Lake of the Ṛṣi.
7. Svay Pancaka—Pancaka mango.
8. Travan Vanik—Pond of the merchant.

Names of Divinities and Persons

A clear distinction between the names of reigns and the posthumous names of the kings is necessary to be made. The pre-Angkorean posthumous names are—Śivaloka, Śivapura, and Indraloka while in the Angkorean epoch they become more numerous. The two suffixes Loka and Pāda which are very close in meaning have been used, e.g. — 1. Parameśvaraloka, 2. Viṣṇuloka, 3. Īśvaraloka, 4. Paramaśivaloka, 5. Rudraloka, 6. Paramarudraloka, 7. Paramaśivapāda, 8. Brahmaloka, 9. Śivaloka, 10. Paramaviraloka, 11. Nirvanapāda, 12. Sadaśivapāda, 13 Paramakaivalyapāda, 14. Paramaniṣkalpapāda, and 15. Paramaviṣṇuloka. Among the interesting names of persons, the following can be mentioned:

1. Namasśivāya (name of a donor)
2. Vikalanetra (name of a slave)
3. Januklesa. and
4. Amṛtavisa.

We have names of women with masculine or rather neuter endings like *Pavitra* and *Tīrtha* which are contrary to the traditional rules. Some ancient Brāhmaṇical texts show that the Kṣatriyas were known as Varmans from the beginning of the Christian era though it would be wrong to suppose that this term Varman became an integral part of the names of all Kṣatriya kings in the earlier periods. It was a mere convention to call Kṣatriya by the general designation—Varman at that time and in a later period it was almost meaningless though it formed an integrated part of the names of the kings in some cases. Barth has remarked that the term Varman was possessive compound meaning who has such and such god as protector.[1] According to him the following translation can be made:

1. Vīravarman—The Varman who is a hero.
2. Udayādityavarman—The Varman who is a rising sun.
3. Jayavīravarman—The Varman who is a victorious hero.

Names of priests often end in Śiva, such as Vāmaśiva, Sikhaśiva and Sadāśiva.

These names of the priests were definitely transplanted from India in their original forms. In the lists of names of Śaiva Āchāryas of the Mattamayura clan Sadāśiva, Sikhaśiva, Vāmaśiva are found.[2] It is just possible that the families of the royal priests in ancient Cambodia were related with these clans in India.

A great number of names of the divinities reveal importance of local cults. Jayaśreṣṭha, Liṅgapurāsana, Champeśvara, and Nāgasthāna are the tutclary deities who are essentially indigenous though the fact reminds us of the cult of Yakṣa in India. It is really surprising to note that even the names of Śiva like Utpaneśvara, Akaleśvara and Amrātakeśvara which are quite rarely met with in India were known in ancient Cambodia. The name Amrātkeśvara find mention in an inscription of Basarh (Vaiśāli, in the state of Bihar in India).

Administrative Terms:

Quite numerous are the administrative terms mentioned in inscriptions written in old Khmer language. The most important ones are:

1. Kulapati—Chief of temple.
2. Kramapāla—Guardian of rules and regulations.
3. Devaparichara—Servant of God.
4. Gunadoṣadarśi—Inspectors of merits and defects.
5. Rājakulamahāmantrī—Minister responsible for the welfare of the royal family.
6. Grāmapāla—Guardian of village.
7. Samantagajapati—Officer incharge of elephants.
8. Kāryādhipati—Superintendent over administrative activities.
9. Vasanapāla and
10. Vasatrapāla—Guardian of clothes.

1. *ISCC*, p. 133, Notes—4.
2. *IHQ*, Vol. XXVI, p. 1.

Technical terms connected with administration are:

1. Rājakārya—administration.
2. Sabhā—court of justice.
3. Varhpanji—sacred register.
4. Dharmādhikarana—court of justice.
5. Pratyaya—entrusted to treasure, tax and revenue.
6. Prasasta—inscribed stele.
7. Ayatya—authority.
8. Śagana—in common.
9. Prasiddhi—exclusive right.
10. Śāsana—royal order.
11. Alakshana—written deed.
12. Rājadharma—royal foundation.
13. Upakalpa—auxiliary.
14. Vyavahāra—law suit.
15. Vyāpāra—employment, occupation.
16. Apavāda—opposition, objection.

Administration of the country were:

1. Grāma—village.
2. Viṣaya—district
3. Pramāṇa—province
4. Nagara—city
5. Rāṣṭra] —country.
6. Deśa

In India, we are familiar with most of these terms and designations. A few which appear peculiar to India are creations of the Khmers conforming to the special administrative structure of their country.

Terms related to Calendar and Numbers

The Śaka era has been used in Cambodia without any exception. The inscription of Chālukya Balaveśvara (Pulkeśin) found in Badami which dates from 465 Śaka corresponding to 543 A.D. is the earliest inscription in India in which Śaka era has been used while the earliest old Khmer inscription bears the date 535 Śaka corresponding to 611 A.D. It is evident from this that the Śaka era spread in ancient Cambodia at almost the same period when it found introduction in Indian epigraphy. Old Khmer inscriptions contain very detailed dates like the era, year, month, fortnight, tithi, nakṣatra and also the day of the week. Khmers used to count their dates in expired years. In the enumeration of the day of the week, words like Vṛhaspatidinavara (Thursday) have been used. The following forms and terms have also been variously used: 1. Pratisamvatasara—every year; 2. Vuddhavara—Instead of Buddhavara; 3. Purnnami; 4. Asujya—Asvayuja; 5. Sankranta--New year, 6. Candradivasavara—Monday.

Ancient Khmer used to express the numbers only with the help of Khmer words for 1, 2, 3, 4, 5, 10, 20 and sometimes multiples of 20 and had borrowed from Sanskrit the word Śata for 100. Such examples are: 1. Mvay—one; 2. Vyar—two; 3. Pramvai—six; and 4. Bhay—twenty.

For counting of slaves and animals, various objects of length etc., this system of counting remained in force for a long time but in old Khmer inscriptions the dates are, however, expressed in Sanskrit words only even in the early period.

Abstract terms

Abstract terms in the inscriptions written in old Khmer are:

1. Svatantra—out of
2. Śākhā—A derivative of śākhā meaning origin, provenance used in connection with slaves.
3. Svargat—to die
4. Nivedana—to address
5. Paripālana—to keep
6. Santāna—progeny
6. Prasāda—gift due to royal generosity
8. Kalpanā.

In relation to other terms, the abstract terms are less numerous and do not reflect any philosophical ideas. In most of these cases these terms carry material sense although their forms have been abstracted. 1. Kalpanā—to appropriate, 2. Dharma—pious foundation, 3. Sthāpana—to establish, 4. Pratiṣtha—to install, 5. Panbhoga—revenue.

Miscellaneous Terms

Among the various other terms, mention can be made of the following:

1. Candana—Sandal (name of an Indian tree)
2. Saptaparṇa—Name of an Indian tree
3. Viṇā—Indian guitar
4. Gurajana—Parents
5. Yugapata—Together
6. Savālavṛddha—Including children and old people, total

7. Satranibadha—Fixation of oblations
8. Mukhadvāra—The inner door.
9. Bhūmipuraskara—Product of Land.
10. Vrahmandira—Royal palace.
11. Kalaśa—Pitcher.
12. Ayoga—Attire.

Another phenomena which is of great interest is the Sanskritisation of Khmer words. From the very beginning old Khmer had the tendency to assimilate the Khmer words of similar meaning into Sanskrit phonetics. We have some words which are written in the same way as the Sanskrit words:

1. Prakola—written as Pragal, which expresses the sense remit, intrust was probably Sanskritised in Pragalbha meaning arrogant.
2. Kula—written as Kule, flexible form in the manner of the Khmer word Khlei which means progeny relative.

A number of Indian classical terms and religious phrases, and the names of deities and demons of Hindu and Buddhist mythology also became current, though most of them suffer a change, becoming Khmerised, guttural and abrupt en route thus:

	Original Indian Classical term		*Khmerised Version*
1.	Garuḍa	—	Krut
2.	Mukuṭa	—	Mkot
3.	Guru	—	Kru
4.	*Rāmāyaṇa*	—	Reamker
5.	Ma-Gaṅgā (Mother Ganges)	—	Mekong
6.	Nagar (City)	—	Nokor

It is from the last that the name Angkor is derived. Like the Arabic Medina, the old Mesopotamian Ur the Indian Puri, Angkor just means The City.[1]

The following are a few remarkable literary styles of the Sanskrit inscriptions dating from the pre-Angkorean and Angkorean epoch:

1. *Double Entente*

In several passages of the inscriptions where every significant word of a sentence has got double meaning:

1. Walker, G.B., *Angkor Empire*, p. 15.

Words		*Different meanings*
Kara[1]	—	Hand, Ray
Kalā[2]	—	An art, A science, sixteenth part of the disc of the moon
Rāga[3]	—	Redness, lustre, passion

2. *Repetition of the same letter*

Very frequently repetition has been done of the same letter or of the same syllable inside one and the same verse:

Letter or Syllable		*Verse*
'bh'[4]	—	vidviḍrāsaṣṭabhrdphūpo bhūbharavibhāvo bhavat
'dharma'[5]	—	dharmapriyā dharman imaṃ rakṣatādharmarākṣasāt
'ja'[6]	—	Jagajjayo so janayaj janesah
'bhu'[7]	—	bhupendro bhupatibhumi-bhusanobhuribhanubhah

3. *Stereotyped Expressions*

Stereotyped expressions conveying generally almost the same idea occur very frequently in the Sanskrit inscriptions:

(a) asid asindhubhupala—mulilalitasasanah.[8]
(b) asid asesabhupala—mastakadhṛtasasanah.[9]
(c) asid asesabhupala—maulimalitasasanah.[10]
(d) asid akhilabhupala—maulimalitasasanah.[11]
(e) rajnam murddhasv ahitasasanah.[12]
(f) samudravasana mahi.[13]
(g) sasati pṛthvim samudraparyyantam.[14]
(h) vijitya nikhilan desan.[15]

1. Han Chey, *Inscription of King Bhavavarman*, v. 8A.
2. *ibid.*, v. 15A.
3. *ibid.*, v. 18A.
4. *IC*, Vol. II, p. 59. Stele of Basak (Romduol).
5. *ibid.*, Vol. III, p. 67, Thmapuok Inscription.
6. *ibid.*, Vol. V, p. 299, Stele of Phnom Run.
7. *ibid.*, p. 230, Kul Prin Crum Inscription.
8. *IC*, Vol. II, p. 106, V. 11-0 Damban Inscription.
9. *ibid.*, p. 200—Pillars of Phimankas.
10. *ibid.*, Vol. II, p. 183, Inscription of the Buddhist Terra M of Angkor Thom.
11. *ibid.*, Vol. V, p. 99—Prasat Ben Vien Inscription.
12. *ibid.*, Vol. I, p. 256—New Inscription of Phnom Bayan.
13. *ibid.*, Vol. II, p. 11, Stele of Prah Kuha Luon.
14. *ibid.*, p. 92, V. 1, Pillars of Lobok Srot.
15. *ibid.*, Vol. V, p. 3, Surin Inscription.

4. *Long Compounds*

The following can be quoted as fairly good example of the use of long compounds in the inscriptions:

(a) hitakulakamalakuncanayaikacandrah.[1]
(b) nissankhyasenasarabhasacaranoddhutadhulipratanam.[2]
(c) antasthanesthitendrapramukhamakhabhujam.[3]

Since the use of long compounds and repetition of the same letter was the characteristic feature of the Gauḍas, M. Coedes believes that the authors of such Sanskrit inscriptions must have belonged to the Gauḍa region.

Among the important literary Brāhmaṇical works of India and Brāhmaṇical way of life and philosophy referred to in the compositions contained in inscriptions, the following are noteworthy:

1. *Pāṇini's Aṣṭādhyāyī*

One stele of Prāsāt Krun of Angkor Thom (one of the last epigraphic productions of Cambodia), in Sanskrit mentions Pāṇini. The inscription reads:

'The castes of the population (or the letters of the theme) deteriorated by the evil of time were restored by this king (Jayavarman), who like Pāṇini, had destroyed this evil, thanks to the practice of the Śāstras'.[4]

2. *Manusmṛti*

Vat Prah Einkosei inscription refers to the text of this sacred book which reads:

'The violent, wicked, greedy men who are the violators of good actions of others, according to Manu, go to hell with their ancestor'.[5]

It has been quoted in many of the inscriptions. Verse LI of the Tuol Ta Pec inscriptions describes the practice of the path of Manu.[6]

The inscription of the pedestal of Vat Easset furnishes us with a fragmentary verse in which we find a reference to someone who traversed the path of Manu.[7]

3. *Vātsyāyana's Kāmasūtra*

In the stele of Thnal Baray (LIX, D. 1) Vātsyāyana appears as the author of Kāmasūtra. The mention of this Indian has been made in the

1. *ibid.*, Vol. IV, p. 121 (face A)—Inscription of Vat Prah Einkosei.
2. *ibid.*, Vol. V, p. 255, Stele of Tuol Ta Pec.
3. *IC*, Vol. I, p, 236, Stele of Prāsāt Tor.
4. *ibid.*, Vol. II, p. 232.
5. *IC*, Vol. IV, p. 127.
6. *ibid.*, Vol. V, p. 253.
7. *ibid.*, Vol. VI, p. 289.

following words—'Nothing but at the very sight of him the wives of elite, as if rivalling with him in beauty and in grace, are found perfectly expert in the science of love, such as was taught by Vātsyāyana and others.'[1]

4. *Patañjali's Mahābhāṣya*

The inscription of Lovek contains reference to Sabdaśāstra (Grammar)[2] and to the Bhāṣya (commentary of Patañjali).[3]

5. *The epics (the Rāmāyaṇa and the Mahābhārata)*

The stele of Prāsāt Barmei dated in the end of the 10th or in the beginning of the 11th century A.D., on palaeographic groups, contain reference to the recitation of the *Rāmāyaṇa* and the *Mahābhārata.*[4] An inscription of Prāsāt Khna (Mlu Prei) speaks of King Suryavarman I who was fond of the stories of the *Mahābhārata.*[5]

6. *Purāṇic Mythology, Legends and Allusions*

The inscription of Prāsāt Sankhan mentions the desire to recite the Purāṇas, the *Rāmāyaṇa* and the *Mahābhārata.*

7. *Yogācāra System*

Pre-Rup inscription contains reference to the doctrine of Yogācāra (Vijñapti).[6]

8. *Setubandha*

Mention of Pravarasena as the author of this book in Prākrit has been made—'This king with an excellent army (this Pravarasena), while making all know the dike (Setu) of law, had vanquished the other Pravarasena, who made only one common bridge.'[7]

9. *Śruti*

In Vat Prah Pinkosei inscription Śruti has been quoted 'Above our own good actions are those of others, says the Śruti' (the revealed science).[8]

10. *Jātaka*

Verse LXXIII of the Grand Stele of Phimanakas tells us that queen Jayarajadevi entrusted her own dancers with giving performances drawn from the Jātaka.

1. *ISCC*, LIX, p. 483.
2. *ISCC*, Vol. XVIII, B, p. 130.
3. *ibid.*, V. 15.
4. *IC*, Vol. VI, p. 216.
5. *ibid.*, Vol. I, p. 202.
6. Verse—CCLXXV.
7. *ISCC*, LVIII, p. 434.
8. *IC*, Vol. V, p. 153, V. 5.

11. *Viśālakṣa's Nītiśāstra*;
12. *Suśruta Samhitā*;
13. *Trayī (Vedas)*;
14. *Vedāntas*;
15. *Buddhist scriptures*;
16. *Gautama's Nyāyasūtra*;
17. *Siṁhavalokitanyāya*;
18. *Harivaṁśa*;
19. *Kauṭilya's Arthaśāstra*.

Allusions to several Indian authors have been found in various inscriptions:

1. Guṇāḍhya has been mentioned as a writer in Prākrit.
2. Viśālaka is mentioned as having written on Nīti.
3. Sura is represented as having triumphed over a rival named Bhimaka.[1]
4. Jina has been mentioned as the author of one of the Purvas.[2]
5. Mayūra has been referred as the author of Sūryaśataka.[3]

Vidyāśramas in the different parts of the country were centres of literary activity where professors and other dignitaries dominated. Teaching of Sanskrit grammar played a very important role in this country. Vedic Studies were popular and as we have seen people had familiarity with the epics of India. Recitations of sacred texts had been a part of daily life of the temple. Arrangements for copying of important treatises existed such as Kasikavṛtti, Śivasaṁhitā and Parameśvara. Some ladies have also been referred to in the inscriptions. They were talented and took part in the literary activities. Since they had easy access to the literary treasures of ancient Cambodia, they could excel in literary compositions like the big praśastis. Use of almost all the Sanskrit metres in the inscriptions tends to show that authors and composers of these epigraphic texts had thorough knowledge of the rules of Sanskrit poetics. It is not to be forgotten here that some of the Brāhmaṇas of ancient Cambodia were extremely talented and it is not at all surprising to note that they were authors of several technical works besides literary ones of Kāvya type.

The presence in ancient Cambodia of local traditions had nothing to do with those of India and the traditions which had inspired the Khmer artists in different epochs to represent the episodes in the bas-reliefs of magnificent monuments.

Cambodian writers of prose demonstrated full knowledge of various Indian sects. The composers of poetry had mastered rhetorical and literary

1. *ISCC*, p. 457, Stele of Thnal Baray, v. C-15.
2. *ibid.*, pp. 457-58.
3. *ibid.*, p. 458, Stele of Loley, v. C-16.

conventions like puns, alliterations and similes. They employed all the varied metres of Sanskrit poetics. Sanskrit and old Khmer language were used simultaneously. Sanskrit which was considered to be a sacred language, was used for writing genealogies, panegyrics of founders of monuments and donors while old Khmer and Cambodian were used for the details which followed.

Sanskrit in Cambodia maintained intimate and close relation with contemporary Sanskrit literature on the mainland—India. Pāṇini's rules were thoroughly known by the composers of verses during the reigns of Jayavarman and Yaśovarman. Many of the verses were so beautiful that we do not find their parallel in India. In the Pre-Rup inscription a new Kāvya style named *Manohara* has been used.

In spite of its richness Sanskrit remained almost static and unresponsive to native elements although most of the vocabulary of the Khmer language was comprised of Sanskrit words. Sanskrit was considered to be a foreign language. There was an apathy towards it which can be seen from its complete disappearance from Cambodia in the modern times. But originally though various elements of Brāhmaṇical culture were implanted by the Indian colonists, Sanskrit language and literature was the first and foremost which opened a new world of culture.

Thus we may say that indeed Cambodia had been effectively Brāhmaṇised. The kings, nobles and priests had Sanskrit names. The Paṇḍits of the royal court wrote the inscriptions—some of which are quite long compositions—in elegant Sanskrit. Princes were educated by their gurus in the *siddhāntas*, Sanskrit grammar (especially the Vyākaraṇa of Pāṇini), the Dharmaśāstras and the six systems of philosophy. *Śāstrotsavas* (literary assemblies) were held in which sometimes Brāhmaṇa ladies also joined and won admiration for their learned discourses. The *Vedas* were carefully studied. Daily recitations without interruptions of the *Rāmāyaṇa*, the *Mahābhārata* and the *Purāṇas* are referred to in a 6th century inscription. We hear of libraries well stocked with books on all the *śāstras*. Yaśovarman's digraphic (written in two scripts, south Indian and north Indian) inscriptions show intimate knowledge of the Indian Epics, *Harivaṁsa*, the *Bṛhatkathā* of Guṇāḍhya, and the works of king Pravarasena, Vātsyāyana, Mayūra, etc. In the inscription of Pre-Rup a very long Sanskrit inscription, there are four references to Kālidāsa's *Raghuvaṁsa*.

Cambodia's social life was greatly influenced by the Brāhmaṇical life of India. The change in social patterns were affected by the marriage of Indian Brāhmaṇas in the royal families, since this class of Indians had a very respectful position in Cambodian society. A new class of people called Brahma-kṣātras sprang up from the marriage alliances of Indian Brāhmaṇas with Khmer brides. Cambodian kings were the guardians of the society. There are numerous references of the kings taking active role in the organisation or re-organisation of the caste system. According to George Coedes, Queen Mahendra Devi had, by two different husbands two sons who ruled as Rājendravarman-II and Harṣavarman-II. This indicates a sociological phenomenon unheard of in a Brāhmaṇic society—the remarriage of a widow.

Various names of individuals which appear in the inscriptions are mixture of Indian and Cambodian names. Names like Mṛtoñ Pṛthvindrapaṇḍita, Mṛtoñ Jayendrapaṇḍita and Loñ Yudhiṣṭhira are clear examples of matrimonial relations of Indians with Cambodians and that the people had liking for Indian names. These names also portray that the mixture was of the Brāhamaṇas and the Kṣatriya classes.

Cambodian social and family life was primarily functioning on the lines of the *Gṛhyasūtras.* Even very minor affairs like saṁskāra and food and drinks were patterned on the lines of the *Gṛhyasūtras.* People of lower class of society could not establish as a rule, relations with the upper class. Palanquins were the mode of transport of the wealthy people. Like the Indians, the Cambodians considered their right hand to be pure and left hand to be impure. People were very keen in their personal cleanliness. Indians, from very ancient times have offered oblations to the spirits of persons related to them and also to them who died without any heir. This practice was followed in Cambodia also. In an ordinance of Yaśovarman, we find reference about oblations to the spirit of loyal soldiers, good officers and poor people old and young who died without any heir to offer such oblations to them. In matters of educational organisation, teachers and subjects of study, Cambodian system wholly resembled India.

As in India, the Cambodians were predominantly vegetarians. Salt, jeerā, ginger and cardamom were the condiments used in preparation of food.[1] Kings in Cambodia wore *dhoti* and a number of ornaments besides mukuṭa veṇu like the Indian kings. Ornaments were worn by both men and women. By putting colours women decorated their hands and feet similar to Brāhmaṇical traditions. They kept their hair knotted on their heads. As in India, so in Cambodia also we find that entertainment on grand scale was organised on festive occasions like Śivarātri etc., in monasteries. Musical instruments of Indian origin like duduṁbhī tāla and veeṇa were played. There prevailed the system of *devadāsīs.* People used to offer beautiful girls for the service of temples. This system was identical with the south Indian system.

2. *CHAMPA*

Like Cambodia, Champa too was fully imbued with the Brāhmaṇical

1. For details of food items, etc., see Majumdar, R.C. *Kambujadesa,* p. 65ff.

culture. In the field of literature she (Champa) felt the vigorous impact of the latter. It is evident from the inscriptions that at least upto tenth century A.D. the classical Sanskrit literature, particularly the kāvya, was thoroughly studied. Sanskrit became the language of the learned.

The kings seem to have taken a leading part in the cultivation of Sanskrit language and literature. Thus king Bhadravarman is said to have been versed in the four *Vedas*. King Indravarman III is said to have been versed in the well-known Six Systems of Philosophy, as well as in the Buddhist philosophy. In addition, he knew Pāṇini's grammar with *kāśika*, and the *ākhyāna* and *uttarakalpa* of the Śaivas. King Śrī Jaya Indravarmadeva VII was versed in grammar, astrology and the dharmaśāstras, notably the *Nāradīya* and *Bhārggavīya*. Whether these kings were as learned as their court-poets would have us believe may be doubted, but that these different branches of Sanskrit literature formed familiar subjects of study in Champa may be regarded as fairly certain.

That the two Epics, the *Rāmāyaṇa* and the *Mahābhārata*, were quite familiar in Champa is evident from a number of allusions to the chief characters or episodes described in them. Thus reference is made to Yudhiṣṭhira, Duryodhana and Yuyutsu, to the glories of Rāma and Kṛṣṇa, to Rāma, son of Daśaratha, to irrepressible valour of Dhanañjaya and to the son of Pāṇḍu.[1] Besides, the story of the destruction of the Tripura-Asuras bears a very close resemblance to what we find in the Anuśāsanaparva of *Mahābhārata*. The allusion to the epithet "Ekākṣapiṅgala of Kuvera, is also evidently based on the Uttarakāṇḍa of *Rāmāyaṇa*. All these point to a very intimate knowledge of the Epics on the part of the people of Champa.

The religious literature, particularly the literature of the Śaiva and Vaiṣṇava sects, must have been thoroughly studied. The familiarity of the people with the numerous epithets and legends of Śiva, Viṣṇu and other gods, cannot be explained except on this assumption. We have also some specific references to it in inscriptions. Thus the minister Ajna Narendra Nṛpavitra is said to have been versed in "all treatises dealing with the Śaiva religion". The minister of King Indravarman III "was versed in sacred scriptures".

The *Smṛti* literature, specially the *Mānavadharmaśāstra* or *Manusmṛti*, must have been regarded as a standard and authoritative treatise. Specific reference to it is found in inscription no. 65, and the *Bhārggavīya Dharmśāstra*, mentioned in inscription no. 81, may also refer to the same.[2] The

1. Cf. Ins. Nos. 41, 74, 12, 23, 39.
2. According to *Manusaṃhitā*, Chap. I, V. 60, the entire text was narrated to Bhṛgu, who originally learnt it from Manu. This is corroborated by Chap. V, vv. 1-3 and Chap. XII, v. 2. Thus the text may also be called *Bhārggavīya*, in the sense that it was narrated by Bhṛgu.

latter inscription also refers to *Nāradasmṛti*.

The great influence of Classical Sanskrit literature, including kāvya and prose romances, is met with in all the Sanskrit inscriptions that have reached us. The writers of these inscriptions show great familiarity with different metres and styles of poetry and prose-writing. Even the extremely artificial style, consisting mainly of *śleṣas* and *anuprāsas* such as is met with in *Kādambarī*, *Naiṣadha-Carita* and *Śiśupālavadha* are not wanting in inscriptions. Artificial prose style, chiefly characterised by placing two apparently contradictory statements side by side is illustrated.

The Chams had evidently a knowledge of the *Purāṇas*. We have reference to a book called *Artha-Purāṇaśāstra* and *Purāṇartha*, both apparently meaning the same thing. The *Purāṇartha* or *Artha-Purāṇaśāstra* seems to have been a commentary to or a Cham edition of an Indian *Purāṇa*.

On the basis of what has been said above we may draw up the following list of the branches of Sanskrit literature which were studied in Champa: The Four *Vedas*; the Six Systems of Indian Philosophy; the Epics; the religious literature of the Vaiṣṇava and Śaiva sects; grammar, notably that of Pāṇini, together with its commentary, the kāśika; astrology; the *dharmaśāstras*, specially those of Manu and Nārada; the *Purāṇas*, and the classical Sanskrit literature including kāvya and prose romances.

Marriage was regarded as a sacred ceremony which laid the foundation of a family life. As in India, the marriage was confined to one's own clan corresponding to *gotra*. We have reference to two important clans—those of Nārikela (cocoanut) and Kramuka (betelnut). These names were derived from a mythical story according to which the founder of each of these clans was discovered, while infant, in a cocoanut (or betelnut) tree by the king who reared him up and ultimately gave him his own daughter together with his kingdom. There were possibly other clans of this type, and the clannish sentiments, although based on mythical legends, superseded all other barriers of the society. Thus we are told that a lady belonging to a noble family would marry even a man of no substance if he belonged to the same clan, and that marriage relations were determined by considerations of clan rather than those of caste. In other words, a man would marry a woman belonging to the same clan but to a different caste.

The details of marriage ceremony such as are recorded in the Chinese texts immediately recall those of India to which they bear a close resemblance. The inevitable match-maker, usually a Brāhmaṇa, as in India, settles the preliminaries. He arrives at the bride's house with some presents, such as a quantity of gold, silver, and jewels, two pitchers of wine, and fish. After the proposal is agreed to on both sides he settles an auspicious day for the ceremony, for, as in India, the ceremony could take place only on certain *tithis* (dates). On the fixed day friends and relations of both—the bride-groom and bride—gather at their respective houses and indulge in joyous festivities amid dance and music. Then the bride-groom goes to the house of the bride who is attired in a splendid dress suitable to the occasion. A priest after introducing the bride-groom to the bride joins their hands together and pronounces the sacred mantras. This finishes the ceremony which is again followed by dance, music and other festivities.

Like the marriage ceremony the relation of husband and wife, too, probably resembled that of India. At least we have undoubted evidence of some of the most important characteristics of that relation. Thus when the husband died, the wife—at least one belonging to a high family—followed him in the funeral pyre, according to the well-known *satī* rite in India.[1] Some inscriptions even record a number of queens burning themselves on the funeral pyre of a king. The case of the Annamese queen of Jaya Simhavarman IV shows how difficult it was even for an unwilling victim to avoid this tragic fate. The traveller Odornic de Pordenone remarks with reference to Champa:

"When a man dies in this country, his wife is burnt along with him, because they say that it is only right and proper that the wife should live with the husband in the other world".[2] Those who did not die along with their husbands mostly lived like Hindu widows the rest of their lives.[3] They led retired lives and did not dress their hair. It is possible that in exceptional cases, the widows were remarried. All these are exactly analogous to what we find in India. On the same analogy we should expect the prevalence of polygamy and this is confirmed by the examples of kings who had numerous wives and concubines.

The sacred ties of marriage, however, sometimes set loosely upon the lower classes of people, if we are to believe in an account preserved in the Chinese Text called *Tao-yi-tchelio*. We are told that when a vessel stopped at a coast-town for some days, the sailors married the women of the locality. The men and women lived as husband and wife during the short residence of the former, and when the time of parting came they took leave of one another amid tears and lamentations. Next year the women again married the new batch of sailors, and so on. We are told that if perchance any one of these sailors returned to the same country after a long time, he was warmly received by his former wife and offered food and drink, but the

1. For details of *Sati* in India, see Thakur, U., *History of Suicide in India.*
2. *T'oung Pao*, pp. 600-601.
3. *BEFEO*, Vol. XIV, No. 9, p. 14.

old ties of husband and wife being once dissolved, could not be automatically revived.[1]

Nevertheless there was a high ideal of womanhood, and feminine virtues are frequently referred to. The good qualities of Pu lyan Rajakula enumerated[2] may be regarded as those of an ideal woman. The women were, as a general rule, very religious, and many inscriptions record their religious gifts and pious endowments. The heroic example of a lady determined to save her honour even at the cost of her life has been referred to.

Some of the popular customs and ceremonies of Champa have been recorded by Chinese historians. These were held on fixed dates in accordance with the Brāhmaṇic calendar which was in vogue in Champa. The year began with the month of Caitra, and months ended in *amāvasyā* or new moon. Many of the Brāhmaṇic festivals were observed there. A few peculiar ceremonies are recorded below.

On the New Year's day an elephant was taken out of the town and let loose; for they believed that they would thereby get rid of the evil spirits for the year. In the month of Āṣāḍha they held grand boat-races in which even the fishing boats took part. At the feast of the winter-solstice, which took place on the full-moon day of the 11th month, the people presented the king with samples of their agricultural and industrial products. Lastly, on the 15th day of the month of Caitra, a wooden tower was constructed outside the walls of the capital city; the king and people of all ranks placed there clothes and perfumes which were then burnt as sacrifice to God.

Maspero regards all these customs as of indigenous origin, but this may be doubted. The practice of letting loose an elephant particularly when there is no heir to a king occurs in many old stories of India. The annual boat races are held even to this day on the Dussera festival in various parts of Bengal. The practice of presenting the "first fruits" to kings, landlords or greatmen is a well-known custom in this country, and the last festival mentioned above has its counterpart in the modern Dolayātrā festival. The festivals in Champa recorded above may thus be regarded, like many others, as ultimately derived from India, although modified by local ideas.

There were many popular festivals connected with harvest, as we find in India. Even the king took part in them and was to give the signal for harvest by himself cutting a handful of rice.

Some of the customs and ceremonies were horrible and barbarous. Thus every year on the 15th day of the first month and the 15th day of the 12th

1. *ibid.*, p. 37. Similar forms of short-term marriage are said to be prevalent even now among the mariners of Hue.
2. Cf. Ins. No. 36, VV. 8ff.

month, the people were authorised to procure the galls of living persons and sell them to officials. These galls were mixed with an intoxicating drink and taken by the official with his family. They believed that they would thereby be feared by other persons and be safe from infectious diseases.[1]

The funeral ceremony was analogous to that of India. The usual practice was to burn the body on a pyre. The cremation took place the very next day in the case of the ordinary people, and three or seven days after death in the case, respectively, of nobles and kings. The dead body was soaked in beer and placed on a hearse. It was then taken to the burning place to the accompaniment of music. All the members of the family, both male and female, with shaved heads, accompanied the procession uttering loud shouts of lamentations all the while, until they arrived at the river-bank. There they burnt the body on a pyre, and having collected the ashes in an earthen pot and thrown it into the river, returned to their house in profound silence. If the deceased belonged to any noble family, or had performed any high functions in the state, the burning ceremony had to be performed near the mouth of a river, and the ashes were placed in a copper pot. In the case of the king this pot must be of gold and it had to be thrown into the sea. Thus the distinction of ranks was carefully preserved even after death.

For a period of two months the members of the family came to the pyre at the end of each week with incense and perfume, and uttered wails and lamentations over the remains of the departed. On the hundredth day, and again in the third year, some ceremony had to be performed in honour of the dead.

Although cremation was the usual rule, the practice of exposing the dead body was not unknown. In accordance with the custom prevalent among the Parsis, and among several peoples in ancient India, the dead body was left in an open field and devoured by the sacred vultures. After a few days the family of the deceased collected his bones, burnt them to ashes and threw them into water.

3. *BURMA*

Brāhmaṇical elements are found in abundance in the early Mon inscriptions of Burma. The use of Sanskritic religious terms (e.g. Svar for Svarga, Dharma, etc.), royal names and styles, and certain religious and social observances occur frequently, but they are common to both Brāhmaṇism and Sanskritic Buddhism. As to the use of Sanskrit terms too, it may be urged that that form of Buddhism using Sanskrit as its sacred language had probably existed in Burma from early times. Even making

1. *BEFEO*, Vol. XIV, No. 9, p. 37.

all such allowances there are strong reasons for believing that Brāhmaṇism had its share of responsibility for the strong Sanskritic element present in the early Mon records. The numerous references to Brāhmaṇas in these records show their great influence in the Buddhist courts. Rituals and ceremonies performed by them are partly Brāhmaṇical in character, and the god who is invariably worshipped has been identified as Nārāyaṇa-Viṣṇu.[1] We also have the story of one of the most celebrated kings of the Pagan dynasty—Kyanzittha was his name who in one of his former births was once Viṣṇu, and on another occasion was born in the family of Rāma, king of Oudh.[2] This legend has a unique interest inasmuch as it shows a distinct blending of the Buddhist theory of re-birth with purely Brāhmaṇical legends. It is no less remarkable that in the same records we find mention of the "four castes" who are directed to perform their respective duties.

"A remarkable proportion of loan words in these records is of Sanskrit origin, not Pāli. . . . As to the reason for their presence in early Mon, allowance must be made for the fact that Brāhmaṇas, who are often mentioned in the inscriptions, played a great part at all the Indo-Chinese courts, from Burma to Champa. Vestiges of Brāhmaṇism have been found in lower Burma, though they are not so common as in several other parts of Indo-China. But there is much reason to believe that some form of Buddhism using Sanskrit as its sacred language also existed there in former times, just as it did, for example, in Kamboj.... The soundest inference seems to be the one drawn by Finot that Sanskrit and Pāli (and the several forms of religion with which they are respectively associated) were more or less concurrent influences in the Mon country from an early period. Whatever may have been the channel or channels through which Sanskrit words came in, they are present in such numbers that the strength of the influences that introduced them must have been considerable and probably extended over a fairly long period."[3]

To have an idea of the strong Brāhmaṇical element in the Mon inscriptions, we shall here quote only a few selected passages from the records already referred to, Mon Inscription No. IX (found near the Tharaba gate, Pagan)[4] has the following passages:

"The Brāhmaṇa astrologers went (and) drew water...and (bathed) the side pillars, the yas pillars, the atas pillars, etc., etc... (At) All these seventeen places, they made a decoration of plantains, adorned with young plantains, (and) sugar cane (and set?) water (in) vessels of gold (and) silver (and) water (in) conch-shells wherein (they) put cleaned rice (and)

1. *Ep. Birminica*, Vol. III, Pt. I.
2. *ibid.*, Vol. I, Pt. II.
3. *ibid.*, Vol. I, Pt. II, p. 76.
4. *ibid.*, Vol. III, Pt. I.

dubbā grass (and) spread mats (with) golden flowers, altar oblations and altar candles. Having (arranged them?); they made in honour of Nārāyaṇa, decoration of plantains...then the Brāhmaṇa astrologers worshipped Nārāyaṇa".[1]

We notice here the characteristically Brāhmaṇical ritual of using plantain trees as well as *dubbā* grass in a religious ceremony. At the auspicious time. . .godhūli (evening) lagna, the expert Brāhmaṇa astrologers bathed the side pillars, etc. . .[2] An essentially Brāhmaṇical custom was made use of in a Buddhist coronation ceremonial presided over by Brāhmaṇa priests when the different pillars referred to above were bound by sacred Brāhmaṇical threads in a hundred and eight spools. "The thread wherewith they bound up the pillars, tender maidens, young damsels, daughters of Brāhmaṇas, had spun (it and) made (it on) a hundred and eight spools. Then the Brāhmaṇa astrologers recited and sprinkled water and after that they bound up pillars".[3]

These and numerous other similar references clearly indicate the existence of a considerable number of Brāhmaṇas in Burmese courts as priests, astrologers, and experts in house-building, who must have occupied positions of influence and importance there. And not only were there the Brāhmaṇas, the other three castes as well of the Brāhmaṇical fold were there. Thus we read the pious wish of a pious king "All the monks shall be full of virtue and good conduct. All the Brāhmaṇas, who know the *Vedas,* they shall fulfil all the Brāhmaṇa Law. All the princes shall carry out the law altogether. The 'four castes' shall fulfil their law also".[4]

Brāhmaṇism was not the religion of the State nor of the people in general, but the records referred to above seem to show that there was a considerable number of followers of the Brāhmaṇical religion, not exclusively Brāhmaṇas, but of other three castes as well, who were free to perform their own religious ceremonies. Brāhmaṇical influence is also indicated by certain ancient place name of both Upper and Lower Burma. Such a name is Bissunomyo, which is equivalent to Viṣṇupura or the city of Viṣṇu. The name was in ancient times applied to old Prome of Hmawza which had obviously been a centre of Viṣṇuite influence. The tradition of the foundation of the ancient city of Prome as contained in the *Mahayazawin*, a late Burmese chronicle, is associated with Viṣṇu and

1. *Ep. Birminica*, pp. 42-43.
2. *ibid.*, Vol. III, Pt. I, p. 36.
3. *ibid*, pp. 50-51.
4. *ibid.*, Vol. I, Pt. II, Mon. Insc. No. 1, Sec. G., p. 127. But regarding the mention of 'four castes' Blagden is, however, of opinion that this is a merely conventional phrase used to denote "people in general". "There is no reason", he says, "to believe that apart from Brāhmaṇas who were of foreign introduction, any real division into castes was recognised" (p. 75).

his vāhana, Garuḍa, as also with Caṇḍi and Parameśvara equivalent to Durgā and Śiva respectively.[1]

The existence of a Brāhmaṇical population (mainly Vaiṣṇavite in creed) in Burma at an early period cannot, therefore, be doubted. It can easily be surmised that this Brāhmaṇical community would have their own gods whom they could worship in accordance with their own religious rites. In those localities where the Indian element was permanently represented either by a more vigorous commercial intercourse or by settlement and colonization, it was likely that their gods would have permanent habitats there in temples. These temples having been usually built of brick gradually fell into decay and finally disappeared with the singular exception of the one that is now standing at Pagan. But most of the images which had been once enshrined in these temples are now emerging out of the debris of ruins of centuries. Thus, at old Hmawza, a locality known in ancient times as Bissunomyo, at least three different types of stone images of Viṣṇu have been discovered, one of which belongs to the 6th or 7th century A.D.,[2] along with images of Gaṇeśa, Brahmā and other Brāhmaṇical deities. At Mergui in the Tennasserim province images of Viṣṇu, Gaṇeśa, Hanumāna and Brahmā have been found.[3] There stone slabs, belonging stylistically to about the latter half of the 9th century A.D., have in recent years been brought over from Thaton to the Rangoon Museum. Two of these slabs depict in bold relief the Ananta-sayyā episode of Viṣṇu and the third represents Śiva with Pārvatī seated by his side. At Thaton, the walls of a pyramidal stage of a Buddhist pagoda are decorated with rectangular stone panels purporting most probably to depict a Brāhmaṇical mythological story. Of the slabs that still remain, two certainly represent Śiva with his trident. In Arakan where Brāhmaṇical influence had been more pronounced from earlier times, archaeological exploration has discovered in recent years images of Viṣṇu, Durgā, Sūrya and other Hindu deities. Of these, the image of Durgā can in no way be dated later than the 8th century A.D. Coins and terracotta tablets bearing the Śaivite symbol of the trident and the representation of the bull Nandi have been found in large numbers at Mrohaung and other localities in Arakan as well as in other place of both Upper and Lower Burma. Coins with the Vaiṣṇavite symbol of a conch-shell are not also infrequent.

It is interesting to note that the Burmese law-books or *Dhammathats*[4] which are still recognised as legal authority regulating inheritance and

1. *An. Rep. A.S. Burma*, 1910, p. 18.
2. Phongyi Kyaung Museum Shed near Hmawza Ry. Station, Exhibit No. 23.
3. Rangoon Museum Exhibits No. 1/6, 2/6, 3/6.
4. Forchhammer, E., *Jardine Prize Essay*; Jolly, J., *Grundriss der Ind.*, Ar. Phil. 1896, pp. 41-44; M.H., *Pali Literature of Burma*, p. 83ff.

other domestic matters are Brāhmaṇic in origin and do not betray any trace of Siṁhalese influence "although since 1750 there has been a decided tendency to bring them into connection with authorities accepted by Buddhism."[1] The earliest of these codes are those of *Dhammavilasa* (1174 A.D.) and of Waguru, king of Martaban in 1280 A.D. They are based on the authority of Manu, and in matters of purely legal topics correspond pretty closely to the *Mānavadharmaśāstra* or *Manusmṛti.* But in all these, the prescriptions involving Brāhmaṇical religious observances such as penance and sacrifice have been completely omitted. The theory of punishment is also different and inspired by the doctrine of Karma, that is evil deed must bring its retribution. Thus, the Burmese codes ordain for every crime not penalties to be suffered by the criminal but merely the payment of compensation to the aggrieved party, proportionate to the damage suffered. Scholars generally believe that "the law-books, on which these codes are generally based, were brought from the east coast of India and were of the same type as the Code of Nārada which, though of unquestioned Brāhmaṇic orthodoxy, is almost purely legal and has little to say about religion".[2] Later on, a subsidiary literature grew up embodying local decisions, summarized by a Burmese nobleman Kaingza in about 1640 A.D. in the *Mahārājadhammathat.* In recognition of his services and scholarship he was given the title of Manurāja by the king and the name of Manu was connected with his code. This code superseded all the older law-books and during the reign of Alompra who remodelled his administration, several other codes were also completed, but these also preserved the name of Manu.[3]

4. *SIAM*

It appears from available sources that Brāhmaṇism and Buddhism took parallel paths in early Siam without seriously colliding with each other until they obtained a happy coalition in the cross-road of Tāntric Mahāyānism. As a result of this, at present the Thais have a great devotion for Paurāṇic Brāhmaṇism although they are upbread by the strong veneer of orthodox Buddhism, i.e., the Theravāda or the Hīnayāna institution. In the place names, dance, drama, language and literature, festivals and ceremonies etc., of present Thailand a subtle and subterranean flow of Brāhmaṇism may be easily detected just beneath. The uppermost thin layer is of Thai Buddhism. All of them are primarily inspired by the Brāhmaṇical mythology and the *Rāmāyaṇa* (Thai, *Rāmakīrti* or *Rāmakien*).

1. Eliot, *Hinduism and Buddhism*, Vol. III, p. 66.
2. *ibid.*, Vol. III.
3. *ibid.*, p. 67.

Certain ancient place names of Thailand are similar to the Brāhmaṇical names.

The Pāli work *Mahā Niddesa* refers to a certain port named "Takkasilā" (Takṣaśilā), which apparently lay in the trans-Gangetic India, among many other ports of India and the Far-East. This port seems to be better identified with Muang[1] Takkasilā or Tak near modern Raheng in Siam. The place was navigable by the river Meping, as it is still navigable today.[2] In the *Kathāsaritsāgara* (Taranga 57, v. 76) and in Baṇa's *Kādambarī* there are references to sea side country in the Far-East called Kāñcanapura or Suvarṇapura. Bāṇa describes this place as near the waves of the eastern ocean (the Pacific?). Here it may be suggested that this particular Suvarṇapura was identical with the ancient city Suphanburi on the banks of the river Tacin or Suphan (Suvarṇa). If Kāñcanapura was not synonymous with Suvarṇapur, we may also identify it with Kāñcanburi, which lay in the neighbourhood of Suphanburi. As old Kāñcanaburi lay at the confluence of the two rivers Meklong and Nam Saiyok, the place, it seems, was regularly visited by the Indian as also the Chinese, Indo-Chinese and the Indonesian vessels. Here, it is interesting to note that in the *Kathāsaritsāgara*, Suvarṇapura is somehow connected with Suvarṇadvipa (Sumatra?), while describing the voyage of merchant Iśvarvarman. Now major Erik Seidenfaden, who should be regarded as one of the most prominent scholars on the history of Siam, thinks on valid grounds that "Suphanburi", gets its name from Suvarṇapuri ("the golden city"), probably due to its "ancient relation with Śrīvijaya empire that lay in Sumatra".[3] Similarly, there may be some references to Siam in the "Kiṣkindhyā Kaṇḍa" of the Bengali *Rāmāyaṇa* of Kṛttivāsa as also in one of the ancient Bengali folk tales and the 'Gorakṣavijaya', or 'Mīncetān' a religious treatise of mediaeval Bengal. In the latter work, a country is referred to as "Kadulīr Deś" (i.e. 'the Land of the Bananas'), which is possibly no other than the major portion of the trans-Gangetic peninsula comprising parts of Siam and Burma. Apart from these, possibly, there are some vague references to Siam in the *Mangal Kāvya* literature of the early mediaeval Bengal.[4]

The Thai language has similarity with the Sanskritic languages.[5] The reason should be found in its origin to a great extent from and can be felt in the monosyllabic character of the Thai language. There are

1. Muang—City or Country.
2. Levi S. *Etudes Asiatiques*, Vol. II, pp. 1-55, 431. He places it in Arakan. Vide, also Majumdar, R.C., *Suvarnadvipa*, p. 57.
3. "*Guide to Nakon Patom*", pp. 19-20.
4. Das Gupta, T.C., *Some Aspects of Bengali Society*, Ch. I.
5. The language is pronounced with regular hiatus, not in one motion as it is done by the peoples speaking the Indo-Aryan languages.

hundreds of words in the Thai language, which are just like Sanskritic words (Bengali, Hindi, etc.), examples of which are given below:

English	*Bengali*	*Siamese*
Clever	Cālāk	Chalād
Sky	Ākās	Ākās (pronounced as Ākāt)
Chariot	Rath	Rath (pronounced as Rot)
Great	Mahā	Mahā
Place	Sthān	Sathāni
Obstruction	Antarāi	Antarāi
King	Rājā	Rāchā
Wheel	Cakra	Cakra (prononuced as Cak)

The pronunciation of the language is very difficult and meanings of words depend entirely on intonations, which possibly show some amount of similarity with the linguistic slow pronunciations and intonations current in different parts of Bengal. One peculiarity which can be marked in the Siamese language is that the Thais do not pronounce as they write. This difference between the writing and the pronunciation also can be found in the Bengali language.

The Thai language has 18 vowels and 23 consonants, specially in Northern Thai. This is exactly what is found in the Ahom language of Assam. It is not surprising because Ahom and Thai both came from the same common stock, common land and common Indian cultural influence in Yunnan in South China, called Gandhāra by the Indo-Chinese. The Thai language has only seven consonantal endings viz., k. t. p. m. n., etc. The Thai people read the conjunct consonants with their members pronounced separately and fully one after the other.

Brāhmaṇical cultural impact in Siam has left a deeprooted influence on the language of the country. "Any one visiting Bangkok today", says S.R. Sehgal[1], "would be amazed by the multitude of words in every-day speech which are derivatives from Sanskrit". Any one listening to the radio broadcasts of these countries will be struck by the frequent occurrence of these words. There are no synonyms of these words both in Thai and Lao languages to express these ideas. It is in the Thai language that we have more of Sanskrit elements. The Sanskrit words have undergone such phonetic changes that at times it is rather difficult to notice their Sanskrit origin.

A few examples of Sanskrit words will not be out of place. A popular word for greeting in Thailand is Sabaidi Krap which has its origin in Sanskrit word *svasti* which finds mention as early as the *Ṛg Veda*. The

1. Sehgal, S.R., Sanskritistic culture in South East Asia, in Sanskrit (Dr. Aditya Nath Jha Felicitation Vol.), Vol. III, (English), p. 474.

word *velā* is used in the same sense of time as in India. The leader of the Buddhist monks blesses the devotees with the words *sukho hotu* 'may you be happy'. The word for wedding in Thailand and Laos is *vivāha*. The illustrations can be multiplied. Thus, we see that there are thousands of Sanskrit words which are adopted by the Thai people without any phonetic modifications.

But the percentage of Indian words which have undergone phonetic changes in Siamese is numerous. The system of these changes has been studied to some extent[1] though more work still remains to be done in this direction.

KA VARGA: *ga* and *gha* of Sanskrit words are changed into *kha* in Siamese pronunciation. For example—gantha→khantha, gupta→khupta, go→kho, samgiti→samkhiti, samgha→samkha.

CA VARGA: The examples of *ca* changing into *ja* are: candra→janthara, catura→jathura, cakra→jakara. The Mahāprāṇa *cha* changes into ca: Pali *vinicchaya* (Sanskrit *Viniścaya*) *vinicaya*. The change of ja into cha can be seen as: jiva—chip, jaya—chaya, jambu—champhu.

ṬA VARGA: The *ṭa* of Sanskrit words is changed into *ḍa*. For example—piṭaka→piḍok. The letter *ḍa* of Sanskrit words becomes invariably *dha* in Siamese. The example of manḍapa mondhop can be cited.

TA VARGA: The *ta* of Sanskrit words changes into *da*. Such examples are: ṛtu→radu, trūya→duriya, tuṣita→dusit. But *da* changes into *tha*, for example—desa→thet, dukha→thuk, deva→thep, dasa→thasa. It may be noted in this connection that there are also words in which *da* changes into *ta*. For example—Śrī Deva the famous town of the second wave of Indian colonies is called Śrī Tep. The letter *dha* of Sanskrit has the tendency of changing to *tha*, e.g. dhanuṣa→thanu, dharma→(Pali dhamma) thamma, dharani→tharani, Dhanapuri→thonburi, Dhatu→thatu, Ayodhya→Ayuthia.

PA VARGA: *pa* changes into *ba*. Examples are not rare. A few of them are: apsara→absona, puspa→butsa, Pali→Bali, bhupa→phuba, upasika—basika, Lavapuri—Lopburi. *Ba* changes into *pha*, e.g. Buddha→Phut, brāhmaṇa→phrām or prām.

The following words may be taken as illustrations of letter *bha* changing into *pha*, e.g., bhava→phab, bhupa→phuba, bhaga→phak, bhaya→phai.

ANATAHSTHA LETTERS: The Sanskrit later *ra* and *la* change into *na* in Siamese. Earlier the change of *na* into *la* has already been pointed out in discussing tavarga. But here it must be noted that *la* also changes into *na*. In fact both *na* and *la* are interchangeable. According to

1. Bapat, *Indo-Asian Culture*, Vol. IX, No. 2, 1960, pp. 189 ff.

Sanskrit grammar there is practically no difference between *ra* and *la* ralayorabhedaḥ and both the letters have the tendency to interchange in Sanskrit words. There is no surprise, therefore, that both *ra* and *la* of Sanskrit words change into *na* in Siamese. A few examples will illustrate this point: vihāra→vihana, sagara→sakhon, nagara→nakhon, Mara→Mana, akara→akana. A few examples of *la* changing into *na* are as follows: sula→suen, pala→van, Sila→Sin, yugala→yukon, etc.

The letter *va* changes into *pha*, e.g., Viṣṇu→phisanu, vara→phara, vṛksa→phuk, vinaya→phinai, svayamvara→sayamphon.

The dental *sa* changes into *ta* e.g., rasa→rot. In Siamese Sanskrit ṛ has been preserved as ru: vṛkṣa→phruk=phuk, vanamṛga→valamoruk. Thus it is clear that Brāhmaṇical influence in Siam was wide, varied and deep.

The Thai literature is replete with the Brāhmaṇical faith and Sanskrit influence. *Tao Sri Chulalak*[1], a Thai literary text mentions the Brāhmaṇical ceremonies like loy *kratong* or festival of lights. This book was composed by Nang Napamas or Tao Sri Chulalak, the consort of king Rama Kamheng. She was the daughter of the court Brāhmin and astrologer. According to her, this ceremony was of Brāhmaṇical origin and spread in Thailand perhaps in early period. This ceremony was performed for worshipping three Brāhmaṇical gods, viz., Isaun (Śiva), Bhrom (Brahmā), and Narai (Nārāyaṇa).

Nobles, princes and kings were the patron of literature in Thailand and they bear the full impact of Brāhmaṇism, which is clear from the four important Brāhmaṇical works of the Ayudhya period. They are (i) *The Oath to the King*, (ii) *Tosarot Teaching Rāma*, (iii) *Palee Teaching his brother*, and (iv) *Aniruddha*.[2] *The Oath to the King* was the oldest piece of work which was written by Brāhmins. It described the kings desire of power and the need of a king for the running of the country. It then describes that nobles must be faithful to the king. The rest three Brāhmaṇical literatures were written in the reign of king Narai.[3] The latter's court was honoured with the greatest Thai poets called Sri-Prat, the son of the court Brāhmin, Phya Horathibodi. King Narai himself wrote *Palee Teaching his brother*, and *Tosarot Teaching Rāma*.

The destruction of Ayudhya by the invasion of Burma caused heavy losses to the Thai literature. Naturally the later kings of Thailand collected literary men for rewriting old literature apparently lost during the invasion. King Taksin or Boromraja IV of Dhonburi tried to rewrite certain scenes from the *Rāmāyaṇa*.[4] King Rama I, the founder of Chakri

1. Nopamas, Lady, *Tao Sri Chulalak's Text Book*, p. 8 ff.
2. For details see, Jumsai, M.L. Manich, *History of Thai Literature*, p. 151.
3. Na Nakorn, Plaung, *History of Thai Literature for Thai Students*, p. 78.
4. Jumasi, M.L. Manich, *op. cit.*, p. 196.

dynasty of Bangkok continued with this work. He was the famous author of the Thai version of the *Rāmāyaṇa* (Rāmakien)[1] which is still read throughout Thailand.

It would not be out of place here to mention some of the important Brāhmaṇical literatures of Thailand which fully bear the impact of Sanskrit influence. They are the *Rāmāyaṇa*, *Lakshanawongse*, *Sakuntalā*, *Nala*, *Madhanabādhā*, *Śāvitrī*, and *Ilarāt*. The details are as follows:

THE RĀMĀYAṆA

The Siamese *Rāmakien*, though obviously written for performance, is not divided into acts and scenes as the drama modelled upon the classical Indian or Greek types. It is one long story without division though accompanied throughout by stage directions. For the sake of clarity we may treat the long story as composed roughly of three parts:

1. an introductory part, dealing with the origins of the three races inhabiting the world of the time adopted for the drama, namely, the human, the demoniac and the simian, tracing origins mostly from the Hindu heavens as accepted in Buddhist literature;
2. a narrative of the story of Rāma following in main details the gist of the world-renowned Sanskrit literature though not included in the classical epic of the *Rāmāyaṇa* with an additional episode of the wandering of Rāma in the forest to relieve his mental agony in losing again his beloved Sīdā, remarkably told with geographical locales reminiscent of the valleys of the Caopraya and the Mekhong.

Considerable divergence of opinion exists as to where the plot begins. The murals in the galleries of the Chapel Royal of the Emerald Buddha commence with the discovery in the bowels of the earth of Sīdā. Versions of our neighbours, such as the *Rāmāyaṇa* of Vālmīki, the *Javanese Rāmāyaṇa Kakawin* and the Cambodian *Rāmker*, commence with the reign of Daśaratha, Rāma's father, prior to the birth of his four sons. The bas-reliefs of Prambanan begin their story with the circumstances leading to the birth of Rāma and his brothers, tracing it back to the invitation of the gods extended to Viṣṇu to reincarnate in the world to exterminate the evil race of demons. We have decided consequently to begin our narration with the birth of the hero and his brothers as well as that of Sīdā from Monto, Queen of Loṅka. The baby-girl's horoscope indicates disaster for her father and his family of demons. Tośakanth has her thrown into the waters; but she is picked up by Janok, King of Mithilā

1. Rama I, King, *Rāmakien*, Vols. I-II, p. 166.

who had doffed kingly robes to assume the life of a hermit in the forest. Feeling the impropriety of a hermit celibate living along with a female even though she is a mere baby, he buries her in the ground, praying to heaven to take care of her till she grows up and is able to take care of herself. Meanwhile the young sons to Tośaroth of Ayudhya (Ayodhya) grow up under a training destined for royalty. Rāma is then sent with Lak (Lakṣmaṇa) to the forests to the rescue of hermits who have been molested by the demon crow and her inhuman ruffians, whom he succeeds in exterminating. Wandering forth further with their preceptor they come into Mithilā where King Janok is holding a tournament to lift an ancient bow the prize of which is to be the hands of his daughter. Sīdā, now restored to her father's court and grown to be a beautiful damsel. When all the contestants had failed in the tournament, Lak is sent in by Rāma, and though he is able to lift it he does not consummate the effort, leaving it to his brother, who of course lifts the bow and wins the hand of the princess.

We are then told about the intrigue of King Tośaroth's young queen in extracting the promise of the throne from her ailing husband for her own son Prot (Bharata) to be coupled with the exile for fourteen years of the rightful heir Rāma. Rāma insists upon observing his father's promise to the latter and leaves with his consort Sīdā and his favourite brother Lak for the forest. The ailing King, Tośaroth, is heartbroken and dies. The claim of the young queen for the throne on behalf of her son Prot is rejected by all including Prot himself who is too loyal to his brother to accept the high honour. He heads a deputation to discover Rāma in his exile in the forest to invite him back to reign in accordance with his right. Rāma, however, refuses to break his father's promise and at the insistence of Prot gives the straw sandals he is wearing to Prot to place on the throne to signify his personal rule.

Rāma with his wife and brother Lak goes further into the forests and meets with a series of adventures. First of all they meet a young demon maiden, a sister of King Tośakanth of Loṅka, named Sammanakhā (Surpanakhā), wandering about in the wilds in search of males. She makes love to both brothers and threatens Sīdā. Lak is furious and drives her away after cutting off her nose to defame her looks. She hurries to report the wrong done to her brothers, Tut, King of Carik and a brother of Tośakanth, who goes out indignantly to avenge the dishonour rendered to his sister but is killed in the battle. Another brother Khorn meets Rāma and is duly killed in battle. Yet another Trisian, meets a similar fate.

Sammanakhā now goes to Tośakanth and succeeds in persuading him to try to abduct Sīdā from their hermitage. Māric, a relative of the King of Loṅka, disguising himself as a golden deer walks past the hermitage and arouses Sīdā's wish to possess the beautiful golden animal. She begs her husband to go and catch it. Though at first reluctant to leave her and rather suspecting that deer, Rāma cannot resist his wife's desire and, leaving her in the charge of his brother Lak follows the deer and shoots at it in the suspicion of something foul. The demon cries out in Rāma's voice for help: and Sīdā sends Lak much against his good sense to rescue Rāma. Tośakanth now appears in the guise of a hermit, abducts Sīdā on his flying chariot and speeds away. Rāma returns to meet Lak and both hurrying back to their hermitage find that Sīdā has disappeared. Tośakanth on his aerial flight meets with the king of birds, Sadāyu, who tries to bar his way but is killed, though not before meeting Rāma and Lak to whom he relates what happened.

Another incident of their peregrination is the meeting with the monkey Hanumān who turns out to be Rāma's most valuable officer. The latter is instrumental in effecting an alliance between Rāma and Sukrib king of the simian kingdom of Khidkhin, who places his simian army at the disposal of Rāma for the recovery of Sīdā. This force is augmented by another simian army of Jompū.

A reconnaissance party led by Hanumān, Jomp'ūpān and Oṅkod is now despatched; and, meeting with the eagle Sadāyu's brother, is taken on the bird's back to obtain an aerial view of the enemy terrain. Coming back to the eagle's nest, Hanumān jumps across the ocean to Loṅkā, and discovers Sīdā confined to the royal park. She is desolate and just about to commit suicide by hanging. Delivering Rāma's message he offers to take her back; but Sīdā refuses on the ground that it would seem improper to be carried about first by a demon (Tośakanth) when he abducted her and then carried back by a monkey. She sends back, however, a message urging Rāma to hurry up rescuing her from the demons by coming at the head of an army and heroically vanquishing the enemy; in a wanton mood for revenge Hanumān wrecks the park. Successive forces are sent to catch him; but do not succeed till the redoubtable Indrajit, champion of demons, comes out and brings him by force into King Tośakanth's presence. Every imaginable method is used to kill the monkey warrior without avail till, in answer to Tośakanth's enquiry, Hanumān suggests clogging by fire. This done personally by the Demon-King, Hanumān jumps about setting fire to every corner of the palace and escapes. On his return to Rāma's camp he is rebuked for thus destroying buildings even though they belong to the enemy.

Rāma now moves his camp to the sea-shore opposite the enemy's citadel in Loṅkā. Meanwhile in Loṅka, Pipek, Tośakanth's brother, urges his brother to be fair and restore Sīdā to her husband. He is banished for this advice. Being an astrologer, he sees doom threatening the race of demons, an incarnation of Viṣṇu being already on earth in the shape of

Rāma to work out their extermination. In the hope of minimising the national tragedy he goes straight into the camp of Rāma; and, on being caught, offers his service on condition that he should not have to inform against his relatives except when asked by Rāma.

Tośakanth now resorts to a ruse by which his niece, Pipek's daughter Banyakai, is disguised as Sīdā floating in the water as if dead past Rāma's camp in the morning. Rāma, coming down to the sea-shore, is deceived; but Hanumān, ever clever, suggests and arranges for a cremation of the dead lady, who of course rises into the air to escape and is caught by the monkey general. She confesses and after some punishment is set free.

Rāma, then orders bridging of the channel of sea. The monkey leaders Hanumān and Nilapat head the workers, but quarrel and come to blows. The latter is sent back to Khidkhin by way of punishment. Hanumān is in sole charge. Finding that stones thrown into the sea disappear for no apparent reason he dives below only to find a queen-fish leading her fishes carry away the stones. She is caught by Hanumān; the two fall in love; a promise is made by the queen-fish to cease the obstruction. The queen-fish duly gives birth to a son in the shape of a monkey with a fish-tail, who in later years becomes one of the leaders of Rāma's brother's army fighting later demon enemies. Rāma now crossed over the causeway and set up camp on thc island of Loṅkā.

In order to be correct in etiquette Rāma sends an official envoy, Oṅkod, into the citadel of Loṅkā to offer terms of peace. The mission is a prominent feature in most versions of the Epic and is believed to have served as one of the early drastic episodes for the Indian shadow play.

To satisfy his curiosity of the strength of the enemy, Tośakanth sets up his gigantic canopy over the citadel on which he and his court go up. Sukrib is sent up to destroy this contrivance with the result that Tośakanth and his party fall headlong to the ground, which indignity is highly resented by the demon-king.

The war in Loṅkā may now be said to commence from this point, and instead of following the detailed narrative we need only give just a summary of the battles since the successive demon leaders who take part in the battles provide many artistic marks.

(1) The campaign of Maiyarāb, the magician, with its fanciful account of obstacles set up by him down to his citadel in the bowels of the earth. Maiyarāb is finally killed by Hanumān.

(2) The campaign of Kumbhakarṇ, brother of the demon-king, in four episodes; but is finally killed in battle by Rāma.

(3) The campaign of Indrajit, son and heir of Tośakanth, who values him as the most redoubtable of his commanders. After causing a lot of trouble he is killed in the fifth battle.

(4) Maṅkarakanth fighting a delaying battle during Indrajit's sacrifices loses his life also in battle.

(5) The death of Indrajit brings out Tośakanth to battle without result.

(6) Next comes Sahassadeja, a gigantic ally distinguished for his lack of intelligence; followed by demon leaders, namely; the former's brother Mulaphalam. Saṅ-ātit, nephew of Tośakanth, Sataluṅ and Trīmegh, the latter also a nephew of Tośakanth, all four distinguished for valour, take their turns but are finally killed.

The king of Loṅkā now comes out to battle without any result. Just before this last battle Tośakanth holds a great sacrifice underground to attain invulnerability but is foiled in the attempt by three simian generals. He summons therefore, on old ally Satthāsūra and another nephew Viruñcambaṅ to his aid. The former has a short battle and is killed; the latter an expert spearman and a redoubtable horseman who can disappear at will with mount gives some trouble but escapes to the ocean hiding himself in seafoam. He is tracked and killed by Hanumān.

Tośakanth appeals to the Brahmāna-ancestor of the demon world. Mālīvan, who comes down to earth to try to effect reconciliation. Holding a trial at which the King of Loṅkā is plaintiff and Rāma is defendant he gives judgment in favour of the latter on the strength of the evidence of witnesses; and thus enrages the demon-king who decides to hold another sacrifice with the object of demolishing heaven where the denizens have been witnesses in favour of Rāma. In order to prevent the planned Gotterdāmmerung the god Śiva summons Pāli, now a deva, to foil the sacrifice for at the sight of him the valiant Tośakanth recoils quickly.

As on former occasions of disappointment the King of Loṅkā gives battle and this time succeeds in wounding very seriously Prince Lak, brother of Rāma. He is, however, revived after a difficult search by Hanumān for rare medicaments. Other relatives—a brother Tapanāsūra and two sons by an elephant mother—are sent into battle and lose their lives. Tośakanth is finally killed on the field of battle after Hanumān and Oṅkod have secured his physical heart and crushed it in sight of the owner, Tośakanth.

Though here we should have reached the climax, the romance goes still further. On the march back home after crowning Pipek as King of Loṅkā and the famous ordeal of fire insisted on by Sīdā to prove her innocence during her confinement at the demon court, Rāma is caught up by Asakarn, an ally of Tośakanth, who is killed by Rāma. A son of the demon-king, Banlaiyakalp, who has been brought up in the court of his maternal grandfather the king of the Nāga-world, tracks the army of Rāma and is met by Hanumān who succeeds in putting an end to him.

There is yet a considerable amount of material concerning further wars and Rāma's domestic trouble which we have taken the liberty for convenience sake to designate as the third section of the whole story. The narrative commences with the rule of Pipek in Loṅkā, where the learned king, lacking in military experience, faces a revolution and is only saved by Rāma sending Hanumān to put things in order. The affair is aggravated by the interference of Cakravat, King of the demon state of Malivan out of his sense of loyalty to his friend, Tośakanth. Deeming it unwise to leave things as they are even though the revolution has been successfully put down, Rāma carries war into the Malivan territory with his brother Prot in command. The description of this war is but a parallel of the one in Loṅkā. In place of Rāma and Lak, we have Prot and Satrud (Bharata and Śatrughna); the army of Khidkhin accompanies the princes but instead of Hanumān as champion, even though he is in that army, we have his rival, Nilapat. On the demon side we also have parallels, because in place of Tośakanth there is King Cakravat with his three sons who take the places of Khumbhakarṇ, Indrajit and Maṅkarakarṇ. The gigantic Sahassadeja is replaced by King Vayatal. After details of fighting which is considerable, though not as lengthy as in the case of the war of Loṅkā, Cakravat is killed and the war ended.

We are now told of a court intriguc. In an absence for the day by Rāma, a maid becomes possessed by the spirit of a rākṣasī bent on vengeance and implores Sīdā to draw a picture of the demon-king of Loṅkā. As soon as the drawing is finished Rāma returns. Fearing the anger or jealousy of her husband Sīdā pushes the drawing under her lord's bed. Its magic spell makes Rāma restless and unwell. Searching for the cause of his indisposition Rāma discovers the drawing which Sīdā admits having drawn for the curiosity of her mind. Jealousy is aroused to such an extent that Rāma orders his brother Lak to deliver a severe penalty by killing his beloved consort. Lak accompanies his sister-in-law out of town and leaves her in the forest instead of killing her. Sīdā eventually takes refuge with the hermits. She eventually gives birth to a son who is named Mongkut. One day she goes out to gather fruits for daily sustenance leaving her baby in the care of the old hermit but later comes back to fetch it. The hermit in his meditation does not notice Sīdā coming back; but later opens his eyes to find that there is no baby left. Alarmed at having lost his charge he creates by magic another baby to take its place. On Sīdā's return she is delighted to find another baby Loh and the two are brought up together as twin brothers. As the boys grow up they are taught the letters as well as martial prowess as becoming to royal children. Their archery practices stir up atmospheric commotions to such an extent that it is heard in the capital of Ayudhyā. Rāma sends Hanumān to find out what it is all about by following a royal horse-mount labelled as such with the law quoted that whoever mounts it commits an act of treason. As it wanders into the forest it comes near the hermitage and the boys catch the horse and ride on it for pleasure with the remark that we don't care or know what treason is. Hanumān advances to catch the boys whom he has no means of recognising; and is caught and bound up by the boys. Prince Prot, following with soldiers, tries to rescue Hanumān and is forced to use his bow against the boys eventually succeeding in capturing the elder of the two, who is brought into town and exposed for punishment in the middle of it. However, he finally escapes back to the hermitage. Rāma now comes out to catch the boys and has to use his weapon though without avail. Upon enquiry Rāma discovers that they are his sons. He tries to tell them but they would not believe him and escape to the inner room of the hermitage. Meeting Sīdā here Rāma apologises for his treatment of her, tries to persuade her to return which the princess refuses, though allows the children to return with their father. Every means for the restitution of their normal relationship failing, Rāma sends Hanumān to bring Sīdā back to a feigned cremation of himself. On discovering the fake she uses her right of returning to Mother Earth by a magical submergence into the ground to take refuge with the King of the Nāgaworld, who has a separate palace built for her.

The last part of this third section describes how desolute and worried Rāma becomes that he invites Pipek to Ayudhyā to advise him about his trouble. The latter recommends a year's exile which Rāma carries out. The exile is to be towards 'the East where malignant spirits still abound'. Lak and Hanumān are to go with him and Prot, Satrud and the two sons remain to take charge of state affairs. The exile to the East is accompanied by a few adventures. First a gigantic demon eagle fights with simian leaders who have by now joined Rāma. In the end the eagle is killed. In his wandering in exile Rāma with his simian army trespasses into the part of King Unārāj, a demon chief, who at once engages Rāma. He is finally vanquished and sent flying by force of the hero's grass-arrow to a cave wherein he is doomed to remain in punishment for some 1000,000,000,000 years, stuck to the ground by the grass-arrow. Having concluded his term of one year's exile Rāma returns to his capital. Śiva in heaven learns now how desolate Rāma is owing to the refusal of Sīdā to be reconciled; summons both parties and effects a reconciliation.

There remains yet another expedition to be carried out. The King of the demicelestial Kondhan (gandharvas),—represented in Thai are as demoniac people,—tours the forest and comes to molest hermits who have come out for solitude and meditation and advances to the city of Kaiyakes, the King of which is related to the House of Ayudhyā. The latter appeals to Rāma for help; Rāma sends a combined army of his own men of Ayudhyā, and an army from the simian state of Khidkhin under the command of

Prot, Satrud and his own sons. The aged monkey general, Jampūvarāj is delegated as envoy to warn the enemy. This being ignored hostilities commence with the result that the two sons of Rāma kill the gandharva king and his son. The four princes then enter Kaiyakes and later go out to seek the aged monarch of that state, the maternal grandfather of Prot; and restore him to his throne. The princes return to report to Rāma who in turn sends his two brothers, Prot and Satrud back to Kaiyakes to assist the old King. Here all ends happily.

LAKSHANAWONGSE

Prommatat and his queen, Suvarnaampa, had a son called Lakshanawongse. One day they went into the forest and found a wicked ogress. The ogress accused Suvarnaampa and Lakshanawongse for plotting against the life of the King. The latter ordered their execution, but the executioners out of sympathy for them let them escape. On the way in the forest a giant came and stole away Suvarna Ampa. Lakshanawongse now went in search of his mother and came to meet a hermit and a maid called Kesorn.

The hermit taught him the art of fighting and gave him an invincible bow. He also gave him a magic horse which carried him through the air to the giant city where his mother was. He killed the giant, came to his father's town with an army of giants and caught the ogress in disguise. Lakshanawongse now went in search of Kesorn. The hermit was dead and Nang Kesorn was saved by five Kennari maidens, who all became the wives of Lakshanawongse. On their return journey Kesorn was abducted by a Vichātorn, but they were attacked by another Vichātorn. Both Vichātorns killed each other and Kesorn now disguised herself as a Brāhmin in search of Lakshanawongse. The latter also went in search of Kesorn and came to a great town where he met Yisun who became his wife. The disguised Brāhmin now arrived at the town but Yisun accused the Brāhmin of trying to make love to her. Lakshanawongse ordered the Brāhmin's execution. Before her death the disguised Brāhmin had as yet time to deliver a son. Lakshanawongse discovered Kesorn's identity but it was too late.[1]

After the lull of three reigns Thai literature was soaring up high again during the reign of King Rama VI (1910-1925).[2] Rama IV was educated in England. He knew the ways of the West and could write equally well in English and French as well as in Thai. He drew inspiration sometimes from English and French literature, but very often also from Sanskrit and Brāhmaṇical literature, for which he had a great liking.

1. Na Nakorn, Pluang, *op. cit.*
2. *ibid.*

ŚAKUNTALA[1]

It was translated into Thai by King Rama VI in the year 1910.[2] Śakuntala was an adopted daughter of the hermit Kanavamuni. One day King Tusyant came to the forest, met her and married her. He gave her a ring and went back so that she could follow him with a grand procession afterwards. One day a hermit visitor came to her door and asked her to open it. She came rather slowly and the hermit was angry cursing her that she would be unlucky in love. She asked for forgiveness and so the hermit relented saying: The King would recognise her after having a look at the ring. Śakuntala went to the palace in a procession, but on the way she dropped the ring into the river. When she turned up at court King Tusyant could not remember her. She went away and a goddess took her away to heaven. One day a fisherman found a ring in the stomach of a fish and brought it to the King. Memory came back to him and he went in search of Śakuntala. He met a giant, overpowered him and finally Īndra, the God of Heaven, took him to see Śakuntala, who by now had a son. The three then returned to their kingdom together.[3]

NALA

Nala was written in 1913 A.D. by King Rama VI. It is based on the story of Sanskrit literature.[4]

At the wedding ceremony of Nala with Princess Damayanti, the gods blessed the couple. But two devils, Kali and Twaborn, could not come in time and had rancour in their hearts against the couple. Kali persistently persecuted Nala so that he would have all the bad luck. So he lost at chess to his brother, Buskorn, and had to leave the country with Damayanti, but Kali still persecuted him until he was mad and left Damayanti. He then met a royal serpent, the nāga, who was about to be burnt up by a forest fire. Nala saved the serpent. The nāga then changed the figure of Nala into something else and gave him a magic cloth. He could get back into his former shape when he put the cloth on. The serpent took him to live with Ratubarn, the master of chess. Nala became his charioteer. Damayanti now returned to her father's house and sent out spies to find out Nala. One spy came back and told her that Ratubarn's charioteer looked very much like Nala. Damayanti then proclaimed a ceremony for the chosing of a husband. Ratubarn also hurried forward to the ceremony and gave a chess winning magic to Nala so that he would make the horse

1. According to Thais, there is no term SAKUNTRA, but SAKUNTALA, the daughter of the bird.
2. Jumsai, M.L. Manich, *History of Thai Literature*, p. 212.
3. Rama VI King, *Sakuntalā*, pp. 1-562.
4. Na Nakorn, Pluang, *op. cit.*, p. 365.

go quicker. Nala went back with Damayanti to play chess with his brother and won back his kingdom.[1]

THE STORY OF MADHANABADHA[2]

The god Sutet was in love with the goddess Madhana, but she would not love him. The god therefore sent her down to earth in the form of a rose, but on full moon she would become a woman for one day and one night until she loves a man then she could become a woman, but her love will be fatal to her unless she consented to love him at last. So Madhana was born on earth as a rose near to the hermitage of Kalastassin. The hermit loved her as his own daughter when she came out in her own form.

One day King Chaiyasen passed by, saw her, fell in love with her and asked for her hand in marriage from the hermit. Chaiyasen had another queen, Nang Chantee, who was jealous of her, and sent message to her father to come and attack Chaiyasen's kingdom. She also accused her of being unfaithful and had secretly given her love to one of his own generals, Subhang. In fury Chaiyasen ordered the execution of Madhana after he had beaten the enemy off. The hermit came to save the life of Madhana and took her back. When the fact was known that Subhang was his most faithful general and that Madhana had not batrayed him, Chaiyasen followed Madhana to the place of execution but found her escaped. He followed her to the hermitage.

In the meantime Madhana asked to see Sutet and begged of him to allow her to live in peace. Sutet was very angry and turned her into a rose for ever, and never to come out again in a human form. Chaiyasen could only transport the rose-tree back to his palace.[3]

ŚAVITRI

The King Rama VI has written this book in the year 1925,[4] on the basis of Sanskrit literature. It described the harrowing scene of a poignant love of a woman for her husband. Sāvitri was allowed by her father to choose her own husband, and she chose Satyavān, in spite of the fact that the hermit reminded her that he had only one year to live. She followed him to live in the forest, for Satyavān had lost his kingdom. On the last day of Satyavān's life, she made a fast and followed him into the wood to cut trees for firewood, when he died in her arms. Then she saw Yama, the God of Death, approaching and finally taking her husband's soul away. She followed Yama closely behind and tried hard by all the sweet and humble words asking Yama to give her husband back. Yama was adamant and

1. Rama VI King, *Nala*, pp. 8-479.
2. Jumsai, M L. Manich, *History of Thai Literature*, p. 239.
3. Vajiravudh Rama King (Rama VI) *Madhanabadha*, pp. 6-164.
4. Na Nakorn, Pluang, *op. cit.*, p. 301.

would give her anything she asked except his life. In the end Sāvitri asked to be blessed with one hundred children. The God agreed. Then Sāvitri said how could she have hundred children if her husband could not be returned to her. God Yama was beaten and had to allow Satyavān to go back to the hermitage.[1]

ILARAT

The story was taken from a tale in Indian literature by Phya Sri-Sunthorn Voharn, the Chief of the Royal Scribes.[2] Ilarat went into the forbidden garden of Śiva and was therefore cursed to become a woman for one month and a man for another month and so on alternately. When he went for a swim in a pond, a hermit, found him, took him to wife and kept him. The hermit knew that he was cursed and kept him as his companion. Ilarat kept on changing his form month after month for quite some time until he had a child with him. When Ilarat became a man the hermit invited other hermits, his friends, to come along and perform a ceremony to appease Śiva. Ilarat was at last forgiven by the powerful god, and he returned to his country with his son.[3]

The Siamese music remains just in a kin relation with the subtle art of the Thai dance. Its general tendency is to be melodious with enchanting vibrations, which produces a master effect upon the hearers, if produced in accompaniment of classical Siamese dance. Apart from the melodious characteristics, the Siamese music also possess the capacity of producing sweet and rhythmic sounds, which easily fascinate one's mind.

Among the musical instruments of the Thais, the most important are types of Xylophone (viz. Ranād Ek, Ranād Thong Ek, Ranād Thume etc.), Celesta (Gong Wong Lek), Timpani (Klong Thand), Cymbals (Chārb Lek, Chārb Yai, Ching etc.), Clarinet (Pi, Nai), and big and small drums (Klong Thad, Song Na, Taphone etc.) Many of these greatly resemble with their equivalent Indian musical instruments. Particularly, the Siamese cymbals are very similar to the Indian cymbal 'kartāl'[4] of different sizes. Again the 'Song Na, the 'Taphone' and the 'Klong[5] Thad' greatly resemble the Indian drums like 'dhol', 'khal', and 'dhāk' respectively.

The paintings of Siam prior to the days of the downfall of Ayuthia do not exist today. As almost all the paintings, which we notice in Siam date from the beginning of the Bangkok period; the archaeologists have given very little attention to them.

1. Rama VI King, *Savitri*, pp. 1-285.
2. Na Nakorn, Pluang, *op. cit.*, p. 390.
3. Jumsai, M.L. Manich, *History of Thai Literature*, p. 250.
4. It is especially used by the Vaiṣṇava 'Kirtaniyas' of Bengal, who are a class of mystic singers.
5. It is very favourite among the Bengali 'Kirtaniyas'. It was also imbibed by the Manipuri Vaiṣṇavas from the Bengalis.

The paintings of Siam of the Ayuthian period virtually do not exist mostly due to their perishable nature.[1] The old paintings of Bangkok and Thonburi generally depict the scenes of Rāmāyaṇa, the Buddhist Jātakas, the life story of Buddha as narrated in the Nidānakathā and other sacred Buddhist texts, and the different episodes of the Siamese history. These paintings have been wonderfully executed by means of vegetable colours and gold leaves on the inner sides of the temple walls, as it may be seen in the various "Wats", viz., Wat Phra Keo, Wat Pho, Wat Benchama-bopit, Wat Rajapradit and others. Among such mural paintings, the most notable are those of Wat Phra Keo and Wat Pho. In a large gallery of the former temple the scenes of the important Rāmāyaṇic episodes have been drawn with vivid colours and uncommon sensitiveness. But there is quaintness in these paintings, which may be discerned in the occasional introduction of modern elements like the arrays of European soldiers of the mid-eighteenth century and the modern "Samlors"s (a sort of vehicle drawn by bicycles), in the frescoes revealing the battles between the troops of Rāvaṇ and Rāma, as well as, in the scene showing the lamenting feature of Sītā in the royal orchard of Laṅkā. Such anachronistic discrepancy to some extent characterised the mural paintings of modern Siam—i.e., the early Bangkok period. Now, before finishing our discussion about Siamese paintings, it should be remembered from the article of Quaritch Wales that "to appreciate them to the full one must go to Siam. There when one passes from the brilliant tropic sunshine into the half light of the temples, the deep rich colours are toned down, far from the earliest times it was in this half light that the frescoes were intended to be seen. Thus the enchantment of the whole impression is enchanced and the observer is led into a legendary dreamland."[2] (The opinion of Q. Wales undoubtedly affords a right perspective about the paintings of Siam).

The Siamese dance is a notable factor in the cultural history of Greater India as since remote times it has been giving a most romantic and lively touch to the poetic expressions of the Brāhmaṇical episodes of emotional nature. Unlike modern India, the whole of Siam is still a veritable stage of the *Rāmāyaṇic* and other ancient *Purāṇic* plays, and even now these performances inspire the Siamese people.

In Siam shadow plays are very popular, although it now represents a dying phase holding only a feeble stand in the enactment of minor plays like "Nang Talung" in the simple circles of the common people. Plays

1. According to Silpa Bharasri "While statuary had reached its classic period in Sukhothai, Siamese architecture and painting and decoration developed fully in Ayuthian time." He also thinks that "the first examples of Bangkok must represent the art of painting in its best period". "*Mirror*", Vol. I, No. 9, p. 42. See also, Dohring—*Siam*, Munich, Pl. XXIV—XXVIII.

2. *op. cit.*, p. 106.

enacted by shadow dances were not unkown in ancient India and we have the reasons to believe that the "Chāya Nātakas" (shadow-dramas) got in early days a fascinating response from the appreciative mass of country.

In Siam shadow-plays are known at *Nang*, shadows are thrown on the screen from the back by the use of hides or papers cut in fashion of the actors and thereby, silhouette like impressions are produced before the audiences.

In these pictures some dancers will take by their two hands and dance in such a manner that their shadows will move like those of actual actors and create a very keen interest to those who see them. As a matter of fact shortly after the beginning of the performance audiences forget the intrinsic disadvantages of the shadow-plays and start to imagine them as living heroes and villains of their age-old dramas. Rāvaṇa really looks like fighting against Rāma, and Hanumān combating the demon generals. The shadows recede and come forward with such a lively movement that it seems that they are fighting mortal melees in the decisive battles of Laṅkā. Even a man with a most ultra-modern outlook will be absorbed with dramatic interest unawarely, while attending the shadow-plays relating to the stories of the *Rāmāyaṇa* (known as "Rāmakien" in Siam).

Brāhmaṇical festivals and ceremonies played an important part in the religious life of the people of Thailand. Majority of the Thai people even today practised and observe a large number of Brāhmaṇical festivals and ceremonies. Most important amongst them are as follows:

The Tiruvembavai-Tiruppavai festival

Among the various popular Brāhmaṇical festivals and ceremonies which are known to have enjoyed the royal patronage of the Thai rulers, the festival of *Tiruvembavai* (or *Triyampavai-Tripavai*) the term transcribed in Thai in such works as *Ruang Phraraja Phidhi Sib Song Duen* Royal ceremonies for the twelve months of the years[1] and *Ruang Naphamas* the story of lady Napamas is of great significance, for the ceremonies concluded by the court Brāhmaṇas and the sacred hymns they recite on the occasion are vitally related to the concept of Devarāja.

The festival of Tiruvembavai-Tiruppavai is so called after the titles of the Tamil Śaivite (Tiruvembarai) hymns of twenty stanzas of saint Manikkavasagar and of the Tamil Vaiṣṇavite (Tiruppavai) hymn of thirty stages of saint Andal, which were recited by the course Brāhmaṇas at the ceremonies connected with the festival and the ceremonies were held in the Brāhmaṇical sanctions of Śiva and Viṣṇu.

1. Nopamas, Lady, Tao Sri Chulalak's Text Book, p. 8 ff.

The swing festival or Loching Chā

This festival was celebrated in various parts of Thailand (e.g., Sukhodaya, Ayudhya, Nakors Sri Dharamaraja, Bangkok etc.) for swing was a major event of popular interest and it was also of great symbolic significance. It was observed in the first Thai lunar month (the period between mid-December and mid-January), though it is said to have been changed later to the second lunar month corresponding to the period between mid-January and mid-February.

In South India the Tamil lunar month of Markali (mid-December, mid-January) has been since the mediaeval period, an annual occasion when the devotees of Śiva and Viṣṇu, particularly young maidens participated in congregational singing of the Tiruvembavai and the Tiruppavai hymns, ritual bathing and worshipping the *pavai* of deities, and praying for rain and spiritual bliss.

The significance of the ceremonies and the recitation of hymns in praise of Śiva and Viṣṇu was based on the belief that the great gods of Brāhmaṇism came down to earth during the festival to confer blessings on their devotees. When the festival was celebrated in the former days, the Thai ruler himself represented Śiva or Viṣṇu, or he appointed a nobleman to represent him as well as the gods at the festival. When the king or his representative was seated at the time of the circular dance, people would come and kneel in front of him in the firm belief that they were indeed paying homage to the Royal god[1] (Devarāja) who would bestow symbolic gift to the people which was equivalent to the divine gift of the gods.

It would seem thus that in Thailand the Brāhmaṇical South Indian devotional hymns of the Tiruvembavai, and also the Devaram hymns of the Śaivite saints were used at the swinging festival[2] and also at the coronation ceremony, not only as sacred hymns in praise of the great gods of Brāhmaṇism—Śiva and Viṣṇu, but also as an effective means of stressing the divine nature of the kings. The devotional hymns were thought to be freely in praise of Devarāja, the Royal God.

Coronation Ceremony

The Thai coronation ceremony, since the time of the inauguration of the Chakri dynasty had been carried out in accordance with the reconstructed system drawn on the basis of the surviving information concerning the coronation ceremonies of the Ayudhya period by the royal commission appointed by the founder of the dynasty, King Rama I. The ceremony consists of the benediction of the royal precincts by the Brāhmaṇas and the Buddhist

1. Thompson, Virginia, *Thailand : The New Siam*, p. 233.
2. Bose, P.N., *The Indian Colony of Siam*, p. 110.

monks,[1] Brāhmaṇical rituals to invoke the blessings of the Brāhmaṇic deities, purification and anointing rituals for the king, the recitation of devotional hymns for Viṣṇu to pervade the person of the king, the presentation of the royal regalia[2] to the king by the Brāhmaṇa, the first command of the king, its acceptance by the chief of the Brāhmaṇas on behalf of the people, and finally, a formal audience granted by the king in the throne hall.

An important part of the ceremony seems to have been the recitation of the devotional hymns by the Mahārājaguru (the chief of the court Brāhmaṇas) thereby inviting the god Śiva and Viṣṇu to pervade the person of the king. The hymn chosen for this purpose, namely the Tamil devotional hymns (known as Devaram) of the Śaivite saints and also of the Vaiṣṇavite saints (known as Divyaprabhandam) who lived in South India between the seventh and the ninth centuries A.D., have been rather appropriate, for they are in fact sacred hymns in praise of Śiva and Viṣṇu. The hymns which are entitled in Thai as "Perd Pratū Śivālai" or opening the portraits of Śivālaya, "Pid Pratū Kailāsa" or closing the portrait of Kailāśa[3] and Loripavai (named after the refrain reading Elor Embavai) have been identified as the first eleven stanzas of the Tirumurai (sacred scripture) collection of hymns attributed to the Śaivite saint. Sambandar, the first ten stanzas of the fourth Tirumurai hymns of the Śaivite saint appear, the Tiruvembavai hymns of the Śaivite saint Manikkavasagar, and the Tiruppavai hymns of the Vaiṣṇavite saint Andal respectively.

The tonsure or the shaving of the top-knot ceremony

The shaving of top-knot is a very ancient ceremony and practised in many countries. It figures as a religious observance, symbolical of a change of life and purpose. In Thailand it exists as a civil rite marking the end of the period of childhood. Indeed, it typifies a complete change of condition or purpose; it marks a rebirth. When the child reached puberty, the tuft of hair of the head is shaved with great ceremony. Though it is purely a Brāhmaṇical system, yet it has survived in the Buddhist country of Thailand. In other words, we may say that this tonsure ceremony is the reminiscence of the Indian Vedic custom, the sacred Muṇḍana ceremony of the Brāhmaṇas.[4]

The whole ceremony is now a complex mixture of both Buddhist and

1. Wales, H.G.Q., *op. cit.*, p. 67ff.
2. Royal regalia includes the crown, sword, golden sandals, fan, scripture, and also the Śaivite girdle and the Vaiṣṇavite discus.
3. Singaravelu, S., "Some Aspects of South Indian Cultural Contacts with Thailand", *PFICDTS*, Vol. I, pp. 22-23.
4. For a detailed and clear idea of the ceremony see Young, Ernest, *The Kingdom of the Yellow Robe*, pp. 66-72.

Brāhmaṇical rites, but there is very little difference between the parts enacted by the Buddhist priests and the Brāhmaṇical priests. The latter however, have a special set of chants of their own, and these they repeat during the first day's ceremonies. The object of their prayers is to entreat a member of their own supernatural beings to grant their approval of all that is being done. They appeal to the Devas, and to Śiva sitting on his porpoise they invoke the blessings of Viṣṇu as he rides on the back of the serpent king in an ocean of milk, the four armed Brahmā on his golden swan; the god of the winds riding swiftly in his chariot of clouds; and Indra on his wonderful elephant with the three and thirty heads. They recall to the minds of these deities the past existences of the tonsorial candidate. They remind them of the good actions he has previously performed, and wind up with a powerful and poetic appeal that they will combine to endow the subject of their prayers with a long and prosperous existence.[1]

So important to the individual is this ceremony of shaving of the top-knot, that were it omitted in the case of any single person, the unlucky one would believe himself ruled by evil influences for the rest of his life, and would unfailingly attribute every disaster in after-life to the fatal omission of the ceremony. Yet there are many people who have neither money, nor friends, nor relatives from whom they can borrow it. Were it not for the kindness of the Government, their unfortunate off-springs would never be able to enjoy the advantages conveyed to them by the celebration of the tonsorial ritual. The Government, however, hold a public ceremony which is less impressive and expensive than the private one, at which all who are too poor to afford the ceremony at home, may have their heads shaven by Brāhmaṇa priests gratuitously. Each child receives also a present of a small silver coin worth about two pence. This public function is held immediately after the close of the "Swinging Festival" and three or four hundred people annually avail themselves of the opportunity thus afforded them to get their children's top-knots removed.

In the case of children of royal birth, the celebrations are of a still more imposing character. The essential details are similar, but various modifications are introduced in order to emphasise the extra importance of the rite to those belonging to the royal family. On these occasions the shaven candidate is not bathed upon a mere canopied dais. In the court-yard in front of the royal palace, a hillock is erected in imitation of Mount Kailāsa, the adode of Śiva. It is a hollow structure, built up of plaited bamboo, supported on poles, and covered with tinsel. Upon the summit of this artificial hill is a central pavilion beautifully gilt, elaborately

1. For other details see Young, Ernest, *op. cit.*, pp. 72-77.

decorated, and adorned with tapestry and cloth of gold. A fence of prescribed pattern encloses the pavilion. It is an open framework with small rhomboidal openings in each of which is hung a small gilded heart shaped lozenge. Conical umbrellas with seven tiers occur every two or three yards. There are four pavilions, also lavishly decorated, one at each corner of the hill. At one side, an artificial grotto is constructed in which the bathing takes place. In the walls of the grotto are representations of the heads of the horse, the elephant, the lion and the bull. Over the entrance appears the head of the hooded snake, these heads are connected with the water-main, and are so placed that the five streams of water from the five mouths all converge to the central spot which the candidate occupies when he takes the bath. The floor of the grotto is a miniature lake in which are placed golden models of water beetles, fishes and other aquatic creatures. Rare flowering plants and ferns complete the internal decorations of the place. A little passage leads thence to the pavilion where the young prince or princess will change his or her attire on the completion of the ceremony. On the ground, four lath and plaster elephants covered with tinsel of different colours, face the four points of the compass. Here and there about the hill is a multitude of mechanical toys, plaster casts, waxen flowers, real plants and models of animals. The candidate is carried round the palace each day with an imposing procession of priests, members of the amazon guard, soldiers and attendants.[1]

From the above it is clear that the tonsure ceremony is very important amongst the people of Thailand. An auspicious day is fixed for this purpose, when all the friends, relatives, and monks come and bless the child. The child receives presents from all, which is followed by a great feast. The tonsure ceremony of royal prince is also performed with great pomp and all Bangkok enjoys holidays. Every boy is required to enter the monastery as novice after this ceremony. Even the Thai Prince is not exempted from this rule, though prince like Chulalongkorn would not like to stay in the monastery for more than three days.

The Songkran festival

This festival of Thailand is the Holi festival of India, for there is great similarity between the two. The Thai word "Songkran" literally means a move or change. According to the traditional Brāhmaṇas reckoning Songkran is the astrological New Year and falls on April 13, the date of the assumed entrance of the Sun into Aries. It is a kind of folk festival of throwing water as well as the setting free of fish and birds. Water throwing was accompanied by dances in the streets with young girls

1. For details see, Young, Ernest, *op. cit.*, pp. 66-84.

their best attires displaying all kinds of bright colours, walking and dancing through the streets in a big procession towards the temples. It is also the best occasion for a young man to know beautiful girls by spotting out the most attractive ones and to squirt water at them as a sign of blessing for the New Year. The water is supposed to be scented or perfumed, but sometimes they use unclean or dyed water in order to worry other people and laugh at their plight. However, it is taken as a joke and nobody bears malice on that day. Waterthrowing sometimes results in a sort of battle between two parties when both try to squirt pails and pails of water at one another, but neither gets offended even when they became shockingly wet. Old folks clean the Buddha images by pouring lustral water in the temples with great celebrations. At home they fetch out Buddha images from the altars, and clean them with perfumed water. It is also a spring cleaning day for the people, when everything in the house is cleaned up and put in order. The idea is that they should start everything new and afresh with luck and happiness in the new year. Old people and relatives of sixty years of age or over are visited and perfumed water poured on their hands while asking for their blessings. They are also presented with gifts, usually white cloth.

Buddha sihing, the famous image of the Buddha in Bangkok was taken out of the palace and exhibited to the public on the *pramane* ground in front of the Grand Palace, so that people could come and pour lustral perfumes on the image. The occasion was accompanied by the offering of food to the priests in the morning as an official event with the general public participating and a great fair was held for three days and three nights for the public. People also paid their respects to the relics of the dead kept in urns, on this memorable day. It was an occasion when they could think of their ancestors every year. The ceremony was marked by a grand procession at Phra Pradaeng just outside Bangkok. Young girls in their beautiful attires carry fish in procession towards the river and free them into water as an act of great merit with a big crowd watching them. Other people release birds to freedom from their cages on this occasion. In the Mekong river, people have boat races with government boats moving in the river fully illuminated at night with a thousand lights, especially in front of Vientiane. People hold procession, sometimes with crude masks and abnoxious male sexual organs exposed. It is supposed to be a fertility rite, and prayers are made for a lot of rains for the next rice season.

The festival is at its best in Chieng Mai in the North of Thailand and closer to Bangkok at the village of Paklat. It is still widely observed in Thailand especially in the provinces, though the civil new year (January 1) has been now fixed.

The Loykrathong festival

According to an old saying in Thai[1], a man can grow from infancy to adulthood because of the nourishment of rice and water. Children in the ancient times were taught to give their thanks to the goddess of rice called Mae Bhosop, who guarded rice crops. This was based on *maniscalm*, belief that there was a protective god or goddess for everything in nature.

"After every meal we used to join our hands in reverence to the goddess of rice, but not yet to one of water. In ancient times people had water in form of rain, then water in the rivers and canals all of which had regularly sustained their lives. This water flowed down from the Northern highlands, mainly during the beginning of the rainy season (around July or August), carrying with it mud and soil. This gave the water various colours, depending on its mixture."[2]

Generally it was not until the month of November (on the full moon day of the twelve lunar month) that most of the mud, soil and other foreign bodies settled down to the bottom of the river. Then the water became most clean and the people took delight in storing it for drinking and using purposes. They were more delighted on the full moon day of that month when everything, the moon, the sky and the water were seen to be all clean and clear at the same time. It was on this occasion that there occurred the thought that a thanksgiving should be arranged for the goddess of water called Mae Kongka in addition to the goddess of rice Mae Bhosop. The best possible way thought of at that time was to float leafcup baskets on the water as token of their homage. This custom later developed into tradition and still later had art incorporated into it, with the result that the leaf-cups have been made with various ornate designs. Those who want to know about the origin of this ceremony may have the answer from Brāhmaṇism that it is meant to float away whatever evils the floaters have done. This is in the same spirit as the person taking a bath in the Ganges can float away his sins in its water.[3]

The Brāhmaṇical records[4], however, give another information. They say that Loy Krathong is an act of worship aimed at the three Brāhmaṇical gods of Isuan (Śiva), Phrom (Brahmā), and Narai (Nārāyaṇa) and that the releasing of lighted boats is a part of this religious rite.

The probable answer is that the Thais have taken the various ceremonies that comprise Loy Krathong from the old Indian civilisation, which exerted a strong influence over early Thai culture. and have gradually made them a part of Buddhist rituals, as for example, when they perform

1. Rama V, King, *The Royal Ceremonies of the Twelve Months*, p. 25.
2. Priññāno, Bikkhu, *Traditions & Customs of North-Eastern Thailand*, p. 32.
3. *Loy Krathong*, Holiday Time in Thailand, T.O.T., Vol. 14, No. 2.
4. Nopameas, Lady, *Tao Sri Chulalak's Text Book*, p. 54.

them, as an act to worship the Buddha's foot-print on the bank of the Nammatānatee river. Loy Krathong is performed in every part of Thailand and is one of the famous ceremonies of the country.

Śivarātri Festival

This festival was celebrated from very early times in Siam[1], but was discontinued after the fall of Ayuthya. It was, however, revived by the King Rama IV. It occurred on the full-moon day of the third month (Māgha), and was of course a strictly Śaivite festival.

In the evening the High Priest of Śiva (Phra Mahārāja Guru) carried out the usual preliminary rites common to all Brāhmaṇic ceremonies.[2] He then set up four poles from which was suspended, by means of strings, an earthen pot full of water with a hole in the bottom. Under the pot was placed a stone liṅga, symbolic of Śiva, which stood on a bass having the form of a yoni, symbolic of Umā. The Yoni was provided with a spout from which the water which dripped from the pot over the liṅga and ran down into the Yoni, was collected in vessels. This went on all through the night, and just before dawn the Brāhmaṇas cooked some rice mixed with honey, sugar, milk, and butter, which was distributed and partaken of by all those present. At day-break they all went down to the canals and bathed, and then they returned and anointed their heads with some of the water which had been collected from the liṅga. It was a rite of purification, and the Brāhmaṇas believed that the consecrated water washed away all impurities and sins.

In Siam the festival can hardly be regarded as a royal ceremony, or it was rather a ceremony performed by Brāhmaṇas for their old benefit. But it was probably fostered by the Siamese kings as the means by which Brāhmaṇas purified themselves before performing more important ceremonies connected with the welfare of the King and the State.

Swing Ceremony

The Swing Ceremony is known in Siam as Loh Chingchā (loh=to swing, to pull, chingchā=swing). This ceremony occurs on the seventh and ninth days of the waning moon of the second lunar month, dates falling between the later part of December and the middle of January and takes place only in Bangkok.

The ceremony is conducted as shortly before the appointed date a nobleman, a different person each year but always a Phaya Pan Thong or noble of the "Golden bow" rank, is appointed by the King to fill the chief role, that of the God Phra Isuan (Īśvara). A few days later the open

1. Rama V, King, *op. cit.*, p. 13.
2. Wales, H.G.Q , *Siamese State Ceremonies*, p. 297.

square in which the great swing stands is prepared. Finally a footboard is suspended from the cross-bar of the swing with six strong ropes of ratlan, at a height of about fifteen feet from the ground. The board is some six feet long by eighteen inches broad, the greatest length at right angles to the cross-bar, and an extra rope hangs from it, by pulling on which from below, the swing is got into motion. A long bamboo is planted in the ground at the short distance on the western side of the swing, to which a small bag of money is fastened when the ceremony takes place. On the day of ceremony four muscular looking individuals wearing appropriate dresses and a high hat made to resemble the head and neck of snake, are hoisted amid cheers on to the varing. Their headdress proclaims these neither satellites of Phra Isuan nor men, but representative of the underworld kingdom of Phaya Nāga, King of Snakes and the producer of rain, sent, it is pretended, to perform for the delectation of Great Śiva before the eyes of men. The Brāhmaṇas now enter the sentry borces specially built for the occasion and intone prayers, and assistant pulling on the dependent rope, the swing begins to move to and fro. The momentum increases gradually, the performers bend their bodies in the attitude of saluting deities and at the same time increasing the area of the swing. At last the momentum brings the swing close to the bamboo with a bag of coins, and one of the swingers, leaning far out and watching his opportunity, makes a grab with the mouth and secures the bag in his teeth. Custom has decreed that to complete the ceremony the swing must take place three times and to that end three small money bags are provided by the Royal Treasury, the first containing twelve ticals, the second ten, the third eight. This brings the ceremony to an end, and Phra Isuan is allowed to place his raised foot on the ground once more and after receiving the prayer of the Brāhmaṇas to depart with his satellites in the procession the way he can. The ceremony is repeated on the next day, but one, with the same observance, and is then over for the year.

The first Ploughing Ceremony

Brāhmaṇa rite and pageantry are the colourful keynote of the Ploughing Ceremony—Rack Nan Khwan in Thailand.[1] This important and picturesque ceremony may only be performed on certain days of the sixth lunar month: the 2nd, 3rd, 4th, 6th, 12th, 13th and 14th days of the marcescent moon, and on the 2nd, 3rd, 4th, 9th, 11th, 12th and 15th days of the waxing moon. Additionally the day fixed must be Monday, Wednesday, Thursday or Friday.[2]

The selection of an auspicious date is important because the rites which constitute the ceremony are Siang Tai, or prophetic in character. Rigidly

1. Chu, Ualentin, *Thailand Today*, pp. 53-54.
2. Rama V, King, *op. cit.*, p. 396.

adhered to are the previously predicted auspicious times at which important portions of the ceremony must be performed. At this year's ceremony, for instance, the Phya Rack Nah, Lord of the Festival of the First Ploughing must arrive at the ceremony site shortly after 7 a.m.[1]

According to ancient custom Phya Rack Nah represents His Majesty the King of Thailand.

Immediately after Phya Rack Nah arrival, the ceremony's first procession is formed; flanked by Peung Pruat (ceremonial drumbearers elaborate red costumes) beating a rythmic measure and processional umbrella-bearers, preceded by senior Brāhmaṇa officials chanting rituals and blowing conch-shells, followed by bearers of his ceremonial dress and four Nang Thepi (consecrated women) taking part in the ceremony the Phya Rack Nah is escorted to the Brāhmaṇa ceremonial pavilion.

Incense sticks (Thoop) are lighted by the Phya Rack Nah before an altar bearing images of the deities. Then will occur the first of the Siang Tai (prophetic) rites: presented with a pile of three Phanungs (a cloth worn about the waist) each of a different length-long short and medium-Phya Rack Nah selects one to wear during the subsequent proceedings. The choice made is significant and important. The short Phanung forecasts a plentiful supply of water during the coming year, the long Phanung denotes an insufficiency of water and the medium length an average supply. By way of explanation, it is natural to raise one's Phanung (or trousers) up and out of a flood of water.

His Majesty the King is scheduled to arrive at the ceremony site soon after 8 a.m. will proceed the royal pavilion overlooking the ploughing area.[2] This year the auspicious time for enactment of the most important part of the ceremony is between 8.21-8.46 a.m. Within the space of these twenty-two minutes the Phya Rack Nah must be escorted in a second procession from the Brāhmaṇa pavilion to the stall holding the sacred bulls which are caparisoned in velvet and gold.

The Phya Rack Nah will then anoint the sacred bulls: anointed, the bulls are harnessed to the great and gilt plough and ploughing begins. Led by Brāhmaṇas[3] blowing conches and followed by the Nang Thepi carrying gold and silver Kaboong (baskets) containing seed-rice hallowed by Brāhmaṇa and Buddhist Mantras (ritualistic formulas), the Phya Rack Nah will first plough the Tai-da—three concentric furrows; then are ploughed the Thai Kwang, three other concentric furrows at right angles to the Tai-da. Phya Rack Nah will then sow the seed-rice carried by Nang

1. *Thai Ratha Newspaper*, 14th May, 2519.
2. *Thai Ratha : Newspapers*, 14th May, 2519.
3. Chu Valentin, *Thailand Today*, p. 54.

Thepi, this portion of the ceremony is concluded when the furrows are covered—Tai Klob.

The sacred bulls are next unyoked and, to the chant of other rituals and more blowing of conch-shells, presented with seven varieties of food; paddy (seed-rice), maize, beans, sesamum, grass water and rice spirit. This part of ceremony is again Siang Tai, prophetic in character. The Brāhmaṇas carefully note the food the bulls select, they will then declare which crops will be plentiful during the coming year. "Thailand will enjoy an abundance of rice, fruits and vegetables, as well as improved international trade."[1]

Thus ends the ploughing ceremony itself and the Lord of the Festival and his entourage leave in procession for the ministry of agriculture. The King and Queen take their leave too, and onto the scene rush the farmers to collect grains of seed sown during the ceremony, believing that mixed with their own seeds and planted on their farms a good harvest will ensure. With their families, farmers from all over the country come to Bangkok for this ceremony. It is the end of their rest period and the beginning of the busy farmwork ahead when all the family will be active from dawn to dusk in the paddy fields. Extreme importance is attached by the farmers to the rituals and predictions which take place on this day.[2]

Three-day old Propitiatory Ceremony

The propitiatory ceremony for[3] the three-day old baby has its origin in the superstitious belief that the spirits are responsible for the birth of a child and its physical and mental characteristics. According to this belief, the spirits are continually engaged in moulding human forms from a human reservoir of great depth. These are on the look-out for stray souls with which the ready-made human shapes are to be invested. The combination is then put into the body of the mother, resulting in what is known as conception. Thus, it is believed that the newborn was formerly owned by the spirits.

This ceremony takes place on the third day after the birth of the child, and may be described as follows:[4]

First, the baby is tossed in a type of winnowing basket while an incantation, supposedly addressed to the spirits, is recited: "Three days still a ghost-child, after that a human child. Let the owner of this child come forth and take it."

1. Rama V King, *The Royal Ceremonies of the Twelve Months*, p. 396.
2. *First Ploughing Ceremony Holiday Time in Thailand*, J.T.O.T., Vol. 30, No. 5, p. 56.
3. Diskul, Princess Poon Pimsai, *Thai Traditions & Customs*, p. 1.
4. Sondhirak, Plak, *Praphene Thai*, p. 79.

At this moment an old matron comes forth with a cowrie shell, (a former form of currency) and offers to buy it. This old woman is from that moment onwards known as *mae sue*, or "bying mother."[1] During these three days the baby is believed to be in mortal danger. The belief probably reflects on the state of medicine in former time, when infant mortality must have been exceedingly high. The child, at this time, is called a host-child, since no one can guarantee that it will live.

The baby is now put on the bed and a taper of about one foot in length is lit and placed at the head of the bed. This taper, called *kalamed* candle, must be kept burning uninterrupted for one month. The practice probably has its origin in the fire sacrifice of Brāhmaṇism. Fire sacrifices were based on the belief that fire is the giver of light and warmth, and the killer of all diseases. Hence, fire may be regarded as the great source of life. For this reason every human being must be furnished with a light at the moment he comes into the world. At his death the same candle is to be lit again. At this time the candle is used to light his funeral pyre. Since this fire is lit by means of a magnifying glass it is termed a celestial fire.

The child is now considered out of danger and is henceforth a "human child". The occasion naturally calls for due celebration. This ceremony is usually confined to the family circle.

The prescribed requisites for this ceremony are:

(i) *Baisi*, or a cone-shaped container made of banana leaves tipped with a hard boiled egg crowned with a small pinnacle of fresh flowers. This Baisi is filled with boiled rice. It is then placed in a beautiful bowl and surrounded by three horse-shoe crabs made of banana leaf, filled with bananas, cucumbers and sweet-meats. Alternating with the banana leaf horse-shoe crabs are three small banana-leaf cones decorated with flowers and pieces of sacred thread.

(ii) A small candle on a candlestick.

(iii) A bowl of perfumed powder for anointment.

(iv) A bowl of tepid water and a small spoon for feeding the baby.

At the auspicious moment, the senior members of the family lighted candles and gass-sticks to pay homage to the triple Gem of Buddhism. A prayer invoking the blessing of the gods is then chanted. The Baisi is placed on the baby's bed which is then held before the officiate. He proceeds to charm away all the evils threatening the child by gently rubbing the baby's limbs with the sacred thread, one piece for each limb. This

1. Anuman Rajadhon, *Nation, Religion and Civilization of Thais*, p. 370.

done, all four pieces of sacred thread are burned. Pieces of new thread are then blessed and knots tied in the centres. These are tied to the wrists and ankles of the baby. After this, the baby is anointed and fed with three spoonfuls of water from the water bowl. Thus ends the ceremony. At the end of the ceremony, the food in the Baisi is offered to the spirits, while all the banana-leaf accessories are put under the baby's mattress and left there for three days. At the end of the three days they are thrown into the Menam (river).

One month old Propitiatory Ceremony

After the lapse of one month, there is reason to believe that the baby is completely out of danger. Another ceremony is then held to celebrate the occasion and make known to members of the family the fact that a new member has been added.[1]

This ceremony is celebrated on larger and more elaborate scale than the first one.[2] A service is performed by a class of Bhikkhus on the eve of the auspicious day which has been fixed by the astrologer. Next morning food is offered to the monks and there is then a Brāhmaṇical ceremony of propitiation which runs as follows:

When the auspicious moment arrives, the astrologer announces the fact by sounding of gong. The official then dabs at the baby's head with a finger wet with lustral water from a conchshell, and touches the hair with the tonsure knife symbolizing the act of tonsure. The monks then chant blessing followed by Brāhmin and Thai orchestral music which is played on conchshells, and a small drum. When the tonsure is over (in some cases there is no actual tonsure) the Brāhmins proceed to bathe the baby in lukewarm water mixed with lustral water prepared on the previous day. This ceremony may well be compared to Christian baptism. The baby is then handed over to a member of the family, usually a grandmother, who holds it in her arms before a *Baisi*.

The Brāhmaṇa then proceeds to charm away evils by means of sacred thread which is later burnt. The baby is anointed and fed with spoonfuls of coconut milk. Three candles, each fixed to a flat candlestick, are lighted and blessings are repeated three times. The candles are then handed round clockwise, one by one, with the baby to the right. This is based on the belief that the right side brings good luck. All this is performed to the accompaniment of a full Thai orchestra. After the candles have been handed round three times, they are handed over to the Brāhmin who sticks them one by one, in a rice bowl. The three candles are then kneaded into one and the flame snuffed out with betel leaves. The smoke thus

1. Diskul, Princess Poon Pismai, *Thai Traditions & Customs*, p. 4.
2. Anuman Rajadhon Phya, *Introducing Cultural Thailand in Outline*, p. 18.

produced by Agni, the fire god, is then fanned towards the baby. The candle rotation ceremony over, the Brāhmin makes the baby's bed and places the baby's various gifts in the corners of the cot and under the mattress and pillow. A clean cat, with a chain around its neck to show that it is a pet, is then brought along, placed in the cot for a few seconds and then taken away. This is a mystic gesture of giving the bed being made, the baby is put into the cot by the Brāhmin who proceeds to put it to sleep. The ceremony now over, the relatives come forth with their gifts and put them into the cot with the baby.

A further ceremony is then held in which two coconuts, called gold and silver coconuts are taken away to be buried together with the placenta in a plot of land which is destined for the child. The gesture is again symbolic of giving.

For the ceremony the following articles are required:

A set of tables of varying sizes for offering a Buddha image, the baby's horoscope, a bowl of lustral water, a ball of sacred thread, vases, flower bowl, a joss-stick bowl and a pair of large tapers.

These articles are set out on the tables at one side of a platform prepared for the Bhikkhus to sit on. It is covered with white cloth and cushions, hot and cold beverages, cigarettes, betel nuts and spittoons are provided. Next morning, food is offered to the Bhikkhus, each Bhikkhu being served with an individual set of dress.

A Brāhminical rite follows, for which the following articles are required:

(i) Baby cot, usually installed in the centre of the room to facilitate the candle rotation ceremony.

(ii) *Baisi* which is made in a varying number of tiers, from three to seven, according to the rank or nobility. This Baisi is tipped with flowers decorated with silver nickel or gold according to the rank and filled with sweets. It is then covered with brocade and placed on a low table at the head of the baby's cot and within reach of the officient. Besides the Baisi, there are the following articles on the table:

(a) A wash basin containing three knives placed on a small raised tray, a bowl for the shaven-off hair, a bronze bowl of lustral water, a conch-shell containing lustral water, and a bale leaf.

(b) A well husked coconut on a raised tray and a small spoon (coconut milk is held to be the purest liquid available).

(c) Two toy ducks, one yellow and one white, made of flour and symbolical of gold and silver.

(d) A bowl of perfumed powder.

(e) Five to seven betel leaves for snuffing out the candle.
(f) Candle and matches.

All these articles are placed on the table alongwith the Baisi.

(iii) A baby bath tub which is put on one side of the cot together with imitation fish and crustaceans made of light wood and covered with gold and silver paper. These toy creatures are set on a miniature raft made of banana stalk until the time they are immersed in the water, by the Brāhmin prior to the baby's ablution. This is suggestive of the sacred river according to Brāhmaṇism.

(iv) A large bowl filled with uncooked rice and three flat candle sticks holding three candles is for the rotation ceremony. This bowl is placed before the table bearing the Baisi.

(v) Two sprouting coconuts, one covered with gold paper and the other with silver paper, which are placed beside the bath tub.

(vi) Bags of various vegetable seeds are placed beside the cot. These are meant to be sown by the child when he grows up.

(vii) Articles indicative of the future career of the baby, if it is a girl, then sewing needle, thread, knife and scissors are put into the cot together with the baby. If it is a boy and destined for the career of an artisan, the tool of his trade is placed beside him.

(viii) An image of the god Vessuvan, the demon king, is hung over the cot or on the mosquito net to ward off evil spirits.

(ix) Baby clothes to be worn after the bath.

(x) Mattress and pillow to be put into the cot. These are placed besides the cot together with the gifts to the baby.

Thus, it may be understood on the basis of the above that the Brāhmaṇic culture of India and Thailand (Siam) are intimately knit together from time immemorial. It cannot be doubted that the spirit of this unity can be discerned in about all of the manifold aspects of Siamese culture and civilisation. Music, paintings, drama, language and literature, festivals and ceremonies and other traditions of Thailand seem to represent the extension of the Brāhmaṇical culture in the extreme orient. Of course, here it may be pointed out that in spite of the immense Brāhmaṇical-Buddhistic influences in the culture of the Indo-Chinese peninsula, there is a subtle flow of a primitive culture in it, which may be partly the reminiscences of the pre-historic civilisation of Oceania and South-East Asia. This flow is no doubt far less pronounced in the Thai culture, in comparison with its force in the beliefs and customs prevailing amongst the various primitive tribes living in the solitary forests and mountains of the Trans-Gangetic peninsula.

5. LAOS

The land of the kingdom of Laos popularly known as "The land of the million elephants and of the white parasol" was known as Suvarṇabhūmi (the land of the gold) in early time.

In the absence of authentic historical records bearing on the early history of Laos, it is difficult to assign any definite date of contact between India and Laos. Nevertheless it can be safely presumed that relation between the two countries in the field of culture, religion and society existed since pre-historic days.

Before the introduction of Brāhmaṇism and Buddhism into Laos, the country was clustered with the cult of spirits and animism in all its forms. As in India, life was dependent on supernatural forces which swayed the destiny of man. It may be observed here that the syllable 'Om' recurs very often in the beginning while invoking a particular spirit:

"Om, Oh White herb;
I use the talisman of the White Angel:
Om, I invoke the power of Phra In,
I invoke the power of Phra Prom
I invoke the power of internal spirits:
Om, Maha Saming:
I invoke the Great Genius of living being."[1]

Even today the majority of the Lao people practice both religion and the cult of spirits (popularly known as the cult of Phi[2]) in their daily life and public festivals. According to Georges Condominas, the word Phi encompasses a great number of motions, which must be translated for us by words carrying a multitude of different meanings, such as "Śouls of the dead", "maleficent spirit", "tutelary god", "natural divinity" etc.[3] The Phi cult was so popular that during the sixth century of the Christian era, the Khmers built sanctuary, Wat Phu Champassak on the hill known as Liṅga parvata which already contained the famous sanctuary dedicated to God Bhadreśvara Śiva overlooking the place where śreṣṭhapura, the capital of Chenla lay. Once in a year the king, guided by a thousand soldiers, proceeded to offer human sacrifice there. According to local tradition, Phya Kammatha (the builder of Wat Phu Champassak and That Phanom) went up to that sanctuary and presided over the sacrifice

1. Phouvong, Phimmasone, *Kingdom of Laos*, pp. 336-37.
2. For details see Condominas Georges, *Rites et Ceremonies en Milieu Bouddhiste Lao*, p. 171.
3. For detailed interpretation of the various *phis*, see *ibid.*, pp. 185-92; see also U. Thakur, "Elements of Hindu Culture in Laos", presented to the 7th Conference International Association of Historians of Asia, Bangkok, 22-26th August, 1977.

of a pair of virgins, and a bowl of alcohol was also offered in the sixth month when the red jasmine started to shed its fragrance.

The ritual continued to be practiced uninterruptedly every year with the same pomp and pleasure at Wat Phu though the human sacrifice was substituted by buffalo sacrifices in later times because it came to be popularly believed that the 'blood of a buffalo, is of equal value with the blood of a man'. The sacrifice of the buffalo as in many temples in India, is still performed both in Vientiane (the Capital of Laos) and Luang Prabang (the residence of the King), usually in May or June. The people of Laos believe that the Spirit or Phi can help and give good fortune in life and impelled by this notion they offer the god, flowers, candles, incense, and blood of the animal etc.[1]

Important Sanskrit inscriptions of Cambodia have been found in Laos. A digraphic inscription (written in the usual Pallava script of South India and also in North Indian script akin to Bengali, Post-Gupta Brāhmi) of Yaśovarman, the founder of Angkor, has been found in Laos.[2] A late eleventh century inscription of Jayavarman VI, found near Bassac in Laos, gives a beautiful description of the beauty and vast learning of the Lady Tilak:

"In her youth not only had she a beauty most excellent coupled with right conduct...but by the elders, the royal Guru, and the most learned, she was honoured publicly and proclaimed as the goddess Vāgiśvari (Sarasvati), and in contest of learning being reckoned the foremost, she decked with jewels", she was the mother of the Court Paṇḍita Subhadra of King Jayavarman VII.[3]

It would thus be seen that Laos, the cradle of the early Kambuja realm, witnessed the process of Indianisation in full swing and got the name of Lava, i.e., the Land of Lava, the son of Rāma, in learned circles. There is still a city named Lavapuri, popularly pronounced as Loppuri (or Lopburi) in Thailand.

As regards literature and script it would suffice to say that with the introduction and popularity of Sanskrit language it had come to occupy a dominant place in all these regions. Majority of the inscriptions of the early period, found in different parts of Laos referred to above, are in beautiful Sanskrit which clearly testify to the wide prevalence and popularity of the language. It is true that no early works in Sanskrit have been found in Laos, but there is no doubt that the earliest Lao literature is replete with Sanskrit and Pāli origin. Sanskrit and Pāli grammar, lexicography and prosody have influenced Lao language and literature. The classical period of Lao litrature was in its full splendour from 1547 to 1571

1. Archaimbault Charies, *Kingdom of Laos*, pp. 156-57 and p. 162.
2. Majumdar, R.C., *Suvarnadvipa*, Pt. II, pp. 99-101.
3. *ibid.*, p. 17.

under the rule of Sethathirat, a Sanskrit name which is as Śri Jayajyeṣṭha or in local pronunciation as P'ra Jaya Jettha. The reign of King Suryavathsa (1637-1694) also witnessed the classical period of Lao history and culture, and Laos, during this period, was mighty centre of intellectual and religious activities. The diversity, richness and the characteristics of Lao culture and literature are essentially Indian.

In 1283 A.D. King Ram Kamheng of Sukhodaya introduced the Lao script which marks the common origin of Thai and Lao alphabets. It was in this year (1283 A.D.) that Pāli scriptures from Ceylon were introduced into the kingdom of Sukhodaya and from this moment Sanskrit was replaced by Pāli.

The Lao script and language are derived from Sanskrit and Pāli. There is a great similarity between Sanskrit and Lao words. For instance the names of some Indian flowers such as Gulāb, Campā and Sabhā etc., are exactly the same in Lao language. The words Dharmaśālā in Sanskrit and Sālā Dham in Lao have exactly the same meaning.

The classical Lao verses follow the metrics of Indian prosody and the metre is regulated by the number of syllables and their quantity. Infact, "the true classical Lao poetry is formed of translations of Indian poems and even Lao folklore is peopled by the Indian pantheon." The religious songs of the Bhikkhus (Bhikṣus) developed upto the nineteenth century and they inspired large number of stories which became popular both in verse and prose. The Lao people sing of "the beauty and charm of nature, and of love and its attractions. Their dances, gestures and movements recall Indian origins, the themes of which are taken from Brāhmaṇical and Buddhist stories, the epics (the *Rāmāyaṇa* and *Mahābhārata*), historical and legendary episodes as well as Indian fables, supplying interminable topics of gallantry and tenderness. The Molam is an important genre of literature which "evokes the marvels of paradise, the powers of Indra, the cruelty of Yama, the atrocities of hell, and on the other hand, the beauties of full moon, the enchantments of woods and seasons". The story of Rāma (Rāmakathā, The Phra Lak Phra Lām or The Phra Lām Sādok, a Lao version of the story of Rāma[1]) is as popular in Laos, Thailand and other countries of South-East Asia as it is in India. Infact, "the abiding and fundamental human values and social ideas of the Rāma legend have contributed to the central place it has come to occupy in the cultural life of the peoples of most South-East Asian countries. In each country, while the central theme of the Rāma legend has been maintained, the narration of the epic has evolved considerably in such a way as to reflect the environment, civilization and

1. Edited, Critically for the first time by Sahai, S. 1973.

culture of each country which has resulted in the emergence of classical masterpieces of literature."[1]

Besides literature, the classical Lao theatre has Brāhmaṇical origin and had been imported from Khmer in the 14th century. It was mainly developed in the 16th and 17th centuries. Gestures and movements remained one of Indian choreography and the scenes represented in general the episodes of the *Rāmāyaṇa.* Didactic stories, judicial stories, comic stories, legends and histories, canonical (Buddhist) and extra-canonical literature, and technical literature form the different branches of the vast classical Lao literature which betray undoubted Brāhmaṇical origin and influence. In this connection it is interesting to note that the age-old Indian gurukula system still exists in Laos.

Minds of Lao people are so impregnated with Brāhmaṇism that some Brāhmaṇical rites are still practised alongside Buddhism, especially on great occasions such as birth, wedding and death. The names of Brāhmaṇical gods. . . Indra, Viṣṇu, Śiva etc., are quite familiar to the Lao people, and in their prayers to Lord Buddha, they never fail to invoke these Hindu divinities.[2] The Rāmakathā is as much popular in Laos as in India.

The Baisi ceremony is just one of the many instances which show how deeply Brāhmaṇism is entrenched in the religious life of the Lao people. The term Baisi or Sukhuan (officient, palm) is etymologically derived from Brāhman, and this rite is celebrated on many occasions such as New Year, marriage, birth, etc. Though the Brāhmaṇas and the Bhikkhus were in their country of origin (India) quite unaccommodating antagonists for a long time and the Brāhmaṇic religion virtually eliminated the Buddhist monks, yet they incorporated some of the ethical achievements of Buddhism[3] of which Baisi is a living example. The chief of this ceremony is called Brāhma who is chosen from amongst the elders of the village. He performs the ritual ceremony according to the Brāhmaṇical rites. Thus, Brāhmaṇical religion combined with Buddhist rites have taken deep roots in Laos and whenever the Lao people perform Buddhist rites and other festivals, the Brāhmaṇical ceremony also follows at home and in the temple.

Should any one have the opportunity to visit Laos and stay for some time with a Lao family, he would certainly notice that the Brāhmaṇical and Lao manners and customs are very similar in many respects. The way of greeting a friend or high personality by joining the hands at the level of the heart with a slight bow of the head is just one instance to cite. The simple way of dressing, especially by a male, consisting of *lungi* made

1. *ibid.*, p. XIII.
2. For details see, *Rites et Ceremonies en Milieu Buddhiste Lao*, p. 182.
3. Tambiah, S.J., *Buddhism and Spirit Cults in North-East Thailand*, p. 252.

of silk or cotton, a shawl carelessly thrown upon the shoulders, a light shirt and, on special occasions, the *bundhgalā* (closed neck) coat and *dhoti* are all believed to have come from India.

We possess an important collections of Lao stories. The majority of them are derived from the *Pañcatantra.* In fact *Pañcatantra* stories are widely diffused throughout the Indo-Chinese peninsula.

The stories may be divided into three categories; viz., *Pañcatantra* stories, judicial stories and comic stories.

The Lava *Pañcatantra* consists of five works termed Pakon (=Prakaraṇa). Their names are : (1) Nanda Prakaraṇa (Nanda is the name of a bull), (2) Maṇḍūka Prakaraṇa, (3) Piśāca Prakaraṇa, (4) Śakuṇa Prakaraṇa, (5) Saṁgha Prakaraṇa (which is in the form of a gloss to the text of *Vinaya*).

The narrator of the stories is a queen called Tantai Mahādevī, a name which corresponds to Nang Tantrai of the Siamese version, and Dyah Tantri of the Javanese version of *Pañcatantra.* Tantai, Tantrai are alterations of the Sanskrit "*Tantravāya*" (the weaver of tales).

There also exists another collection of stories entitled *Mulla Tantai* resembling the Kambuja work *Koeng Kantray* which is a sacred book of laws. These are judicial stories. *Kantraya* is probably the Sanskrit *Karttri* (spinner). *Cantrai, Cantai, Canti* are also used to denote the narrator of stories *Mulla Tantai* is Sanskrit *Mula-Tantra.* These are used as commentaries on different articles of the Code of law. In general they have an ancient tinge about them. One of the best known works of this genre is *Ay Cet Hei.* It is in verse. It is based on elements which are grotesque and miraculous. Another work which may be mentioned is *Hua Lan Bua Hei* "the horse poisoned by mushrooms".

The principal historical legendary works are the following : (1) *Nitan Khun Borom* : Khun Borom is the son of Indra who was sent from heaven to found the kingdom of Lan Xang. The events come to end in 1571. (2) *Pongsavadan Muong Lao.* (3) *Pongsavadan Kasat Vieng-Cah*: It is a chronicle of the kings of Vientiane. It comes to end in 1901. (4) *Pun Pra Bang* : It is a history of Pra Bang. (5) *Pun Pra Keo* : It is a history of the emerald statue of Pra Keo. (6) *Nitan Praya Cuong Lun* : It is a chronicle of the western principality of Lava during the last three quarters of the 12th century. (7) *Uranganidana* : It is a heterogeneous text comprising predictions of Buddha, of his different births and miracles, and of kings of Lava in the 16th century.

Lava words of Indian Origin :

Here under we give a few :

Praya Then, Then Fa, Phi Fa=Indra

Pissanukam, the celestial architect=Viśvakarmān.

Nang Thorani=Devī Dharaṇī (the earth)

Nang Mekhala=Devī Mekhalā, Maṇī Mekhalā (the goddess of the Ocean)

Praya Nak=Nāgarāja. These are serpents who live in rivers and can take human form.

Prom=Brahmā

Rusi=Ṛṣi

Si Ayudhya=Siam

Hongsa=Pegu

Setthi=Śreṣṭhi (a merchant prince)

Kumara=Kumāra (prince)

Sut=Sūtra.

6. *JAVA*

On the basis of legends and local traditions we are able to know about the introduction and prevalence of Brāhmaṇism in Java. The leader of the first colonists, the cultural hero Aji Saka (lit. "Lord Saka-era"), is for instance associated with the heroes of the Mahābhārata ruling at Hastināpura.[1] That he is called after the Saka-era beginning 78 A.D., which was also used elsewhere in Greater India, may be regarded as a reminiscence of the permeation of the higher culture of south India, where this era was very much in use. This legendary personification was indeed not only held to be the introducer of a new religion and a new social order, but also of a new script and a new calendar. According to another, and in all probability, younger version of this legend Aji Saka and the descendants of the Epic princes were natives of Gujarat.

These traditions—similar to those current in southern India—cannot, of course, be regarded as reliable historical data. This is also apparent from the existence of a concurrent tradition relating the introduction of the Brāhmaṇical calendar and the Hindu mode of divine worship to the Brāhmin Tritṛṣṭa who has its peer in the Brāhmin founder of Fu-nan in Cambodia.[2] Taken collectively they may, however, be regarded as a welcome supplement to the Indian, Chinese and Western references to

1. For this tradition see Raffles, Th. S., *History of Java*, II, p. 66ff.
2. The inference that the first Indians arrived in Java in 78 A.D. would be completely unwarranted. The earliest Indonesian inscriptions are undated.

early trade intercourse between the Indian mainland and South-East Asia, including the Archipelago.[1]

Legend of Mahāmeru

An interesting tradition is preserved in a Javanese book which probably was compiled in the sixteenth century. In this *Tantu Paṅgelaran*[2] which is a sort of "religious history" of Java, narrating *inter alia* how different gods introduced various arts and crafts into that island, much attention is drawn to the Mahāmeru, the central mountain. This mountain was, according to the detailed description, with great difficulty transported from Jambūdvīpa to the island of Java to be the abode of Bhaṭṭāra Guru, the highest Javanese god of later literature, who, also called Parmeśvara, has a strong resemblance to Śiva, the teacher (also called Guru) ascetic and husband of Umā. The significancc of this mythical tale must have been considerable and the story of its transference—which was only partially effectuated, half of the mountain (interestingly enough !) remaining in India—cannot be said to be a mere reflection of the well-known fact that after the cultural spread of Brāhmaṇism many Indian geographical names were given to rivers and mountains of South-East Asia.[3] Nor was it merely an occasion for its inventors to combine and supplement a number of Indian mythological motifs, such as for instance Viṣṇu's acting as a serpent and Parameśvara's drinking the "water" Kālakūṭa which rushed forth from the mountain, when the gods, semi-divine beings and ṛṣis turned round the Meru—which is also called Mandara—in order to pull it loose. The Meru is not only in this work called thc liṅga of the world, but was obviously, in accordance with Indian concepts, believed to be the centre of the universe. The purpose of the removal of the mountain to Java, as in the text itself,[4] said to have been the stabilisation of the island. Thus the narrative in all probability reflects a ritual settlement of the new country. To settle and to organize a new territory is an act of "cosmicization", a consecration, repetition of the paradigmatic work of the gods. Around the mountain, the representative of the cosmic exis, a territory becomes habitable. The removal of the mountain to Java—where it has up to the present day remained as mount Smeru (Sumeru)—was on the one hand to make human existence in the new surroundings possible and on the other

1. Chatterjee, B.R., *India and Java*; Majumdar, R.C., *Hindu Colonies in the Far East*; Coedes, *Les etats hindouises d' Indochine et d'Indonesie*; Sastri K.A. Nilakanta, *South Indian influence in the Far East*; Quaritch, H.G. Wales, *The Making of Greater India*; Warmington, E.H. *Commerce between the Roman Empire and India.*
2. Edited and translated (into Dutch) by Pigeaud, Th. G., *Tantu Pangelaran.*
3. Pelliot, P. *Bulletin de l' Ecole Francaise d' Extreme-Orient*, p. 157.
4. *Tanty Pangelaran*, p. 63.

to identify these with India, the country of its origin. This is neither to say that those who first ritually identified a Javanese mountain with the Indian Meru or who invented and promulgated the myth in the form known to us were the leaders of a group of colonists in the proper sense of the term, or that they were the first colonists themselves; to express an opinion about a factual transference of what might be called a sort of palladium. It is, further, easily understandable that the name Meru was, in Indonesia as well as in India proper, also given to a towering form of temple structure—the term is still usual in Bali[1]—not only because a temple was regarded as an earthly counterpart of the heavenly dwelling of the deities to which they descend from their cosmic mountain home, but also and, no doubt primarily, because a temple is likewise a representative of the cosmic axis and, hence, of the cosmic mountain.[2]

It is interesting to add that the Malays of Perak are convinced that the first Malay king came down from the mountain Saguntan Mahameru and appeared suddenly in Palembang (Sumatra) riding on a white bull. There is, however, often occasions to consider traditions of this type with reserve, because personal, tribal, geographical names may have been introduced at different times. We are for instance by no means sure that some names of tribal subdivisions, which are unmistakably South Indian, among the Karo-Batak of Sumatra (Coḷiya, Pāṇḍya, Meliyāla, etc.) were received by that people at an early date, although it is true that there is a sufficiency of date to prove an early Indian presence in the West of Sumatra and especially the existence of commercial relations with Barus. Sometimes also apparent identity of names does not furnish us with absolutely reliable information. A combination of the Indonesian usage to call Indians Kalinga or Klin and the ancient Chinese names of Java Ho-lin, which is identified with Kalinga, should not induce us to give all credit for the "Colonization" of the Archipelago to the people of Kalinga, or to maintain that "the leading kingdom of Java" was named after that Indian region, and "dominated" by immigrants from that coastal area.[3] A more cautious conclusion is to assume that the region had already at an early date an important share in the commercial relations with South-East Asia in general and that the Chinese recognised Java as a country touched by Brāhmaṇical culture.

The beginnings of the Brāhmaṇical influence in Indonesia are indeed shrouded in mystery. When, in the early fifth century A.D., the oldest historical sources begin to furnish us with scanty information they show

1. Zoete, B. De and Spies, W., *Dance and Drama in Bali*, p. 337.
2. See Kramrisch, S., *The Hindu Temple*, p. 277ff; Wales H.G.Q., *The Mountain of God*, p. 120ff; Zimmer, H., *The Art of Indian Asia*, I, p. 315.
3. Majumdar, R.C., *History and Culture of the Indian People*, III, p. 641; For a discussion of this question see Krom, *Hindoe-Javansche geschiedenis*, p. 88ff.

that Sanskrit and Brāhmaṇical religion had already found their way into the Archipelago.[1] It is, however, by no means certain that then already the higher Brāhmaṇical culture had brought about many modifications in the beliefs and customs of the population in its entirety. The script of the oldest records resembles the manner of writing in use in Coromandel during the Pallava rule.[2] This does not however mean that no other region of India was concerned in the colonisation, nor that the Indian names of the kings mentioned in the inscriptions were borne by Indian immigrants. They may have belonged to Brāhmaṇised Indonesian chiefs. We have no certain information on the commercial relations which had led to the introduction of Brāhmaṇic culture. We do not know names of scholars and teachers whose activity made it possible that king Mūlavarman of Kutei could eternise, through the erection of stone yūpas with seven inscriptions referring to other sacrifices and donations[3], the performance of a *bahusuvarṇaka* sacrifice. The ceremony was carried out by Brāhmaṇas, but we grope in the dark as to the king's allegiance to a definite god. Nor can we be certain whether these inscriptions really testify to a considerable predominance of Brāhmaṇas and Brāhmaṇical religion in Borneo. Viṣṇu is on the other hand mentioned in an inscription commemorating another king whose name—like those of many rulers in India and Further India—ends in 'varman', viz., Purnavarman, reference to whom has already been made. His feet, depiction of which is added to the inscription, are said to equate the footsteps of Viṣṇu. In another inscription likewise accompanied by a hardly visible pair of human footprints, these feet are *inter alia* stated to have been salutary to devoted princes, but a thorn for his enemies.[4] In view of the relations existing, in India and Further India, between Viṣṇu and kingship it is by no means certain that this god was the ruler's *iṣṭadevatā*. The exact significance of these footprints—which are widely believed to be depositories of the essence of a divine, human or demoniac person—is disputed: were they to mark the spot of the king's cremation, or to commemorate the occupation of his country, or—what seems least improbable—were they "no more than mementos of the valour and heroism of a great king" ?[5] Anyhow, there does not seem to be sufficient reason for doubting that king Purnavarman was, after his death, more or less deified and made

1. Coedes, *Lesetats hindouises d' Indochine et d'Indonesie*, p. 33ff; Bernet Kemper, *Ancient Indonesian Art*, p. 8ff.
2. Chhabra, B. Ch., *Expansion of Indo-Aryan Culture during Pallava rule as evidenced by Inscriptions*, *JASB*, I (1935), p. 1ff.
3. Chhabra, B. Ch., Three more yūpa inscriptions of king Mūlavarman, *Tijdschrift Bataviaasch Genootschap*, 83, p. 370ff.
4. For these inscriptions, see Kern, H., *Verspreide Geschriften*, VII, p. 1ff; 129ff.
5. Nilakanta Sastri, *op. cit.*, p. 108.

the object of worship. The worship of footprints of gods and saintly persons is indeed well-known in India.[1]

To the Chinese pilgrim Fa-hien,[2] who made in 441 A.D. a perilous voyage from Ceylon to China, during which he was driven out of his course to an island called Yeh-po-ti, which must be Yavādvī (pa), that is, in all probability, Java, we owe the information that at that time besides heresy and "Brāhmaṇism"[3] there was in that island a concept "hardly worth mentioning".

From inscriptions dealing *inter alia* with the erection of sanctuaries, and archaeological remains it appears that Central Java was in the 8th and 9th centuries—the intervening period is almost completely wrapped in darkness —the scene of a Hindu-Javanese culture which from the religious point of view must have been Hindu, Buddhist, and indigenous (ancestor worship, etc.) influenced by Brāhmaṇism. Here again there is much scope for controversial discussion and for a premature exercise of ingenuity and imagination in constructing theories on too insufficient data derived from inadequate sources. How far do these scanty sources give us a reliable idea of real historical facts ? How far has, in that period Brāhmaṇism—Buddhism must be left out of consideration here—on its turn been influenced by indigenous religious cults and concepts ? The fact that in the eighth century the Sanskrit language in the inscriptions replaced by old-Javanese can not be without significance, but what parts of the entire population were really involved in the religious evolution which, perhaps, is reflected by this change ? How far were, in that period, the various strata of society really penetrated in the Indian religious belief ? Is it, in view of the few documents available, not premature to discuss the question, whether Śaivism or Buddhism was more inclined to adapt itself to its Javanese environment ? It is true that the Śaivite sanctuaries are more numerous and more widely spread than the very impressive Buddhist monuments which seem to have been founded only in a limited region, but does it follow that the court was Buddhist and the common herd largely Śaivite ?[4] The very fact that it was, as far as we are able to see, this period in which the Old-Javanese *Rāmāyaṇa* was written—and we now know that this beautiful poem, at least for its greater part, follows the difficult Sanskrit *Bhaṭṭikāvya* —proves that Brāhmaṇism must have obtained a firm footing also in the cultured milieus of scholars and aristocracy.[5] It is not only the popularity of the *Rāmāyaṇa*—which was also very well-known in Champa of the seventh century—which induces us to make this observation, but above all

1. For the symbolism see also Kirfel, W., *Symbolik des Hinduismus and des Jinismus*, p. 90.
2. Giles, H.A., *The Travels of Fa-hsien or Record of Buddhistic kingdoms*, p. 78.
3. For a discussion of "heresy" (which may include Paśupata Śaivism, a persuasion dominant in Cambodia) see Kern, *Verspreide Geschriften*, VII, p. 137.
4. Kern, *Verspreide Geschriften*, VII, p. 199.
5. Krom, N.J., *Over het Civaisme van Midden-Java*, (58, 8).

its beauty and the high degree of skill and proficiency of its poet who succeeded in using a variety of metres and in making his work an exemplary product of kāvya technique.[1] There was, moreover, a Śaivite dynasty called after king Sañjaya who had, presumably, founded it, one of its kings probably lending assistance to another[2] Buddhist dynasty on the occasion of the consecration of a Buddhist temple. How are we to conceive an Idea of this cooperation ? Was it a religious or a merely political affair ? Many particulars related to the erection of religious monuments—date, purpose, founder, etc.—are indeed unknown or only a matter for conjecture. Thus the impressive complex of temples at Prambanan known as Lara Jongrang poses some puzzling questions. Is the traditional supposition (founded by king Daksa in the beginning of the ninth century) right ? Or was it built in the middle of the ninth century and was it intended to be a Śaiva counterpart of the famous Buddhist monument, the Borobudur ? King Sañjaya had in 732 A.D. a Sanskrit inscription (found at Cangal) engraved in which homage is paid to Śiva, Brahmā and Viṣṇu and mention is made of the erection, on a mountain, of a liṅga—in all probability, a palladium considered like similar emblems in Further India a donation of the god, conveyed through the intermediary of a Brāhmaṇa and of a wonderful sanctuary dedicated to the worship of Śiva and somehow connected with a southern region of the India mainland, called Kuñjarakunja. This district has not improbably been supposed to be identical with Kuñjara or Kuñjaradari in southern India, where was a mountain "created by Śiva" and the abode of the sage Agastya. The fact that Śiva is mentioned first in the Trimūrti may no doubt be taken to testify to his great popularity. We know that in Further India the same god seems to have, alone of the trinity, been set up for special worship, while Viṣṇu was looked upon as an accessory deity.[3]

The legal system of Java was mainly of Brāhmaṇical origin, though modified by local traditions. There were written law-codes in Java and Bali, and these resembled the Brāhmaṇical Law-books Dharmaśāstras or Smṛtis to a large extent, both in form and substance. How far these Law books were promulgated by constituted authorities and represented the actual conditions of society is a common problem both for India and her colonies. But the general picture afforded by these books may be taken in either case as a safe guide for obtaining a broad view of the state and society in the past. The variations of rules and principles noticed in different law books must be attributed, as in the case of India, to varying indigenous customs in different localities and in different ages. To this we

1. For the Javanese *Rāmāyaṇa* sculpture, see Stutterheim, W.F., *Rama-Legenden and Rama-Reliefs in Indonesian.*
2. Hooykaas, C., *The Old-Javanese Rāmāyaṇa.*
3. Geity, A. *Gaṇeśa.*

may perhaps add the influence of the different Brāhmaṇical law books introduced, perhaps at different times, in Java.

Among the more important Law-books of Java which are known to exist at the present time, the following deserve special mention:

1. *Sarasamuccaya* : It consists mostly of Sanskrit verses, followed by an old-Javanese translation. It begins with an account of Viṣṇu who came to Mdang, ruled there as Rahyang Tavkan Dyavan, and had four sons.

2. *Svara Jambu* (Probably corrupted from Svayambhu)[1] is mostly the translation of the eighth book of the *Mānavadharmaśāstra*. Only the last part, written in later dialect, deviate from this source.

3. *The Śivaśāsana*, written in pure Old-Javanese is referred to in an inscription of 991 A.D., and is associated with king Dharmāvaṁsa teguh Anantavikramottungadeva.

4. The work generally known as Purvadhigama, and designated at the end as Śivaśāsana sarodhṛta may be regarded as a later redaction of No. 3.

5. *The Devāgama*, also known as Kṛtopapati, quotes many rules from *Mānavadharmaśāstra*.

6. *The Kūṭāra-mānava* is also largely influenced by *Mānavadharmaśāstra*.

7. *Gajah Mada*, a law book attributed to Gajah Mada, the famous Prime Minister of Majapahit. The existing text is undoubtedly more modern, but as Gajah Mada is credited with a knowledge of law it is not unlikely that he was the author of the original work.

8. *Adigama* : This is one of the law books now regarded an authentic in Bulelng (Bali). It is attributed to Kanaka, the Prime Minister of Majapahit from 1413 to 1430. The date given in the manuscript is 1401. A.D.

Among the texts mentioned above, the *Kūṭāra mānava*[2] No. 6 which is now held authentic in Bali, may form the basis of a detailed study of the Indo-Javanese law. The book was regarded as of the highest authority in the flourishing period of the Majapahit empire. This is indisputably proved by the Bendasari inscription dating from the middle of the fourteenth century A.D. It is a record of a judgment in a civil case (dispute over the possession of land) and describes the way in which the judges came to a decision. There were six of them referred to as 'Dharmapravartak

1. Cf. Majumdar, R.C., *Suvarnadvipa*, p. 1ff.
2. Edited with a scholarly introduction and Dutch translation by J.B.G. Jonker (Leiden, 1885).

Vyavahāra-vicchedaka'. They heard the statements of both the parties, and in accordance with established practice, interrogated some impartial local people about it. Then they took into consideration the law, as enunciated in legal texts, the local usages and customs, the precedents, and the opinions of religious teachers and old men, and ultimately decided according to the principles enunciated in *Kūṭāra-mānava*.

That the *Kūṭāra mānava* was regarded as of the highest authority also follows from another inscription, dated 1358 A.D. in which the judges, seven in number, are described as "Kūṭāramānavadi-śāstra-vivecam-tatpam" i.e., persons skilled in the knowledge *Kūṭāra-mānava* and other law books.

The language of the existing text of the *Kūṭāra-mānava*, however, shows that it is a later redaction of that work, though it is not easy to determine the nature and extent of the modifications introduced in later times. The text, as we have it now, is a compilation from various sources, some of which are named in the book itself, and others are referred to in general terms, such as 'so say the wise people,' etc. The arrangement is also somewhat irregular, the same topics, even the same rules, recurring in different parts of the work and sometimes there are different rules about the same topics. This is more particularly the case with regard to rules about slaves, pledge, the marriage price, and adultery. The legal principles and detailed rules betray clearly the influence of indigenous laws and customs. The influence of indigenous law and variations from or modifications of Indian law are clearly much greater in the earlier than in the later part, and this has given rise to the question whether the whole of the present text formed part of the original work. The unity of the language is in favour of this view. But Brandes thinks that it really consists of two parts, the Kūṭāra, inspired by Bhṛgu, and the Mānava, inspired by Manu. Brandes also refers to a Malay chronicle according to which it was composed under Surya Alam, king of Demak.[1]

About the indebtedness of *Kūṭāra-mānava-śāstra* to different Indian Law books we find the following interesting passage in the book itself:

"A buffalo or a cow, given in pledge, is forfeited to the creditor, if it is not redeemed within three years. Thus say Kūṭārāgama. According to Mānavāgama, the period is five years. One of these two must be followed. It is wrong to suppose, however, that one of these law-books is better than the other, both being authoritative. The *Mānava-śāstra* was communicated by Mahārāja Manu who was like god Viṣṇu. The *Kūṭāra-śāstra* was communicated by Bhṛgu in the Tretāyuga; he was (also) like god Viṣṇu; the *Kūtāra-śāstra* is followed by Paraśurāma and by the whole world. It is not a product of the present time. In many other sections also, the different rules of *Mānava-śāstra* and *Kūṭāra-śāstra* are placed

1. Cf. Majumdar, R.C., *Suvarṇadvipa*, pt. II, p. 5.

side by side. There is no doubt that this circumstance explains the title of the law book. References to Manu or *Mānava-śāstra* are, however, more frequent."

What Brāhmaṇical law-book is meant by *Kūāra-śāstra*, we do not know. The reference to Paraśurāma makes it plausible enough to derive Kūṭāra from Kūṭhāra, but that does not help us much in tracing the original work.[1]

As regards *Mānava-śāstra* there cannot, of course be any doubt, that it refers to the famous Brāhmaṇical law-book, *Mānava-dharmaśāstra* or *Manu-saṁhita*. An analysis of the contents of the Javanese Law-book shows that this work formed its chief source. Not only numerous isolated verses, but sometimes a whole series of them, are reproduced, with slight variations and modifications in many cases. These variations are some times the results of the misunderstanding of the original text but are also in some cases undoubtedly due to an effort to bring the law into line with Javanese conditions.

The fundamental basis of the Brāhmaṇical society, and one which distinguishes it from all other known societies, is the system of caste. That this was introduced in Java is clear from the occurrence of the word *Caturvarṇa* in early records, and frequent references to the Brāhmaṇas, Kṣatriyas, Vaiśyas, and Śūdras in literature and inscriptions. It will be however, too much to assume that this caste-system was the same as is prevalent in Brāhmaṇical society today, and we are not sure if the caste-system there meant anything more than a theoretical recognition of the division of the people into four grades.

The study of Sanskrit literature led to the growth of a vast literature in Java, generally known as the old-Javanese literature, which forms one of the most characteristic features of the Brāhmaṇical culture in Indonesia. Nowhere else outside India has Sanskrit literature been studied with so much care and with such important results.

The old-Javanese literature, which flourished during the Hindu rule in Java, is marked by several important characteristics. Its poetry follows rules of Sanskrit metre, and it has a strong predilection for using Sanskrit words and quoting Sanskrit verses. But even in subject-matter the deviation from the Sanskrit original is often considerable. The two oldest books were the old-Javanese versions of a Sanskrit lexicon of type of *Amarakośa* and the great epic the *Rāmāyaṇa*. The Old-Javanese *Rāmāyaṇa* is one of the best and most famous works of Indo-Javanese literature. It is not a translation of the Sanskrit epic, but an independent work. Its subject-matter agrees quite well with that of Sanskrit *Rāmāyaṇa*, but it concludes with the reunion of Rāma and Sitā. Sitā after the fire-ordeal continues to live according to it, and does not contain the story of her banishment

1. Majumdar, R.C., *op. cit.*, p. 5.

and death. The next important landmark in connection with the development of Old-Javanese literature is the prose translation of the great epic the *Mahābhārata*. The Old-Javanese translations closely follow the original epic, but are more condensed. Their style is very primitive and lacks literary merit. Their importance, however, cannot be under-estimated, as they made the great epic popular in Java and supplied themes for numerous literary works which exhibit merits of a very high order.

There was also a class of works, corresponding to Sanskrit Purāṇas. Among these the *Brahmāṇḍa Purāṇa* is undoubtedly the most important. It closely follows the mode of Indian *Purāṇa*, though Javanese touches occur here and there. Another work of the same class is *Agastyaparvan*, where Agastya describes to his son Dṛddasyu the creation of the world in right *Purāṇic* style. Out of the two, first we will examine in brief, the *Brahmāṇḍa Purāṇa* with special reference to one of its counterparts in India viz., the Venkaṭeśvara edition.

An inscription from Veal Kantal in Cambodia provides the earliest reference to the recitation of a *Purāṇa* in a temple alongwith the *Rāmāyaṇa* and *Mahābhārata*. The inscription, though not dated, is assignable on palaeographical grounds to the sixth century A.D.[1] In this case the *Purāṇa* is not specified. But since only one *Purāṇa*, namely the *Brahmāṇḍa* in Kawi language, is known to have been discovered from Java, the adjacent country, there could be a possibility that the *Purāṇa* referred to in the inscription was perhaps the *Brahmāṇḍa*. But there appears to be one serious objection in this identity, i.e., Gonda, while editing the Javanese *Brahmāṇḍa*, has assigned it to the 10th century A.D.[2] If Gonda's date be accepted, the logical conclusions would be that the Purāṇa recited in the temple of Cambodia alongwith the Indian epics, was probably in Sanskrit and that Kawi adaptation was made round about the date fixed for it by Gonda.

The author begins with the topic of creation and after describing the Prākṛta and Vaikṛtasarga, he deals with the legend connected with the eight names of Rudra, which is followed by Svayambhuva Manu and Śatarūpā's progeny. There is an absence of material on the Paśupatayoga of the *Vāyu Purāṇa*, as also of the *Agni-Vaṁśa*. The Dakṣa-śāpa-varṇana is given with a little variation. Then follows the genealogy of Svayambhuva Manu, which is further followed by the description of asuras, gods, gandharvas etc. Next are the Yuga-prajā-lakṣaṇaṃ and ṛṣi-pravaravarnana and the following chapter dealing with sistas etc. The chapter thirty-three

1. Chhabra, B. Ch., *Expansion of Indo-Aryan Culture during Pallava Rule*, pp. 82-83.
2. Gonda, *Javanese Brahmāṇda Purāṇam*, Vol. II, p. 254; Cf. Har Prasad Sastri, catalogue of Skt. MSS, *Asiatic Society, Bengal*, Vol. V, p. cxki; In the island of Bali Brahmāṇḍa is said to have been translated into the Kawi by the 5th century A.D.

of *Brahmāṇḍa—II*, is missing, yet chapter thirty-four is given in a summary form. Sākalya's episode, the Brāhmaṇa literature and their tenfold utility sakhabhedas etc., are given. Then there are descriptions of Svayambhuva and other Manus. The Vena-Pṛthu episode is incompletely given, more after the *Brahma Purāṇa*, *Harivaṁsa Purāṇa* and *Śiva-dharma-Saṁhitā*. There are descriptions of Jambūdvīpa, the Meru, the Īlāvṛtam and further details about the seven varṣas of Jambūdvīpa-Bhāratavarṣa. The Bhagīratha episode is followed by the chapters on Constellations, their movements, etc.

The text of this Javanese *Brahmāṇḍa* is on the whole supposed to be similar to that of the *Vāyu* and *Brahmāṇḍa*. It seems to have been written after consulting the other Purāṇas also besides the above two. In some cases, it goes more with the *Matsya Purāṇa*. Thus the author seemed to have consulted many works rather than one or two only. This again is perhaps called *Brahmāṇḍa* inasmuch as the description of Cosmography of the Universe is contained therein.[1] It ends abruptly and is incomplete inasmuch as it is bereft of dynastic accounts. Most probably, this section was of little utility for the people living there.[2]

The Javanese *Brahmāṇḍa Purāṇa* more or less corresponds to the Baṅgabāsī edition of the *Brahmāṇḍa* rather than the Venkaṭeśvara edition. The long chapter recording the long narrative of the birth of semi-divine beings like the *yakṣas*, *rākṣasas*, *vānaras*, *piśācas* and the like, the legends about the birth of Maruts, the Śrāddha-Kalpa, the Bhārgavopākhyānam and the Lalitopākhyanam (besides the dynastic accounts) are all missing in the Javanese text. In other words, a large part of the madhyama-bhāga (also named Upodghāta pāda) and uttarabhāga (also called upasaṁhāra pāda) appear to be later (than the composition of the Javanese *Brahmāṇḍa*) accretions to the *Brahmāṇḍa Purāṇa*. Similarly the chapter on pratisarga, too, would appear to be late enough.

The above contention does not seem to be true for the pañcalakṣaṇa-trait of the Purāṇas is a conception earlier than the compilation of *Amara-Kośa* and the list of contents of the Purāṇas in the *Matsya Purāṇa*, the later roughly datable to the 6th-7th century A.D.[3] The Śrāddha-Kalpa, too, on the basis of mentioning the heretics (the Jains and Buddhas) as *nagnas* and so unholy that an ablution with clothes on was prescribed on their mere sight, has been taken to be the post-Kuṣāna composition. Therefore it seems to be evident that all that has not been included in the Javanese *Brahmāṇḍa* need not necessarily be taken as belonging to later times, rather the author had his option of pick and choose from the Indian text.

1. Gonda, The Javanese Brahmāṇḍa Purāṇa, *Purāṇam*, Vol. II, p. 254.
2. *ibid.*, p. 267.
3. Hazra, R.C., *Studies in the Purāṇic Records*, p. 4.

The matter accreted to the *Brahmāṇḍa* (Venkaṭeśvara edition) in the post-Gupta times, namely the two upākhyānas, however, do not seem to have any effect on the Javanese text. The Pañcāvatana (adoration to five principal deities)—character of the present *Brahmāṇḍa* (Venkaṭeśvara edition) was undoubtedly not introduced to the Javanese people. Thus the deities introduced to them were Brahmā (Svayambhūva), Viṣṇu, Rudra and Sūrya. However, Rādhā-Kṛṣṇa, Gaṇeśa, Bhadrakālī, Lord Sadāśiva and Lalita Tripurasundarī extolled in the Bhārgavopākhyānam and Lalitopākhyānam could not have reached that island, much less the tāntric character around these deities.

Among the many ancient Javanese texts which are either translated from Sanskrit or deal with subjects borrowed from the Brāhmaṇical traditional literature and which, therefore, are as a rule, of the highest importance for any student of Indian civilization, there are some which excite our special interest because their Indian model or prototype has hitherto not been traced. One of these works is the so-called *Agastyaparva.* This interesting treatise, of unknown date—it may at a rough estimate have been compiled in the eleventh century—and of considerable length, consists in the usual Indian way of a conversation between a *guru,* in this case the famous Agastya, and a disciple or interrogator, his son Dṛddasyu, the former doing, of course, most of the talking. As to its contents and composition the book may generally speaking, said to be a compilation of the *Purāṇa* variety. Although it is interlarded with Sanskrit quotations (about 155 in number), part of which can easily be amended, and although the sage Agastya appears, also in India, in many works or episodes as the author or narrator, it is as yet impossible to say whether it was, like the parvans of the *Mahābhārat*, the *Brahmāṇḍa Purāṇa* etc., modelled upon, or even meant to be, an adapted version of a Sanskrit text. We do not even know whether it is a complete work or only a part of an originally longer composition. Although the contents of many passages—e.g., those about creation and pralaya (destruction) the Sāṁkhya doctrine of the elements, the *manus* and *manvantaras,* the daughters of Dakṣa, transmigration, heavens and hells, the character of daityas and gandharvas, the churning of the ocean, etc. etc.—can be traced in Sanskrit literature, no single Sanskrit book or part of a larger book has come to my knowledge which is in the main identical with the contents of this Javanese work. Moreover, other passages, especially those of a more theological character—which are embedded in the framework of genealogies—are not always well represented in Sanskrit literature, however much they may resemble, in purport and character and often also in detail, similar episodes of epic, śāstric and paurāṇic books. These are brief treatises of a didactic, theological or philosophical nature which, alternating with short stories or legends, constitute the essential part of the subject-matter. The document is decidedly Śaivite in character, some passages tending towards Tāntrism, and shows that mixture of Sāṁkhya and Vedānta ideas which is common to many Indian works of the paurāṇic variety. It is not surprising that in several respects it appears to be related to the *Vāyu-Brahmāṇḍa* version of the paurāṇic themes dealt with, because it is that version which was, at least in part, translated and handed down in Java. The colophon stating that the work goes back to, or is an adaptation, of subject-matter contained in the *Brahmāṇḍa-Purāṇa* points in the same direction. But which *Agastyaparvan* and which *Brahmāṇḍa-Purāṇa* are meant here, the Javanese texts or their Sanskrit prototypes.

Another riddle propounded by this work is its connection with the Agastya worship which we know to have existed in Indonesia as well as in India proper[1], his role as a saint and the promoter of Brāhmaṇisation and preacher of Śaivism in the island of Java being well attested by epigraphs, sculpture and literature. Although the *Agastyaparvan* stands a fair chance of having enjoyed special popularity because of the spread of that worship, it does not shed much light on it. This is a matter for regret because many problems connected with the cult of that mythical figure in Indonesia are still awaiting a solution. Was for instance the late lamented Bosch right in surmising that the inscription found at Dinaya[2] (760 A.D.)—which, dealing with the erection of a sanctuary for Agastya, is among the documents attesting to intimate relations between the dynasties in power and the cult of Śiva-liṅga—to prove the existence of close connections between the court-Brāhmaṇas and that liṅga cult ? This supposition might be corroborated by an information contained in an old-Javanese poem, *Harivaṁśa* (about 1150 A.D.) about a royal poet—probably also a court-Brāhmaṇa—who is said to be an incarnation of the sage, his patron, however, being an incarnation of Viṣṇu.[3] Another unsolved riddle concerns the very character of this Agastya cult. It is for instance doubtful whether the name Haricandra which from the tenth century accompanies that of the sage applies to another saint or is another name for Agastya himself.[4]

The poetical works written in the old-Javanese language on themes derived from the epics and other Sanskrit works are referred to as belonging to a class called *Kakawin* from Kavi meaning 'kāvya'. The greatest work of this class is the *Bhāratayuddha*, based on those parts of the *Mahābhārata* which deal with the war between the Kauravas and the Pāṇḍavas in the field of Kurukṣetra. It is written in simple but epic style and has all

1. See, Sastri, K.A., *A History of South India*, p. 64ff; *South Indian Influence in the Far East*, pp. 59; 128.
2. Bosch, F.D.K., *De Sanskrit inscriptie op den steen van Dinaja en Het lingga-heiligdom van Dinaja, Tijdschrift voor Indische Taal, en Volkenkunde 57*. p. 410ff and 64p. 227ff.
3. *Harivamśa*, edited and translated (into Dutch) by Teeuw, A. 1, 2; 53, 1ff.
4. Cf. Casparis, J.G. de, *Selected Inscription*, II, p. 290ff.

along enjoyed a very high reputation in Java. According to some eminent European critics, its grandeur is comparable to that of the Greek epics. This work, begun by the poet Mpu Sedah in 1157 A.D. by order of king Jayabhaya, was completed by Mpu Panulub, who also composed another poetical work, *Harivaṁśa*[1] Like its Brāhmaṇical prototype this book deals with the abduction of Rukmiṇī by Kṛṣṇa and the consequent war with Jarāsandha and the Pāṇḍavas who helped the latter. This episode is, however, not in the original work. Another *Kakawin* work *Smāradahana*, was written under a successor of Jayabhaya, named Kamesvara. The theme of this work is the well-known episode of the burning of Smara, or the God of Love, by Śiva, which has been so masterly described by Kālidāsa in his immortal work, *Kumārasambhava*.[2] To the same period belongs also the famous *Bhomakāvya* which describes the defeat of Indra and other gods by Bhoma or Naraka, son of Pṛthivi, and finally he meets his death at the hands of Kṛṣṇa. Reference may be made to two other works, probably somewhat earlier. The first *Kṛṣṇāyana* by Triguṇa, deals with the same episode of the abduction of Rukmiṇī by Kṛṣṇa and his consequent fight with the Jarāsandha, that forms the subject-matter of *Harivaṁśa*. Another work, *Sumanasāntaka* (death caused by flower) is based on the story of the death of Indumati, the queen of Aja and the mother of Deśaratha, which has been so marvellously described by Kālidāsa in the *Raghuvaṁśa*.[3]

Special reference may be made to a *Kakawin* work, *Nāgarakṛtāgama*, which is not based on any Brāhmaṇical work but deals with the life and times of a famous king of Majapahit in Java, and gives very important and interesting information about the king, his capital city, his court and his vast empire to which reference has been made before.

Another class of *Kakawin* work also deserves special mention. It is called *Nitiśāstra-kawin* in Java. It is a collection of stray verses containing wise sayings, maxims, moral precepts, religious doctrines and is somewhat akin to the Indian works such as *Nitisāra*, *Pañcatantra*, *Cāṇakyaśataka* etc. Many of the verses in the Javanese work may be traced to their Sanskrit original.[4]

In addition to the proposed translation of the *Mahābhārata*, there are several works in the same series dealing with some episodes with a considerable variation in details. The *Sarasamuccaya*, an old-Javanese translation of a large number of moral precepts chiefly drawn from the 'Anuśāsana-Parvan' of the *Mahābhārata*, is interspersed with quotations of Sanskrit verses from the epics and other Brāhmaṇical books like the *Pañcatantra*.

1. Majumdar, R.C., *Suvarnadvipa*, Pt. II, p. 155ff.
2. Majumdar, R.C., *ibid*., p. 155ff.
3. *ibid*.
4. *ibid*.

A very popular work in the island of Bali, called *Navaruci* describes the exploits of Bhuma. There is also a prose translation of 'Uttarakāṇḍa' of the *Rāmāyaṇa* in old-Javanese, which is interspersed with Sanskrit verses. It shows some divergences from the original text. There are also prose works on history, linguistic, medicine etc.[1]

The dedication of sanctuaries to deceased kings and the worship of their portrait statues—which would be, likely to have been transferred to a sacred place, there, to reinforce with their virtue the concentration of beneficial energies—belong to those religious practices which may probably be regarded as extensions of south Indian influence into a milieu which was accustomed to ancestor worship.[2] This cult included also ceremonies called śrāddha and intended to bring about the final emancipation of the deceased. On that occasion a sanctuary was erected which was to remain the centre of a cult. It is easily intelligible that the *amṛta* (nectar of immortality), the lotus (symbolizing life and vital power) and similar motifs are often represented on these monuments.

Even to this day the people of Java, though Muslim by religion, retain many traces of Brāhmaṇical culture about them. They still retain some form of idol worship. They like it and love it. They still throng the old Hindu temples with offerings of incense and flowers. Dancing is a popular pastime with them. The masked dance is very much enjoyed by them. The masks are of various types and they help the actors and actresses to display the moods of the heroes and heroines they represent. During the masked dances scenes from Brāhmaṇic mythology are represented before the audience in a vivid form. Lord Śiva is represented with his famous Tāṇḍava dance. In these dances the stories are interpreted by means of physical movement only without any oral explanation.

Rāma, Karṇa and Arjuna are still their favourite national heroes and they often name their children after them. Their language and many of their social customs bear the indelible marks of Brāhmaṇical culture on them. Java is also replete with places, bearing names of pure Sanskrit origin. Like Hindus the people of Java, also consider travelling on certain days of the weeks as inauspicious. Similarly, certain days of the week are regarded as inauspicious for commencing an important enterprise. Some trees are also looked upon by them as holy, for they are supposed to be the dwelling place of the soul of the dead ancestors.

1. *ibid.*
2. Cf. Stutterheim, W.F., The meaning of the Hindu Javanese Candi, *JAOS*, 51 (1931), p. 1ff; Sastri, Nilakanta, *op. cit.*, p. 134. It is however wrong to regard all Javanese pre-Muslim monuments called 'candi'—the term may be supposed to represent the Sanskrit Caṇḍi, a well-known name of the goddess Durgā, out of whose body arose a large number of sanctuaries—as sepulchral in character or to describe them as "soul temples".

The Sultan of Jogjakarta, a city in Java, still retains Hindu title of *Bhuwono Senapati* or the Generalissimo of the world and his palace is one of the palaces where the relics of the ancient Javanese art and culture are still to be found. The letter of Dr Soekarno (Shubha Karṇa), the erstwhile President of the Indonesian republic, which he addressed to Pt. Jawaharlal Nehru and a portion of which is reproduced here, reveals how intimately the cultures of the two countries are connected with each other. Dr Soekarno writes, "Your country (India) and your people are linked to us by ties of blood and culture which date back to the very beginning of our history. The word "India" much necessarily always be part of our life, for it forms the first two syllables of the name we have chosen for our land and race...it is the "Indo" in Indonesia. This *Jogjakarta* (*Yogyakarta*) from which I write this letter...like Java, Sumatra and most other place names is an Indian word. My very name "Soekarno" is itself testimony to the great extent to which we have fallen heir to their rich culture of your ancient land. And at this very moment of writing the first ship to take rice to India is being loaded at the port of *Probolinggo* which is made up of two words *Purva* and *Kalinga*. It was the place at which the first Indians set on the Indonesian (ancient Java)—the Kalingas who came here in search of the *Java* (barley) from which Java derives name".

7. *MALAYSIA*

India's ties with Malaysia are closer and older than is generally recognised. The period of Indian settlements and the Indianized kingdoms in the Malay Archipelago led to the political and cultural contacts between the two countries. It is but natural that Malaysia felt the full impact of Brāhmaṇism in various walks of life. Malaysian arts and crafts, literature and folklore, script and language and theatre are the living examples of the Brāhmaṇical culture.

The designs and methods of Malay arts and crafts bear the impress of Indian mythology and motifs. The hilt patterns of the Malay dagger, the keris, often depict characters from Indian tales, Brāhmaṇical and Buddhist. Hanumāna and Garuḍa, for their superhuman qualities, are some of the favourite figures fashioned to shape. The keris blade may have become wavy to represent the Nāgas, the foes of Garuḍa whom he overpowered.

In textile designs both countries are likely to have influenced each other; the exporter catering to the tastes of the importer and in the process acquiring some of the latter's preferences. The word for silk in Malay is of Sanskrit origin. Both the Indochinese and Indian methods of "tie and dye" are in use, the warp threads being tied before dyeing according to the former method and the cloth stitched firmly in puckers before applying the dye according to the latter method. Malay bronze, silver and gold work are reminiscent of Indian shapes and patterns. The lotus blossom and the side view of the lotus appear in repousse work on jewellery, bowls and caskets. The filigree, sometimes jewelled on brooches, betel boxes, keris sheaths, etc., shows strong Brāhmaṇical influence. The foliation in the old type of large water-bottle stands, pedestals, etc., often carries figures from the *Rāmāyaṇa*. Bronze kitchen utensils popular in India are also used in old Malay households and the general name for all bronze, copper and brass water-containers is the Sanskrit *gangsa*.

In a few countries of the world, theatre is as popular a mass medium as in Malaysia and Indonesia. The favourite themes for dance, drama puppet-shows (wayang orang) and shadow-play (wayang julit) are taken from the Indian epics, the *Rāmāyaṇa* and the *Mahābhārata*. The shadow-play version of the epics was always preferred to their written form but some literary works of this genre have survived. The oldest manuscript of the *Rāmāyaṇa* the *Hikayat Seri Rāma* is based on a Tamil prototype. It is a late text and betrays Muslim influence. An unpublished manuscript of the *Malay Rāmāyaṇa* is in the Royal Asiatic Society Library, London.

Bhārata-yuddha, a section of the *Mahābhārata* and the story of Bhauma (son of Bhūmi, the earth), was originally written in *Kawi* and it inspired the *Malay Hikayat Perang Pandawa Jaya* and the *Hikayat Mahārāja Boma*. Some other Malay works influenced by the Hindu epics and Purāṇas are the *Sejarah Melayu* and the *Hikayat Hang Tuah*. As a matter of literary interest, the *Hikayat Rājarāja passai* embodies specimens of a Tamil verse form called gurindam. Many Malay folk-tales and romances also draw upon the epic literature.

The *Pañca-tantra* (the source of inspiration for Aesop's fables) with its translations found as far west as Iceland and as far east as Java, also influenced the folk-lore of Malaya. So did the Buddhist Jātakas and the *Kathāsaritsāgara* (to which the Arabian Nights indirectly owe several tales). The latter inspired the *Hikayat Rakhoda Mudā* and the *Hikayat Mahārāja Pikrama Sakti*. The Tamil classic *Maṇimekhalai* has also supplied the material for many Malay stories. Another survival of the pre-Islamic period is the Malay translations of the Javanese cycle of Pañji tales which has freely borrowed from the *Rāmāyaṇa*, the *Mahābhārata*, and the folk-lore of the Deccan.

With the coming of Indian Muslim traders to Malacca, the Muslimised folk-lore of Brāhmaṇic India, a mixture of Hindu, Persian and Arab stories, flooded Malaya. The *Hikayat Indra Bangsawan* was a result of these influences. With the coming of Islam Malaya also became familiar with the three world famous cycles of tales, the *Persian Tutinameh*, or the original Sanskrit *Śukasantati*, the *Kalila dan Damina* derived ultimately from the *Pañcatantra* (known earlier to Malaya and Java) and the Bakhtiar cycle. The Malay version of the first cycle is known as *Hikayat Bayan Budiman*; of the second, three recensions were made, one from Tamil in

1835 by Munshi Abdullah, while the third cycle has two translations; the *Hikayat Puspa Wiraja* and the *Hikayat Ghulam*. The fifteenth-century Malay author of the *Sejarah Melayu* or Malay Annals knew, among other languages, words from Sanskrit and Tamil and shows his familiarity with the *Rāmāyaṇa*, the *Gītā* and the Cycle of Pañji tales. The Kedah annals or the *Hikayat Marong Mahawangsa* are full of local folk-lore, and myths from the *Rāmāyaṇa* and the Jātaka tales.

It may be presumed that in addition to the epics, the Jātakas, and works of fiction, Malaya knew of the Indian writings on polity, the *Arthaśāstras*. The works in full or part, or at least some maxims of Kauṭilya, Manu, Kāmanḍaka etc., were known in many countries of South-east Asia. Although no translation of Indian political-legal texts have survived in Malaya, her "*adat Temenggong*' as preserved in the Malacca digest of circa A.D. 1450, the Pahang digest with a later supplement, and a Kedah digest of 1650, is influenced by Brāhmaṇical law, and her port rules contained in the Kedah digest resemble "regulations of the kind India knew from the days of Candra Gupta and embodied in the Mogul *Tarikh-i-Tahiri*".[2]

Two Indian scripts were used in ancient Malaysia and in other parts of South-east Asia, the late Brāhmī from the southern and western parts of India (Karṇāṭa), and the pre-Nagari owing to contact with Bengal and Nalandā. The latter had a temporary existence. The Javanese Kawi (Skt. Kavi, poet), however, is a developed form of the Pallava script. Several inscriptions, clay tablets and thin gold and silver discs largely containing Buddhist formulae written in northern or southern Indian characters have, most of them, been found in northern Malaya and southern Thailand, the regions specially popular with Indian settlers. The greatest number of these remains belong to the period between the fourth and the ninth centuries A.D. By the fourteenth century, the Malayo-Arabic script had evolved, as proved by the Terengganu stone, and to the same century belongs the first specimen of a Malay verse composed in a mixed Malay-Sanskrit-Arab vocabulary on the tomb stone of a Pasai princess. It is written in characters similar to those on the inscriptions of the Samutran King Ādityavarman.

Words from Indian languages, Sanskrit, Tamilised Sanskrit, Tamil and Hindustani, came to Malaysia directly; or indirectly through Javanese with which Malay had a lot in common. It is, in fact, difficult to ascertain the contribution made by Malay and Javanese to each other. The coastal Malays visited the Javanese ports early and must have influenced the local vocabularies of Indonesia through the commercial channels. Javanese

1. See, Sternbach, Ludwick, *The Spreading of Cānakya's Aphorisms over "Grater India"*.
2. Winstedt, R.O., *The Malays, a Cultural History*, p. 91.

influences on Malay infiltrated mostly through the literary medium, such as through the Adventures of Prince Pañji and the Wayang stories, etc.

The number of words of Indian origin in the Malay languages is considerable and they pertain to all spheres of life, such as religion, philosophy, art, law, commerce, government and administration. Some of these are : *Shurga* (heaven), *di-setu-i* (one lays such a spell) etc. upon a person, from the Skt. *astu*, ('be it so'), *budi* (disposition, understanding), *rasa* (feeling, taste) and *asa* in Busang a language of Central Borneo, *guna* (profit, use), *danda* (punishment, penalty), *saksi* (witness) all three in Malay as well as Busang, *seloka* (verse), *bangsi* (flute), *kapas* (cotton), *setera* (silk, Skt. sutra) in Busang, *dipati* (king, regent, Skt. Adhipati), *menteri* (minister of state), *geni* (fire, Skt. Agni) *kata* (to speak, Skt. katha), *mansi* (ink, Skt. masi), *beniaga, berniaga* (merchant, Skt. Vanik), *laksa* (ten thousand Skt. lakṣa), *kapal* (ship), *katil* (bed), *chamcha* (spoon), *baju* (shirt, also banian in N. Celebes and Ambon), *basi* (musty, state), *dhobi* (washerman) etc.

8. BALI

The island of Bali bears impact of the Brāhmaṇical culture to a great extent. Although it is generally known in India and elsewhere that the Indonesian island of Bali possesses a Brāhmaṇical religion, Hindu priests and a Sanskrit tradition, notions are often less exact about the real state of affairs in this respect. Reliable studies of Balinese Brāhmaṇism have been published only intermittently, and our knowledge has thus increased only slowly. In recent years, important material has been brought to light by new publications; yet a comprehensive survey of the field is still awaiting its author. Particularly, about the character of the Sanskrit texts preserved in Bali there has been a great deal of misunderstanding—caused chiefly by the fact that the titles of Balinese manuscripts or text fragments often do not in the least correspond, according to general opinion, with their real contents.

Tāntric Śaivite Text

In a report published in 1849, the Dutch scholar R. Frienderich wrote with enthusiasm about the existence of the *Vedas* in Bali.[1] He told his readers that the Balinese priests possessed in manuscript form important part of all the four *Vedas* and *Saṁhitās,* written by Byas (Vyāsa). They kept these manuscripts in secret and taught their contents to the young generations of Brāhmaṇa priests only. Frienderich succeeded in obtaining the priests' confidence in such a degree that they made known to him the old-Javanese *Brahmāṇḍa Purāṇa.* He was not allowed, however, to have a look into their manuscripts called *Veda.* Had he been able to do this, he would

1. Friendrich, R. *Voorloping verslag van het eiland Bali.*

have found out soon that this Veda in no way represented the Ancient Indian Veda, not even in a fragmentary shape; and in that case he would not have led later authors on a false track. The myth of the Balinese Veda still persisted long after other scholars like Brumund and Kern had found out the real state of affairs. The manuscripts kept back so persistently by the Brāhmaṇa priests are usually written in a mixture of old-Javanese, Balinese, and Sanskrit loan-words; they contain prescriptions for all kinds of ritual, and mystical expositions; and they are interspersed with sacred mantras and hymns. The background of these Sanskrit fragments is chiefly Śaivism with a strong Tāntric tinge. More than ten codices called Veda exist; a far greater number has another name, but more or less the same contents. There are also a few collections of Sanskrit hymns only.

In most cases, the word Veda means practically no other thing than pūjā. Thus the term *Veda-parikramā* stands for the performance of daily ritual, also called *Sūrya-sevana*. Such a performance was attended by Sylvan Levi and described by him in his book *Sanskrit Texts from Bali*. The same ritual has been discussed with much more detail and precision by C. Hooykaas. In the volume mentioned above, Levi published also a *Buddha Veda*, which he presented as the daily worship of the Balinese Buddhist priests. This is a mistake; the *Buddha Veda* contains Buddhist death ritual, and incomplete at that. The daily ritual became known to Hooykaas only in 1959 by means of a copy from a manuscript called *Pūrvaka Veda* Buddha. Levi pointed out that the text called *Caturveda* is in reality nearly identical with the *Nārāyaṇātharavaśīrsopaniṣad*; its four chapters are called in Bali respectively, *Ṛg Veda*, *Yajur* or *Jajur-Veda*, *Samaveda* and *Artha* (*Atharva*) *Veda*. At that, the *Upaniṣad* has been handed down in Bali with such a number of lacunae and mistakes that the Sanskrit has become practically unintelligible. Further, the two hymns labelled *Ṛg Veda* and *Yajurveda-stuti* in reality have nothing to do with what might be expected by their names.

Thus, there is no Veda in Bali in the Indian sense; the only Vedic fragments really found there are:

(a) One pada of the Gāyatri : *Bhargo devasya dhīmahi;*

(b) A śloka to the sacred thread found also in the *Gṛhyasūtras*; here again, the Balinese tradition is incomplete;

(c) The five names of Śiva (*pañcabrahma*) and the usual litany directed to them, as found in *Mahā Nārāyaṇa Upaniṣad* 277. It is present in Bali under the name *Brahmastava* (not yet edited).

It is necessary to add that these remarks apply only to the traditional corpus of manuscripts. At present, the Balinese have obtained more knowledge of the source of their Hindu tradition (thus the whole Gāyatri has been taught to them, already some years ago).

What is the real character of the Balinese Sanskrit literature ? A special position is taken by the dogmatic and mystic expositions of the old-Javanese branch of the *Śaiva Siddhānta*, such as the Bhuvanakośa (probably the oldest), the *Bhuvanasaṁkṣepa* and the *Bṛhaspatitattva*. They consist of Sanskrit ślokas accompanied by old-Javanese paraphrase or commentary. The manuscripts of these works have been presented exclusively in Bali or Lombok. Work has been done in editing them and systematizing their doctrines by Dutch, German and Indian scholars. The results are, however, not yet definite.[1] These texts probably have been composed in the 9th century A.D. or not much later.

Balinese Books on Sanskrit Grammar

A more worldly wisdom has been handed down in the form of two śloka collections called *Sārasamuccaya* and *Ślokāntara*. Besides, there are fragments of grammar and grammatical exercises, which prove that the study of Sanskrit has in the past been seriously cultivated. At present, the Balinese priests have no grammatical insight into Sanskrit. They know the meaning of many words and are able to interpret some fragments by means of old-Javanese paraphrases which are in their possession. The paraphrases and interpretations are, however, many a time quite off the mark. They even until recently did not know the term "Sanskrit" but spoke of "difficult words".

This is not the place to dwell on the rich literature preserved in old-Javanese, of a purely literary as well as of a more technical character, and often labelled with Sanskrit titles. This literature includes parts of a prose translation of the *Mahābhārata*, and a text called *Brahmāṇḍa Purāṇa* which is, however, an adaptation of the *Vāyu Purāṇa*. The motifs of the old-Javanese texts have nearly completely been furnished by Indian religion and mythology, and old-Javanese itself teems with Sanskrit words and phrases. Both the *Mahābhārata* and the *Brahmāṇḍa Purāṇa* in Javanese are still recited in Bali on certain occasions. The old themes have sometimes been adapted into more modern versions.[2]

Stutis and Stavas Recited in Rituals

The greater part of the Sanskrit of Bali is found scattered in the ritual handbooks used by the priests; the *Vedas* mentioned above belong to the

1. Zieseniss, A. *Die Sivaitischen Systeme in der altjavanischen Literatur*, in : Bijdragen tot de Taal—land, en Volkenkunde, Vol. 98, 1939, pp. 75-223.

2. Hooykaas, C. Greater Indian Studies; Present Desiderate; in : *Vishveshvaranand Indological Journal*, Vol. 3, 1965, pp. 287ff.

same class. The syllables of the Sanskrit alphabet are known together with their function in Tāntric mysticism; there are Tāntric bījas like *grīṃ*, *hrīṃ* gmum; and sequences of syllables constituting short formulae (thus, e.g. the Kūṭamantra : Om hrāṃ hrīṃ saḥ Parama-Śivādityāya namaḥ). But above all there is a considerable number of hymns to the gods, called *stuti* and *stava*. They vary in length from two or three to about 25 stanzas. These stutis are said or sung on certain fixed points in the ritual, of which they constitute an inherent part. They have been partly edited in a provisory manner by Levi, within them we find a mixture of different styles and even of different kinds of Sanskrit. Besides hymns written in a high-flown style of impeccable Sanskrit, there are also some pieces in a language which can hardly be called by that name. Their style consists of a medley of Sanskrit expressions without any coherence or syntactical order, strung together loosely as epithets, sometimes even interspersed with Indonesian words or prefixes. Between these two extremes, all intermediate varieties exist.

The following hymn of three ślokas may serve as an example of the second style. It is by no means common in the ritual, but found only in one manuscript, a collection of protective maṇtras. In the text given here, some peculiarities of the Balinese manuscript tradition have already been corrected.

1. Oṃ kālāgnighora trimukha byaḥ kṛṣṇavāyu piṅgalam
   cakra Sudarśa ca mṛṭaḥ atiṣṭha nāma rakṣantu
2. Oṃ Mahāgmi mahābhāras ca jagrabhoktaḥ mahājñānam
   raktavāyu mahāmūrti daṇḍāstra saṅ Śivaḥ smṛtaḥ
3. Atiṣṭha māma rakṣantu atisa tami prayāntu
   Mahākrūra pralīnare ātmarakṣa pūjāyukti.

The words of this hymn are so unclear that even the god or gods addressed to cannot be easily determined at first sight. The name Śiva is mentioned in pada 2nd, accompanied by the purely Javanese word saṅ "holy". But the fact that the rod is called his weapon, and also the colour red in the word raktavāyu points to Brahmā. Further, v. I speaks of Viṣṇu as is shown by the colour black (also in Bali, black is Viṣṇu's regular colour), and by the mention of his weapon, the disc Sudarśana. The text in pada 1 says: sudarśa ca mṛtaḥ, but an emendation into Sudarśana smṛtaḥ would at least bring the meaning to light. Interesting is, that Viṣṇu is called "terrible like the apocalyptical fire" and "three-faced". These characteristics of Viṣṇu are repeated by other Balinese studies and thus form an inherent part of the Balinese tradition about this deity. In the second stanza, which as we saw, has something to do with Brahmā; the word mahāgni may be observed. It is quite well possible that Brahmā should be called a "fire", because the deities Brahmā and Agnī have been identified in old-Javanese and Balinese Brāhmaṇism. Thus a volcano in the east of Java is called up till now Tingger Bromo. "Brahmā's Uplands", because Brahmā was brought into connection with the volcanic nature of the mountain. The overall meaning of the poem might be interpreted thus : Śiva, showing himself as a black and a red wind in the terrible shapes of Viṣṇu and Brahmā respectively characterized by their attributes, is requested to protect the worshipper, in time of great danger, especially at the dreadful apocalypse (pralīnare ?). An attempt further to emend the words of the hymn into correct Sanskrit would not only be impracticable and inadvisable but even faulty from the philological point of view. These three stanzas have never been correct Sanskrit, but have been produced by a Balinese or Javanese author with a fair knowledge of Sanskrit religious terminology, but without any idea of Sanskrit grammar and syntax—or if he had it, he did not use it. This is not to say, however, that some emendation of totally dark passages may not be ventured; for instance, in pada 3, instead of atisa tami prayāntu, we suggest atiṣṭha tama (=tamaḥ) prayātu.

Chaste Sanskrit Recitals

In contrast to the preceding stuti, the one given below is one of the best known of Balinese Sanskrit. It is called *Paṅakṣama Bhaṭāra* means for asking the Lords' "forbearance", and is recited on a certain point of the daily ritual of the Śaiva priest. Here the Sanskrit is much better and generally understandable.

1. Oṃ kṣamasva maṃ Jagannātha sarvapāpanirantaram
   sarvakāryam idaṃ dehi praṇamami sureśvaram.
2. tvaṃ Suryas tvaṃ Śivākāras tvaṃ Rudro vahnilakṣaṇaḥ
   tvaṃ hi sarvagatākāro maṃ kāryaṃ prajāyati.
3. kṣamasva māṃ mahāśakte hy āṣṭaiśvaryaguṇātmaka nāśayet satataṃ Pāpaṃ sarvaṃ ālokadarpaṇa.

Translation :

1. Oṃ, Protector of the world, be gracious to me, who is enclosed by all kinds of evil; grant me this whole enterprise of mine; I bow to the Lord of gods.
2. Thou art the Sun, Thou art of Śiva's form, Thou art Rudra characterized by fire. Thou indeed art of all encompassing form; my enterprise comes into existence.
3. Be gracious to me, O Thou of great power, because thy nature consists of the eight faculties of dominance etc.; He will continually

destroy evil; O Thou who are mirrored by everything (?).

Generally speaking, the language of this stuti can be called reasonably Sanskrit (here again, the manuscripts have been corrected before hand on several points of orthography). Yet the poem shows a certain lack of coherence, especially between the pādas lc-ld and 2c-2d. Moreover, vs. 3 contains several dubious features : the place of hi at the head of 3b; the unexpected third person is nāśayet, the peculiar syntax and use of words in 3d, which renders the meaṇing difficult to recognize. These arguments combined are apt to justify a suspicion about the real correctness of this Sanskrit. Probably the hymn in question is the work of an Indonesian poet who had a reasonable knowledge of Sanskrit grammar, but was not very versatile in the art of composing independent ślokas in that language. It is not impossible that he was an Indian; not all Sanskrit composed by Indians is flawless from the grammatical point of view.

This *stuti* also furnishes an occasion for some other remarks. In the first place, the poem is an expression of a real devotion to a God, called by the names or epithets Jagannātha and Surveśara in v. 1; Sūrya, Śivākāra and Rudra in v. 2; and Mahāśakti in v. 3. The deity addressed is in fact the Supreme God of the Balinese, Śivasūrya or Śivāditya. A pre-Hindu sun-worship may have played its part in causing this emphasis on the solar aspect of the Brāhmanic Śiva. It is noteworthy how Śiva and Sūrya have not only been identified, but are also worshipped expressly as a unity in duality. In general, the figure of Śiva and its characteristics are predominant; Śiva is known also as Rudra, as seen above, and freely addressed with other names such as Īśvara, Giripati, Pañcamukha, and Mahādeva.

Besides, attention is struck by the mention of the eight divine qualities of dominance, etc., in v. 3. These qualities: dharma, jñāna, vairāgya, aiśvarya and their opposites, are well known to the Balinese priests. Just like in India, these guṇas are worshipped on the occasion of the Āsana-pūjā during the performance of daily worship. In India they constitute a stage in the invocation of the deity, called siṁhāsana. In Bali, the function of the worship of the guṇas is the same : Śivāditya's lower manifestations have to be successively attended upon by the priest before he is able to reach God's highest nature. Just like in Indian pūjā, the priest's goal is to identify himself with the divinity during the performance of worship. The way to this, identification in Bali is essentially an adaptation of Indian ideas. The fundamental difference between the two systems lies in the priest's activities after he has become the living abode of God : while in India he worships and entertains the liṅga or image as a divine guest, the Balinese priest's task is to make holy water, cause the God to descend into it, and sell it to the people.

Of course, the hallowing of the water is known also in India, but there it does not constitute the central act of the ceremony. This fact gives to the Balinese way of daily worship, notwithstanding its striking similarities with the Indian method, a quite independent character.[1] In order to avoid misunderstanding it should be added that Liṅga Pūjā is also known, but its performance is non-obligatory.[2]

Different Forms of Pūjā

What is said above about the worship of Śiva does not imply that his liturgy knows no variations. Besides the pūjā performed by the Śaivite Brāhmaṇa priests, there are the pūjā kṣatriya destined for the princes, and the ritual performance of the Buddhist priests. The pūjā kṣatriya has not yet been fully described; its manuscript tradition is unclear and defective. In general, it follows the line of the priests' worship, but in a simplified and shorter way. Although it often uses the same hymns, its manuscripts regularly show deviating readings. Thus, the hymn discussed above is not found as much in the pūjā kṣatriya manuscripts, but there exists a composition much resembling it in the first two verses. This might be illustrated by the following.

Oṃ kṣamasva māṃ Śivadeva Jagannātha hitaṃkara
Sarvapāpavimuktena praṇamāmyahaṃ Sureśvaram.

The Sanskrit of this verse is definitely worse than that of the Śiva priests' variant, and the same might be said of most other stutis of the pūjā kṣatriya.

The most original feature of the pūjā kṣatriya is, that it is of a rather Viṣṇuite character. The Viṣṇuite element is not found in the present verse (except perhaps the epithet Jagannātha which is also freely used for Śiva), due to the fact that the Vaiṣṇava pūjā (just like its Baudha counterpart) does not mind to use purely Śaiva stutis on some occasions. As a matter of fact, the designation "Viṣṇuite" does not imply any important dogmatic difference; it is reached chiefly by a change of the references to one or more of Śiva's manifestations to those used for denoting Viṣṇu, or by adding Viṣṇu's name to some expression. For example, the Kavacamantra : "Oṃ hruṃ kavacāya namaḥ" is found in the pūjā kṣatriya manuscripts as Oṃ hruṃ Viṣṇukavacāya namaḥ. This Viṣṇuite character of the worship of the kṣatriya leads to the hypothesis that, just like the Śaiva Brāhmaṇa priest is able to identify himself with Śiva, the Vaiṣṇava earthly ruler considered himself an incarnation of Viṣṇu and actually endeavoured to reach

1. A comparison of Śaiva ritual in South India and Bali has been made by Hooykaas, C. in Surya Sevana, pp. 141ff.
2. Hooykaas, C., Śivaliṅga, the mark of the Lord in Āgama Tirtha, Five studies in Hindu-Balinese Religion.

identification with this deity during his ritual. It is indeed known that ancient Javanese and Balinese rulers saw themselves and were seen by others as manifestations of Viṣṇu.[1]

The Rāmakavaca and the Rāmāyaṇa

To return to literature, another kind of "protective stuti" is the *kavaca*. Just like in Indian poems of this type, a deity is requested to enter each limb of the worshipper's body by means of his divine manifestations. The finest specimen found in Bali is a Rāmakavaca of 22 stanzas in fairly good Sanskrit. The kavaca proper covers only the verses 1-8; the rest of the poem praises Rāma and Lakṣmaṇa and recommends their worship. It is quite surprising to find that Vss. 15c-17d are nearly completely identical with two ślokas from Vālmīki's *Rāmāyaṇa* (3, 18, 11 Critical Ed. and a variant). The figure of Rāma has inspired already the ancient Javanese (there exists an important court poem in old-Javanese called Rāmāyaṇa; it is an adaptation, partly from the Bhaṭṭikāvya and partly from an unknown source, and up till now Rāma is one of the heroes of the shadowplay (wayang).

We cannot direct attention to all interesting cases of Balinese Sanskrit. Let it suffice to say that the religious worldview expressed by the hymns, in particular those to Śiva, is akin to that of the Śaiva Siddhānta. Śivāditya is the universal God and source of all existence. In the shape of the triad Brāhmā-Viṣṇu-Rudra he creates, governs and destroys the world. He is also known as the fivefold (Pañca)-Brahmā : Īśāna, Sadyojata, Vāmadeva (in Bali : Bāmadeva), Tatpuruṣa and Aghora. Fivefold is also the syllable Oṃ, the primeval sound-manifestation of the Absolute : a-u-m-nada-bindu. The god corresponding with these five parts are Brahmā-Viṣṇu, Rudra (or Maheśvara), Sadāśiva and Paramaśiva. Interesting is, that the word *Śuñya* may be used for denoting Śiva's most transcendental nature.

Other manifestations of Śiva (e.g., the classical eightfold one) are also attested. In general, the theological background of the hymns corresponds with that of the Bhuvanakośa and the other old-Javanese works analysed by Zieseniss. One will not find, however, any of the speculations laid down in the Śivajñānabodham and the south Indian literature inspired by it; when Śaiva Siddhānta was systematized thoroughly in Southern India, the contact with Indonesia had already been broken off.

A few more words on the period when this contact has been realized and on its nature are of relevance here. India has begun to exercise its influence in Indonesia in the first centuries of our era. The spread of Brāhmaṇical culture was caused and stimulated by the trade expeditions which were organized from the subcontinent. Indonesian princes accepted

1. **Stutterheim, W.F. *Indian Influences in Old Balinese Art*. p. 22 (Quoted by C. Hooykaas, Preliminary Remarks on Vaiṣnavism in Bali, *Journal of the Oriental Institute of Baroda*, Vol. 14, 1964-65, p. 326).**

the religious and cultural notions of the voyagers and began to invite Brāhmaṇas to their courts. Afterwards, the Brāhmaṇical culture gradually spread among the upper classes of society. About the exact development of this process there is no certainty, but arguments in favour of the hypothesis sketched above with a few words can be adduced from an analogous situation in later times.[1]

The acme of Brāhmaṇical-Javanese civilization lies approximately in the 8th-10th century A.D. After that, there is a period of gradual "Javanization" of the Indian elements, while new developments in Indian religion and culture are not represented any more in Indonesia. The conclusion may be drawn that the contact with India was not prolonged any more now in the same way as before. The Brāhmaṇical Javanese period ended with the diffusion of Islam in the 15th and 16th century A.D.

In Bali, the signs of a Brāhmaṇised culture are found from the 8th century onwards. One might rightly speak of an independent Brāhmaṇical-Balinese culture besides the Brāhmaṇical-Javanese one of Java; some facts lead to the conclusion that Bali was Brāhmaṇised by direct influence of India without intervention from Java. One of these facts is that the oldest Balinese inscriptions are written in Sanskrit and old-Balinese. From about the year 1000 onwards, old-Balinese is gradually pushed aside by old-Javanese; a sign of the increasing dominance of Java over the much smaller Bali. In the 14th century, Bali even became a centre for the study of old-Javanese literature. The influx of Islam, which did not touch Bali, completed the role of this island as a preserver of Brāhmāṇical-Javanese culture and literary treasures, a role which it has maintained up to these days. In the course of centuries a part of the Sanskrit heritage has been incorporated as loan words in the Balinese language (certainly in this process old-Javanese, which is full of Sanskrit words, played a part). From meaning and syntactical function of these loan words often differ considerably from the Sanskrit originals. For example, the Balinese word manase "to devour" is a descendent of Sanskrit māṁsa "flesh, meat"; biseka comes from Abhiṣeka; gumi; "kingdom" from bhumi.[2]

The preservation of Brāhmaṇism in Bali did not imply that indigenous cultural values disappeared. There is indeed beside the great Brāhmaṇical tradition a great deal of what has been called the "small tradition", limited by factors of geographical, cultural or familial environment; and in some respects the two traditions do not constitute an organic whole. Thus, the function of the Brāhmaṇa priest (pedānda) has not been integrated into the religious life of the people. The pedānda procures his holy water and is indeed held in high esteem; but while he is busy performing his ceremo-

1. Hooyakass, C., "Śivaism in Bali, two hypotheses," in : *Journal of the Oriental Institute of Baroda*, Vol.15, 1965-66, pp. 381ff.
2. These instances are taken from Gonda, J., *Sanskrit in Indonesia*.

nies the laity does not pay attention to him. He does not officiate in the village and family temples, of which a great number exists. Liturgy in and care of these temples are entrusted to other classes of priests, notably the pamangku, who are of non-Brāhmaṇa descent. The word temple should not be understood as "religious building". The Balinese temple is an open yard surrounded by a wall or fence; it contains mainly some pavilions and pagodas and a huge stone seat for Śivāditya, who is not represented by an image.

No attention was given to *Vidi* (Vidhi), the Balinese counterpart of *Daivam* or fate, sometimes conceived as a personal god; nor to the very important death ritual and the role played in it by the god Baruna (Varuṇa) Lord of the sea, who receives his sacrifices on the shore; nor to the representation of Hindu mythological motifs in modern Balinese art; only a few words on the Balinese class division cannot be omitted. The Hindu division of society into the four classes of Brāhmaṇas, Kṣatriyas, Vaiśyas and Śudras is found also in Bali (there are no out-castes) although the Indian situation should not be projected without understanding Balinese society. The Vesyas (Vaiśyas) for example, are a group of indigenous aristocrats and as such hold a higher position like that of their Indian namesakes. The Sudras (Śudras), although formerly often exploited by the Kṣatriyas, always maintain their awareness of belonging to a respectable and privileged society. Indeed the Balinese are proud of their individuality and cultural inheritance. Anyone who has been the worthy demeanour of the pedānda walking about in a Balinese village, will intuitively understand something of India's contribution of human values, which cooperated with the indigenous culture of this remote island in shaping what is known at present as "Agama Hindu Bali".

Like Java, in Bali too, Brāhmaṇical tradition has been kept purer and special Brāhmaṇic features still survive in the religious practices, though it has been cut off from Brāhmaṇical influence for at least six seven centuries on a feast day which generally celebrated the birth of a god or the bringing in of the harvest from the field, offerings consisting of various fruits and rich pastries are arranged tastefully in piles of considerable height. They are brought into a temple by women on their head; they enter the innermost courtyard to the accompaniment of music where they deposit their offerings on splayed bamboo receptacles. Men-folk carry long handled multicoloured sunshades which they pitch to the ground to protect the offerings from the sun. The impact of Brāhmaṇism is clearly visible here.

The holy dances are observed by the Balinese. As the evening proceeds the preliminaries for the holy dance are made. The dance is mostly held under a spreading Vaṭa tree, which the Balinese hold in reverence like the Indians. The dancers proceed to the altar, where they are initiated with *tilaka* and *candana* and receive *caraṇāmṛta* with the blessing of the priest.

The spacious courtyard of the temple serves as the stage. The Vaṭa tree is treated as the background and the star-lit sky, (or moonlit as the case may be) the canopy of their play. Torches and lamps are lighted and musicians with their Jalataraṅga and Rabab, equal themselves on bamboo mattings, while the dancers group themselves in the front. It begins on the lower key and slowly rises in volume. The classical side to the show is supplied by the *Mahābhārata*, the source of inspiration being the Tāṇḍava dance of the Naṭarāja.

The Balinese perform all the ceremonies and sacraments as in past. Their mode of dress is perhaps the same as was prevalent in the time of *Mahābhārata*. Their conception of heaven and hell is based on the doctrine of *karma*. Their attitude regarding life beyond death is inspired by the teachings of the *Upaniṣads*. The poorest pedanda or priest still receives the homage of the richest prince. They celebrate the adventures of the heroes of the epics. The islanders being Śaiva by creed, the Śivaloka constitutes their ultimate goal. The same principle of merits and demerits of the present life governs the transmigration of the soul in whose immortality they have an unshakable belief. The four *Vedas* and the *Geeta* are honoured by them as sacred and authoritative books as in India. Mantras are chanted by the priest at the time of cremation, as is done in India. The dead body is put on a pyre of wood. Then the pyre is set fire to and the ashes are collected the next day and thrown into the river or sea. A kind of Śrādha ceremony is also performed by them.

9. BORNEO

Barhiṇa-dvipa of the *Vāyu Purāṇa* (XL. VIII, 12) is probably the Indian varient of Borneo. Like all other regions of South-East Asia, Borneo, the largest island in the Malay Archipelago too felt the impact of Brāhmaṇism which is evident from the discovery of a large number of Sanskrit inscriptions. The very high degree of development of the knowledge of Sanskrit is proved by the several hundreds of Sanskrit inscriptions and numerous books written in Sanskrit and indigenous language profoundly influenced by Sanskrit. At Kutei on the Maharkam, and at Muara-kaman, where the river meets its tributary the Kaman, have been discovered the oldest inscriptions of the Archipelago, belonging on the basis of their script, to the late fourth century A.D. In fairly correct Sanskrit verse, they are engraved on yūpas, sacrificial or donative posts made of stone. All seven of them, four from Kutei and three from Muarakaman (but sometimes stated to be found at Kutei) commemorate the acts of one Mūlavarman, the son of Asvavarman and the grandson of Kundunga (a Tamil or indigenous name). They reveal him as a performer of great yajñas, and a liberal donor to the Brāhmaṇas.

One of the Yūpa inscriptions states, "the illustrious monarch Mūlavarman, having conquered kings in the battle-field, made them tributaries, as did king Yudhiṣṭhira" (Śrī Mūlavarmmarājendra(h) sama (re) jitva partthi (van) Karadan nṛpatims cakre yathā rājā Yudhiṣṭhiraḥ). *Karadam nṛpatims cakre* is reminiscent of Bāṇa's *Karadekṛta* in the *Harṣacarita* and Māgha's *Karadikritabhupalo* (*Śiśupāla-vaddha,* II, 9). This verse, therefore, implies not only the knowledge of an epic event but perhaps also of the political theory of ancient India (the three types of conquest, of sandhi, of tributaries etc.) on the part of a late fourth century A.D. king in distant Borneo.

Among random individual finds showing Brāhmaṇical influence in ancient Borneo should be mentioned a *Karis-hilt,* interesting for its motif, from Balingian in Sarawak.[1] Made of pure beaten gold it is 92mm. high 33mm. at its widest point, and 34 grams in weight including a piece of wood inside it. The hilt is in the form of a bearded figure with large eyes, fanged teeth, right hand lifted and the left holding a human skull. Karis-hilt generally depict Viṣṇu's mount Garuḍa or a rākṣasa or very rarely Hanumāna, all capable of supernatural feats. According to Heine-Geldern the rākṣasa is a representation of the demon cannibal king Kalmāshapāda of the *Mahā-Sutasoma Jātaka* who was finally reformed by the virtuous king Sutasoma. The local Melenans from whom the golden hilt was recovered deeply venerated it and believed that its wearer would be invested with magical powers.

Bukit Maras and Tanjong Kubur have yielded thousands of pottery fragments which have a striking Brāhmaṇical look but are locally made of native ware. Another line of investigation of the meeting of the two cultures, Brāhmaṇical and indigenous may be sought in the megaliths of pre-historic Sungai Jiong, within two miles of Bukit Maras.[2] In the Limbang board the ring with the dolmen motif is found alongside the ornaments with Brāhmaṇical motifs. A more spectacular precedent is in the Sikuh megalith in the Lawa mountains, east of Solo, Java, with Indian mythological figures and an inscription.

Remains of ancient Brāhmaṇical culture have also been found in other localities in East Borneo. The most notable among these is the cave of Kombeng situated considerably to the north of Muara Kaman and to the east of the upper course of the Telen river.

Twelve sandstone images and several architectural pieces, found in this cave, evidently belonged once to one or more temples in the valley of the Mahakam river, and were secreted here, probably for safety. Archaeological remains of Brāhmaṇical structures have been found also in the valley of the Kapuas river. It is evident that the Brāhmaṇical colonists and Brāhmaṇical culture spread from the seaports into the interior along the

1. Tom Harrison, "A Golden Keris Handle from Balingian", Sarawak, *JMBRAS*, Vol., 30, pt. I, 1966, pp. 145-181.
2. Wales, H.G.Q., *The Mountain of Gold.*

valleys of these rivers. But in most regions, away from these rivers, primitive barbarism continued unchecked.

Thus, the facts referred to above indicate that the inscriptions of South-east Asia are, where specified, generally in Śaka era, and not the Vikrama-samvat, as followed in the north. A fragmentary Tamil record from Takua-pa[1] in Thailand, registers the digging of a tank to be called Avani-naranam by a chief of Nangur (in Thanjavur District), and placing the tank jointly under the famous sea-faring guild of merchants called the Manigrāmattār, the Senāmukattār (or a military unit) and another body respectively. The record is palaeographically datable to early 10th century A.D., or earlier, and the title Avani-naranam was generally held by Tellār-eninda Nandi of the later Pallava line. Choḷa king Rajendra's records mention Talai Takkolam (doubtless the same as Takua-pa) in his campaign route, and place it on the way between Malaya and Kamboja in the direct route. The Sanskrit records of the South-East Asian countries follow also the southern form of Pallava script mostly and not the Nagari form. Even more revealing is the fact that Nandivarman II who ascended the Pallava throne at Kanchi after the death of Parameśvara Varman II (728-731 A.D.), is found, on a close study of the contemporary inscriptions and reliefs at Vaikunṭha Perumal temple at Kanchipuram, to have arrived from the Indo-Chinese territory, from a collectoral overseas Pallava branch. Evidence also exists for the closely linked kinship between the royal family of Campa and the Western Gangas of Talakkad, as mentioned variously in the damaged record[2] at Phnom Bayan of Bhavavarman (c. 561-639 A.D.) referring to a Konguvarma or Gangarayan as the founder of the Campa line, and the Mi-son record[3] (c. 708-717 A.D.) of Prakāśadharma-Vikrānteśvara, calling him as of the family of Gaṅgeśvara (Śrī-Gaṅgeśvara-vaṁśajah), and another record, also for Mison[4] of Śambhūvarman (c. 499-577 A.D.) calling him as Śrī-Praśastadharmadiṇḍika. The term diṇḍika, it is to be noted, is a familiar personal name employed by Gaṅgas of Talakkad, one of the earliest such usage is seen in the Śravaṇabelagola record of the 7th century A.D.

This colonisation and assimilation of the Greater Indian tracts by Brāhmaṇic immigrants, which Sanskrit serving as the *lingua franca*, was indeed a phenomenon doing credit to the immigrant as well as to the domicile. There can be no doubt that in this was also a mingling of bloods occasionally and an ethnic blend, an acquisition of pedigree to own and evolve the parental heritage. The deep involvement of the Javanese,

1. Hultzsch, *JRAS*, 1913, p. 337ff; 194, pp. 397ff; Gopinatha Rao, T.A., *Epigraphia Indica*, Vol. VIII, pp. 71-72; Sastri, K.A.N., *JOR*, Vol. VI, pp. 299-310.
2. Coedes, G., *op. cit.*, Vol. I, p. 251.
3. *BEFEO*, Vol. IV, p. 928; Vol. XVI, p. 190.
4. *ibid.*, Vol. III, p. 206.

Annamites and Cambodians towards the legends of the Indian epics and purāṇas have been most nobly integrated in their temple arts. But, then the temple institutions themselves had been of Brāhmaṇic religion and anciently manned by Indians mostly, and the cults of the Trinity, of Gaṇeśa, of Nārāyaṇa, or Rāma, Hanumāna, Garuḍa, Hayagriva and Harihara abounded, both in the Hindu-colonial and post-colonial local stages of the indigenous metamorphism.

It is interesting also to record that while in Cambodia, as in Java and Bali, Buddhism which reached from north India mainly, and Brāhmaṇism which was drawn from the south Indian kingdoms mostly, had themselves achieved a mutual fusion instead of supplanting each other or creating rivalry. Even the charters present invocations to Buddha as well as to Śiva; Śaiva pantheon was itself amalgamated into the emanating scheme of Dhyāni Buddhas; Śaiva structures even often resemble Buddhist dagobas and vice-versa. Buddhist temple like Chandi Kalasan resembles any other Brāhmaṇic temples in Java. In Bali, some types of priests were even given the appellation buda. It should be noted, however, that Śaiva religion (in which Śiva—as indeed Viṣṇu and Brahmā—was regarded as one of the manifestations of Śūrya) ultimately scored over any lingering Buddhist vestige. The full compliment of Brāhmaṇic usages though not of all the Brāhmaṇic gods is seen in the archipelago, as for instance, the Tirta Mpul of Bali which is a sacred spring, ordered at the behest of king Candrabhaya Simhavarman-deva in 962 A.D. It is the successor of this king that married his son to one of the daughters of a Javanese king called Mahendradatta (and Gunapriya dharmapatni, after marriage)—the couple giving birth to the famous Erlangga who united Bali and Java under one royal banner.

It should be stated that the epics had especially been absorbed and imbibed by the Annamites and the Javanese. The versions that had been adapted and redacted from the various sources make interesting reading, and not only show the sense of belonging generally evinced in the heritage, but also follow the pattern guided by the local myths and predilections.

The Annamite version of Rāma legend[1] is, for instance, entitled 'the king of demons' and there Rāma and Sītā received fanciful names, although Daśaratha and Rāvaṇa were exactly synonymous to their Sanskrit names and are called the ten-chariots and tenheaded. The last redaction of the Rāma legend in Campā from Annamite sources is as late as the 18th century A.D. It is interesting to compare here the fact that in the Tibetan version of the Rāma legend also, we fail to connect any corresponding derivative source of the Rāmāyaṇa in India, but the version generally appears to have followed the narration of the Rāma story in the Vanaparvan of Mahābhārata.

1. *BEFEO*, Vol. V, p. 168.

Epigraphical sources inform us, that the epics were caused to be read also in temples, as is usually the case in south Indian temples. A Kamboja record[1] (c. 600 A.D.), shows that Śrī-Somaśarmā, apparently a Brāhmin, presented *Rāmāyaṇa*, the purāṇas and a complete *Bhārata* to a temple, and made arrangements for their recitation. Even more striking is the information gleaned from an inscription from Tra-kieu in Campā[2], by which Prakāśadharma (653-79 A.D.) dedicated an image and temple to Vālmīki himself.

In so far as the Indonesian situation is concerned, it had been the view of some scholars like Stutterheim[3] that the local *Rāmāyaṇa* version was based on the Indian versions, written and traditional—and perhaps more primitive—and not so much on Vālmiki. The *Rāmāyaṇa* reliefs from Prambanan (west Java) were the most celebrated and ancient (9th century A.D.) and though clearly Indian in character, are not based on Vālmīki's work. On the other hand, strangely, the later Panataran (east Java) scenes of the 14th century A.D. in Indo-Javanese style are more coherent in following Vālmīki.

A valuable insight into the remarkably early context of the assimilation of the *Rāmāyaṇa*, even including the controversial Uttara-kāṇḍa, is gained by the unique though undated record[4] again of the king Prakāśa-dharma, which refers to the cult of Ekasṛnga Piṅgala—about how Kubera got one eye burnt yellow, owing to the impertinence of his having gazed at Pārvatī, soon after he had brought both before him by hard penance. The legend is narrated in Uttara-kāṇḍa 13, 21-31 of Rāmāyaṇa and, curiously, even the phraseology of the versified account as found in the Champa record of Prakāśa-dharma is quite close to the above source. In the Musee Khmer at Phnom Penh[5], there are to be found ten groups of delightful and ancient paintings of Rāmāyaṇa episodes, got from Kamboja version of Bālakāṇḍa, including Janaka's discovery of Sītā, Rāma breaking the bow, Paraśurāma's encounter with Rāma after the latter's marriage etc. Again at Ben Mula[6] sculptured scenes exist of the Yuddhakāṇḍa, depicting the fighting of Rāvaṇa, after Prahasta, the commander had been killed by Nīla (sarga 54), and the restoration of dead monkeys to life by the help of Indra (sarga 120). Again, at the famous edifice of Angkor Vat[7] (10th and 12th century A.D.) bas-reliefs portray the fight between Bālī and Sugrīva, the death of Bālī, and the consequent expression of grief by the women-

1. Elliot, III, 120; *BEFEO*, Vol. XXVIII, p. 149.
2. *ibid.*,
3. *BEFEO*, Vol. XXVIII, p. 506; and *JRAS*, 1926, p. 362.
4. *BEFEO*, Vol. IV, p. 928; Sastri, K.A.N., *JOR*, Vol. VI, 1931.
5. Paramentier, *BEFEO*, XII, No. 3, pp. 47-50.
6. *ibid.*, No. 2, pp. 25-26.
7. *ibid.*, No. 6, pp. 2-4.

folk, the meeting of Vibhiṣaṇa and Rāma, the fire-ordeal of Sītā after the war was over, etc.

Of the other Indian legends, Angkor Vat again depicts the Kailāśa-tolana by Rāvaṇa—a favourite theme of the Indian sculptors and immortalised at the Kailāśa cave, Ellorā. Of some local stylistic interest in this context, is the depiction of Rāvaṇa's heads arranged like a pyramid, and manner of display of his full score number of arms. It is unique in form.

The Purāṇic content of the South-east Asian countries closely reflects the Indian tradition, especially in the formative stages, absorbing the most salient elements of Brāhmaṇical iconography. Concepts like Trinity, Harihara, Anantasayi, Garuḍa-vāhana, Viṣṇu are the most distinctive produts of the genius of hieratic Brāhmaṇic art. Especially the images which are consecrated in worship, as different from those which beautify the temple exterior in formal carvings and the like, would be the real test of the degree of permeation that had been effected of the Purāṇic themes. The Trinity temple at Prambanan in Java, is a case in point. The polarisation of the Trinity takes place in India by at least the 10th century A.D., and it is pleasing to note that the integrity of this concept at Prambanan had dove-tailed with a southern Indian architectural format also. Even more deeply embedded in the local matrix was the Harihara or Śankaranārāyaṇa (as mentioned in the record of Glai Lemov[1] in Indo-China in the valley of Phanrang—Panduranga ?—dated to 801 A.D. of the time of Indravarman) concept, as reflected in a pretty large number of icons of this type variously from Simping, Phnom Penh, Hanoi, etc. An interesting innovation seen in some of these examples is the reversal of position of Hari and Hara. In Indian examples Hari is invariably on the left part of the body. This aspect is seemingly based upon the Mohini form that Viṣṇu took as a sequel to Samudra-manthana (ocean churning) and whose bewitching charm led to Śiva begetting a child out of her, called Hariharaputra. In some of the Javanese examples, Hari is on the right. These examples, further, do not make studies in bold artistic embellishment, but rather in subtle amalgamation of the gods, a few details of apparel and facial moulding alone, by and large, eking out the dichotomy. This is, of course, a pre-mediaeval and early mediaeval trend, mostly, but one that would, nevertheless, differentiate the art-outlook of the countries concerned, the Indo-Chinese area showing a plain and subtly moulded body features and dress. The Javanese figures are, on the other hand, generally informed by richness of drapery and ornamentation, and are close to Chālukyan in this respect than even the Pallava. The Singasari Durgā and Gaṇeśa from Bara are good instances of this. The luxuriant surface decoration of these two figures generally recalls to our mind the later-day Hoyasala crafts, but they are certainly of a much earlier period

1. Majumdar, R.C., *Champa*, Pt. III, No. 24 (b).

in Java. The stance of the two deities, again, is less indebted to the Pallavas and more to the Chālukyas and Gaṅgas. Here again, they have introduced many artistic innovations, as for instance, the gaṇa attendant of Durgā (taken by some as the human form of Mahiṣa demon) in the Singasari specimen, which is not usually known from any Indian examples, and the integration or combination of Gaṇeśa with Bhairava on the same sculpture on its two faces, front and rear. Bhairava-Gaṇeśa is a combination which, like Gajantaka-Andhakari is not unknown in India, and is seen in the Deccan and in the Kalinga coast, but the variation of the idiom consists in the carving of it separately on the two opposed faces; instead of on the same face.

The Rāma reliefs from Prambanan, Java, from a substantial expression of the artistic calibre of early Javanese art, as well as its indebtedness to the Indian epic. The inception of the story has been fittingly made with the invocation of the Lord of Vaikunṭha by Brahmā and the devas, for being born as an incarnation in the world and exterminating the evil spread by Rāvaṇa and other similar rākṣasas. This panel is indeed a Vaikunṭhanātha panel, since the God here is not truly reclining, but is more in the seated posture of *Viralalita.* By his side to the proper left is shown Garuḍa. The importance of showing Garuḍa—which is indeed the national symbol of Java—is to be noted elsewhere also in the Erlangga figure of Belaha. The God in the Vaikunṭhanātha panel at Prambanan is intently hearing the petitions presented by Brahmā, and by his lower left hand, giving the abhaya-dāna also, while the sage's party are in rapt attention following the dialogue. The oceanic setting of the scene received capable treatment at the hands of the similar craftsmen of Java. The figures of Viṣṇu's proper left with the sage-like persons were considered by Groneman as representing Daśaratha and his queens, praying to Viṣṇu. But the presence of four male figures with kirīṭa mukuṭa and a sage-like main leader with jaṭābhara seems to show that this is not correct. Even Havell[1] did not consider the four accompanying figures as female and observed that they could be Rāma and his brothers along with Vāsiṣṭha or Viśvāmitra, praying to God. Since they are males, the greater probability is that they could be Brahmā and the *dikpālas* four in number, namely, Kubera, Varuṇa, Indra and Yama. This would seem to be the most satisfactory answer.

Of a class different both in form and in content, belonging as it does to the Indo-Chinese region, is the Hayagriva figure from Cambodia. The utterly naturalistic and vigorous presentation of the horse-god form assumed by Viṣṇu when he retrieved the Vedas from the nether world, is a very appropriate theme for the overland colonials to imbibe and adapt. The

1. Havell, E.B. *Indian Sculptures and Paintings*, pp. 133-34.

representation of Hayagriva with a completely aquine head also reveals a traditional kinship of these craftsmen with their early Indian counterparts who had also revealed in the presentation of Varāha, Narasiṁha and Hayagriva forms of Viṣṇu in a similar way. Hayagriva being the special presiding deity of wisdom and knowledge in the south Indian Vaiṣṇava iconography and Āgamas, this confirms the thesis that it is primarily the southern tradition that had found a harmonious haven in these Far-Eastern shores. The Hayagriva figures, however, in the Indian parallels, are never made to stand, but are only seated. The Cambodian and Laotian examples, including one in the Musee Guimet, Paris, are all of the standing and two-armed type, and show perhaps an early absorption of the cult and a local translation thereof.

Two outstanding examples of Indian themes seen in the Far-East should now be recounted before closing this brief treatment on the South-East Asian Brāhmaṇical tradition. These two are respectively, the spell-binding 'churning the ocean' tableau in magnificent proportions, on the southern avenue of the Bayon, Angkor Thom temples, and the Viṣṇu on Garuḍa figure from Belaha in Java (dated to 991 A.D.). The former is verily a clever integration of architecture and sculpture and alike in vigour and proportions, as in the highly suggestive local ethnic format, the figure is unparalleled. In the first case, the temple itself is rendered as the cosmic form of the Buddhist deity—as it is said to be Jayavarman, the god king's sepulchral temple following the Devarāja cult—gigantic faces of this Bodhisattva Lokeśvara Samāntamukha composedon the four veneer faces of the śikhara towers. Though it strongly recalls the ponderous but emotional figures carved at Elephantā caves, near Bombay (including the 'Maheśa' panel often called the Trimūrti), the Cambodian example apotheosises the temple as God even more effectively than had been attempted anywhere in India, and is in fact a sure testimony to the fact that the Āgama traditions had already received wide and willing acceptance in these regions and even for Buddhist and sepulchral contexts. The textual personification of the temple as God, here the god-king, had, in effect, received sculptural fulfilment in these remarkable temples. The temples, as also the Caṇḍi temples of Java, have their parallels in the Pallippadai temples in honour of dead kings as founded under the Cholas at many places like Melpadi, Tiruppurambiyam, Tondaimanadu etc. That kings are considered in India as temporal manifestation of Viṣṇu is an old Manu-dharma concept. Incidentally, it discloses the deep involvement of the artists in the work, as it is indeed a prodigious task to carve in situ—as it would seem to have been the case here--the whole elevational profile of the temple towers into mammoth divine busts, maintaining harmonious proportions, modulations and symmetry.

The Belaha example[1] of Garuḍa-vāhana Viṣṇu had been freely interpreted as representing the embodiment of king as god and the figure of prince Erlangga who had consolidated the new kingdom in Java and Bali together in the 10th century A.D. This application of a facet of the Devarāja cult of South-east Asia, as seemingly made in this issue, is *prima facei* valid. But it cannot be denied that truly symbolic, and as it turns out in the mediaeval time, specifically sepulchral traits of the sculptures like hands in añjalī, calm face etc. which should represent royal ancestor worship, would be lacking in this Belaha figure.

There is no doubt that the treatment is that of Garuḍa bearing Viṣṇu, both of whom have—following the stylised depiction of the body and face—a somewhat unconventional appearance. The representation of Garuḍa especially, with human face of only bird-beak is also drawn from the south Indian tradition where, at least by the 14th century A.D. it had become a common event in temples of Viṣṇu to have Garuḍa in the posture of a bearer, kept as a mobile unit, for use during festivals. The earlier tradition of Viṣṇu riding the Garuḍa is only in the Gajendra-varada type, and not found in any other myth, and thus it would be feasible to argue that the Belaha figure is also an extension of the trait of readiness to come to succour that characterises Viṣṇu and which, in turn, could have been ascribed to kings also who are noble and gracious.

Thus Brāhmaṇism was the spring that fed the fountain of the culture in South-East Asia. Moreover, in Indonesia when the Brāhmaṇical spring dried up, due to the arrival of Islam, fountain remained as an ornamental relic of the past but ceased to give the life-giving water. But in Indo-China where the current of Brāhmaṇical culture never stopped by the onrush of Islam, she, continued to thrive, though Brāhmaṇical culture was considerably modified by the indigenous races whom it has constantly endowed with higher and higher elements of civilisation. So Brāhmaṇism still survives as a living force in Cambodia, Thailand, Champa, Burma, and the solitary island of Bali, leaving a trail of memorials behind.

1. Vogel, J.P.H. in *The Influence of Indian Art, the Indian Society*, p. 80.

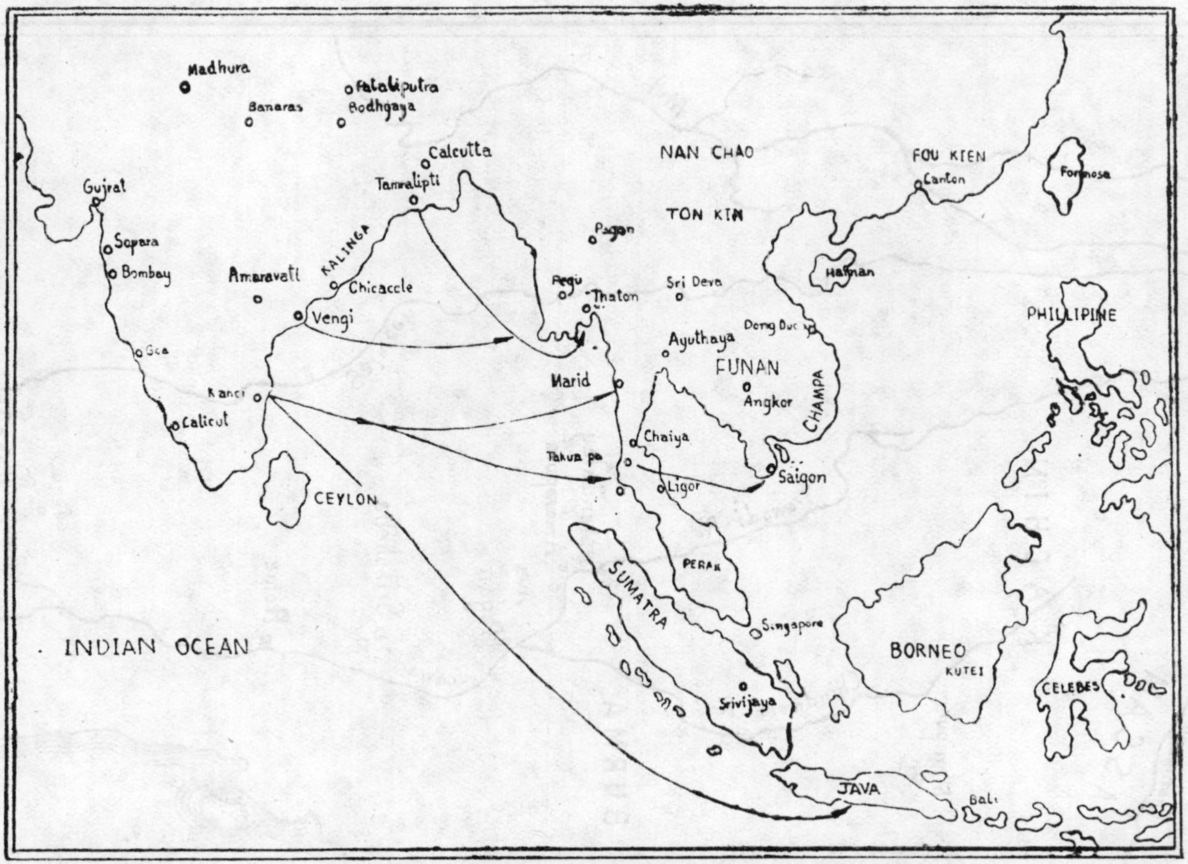

Expansion of Brāhmaṇism

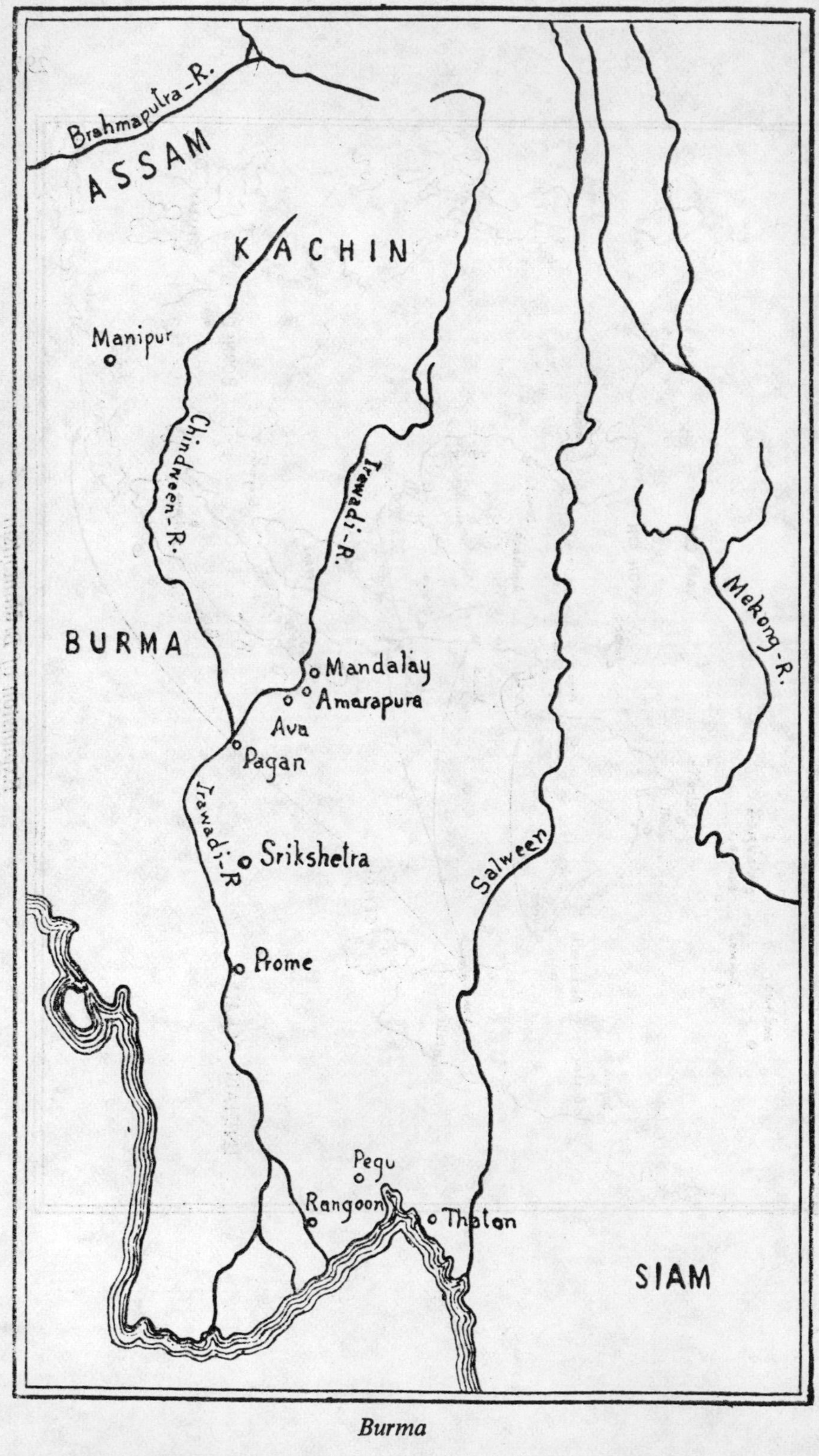
Brahmaputra-R.
ASSAM
KACHIN
Manipur
Chindween-R.
Irawadi-R.
BURMA
Mandalay
Amarapura
Ava
Pagan
Irawadi-R
Srikshetra
Salween
Mekong-R.
Prome
Pegu
Rangoon
Thaton
SIAM

Burma

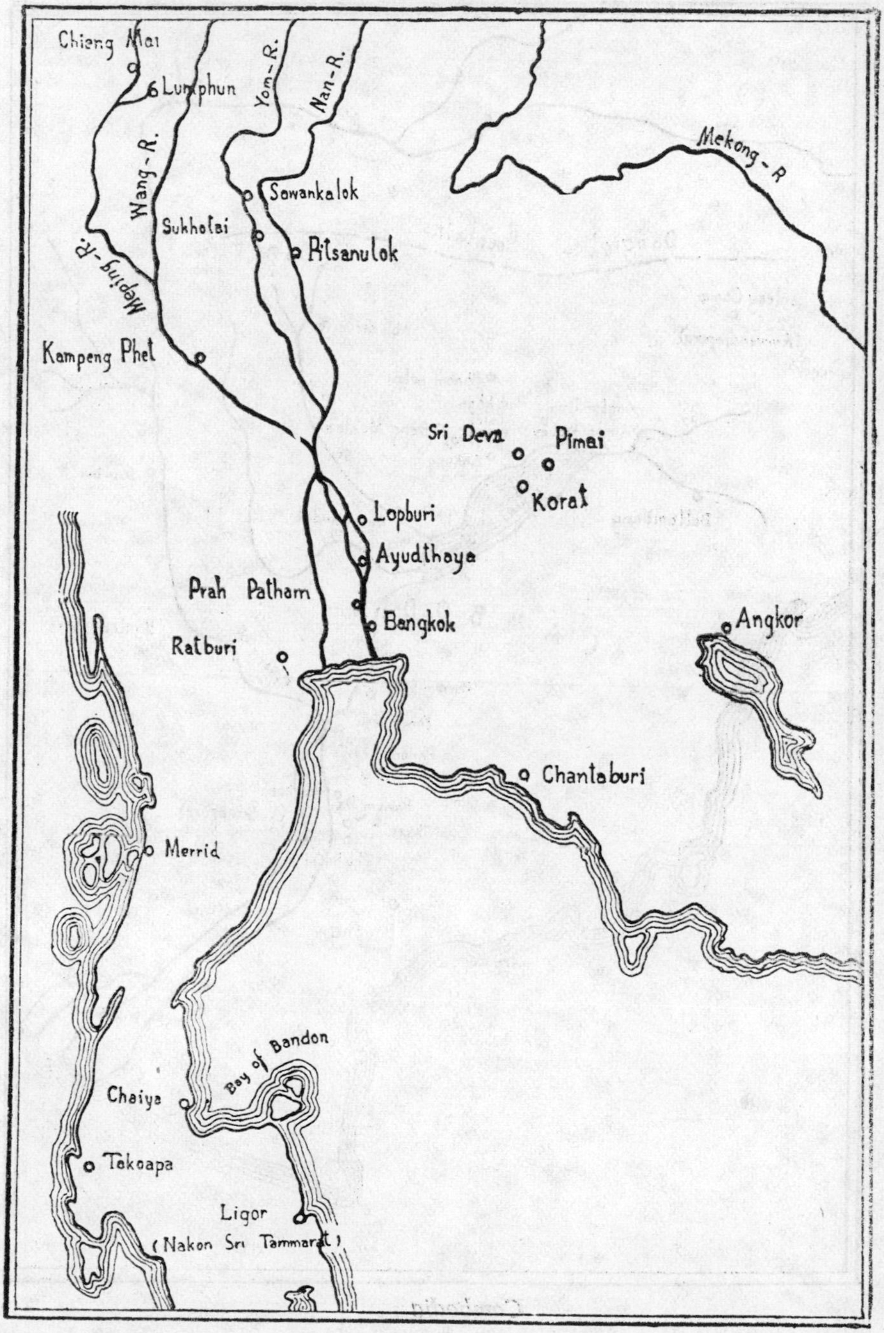
Chieng Mai
Lumphun
Wang-R.
Yom-R.
Nan-R.
Mekong-R
Sawankalok
Sukhotai
Pitsanulok
Meping-R.
Kampeng Phet
Sri Deva
Pimai
Korat
Lopburi
Ayudthaya
Prah Patham
Bangkok
Ratburi
Angkor
Chantaburi
Merrid
Bay of Bandon
Chaiya
Takoapa
Ligor
(Nakon Sri Tammarat)

Siam

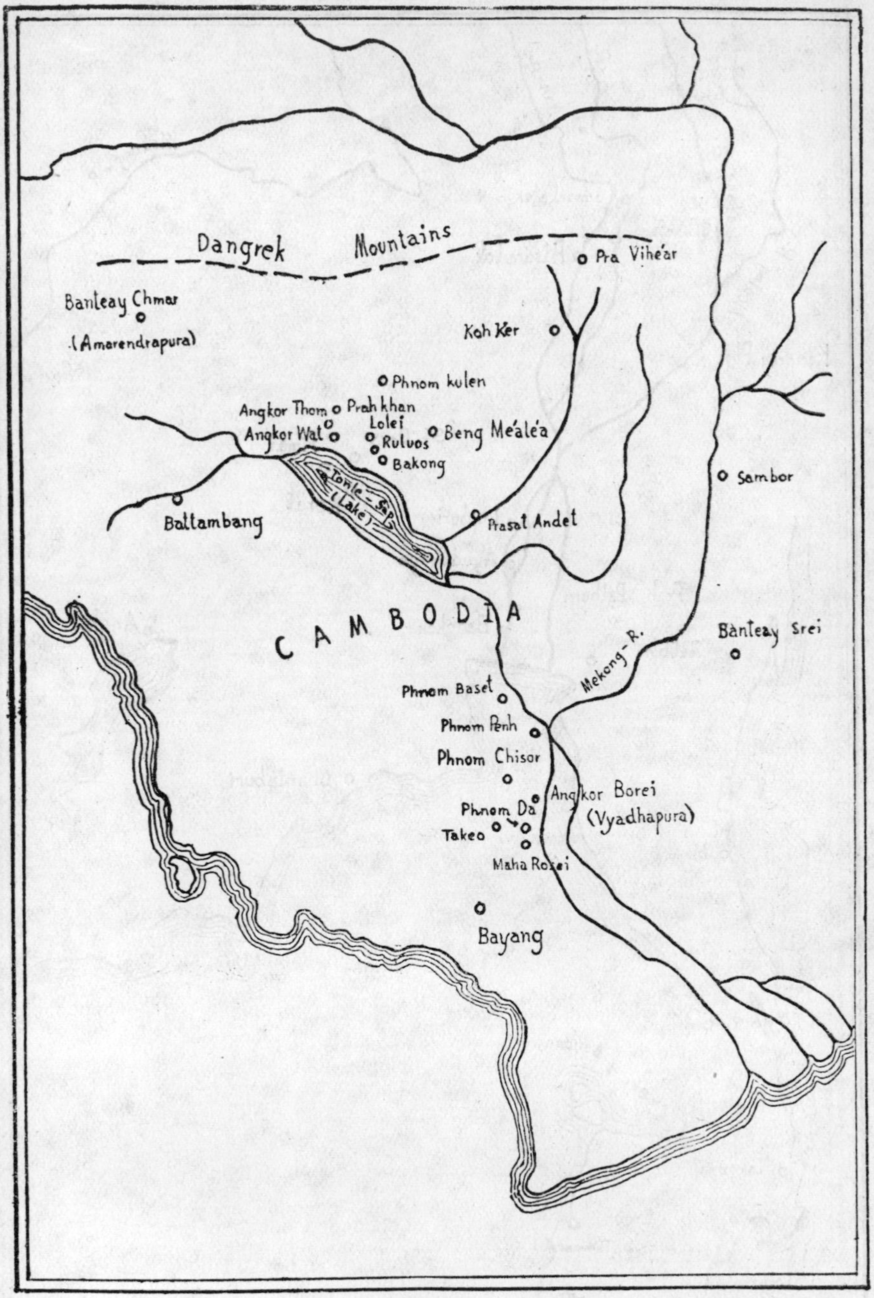
Dangrek Mountains
Pra Vihe'ar
Banteay Chmar
(Amarendrapura)
Koh Ker
Phnom kulen
Angkor Thom
Prah khan
Lolei
Angkor Wat
Beng Mealea
Ruluos
Bakong
Sambor
Battambang
Tonle-Sap (Lake)
Prasat Andet
CAMBODIA
Banteay Srei
Mekong-R.
Phnom Baset
Phnom Penh
Phnom Chisor
Angkor Borei
(Vyadhapura)
Phnom Da
Takeo
Maha Rosei
Bayang

Cambodia

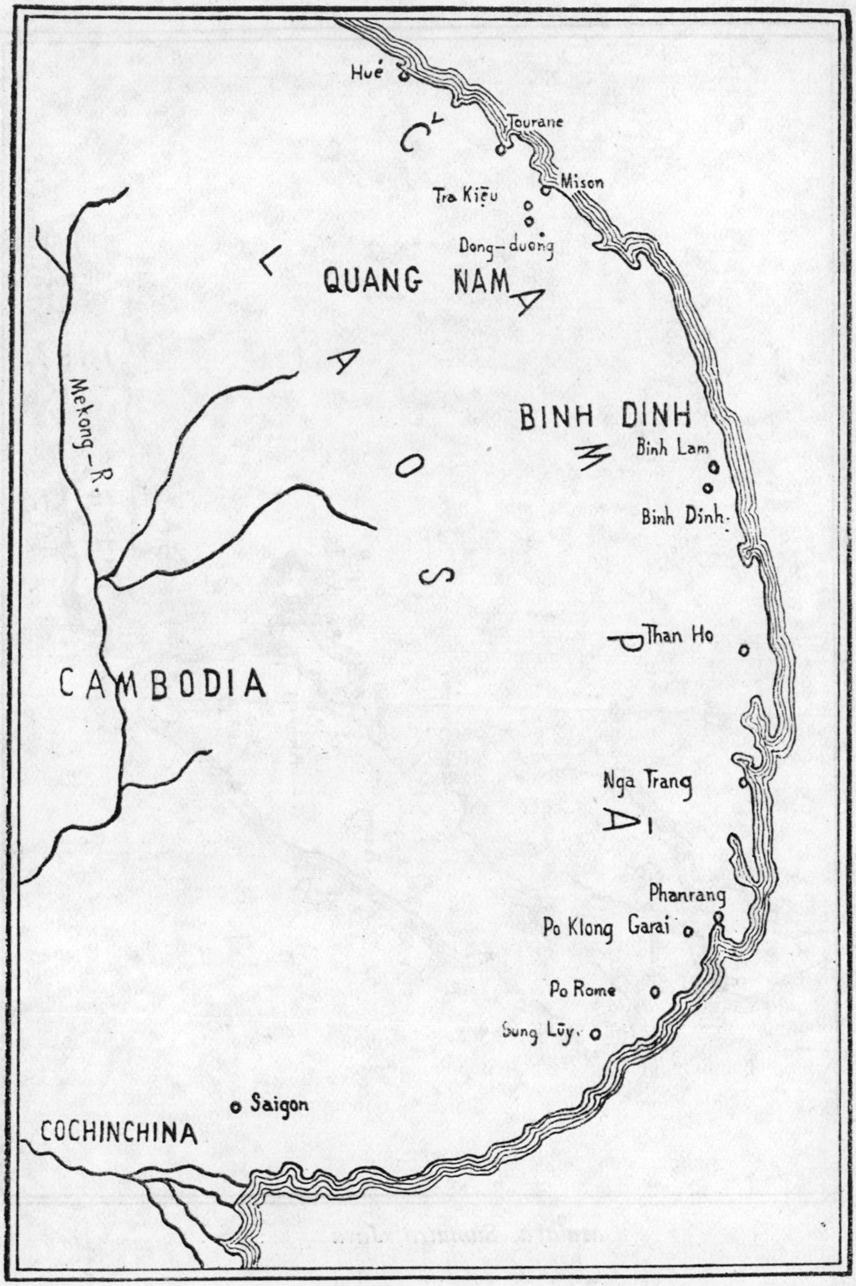

Hué
Tourane
Mison
Tra Kiệu
Dong-duong
QUANG NAM
LAOS
CAMPA
Mekong-R.
BINH DINH
Binh Lam
Binh Dinh
Than Ho
Nga Trang
Phanrang
Po Klong Garai
Po Rome
Sung Lũy
CAMBODIA
Saigon
COCHINCHINA

Champā

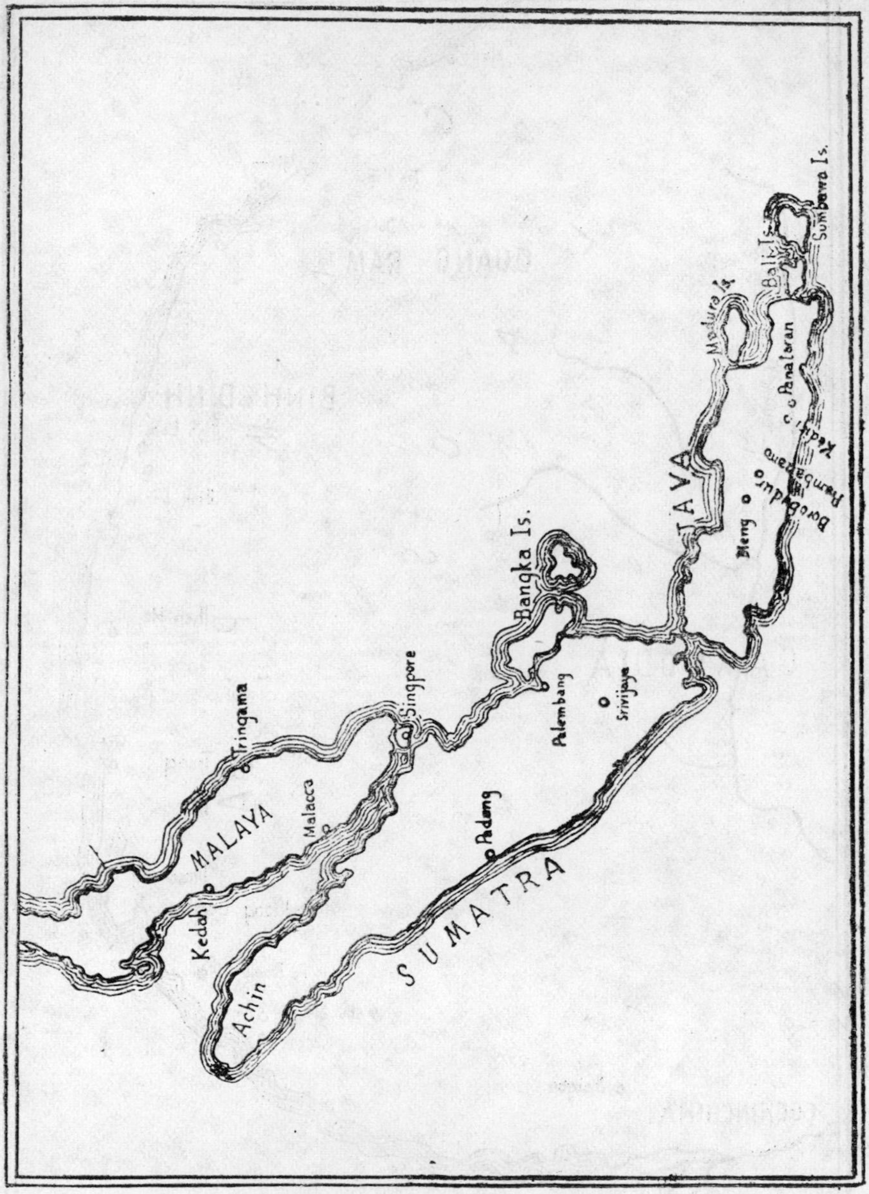

Malaya, Sumatra, Java

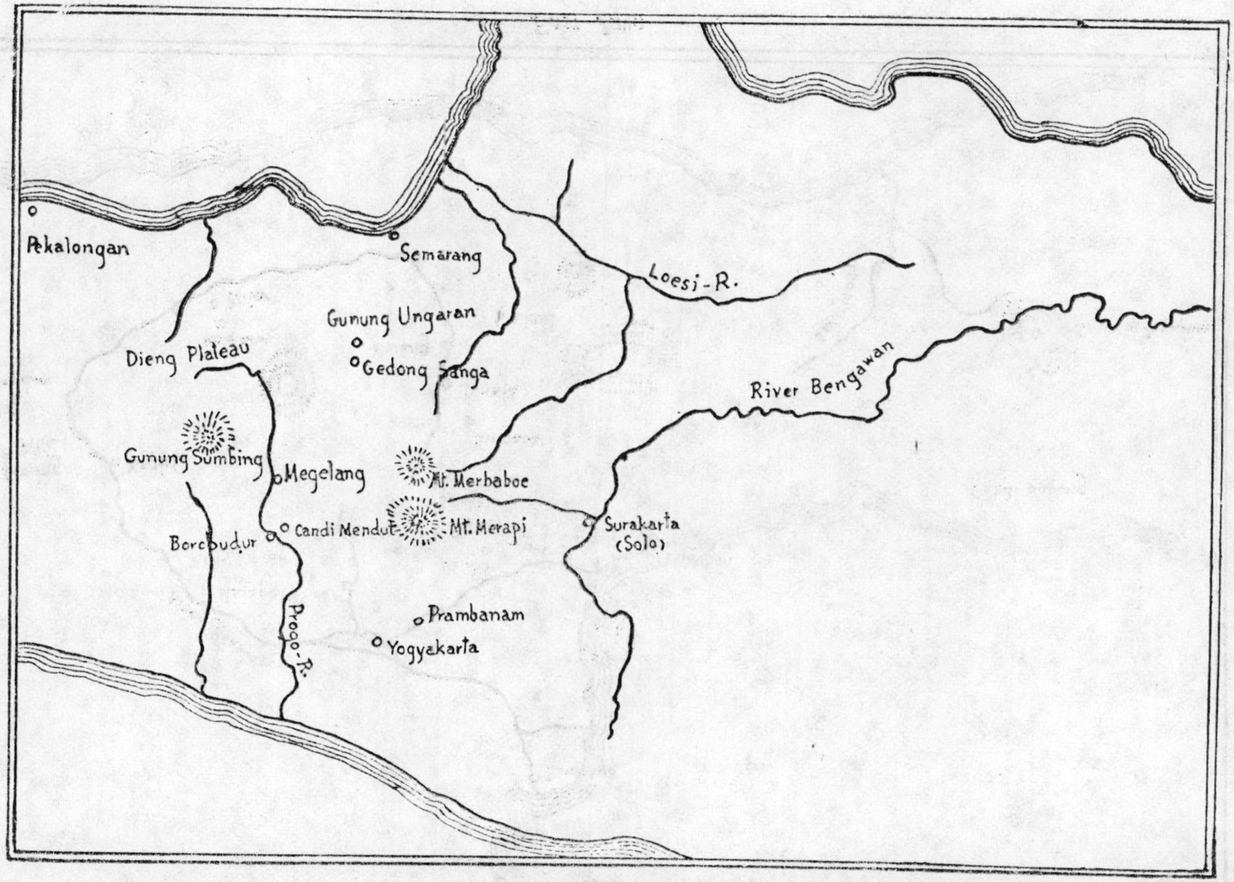

Central Java

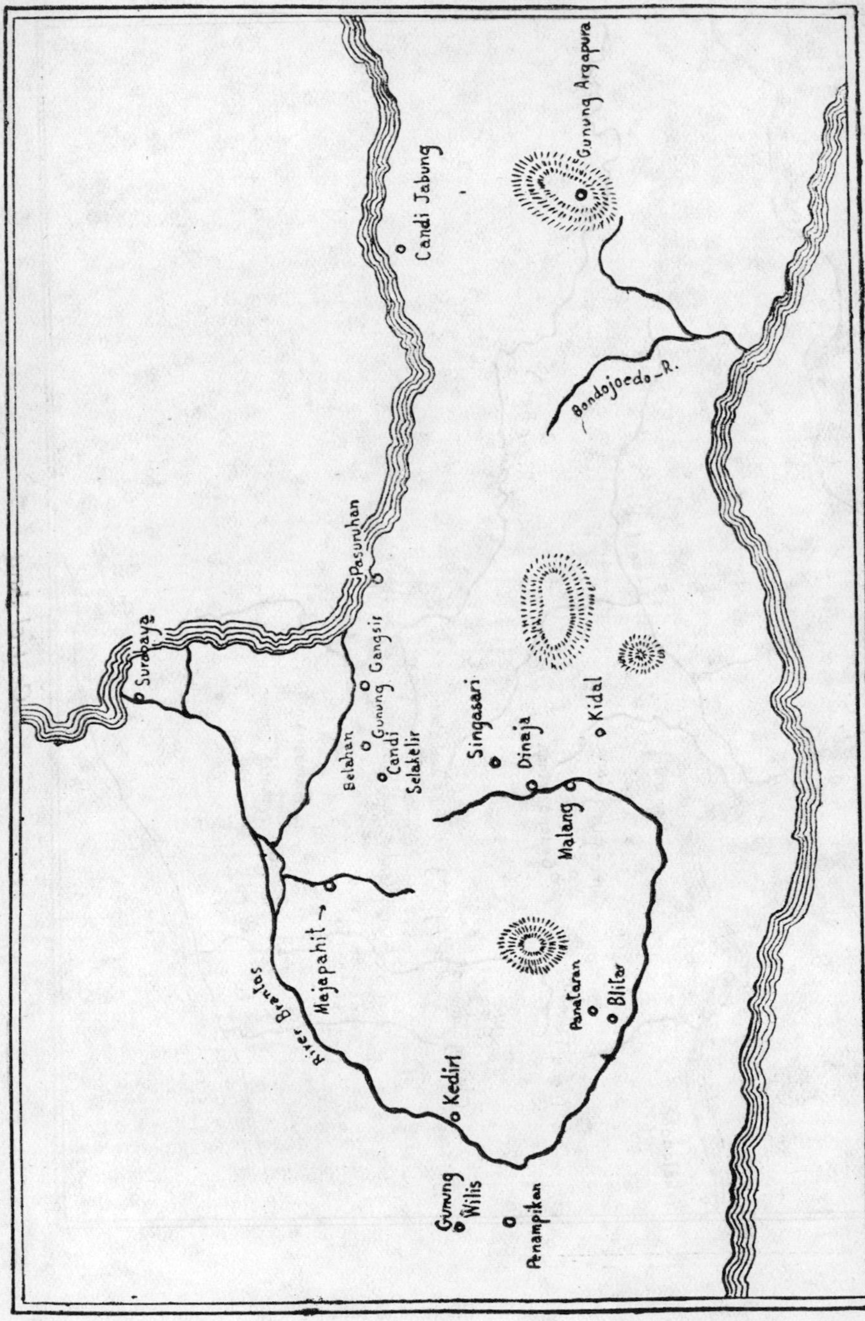
Surabaya
Pasuruhan
Gunung Gangsir
Belahan
Candi
Selakelir
Candi Jabung
Gunung Argapura
Bondojoedo-R.
Singasari
Dinaja
Kidal
Malang
Majapahit
River Brantas
Kediri
Panataran
Blitar
Gunung
Wilis
Penampikan

East Java

SELECT BIBLIOGRAPHY

(i) *ORIGINAL SOURCES*

(a) *Indian Literature:*

Bṛhatsaṁhitā (of Varāha-mihira) : Ed. Kern, H. Calcutta, 1865; with the commentary of Bhaṭṭolpala, Ed. Dvivedi Sudhakara, 2 Vols, Banaras, 1896.

Harivaṁśa : Ed. Tr. into Dutch by Teauw, A. The Hague, 1950.

(b) *Foreign Literature:*

Beylie, De L. : *L. Architecture Hindu an Extreme Orient.*

Coedes, G. : *Les Etats hindouise's d'Indo-Chine et d'Indo-ne'sie, Histoire du Monde*, Paris, 1948.

Friendrich, R. : *Voorloping verslag Van het eiland Bali*, Batavia, 1849.

Gangneux, P. : *L'Art Lao.*

Jean Boisselier : *Le Statuaire du Campā : Recherches Sur Les Cultes et L'iconographie*, Paris, 1963.

Kern, H. : *Verspreide Geschriften*, VII, The Hague, 1917.

Kirfel, W. : *Symbolik des Hinduismus and des Jinismus*, Stuttgart, 1954.

Krom, N.J. : *Hindoe-Javansche geschiederis*, The Hague, 1931.

: *Over het Civaisme Van Midden-Java*, Amsterdam Academy, 1924.

Marshal, H. : *Le Temple de Wat Phu*, Paris, 1943.

Maspero, G. : (Ed.) *Un Empire Colonial Francais l'Indo-Chine*, 2 Vols, Paris, 1929-30.

: *L'Empire Khmer, Histoire et documents*, Phnom-Penh, 1904.

: *To'Oung Po.*

Panikkar, K.M. : *L'Inde et L'Occident La Haye.*

Parmentier, H. : *Inventaire Descriptif des monuments Cams*, Vol. I, Paris, 1939.

Pelliot, P. : *Bulletin de L'Ecole Francaise d'Extreme-Orient*, Paris, 1904.

Pigeaud, Th. G. : *Tantu Pangelaren*, Leyden, 1924.

Souk, Boun. : *Limage du Buddha dans L'art, Lao.*

Stern, P. : *L'Art du Campa et son evolution*, Paris, 1927.

(ii) *SECONDARY SOURCES*

Anuman Rajadhon, Phya : *Nation, Religion and Civilisation of Thais*, Bangkok, 1968.

: *Thailand in outline*, Bangkok, 1973.

Bagchi, P.C. : *Studies in Tantras*, Calcutta, 1920.

Bapat, P.V. : (Ed.) *2500 Years of Buddhism*, Delhi, 1959.

Basham, A.L. : *The Wonder That was India*, London, 1954.

Bose, P.N. : *Indian Colony of Siam*, Lahore, 1929.

Bernet Kempers, A.J. : *Ancient Indonesian Art*, Amsterdam, 1959.

Blanchard, Wendell : *Thailand : Its People, Its Society, Its Culture*, New Haven, 1958.

Bode, M.H. : *Pali Literature of Burma.*

Bowie, T. : *The Arts of Thailand*, Bloomington, 1960.

Brown, P. : *Indian Architecture*, Bombay, 1942.

Briggs, L.P. : *The Ancient Khmer Empire*, Philadelphia, 1951.

Biddja, Pralash : *India and the World*, Hoshiarpur, 1964.

: *Studies in Asian History and Culture*, Meerut, 1970.

Busch, N.F. : *Thailand : An Introduction to Modern Siam*, Princeton, 1959.

Cady, John F. : *South-East Asia : Its Historical Development*, New York, 1964.

Casparis, J.G.de. : *Selected Inscriptions*, II, Bandung, 1956.

Chancharas, Lohapan : *Indians in Siam*, Bangkok, 1943.

Chatterji, B.R. : *India and Java*, Calcutta, 1962.

: *Indian Cultural Influence in Cambodia*, Calcutta, 1965.

: *South-East Asian Transition*, Meerut, 1965.

Chhabra, B.C. : *Expansion of Indo-Aryan Culture During Pallava Rule*, Delhi, 1965.

Chu, Valen Tin : *Thailand : Today*, New York, 1960.

Clarac, Achille & Smithies, Michael : *Discovering Thailand*, Bangkok, 1971.

Clifford, S.H. : *Further India*, London, 1904.

Coedes, G. : *Angkor—An Introduction*, Hong, O.U.P., 1963.

: *The Indianised States of South-East Asia*, Honolulu, 1968.

: *The Making of South-East Asia*, University of California Press, 1966.

Coomaraswamy, A.K. : *History of India and Indonesian Arts*, London, 1927.

: *The Arts and Crafts of India and Ceylon*, New York, 1966.

Corinne Brown : *Understanding Other Cultures*, London, 1925.

Cottnell, L. : *The Concise Encyclopaedia of Archaeology*, London, 1921.

Crawfurd, John : *History of the Indian Archipelago*, Vol. II, Edinburgh, 1820.

Crosby, Sir Josiah : *Siam : The Crossroads*, London, 1945.

Das Gupta, T.C. : *Some Aspects of Bengali Society*, Calcutta, 1955.

Dhaninivat, H.H. Prince : *A History of Buddhism in Siam*, Bangkok, 1960.

Diskul, Princess Poon Pismai : *Thai Traditions and Customs*, Bangkok, 1975.

Diksul, S. : *Art in Thailand*, Bangkok, 1970.

Dobby, D.H.G. : *South-East Asia*, London, 1948.

Duroiselle, C. & Blagden, C.O. : *Epigraphia Birmanica*, 5 Vols, Rangoon, 1919-36.

Eliot, Charles : *Hinduism and Buddhism*, 3 Vols, London, 1921.

Fergusson, J. : *A History of Indian and Eastern Architecture*, Delhi, 1967.

Feroci, C. : *The Siam*, Bangkok, 1967.

Forchhammers, E. : *Jardine Prize Essay*.

Frederic, L. : *The Temples and Sculptures of South-East Asia*, London, 1965.

Gelty, A. : *Ganesa*, Oxford, 1936.

Giles, H.A. : *The Travels of Fa-hien*, London, 1962.

Goloubew, V. : *India and the Art of Indo-China*, London, 1923.

Gonda, J. : *Sanskrit in Indonesia*, Nagpur, 1952.

Graham, W.A. : *Siam*, 2 Vols, London, 1924.

Griswold, A.B. : *Towards A History of Sukhothai Art*, Bangkok, 1967.

Groslier, B.P. : *Indochina : Art in the Melting Pot of Races*, London, 1962.

Grunwedel : *Buddhist Art*, Oxford, 1941.

Harrison, B. : *South-East Asia : A Short History*, London, 1965.

Hazra, R.C. : *Studies in the Puranic Records on Hindu Rites and Customs*, Dacca, 1940.

Hooykaas, C. : *The Old-Javanese Ramayana*, Amsterdam Academy, 1958.

Insor, D. : *Thailand: A Political, Social and Economic Analysis*, New York and London, 1963.

Jumsai, M.L. Manich : *History of Thai Literature*, Bangkok, 1973.

: *History of Thailand and Cambodia*, Bangkok, 1970.

Kramrisch, S. : *The Hindu Temple*, Calcutta, 1952.

Krishna Deva : *Temples of North India*, Delhi, 1954.

Krishna Shastri : *South Indian Images*, Madras, 1955.

Le May, R. : *The Culture of South-East Asia*, London, 1954.

: *A Concise History of Buddhist Art in Siam*, Cambridge, 1938.

London, K.P. : *South-East Asia, Crossroad of Religions*, Chicago, 1949.

Majumdar, R.C. : *Ancient Indian Colonisation in South-East Asia*, Baroda, 1955.

: *Ancient Indian Colonies in the Far East*, Vol. I, Champa, Lahore, 1927.

: *Suvarnadvipa*, Vol. II, Pts. I-II, Dacca, 1937. *Greater India*, Bombay, 1948.

: *Hindu Colonies in the Far East*, Calcutta, 1963.

: *History and Culture of the Indian People*, Vol. III, Cambridge, 1954.

: *Kambujadesa*, Madras, 1944.

Nag, Kalidas : *India and the Pacific World*, Calcutta, 1941.

Na Nakorm, Plaung : *History of Thai Literature for Thai Students*, Bangkok, 1967.

Nopaman, Lady : *Tao Sri Chulalak's Text Book*, Bangkok, 1957.

Pearn, B.R. : *An Introduction to the History of South-East Asia*, Kuala Lumpur, 1963.

Phayre : *Coins of Arakan, Pegu and Burma*, Rangoon, 1949.

Priññāno, Bikkhu : *Traditions and Customs of North-Eastern Thailand*, Thailand, 1965.

Raffles, Th. S. : *History of Java*, London, 1830.

Rajadhon, Phya Anuman : *Life and Rituals in Old Siam*, New Haven, 1961.

Rao, Gopinath : *Elements of Hindu Iconography*, Vol. I, Varanasi, 1971.

Rama V, King : *The Royal Ceremonies of the Twelve Months*, Bangkok, 1911.

Rama I, King : *Ramakien*, Bangkok, 1923.

Ray, N.R. : *Brahmanical Gods in Burma*, Rangoon, 1932.

Rawson, P. : *The Art of South-East Asia*, London, 1967.

Sadanandagiri, Swami : *Thailand*, Calcutta, 1941.

: *Hindu Culture in Greater India*, Delhi.

Sarkar, K.K. : *Early Indo-Cambodian Contacts*, Calcutta, 1939.

Sastri, K.A.N. : *South Indian Influences in the Far-East*, Bombay, 1949.

: *A History of South India*, Oxford University Press, 1955.

: *Srivijaya*, Madras, 1949.

S. Ludwick : *The Spreading of Canakyas Aphorism over Greater India*, Calcutta, 1969.

Smith, V.A. : *Fine Arts in India and Ceylon*, Oxford, 1925.

Sondhirak, Plak : *Prapene Thai*, Bangkok, 1968.

Stutterheim, W.F. : *Indian Influences on Old Balinese Art*, London, 1935.

. *Rama Legend and Rama-Reliefs in Indonesia*, Munchen, 1927.

Syamananda, Rong : *A History of Thailand*, Bangkok, 1973.

Thakur, U. : *History of Suicide in India*, Delhi, 1962.

: *Some Aspects of Ancient Indian History and Culture*, New Delhi, 1974.

: *Studies in Jainism and Buddhism in Mithila*, Varanasi, 1964.

Thompson, Virginia : *Thailand : The New Siam*, New York, 1941.

Vajiravudh Rama King (Rama VI) : *Madhanabadha*, Bangkok, 1927.

Vella, Walter F. : *Siam under Rama III*, New York, 1957.

Vogel : *Indian Art*.

Wales, H.G.Q. : *The Mountain of God*, London, 1953.

: *The Making of Greater India*, London, 1951.

Wales, H.G. : *Siamese State Ceremonies*, London, 1931.

Walker, G.B. : *Angkor Empire*, Calcutta, 1955.

Warmington, E.H. : *Commerce between the Roman Empire and India*, Cambridge, 1928.

Winstedl, R.O. : *The Malays: A Cultural History*, London, 1961.

Wood, W.A.R. : *History of Siam*, London, 1926.

Young, Earnest : *The Kingdom of the Yellow Robe*, London, 1907.

Yule : *Mission to the Court of Ava*, Amsterdam, 1855.

Zimmer, H. : *The Art of Indian Asia*, Vol. I, New York, 1955.

Zoete, B. de and Spies, W. : *Dance and Drama in Bali*, London, 1952.

(iii) *JOURNALS AND PERIODICALS*

Bulletin de la Commission archaeology de L' Indo-Chine.
Bulletin de l'Ecole Francaise d'Extreme Orient.
Bulletin School of Oriental and African Studies, London.
Ecole Francaise d'Extreme Orient.
Journal of the American Oriental Society.
Journal of the Asiatic Society of Bengal.
Journal of the Royal Asiatic Society, Malay Branch.
Journal of Oriental Institute, Baroda.
Journal of Oriental Research.
Journal of the Royal Burma Research Society.
Journal of the Greater Indian Society, Calcutta.
Journal of the Siam Society, Bangkok.
Journal of the South-East Asian History.
Thai Culture : New Series, Bangkok, 1969.
Thailand Official Year Book, Bangkok, 1968.
Vishveshvaranand Indological Journal, Hoshiarpur.

1

Brahmā at Nanpaya Temple, Pagan, Burma, about 11th century A.D.

2

Viṣṇu seated on Garuḍa, the main deity of Nat-hlaung Kyaung. (10-11th century A.D.)

3

Tārā Bronze. 8th century A.D. National Museum, Bangkok, Thailand

4
Brahmā at Eravan, the Government Hotel, Bangkok, Thailand

5
Brahmā at Eravan, the Government Hotel,
Bangkok, Thailand

6
Brahmā at Eravan, the Government Hotel, Bangkok, Thailand

7
Brahmā at Bot Brahm, Bangkok, Thailand

8

Liṅga at Vat Po, Bangkok, Thailand

9

Figure of Rāma, Thailand

10
Figure of Sītā, Thailand

11
Garuḍa, the Vehicle of Viṣṇu, Thailand

12
Figure of Hanumān, Thailand

13

Hari-Hara, Phnom Da style, (557-607 *A.D.*), *Cambodia*

14

Lakṣmē at Prasat Kravan, Koh Ker style, (907-957 A.D.), Cambodia

15

Frontispiece from Prasat Banteay Sarei. (957-1007 A.D.), Cambodia

16

A Lintel of Prasat Banteay Sarei, showing Rāvaṇa raising Kailāśa, Cambodia

17

Apsarāses, Angkor Vat, Cambodia

18

Śiva from Dong Duong, End of the 9th century A.D., Rietberg Museum, Zurich

19

Śiva from Dong Duong, Mid-ninth century A.D., Champa

20

The figure of Brāhmaṇa sacrifice, Binh-Dinh style, Champa

21

The figure of Brāhmaṇa sacrifice, Binh-Dinh style, Champa

22
Hari-Hara from Simping, Java, Indonesia

23
Dancing Goddess from Candi Lara Jongrang, Indonesia

24

Wayang Kulit figure, Java, Indonesia

25

Wayang Klitik figure, Java, Indonesia

INDEX

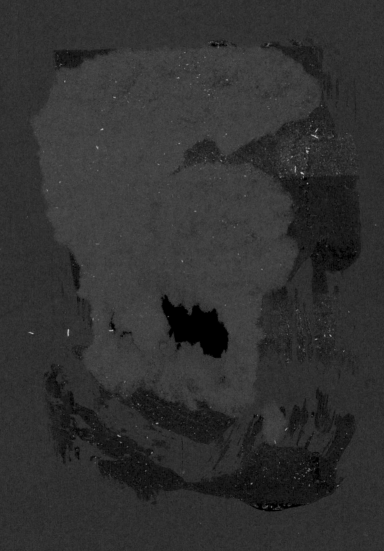